For Joan &
Good friends (patients)
& good, good memories,
Enjoy the book!
Paul

Paul C. [illegible signature]

5-6-09

# My Whole Life

## and Forty-Eight Years of Small Town Family Medical Practice

Paul Alexander Tanner, Jr., M.D.

Eloquent Books

New York, New York

Eloquent Books
An imprint of AEG Publishing Group
845 Third Avenue, 6th Floor — #6016
New York, NY 10022
www.eloquentbooks.com

ISBN: 978-1-60693-298-8
SKU: 1-60693-298-5

Printed in the United States of America

# Dedication and Acknowledgements

Writing my autobiography has been a great thing for me. Reviewing my life has taught me to appreciate where I came from: my mother and father and their families; my two brothers; where we grew up; our friends; and my wonderful wife and our children. I have gotten to know my children individually and have recognized they have created themselves from contact with their parents, siblings, friends, and teachers. This gave them the ability to create who they are and how they live their lives, and teach and help their families become individuals and families of their own. We are so proud of them.

I feel proud of what I have accomplished in my life, the wonderful woman that allowed me to choose her as my wife, and what we together have created and accomplished.

I am so happy that I have fulfilled my lifelong dream of becoming a plain old family doctor who learned everything, most everything I needed to make a successful life and physician. I so appreciate all the patients that allowed me to help them with their health and medical problems.

I know that none of this could ever have happened without my major partner in my life, Elizabeth, my love and my wife.

# Contents

# Introduction

I've finally decided to get started writing my book, on this date—-07-14-07. I've put this off too long now, and I'm not sure I'll live long enough to finish it.

I am now 83 years and 7 months old, lacking 2 days. This will be about a lot of memories and stuff: early childhood in Charleston, Missouri, where I was born; a short few years in Quitman, Georgia; then a return to Charleston, Missouri via Cairo, Illinois during the 1930's depression for grammar school; returning to Quitman, Georgia to begin and graduate from high school. I entered my first 2 years of college at Virginia Polytechnic Institute, Blacksburg, Virginia before the war. I'll write briefly about 3 years in World War II and my time on Saipan, Marianas Island Group in the Pacific Ocean; my return to Virginia Polytechnic Institute, in Blacksburg, Virginia after the war to complete medical school requirements; then entering medical school at The Medical College of Virginia, Richmond, Virginia; interning and 6 months of surgical residency at Mound Park Hospital (now Bay Front Center Hospital) in Saint Petersburg, Florida. I entered into medical general practice in Auburndale, Florida. I retired after 48 years of interesting, busy, sometimes amusing and touching patient contacts, and recording quotes and comments from many, many southern patients with quaint sometimes to me, unusual colloquialisms that perfectly described what they meant. And, what ever else that comes to mind as I glide, cruise, rush, creep, and bumble through history with me in it. I will also write about the ups and downs of life, my marriage, raising 6 wonderful children, and some good friends.

These are my memories. This episode is long and wandering—it's OK by me, so quit reading if it's not OK by you. I just find this stuff so hard to make all these things go in exact chronological order by dates and happenings.

# 1

# Growing Up, the Age of Innocence

I was born in Charleston, Missouri 12-16-1923. My mother, Maurine Finley Tanner, a beautiful, brunette Victorian lady 25 years old, was born 1898 also in Charleston. Mother's father educated his 8 daughters and 2 sons. My mother attended a school in Birmingham Alabama. I think the name was Lilly Compton School for Women.

My Father was 35 years old, Paul Alexander Tanner, born in Austin, Texas, September 30, 1889 of Presbyterian minister father, James Gilbert Tanner, and mother Ida Baskerville Seate Tanner. Daddy was a civil engineer graduate of Virginia Polytechnic Institute, Blacksburg, Virginia, in 1911, working in Charleston, Missouri as the Mississippi County Engineer. Mama and Daddy met, and were married in June, I think, 1921.

Daddy's father was also a graduate of Virginia Polytechnic Institute in 1879. It was named Virginia Agriculture and Mechanical College at that time. His degree was in Mechanical Engineering, later he went to a Virginia Seminary and became a Presbyterian Minister. He died in his 50's of tuberculosis.

Daddy's mother, Ida, spent a lot of her time researching the family genealogy. She went to England to search, and the story is, she traced us back to The Magna Carta days, what King I don't know. Just how important is that? She also traced us back to Thomas Jefferson's grandfather. We had the same grandfather. That's gotta be important! For what? I don't know. I have a lot of scraps of her papers with a lot of her notes, so I know she spent a lot of time writing notes.

My father was in Navasota, Texas when his Father was the Minister at the Presbyterian Church there. Daddy quit school at the age of 16 and joined an engineering team that was responsible for surveying the route to build the railroad going west to San Angelo, Texas, in the far western part of Texas. This is what interested him in becoming a Civil Engineer. He made it his goal to learn all he could about this work and when it was over he wanted to go to Virginia Polytechnic Institute for college.

Daddy had to take an entrance exam and be accepted as a student for his college. He had no financial backing, but was given a job working in the mess hall, serving and cleaning at the college. He also did some work in the infirmary.

After Daddy received his degree, he stayed on as a teacher of mathematics in the engineering school for one year. For some reason I was unable to find in my brain the genes my Daddy had for math. I passed all the required stuff but Daddy was ashamed of my grades in all that stuff, in spite of all his attempts to teach me during the summertime when I was at home. After graduation, and a few jobs, he wound up as County Engineer for Mississippi County, Missouri, and lived in Charleston, Missouri, where he met my Mother.

Mama and Daddy lived in the Barker House, an apartment house after they married, and that's where I was born in 1923 We visited Grandma in Charleston often. After Grandpa Finley died, about 1924, we moved in with Grandma. I have a picture of Grandpa Finley sitting holding me as a little baby on the porch of that Charleston house.

My father, Paul A. Tanner, Sr., Civil Engineer for Mississippi County, Missouri, was traveling through Florida with another civil engineer friend from Charleston, named Clyde Swank, looking to maybe start a civil engineering business in Florida. This was in the 1920's during the well known Florida boom. After their travel in Florida, they happened to drive through Quitman, Georgia and Daddy was intrigued by the pretty, quaint small town, Brooks County, Georgia county seat. Daddy stopped, talked to a few people, and found that Quitman was looking for a City Manager. He applied for the job, and was hired. Returning to Charleston, county seat of Mississippi County, Mo. he made necessary arrangements to leave and brought his wife and their two sons back to Quitman. My little brother Terry was born 9-30-1926 and was a few months old when we moved there.

I remember a 2 story house on North Court Street that we rented. I remember the steps to the front porch of the house. I have a picture of my friend, Harley Mitchell, a neighbor sitting with me on those steps. Harley and I lived two doors apart, and he was a little older than me. I thought he was smart and he taught me a lot of games.

Before too long, Daddy had our home built at 812 North Court Street in Quitman. In the back yard he built a little gold fish pond, about 10 feet long and about 5 feet wide, oval shaped and slanted from all sides, down to about 2 feet deep and made of concrete. In the deepest part was a metal faucet about 4 inches high with a round handle that when turned, drained the pool so it could be cleaned. Around the edge of the pool was an elevated rim about 4 inches high and 4 inches wide with playing marbles sunk into the soft cement before it dried, spelling our names, Paul and Terry. We considered that our swimming pool. We were small enough we could lay down and play like we were swimming, and splash around in the hot summer time. There was a time when there were gold fish and water lilies floating around.

Later when we were older, we would go to the lake at the country club and catch minnows and little perch and put them in the pool. Daddy would take our minnows out and go fishing with them, using them as bait. I think the pool is still there behind that house. Some of the marbles have been removed.

During that time, we had a little fox terrier dog and Mama named him Reenie, for her name Maurine. We ran all over that neighborhood following Reenie all over the place. There was a "nurse" for us that went where ever we went to keep us out of trouble in the neighborhood. She was a black maid named Minnie T. I rode a little tricycle or peddled in my little peddle car, Terry just followed me around. And Minnie T kept me from getting off the sidewalk and into the road.

In those days the ladies in the neighbors would go "calling," socially on their neighbors. They kept up with each other by dressing up a little, with gloves and a hat, and visiting. Nobody ever closed or locked their doors, so the ladies would go to someone's home enter the front door, call their name, greet them, sit and visit a while and come home. If no one was home, there was always a tray, or dish on a table inside the front door for the visitor to leave her card with her name.

I remember some times when a neighbor lady like Mrs. Williams, or "Cousin" Mattie would come, Mama would say, "Now Paul, you and Terry run on outside and play while we visit." She would send

Minnie T out to be with us. Sometimes we would climb up in the big old persimmon tree in our front yard and she'd be scared we were going to fall out of it. We never did. A ripe persimmon was good, but a green persimmon puckered up your mouth really bad.

In my earliest life, my prim Victorian mother never used any bad words, or any of the usual synonyms for body parts or functions. I suppose mothers make up the words that come to be common usage in their families. My mother made up her own when she wanted to know stuff about us. We learned, and used the word "urinate" in the proper and usual manner. There was no word for defecate. When she wanted to know, she would lean over us and gently pat us on our buttocks, and ask, "Do you want to do something back here?" We soon learned that little phrase, and I was nearly grown when I quit using that little group of words, that had become a rapid combination of sounds "dosumpnbackere."

If we had been hit or kicked in the groin or penile area, she would ask, "Did you hurt your little thing?" My little thing to her was my little thing until she quit asking me about it, and I had about grown up and it wasn't any longer any business of hers when it had become, not a big thing, but an adequate thing. She was a sweet, wonderful lady that saw to it we got good upbringing. She and Daddy required that we give the utmost respect to all females, young and old, at all times.

I remember when I was in the first grade in Quitman, Georgia at the beginning of every day at school, we went to the auditorium for Chapel, where somebody said a prayer, and then we'd sing a hymn. One of my favorite hymns was "Onward Christian Soldiers." I liked it because it had a good beat. I often sang a little of the song when I was playing at home. One day after school it was in my mind from singing it that morning. Mama was in the room where I was playing. She stopped me and asked, "What did you sing?" I sang it again. She said," that's not right." I didn't understand until she corrected me. I wasn't able to read at that time, so I was singing what I heard everybody sing, and had memorized…"Onward Christian Soldiers, marching on to war, with the cross-eyed Jesus going on before…" That's what I heard sung, so that's what I was singing, until I was corrected.

One day walking back home from school, I was passing our next door neighbors house, Mr. Williams and their big dog, a bird dog, was sitting right on the walk, in front of their house. I walked up to the dog and petted him on the head. He suddenly jumped up and bit me on my left temple. I ran home crying. Mama took me downtown to Dr. Smith's office. He took care of my wound, by 2 loose stitches after cleaning it. He just lightly pulled together the edges of the wound after thoroughly cleansing it, to guard against infection. A dog's mouth is full of bad germs, and a tight suture line can seal the wound and result in a significant infection. Remember, in the 1920s there were no antibiotics. The scar is still there. Then he started me on Rabies inoculation, requiring 21 injections, 1 weekly for 21 weeks. He gave them in the soft tissue of my abdomen. They hurt, and my abdomen got sore. I was little and 21 shots in my arms would not have been nice, I learned later it was better than getting Rabies.

There was a girl in the first grade with us who I thought was the most beautiful girl I'd ever seen. I remember her bright blue eyes and her wonderful friendly smile. I wanted her to know how beautiful I thought she was, and that I really liked her. Her name was Bessie Oglesby. One day I asked my friend, Harley, who I thought knew a lot more than I, how I could tell Bessie that I liked her. Harley said all I had to do is go up to her, and say, "Hi Bessie, I like you, who do you like?" He said she would then say "thanks, I like you too." Well, after a few days I got up enough nerve to talk to Bessie. I just walked right up to her on the school grounds where we all were playing at recess, and said, "Hi Bessie, I like you a lot, who do you like?" She said with no pause, "Denny Groover." I was crushed and never forgot the rejection. Later in high school, Denny and I became sort of good friends.

To make matters worse, later in high school in Quitman, I dated, very seriously a girl I'll not name here. We dated even a couple of years after we both went to college, and I was overseas during World War II, still writing to each other. One day I received a letter letting me know that she had found her dream man, and was sorry, but she was to be married to "Denny Groover." That was another crushing blow to my ego, due to the same Denny Groover. Well, he's dead long ago. Only recently, after not being able to reach her by phone, due to the area code being changed, I finally reached her. We had talked a few times in recent years, and Elizabeth and I moved and had a new phone number. When I talked to her recently, after 3 years, I was about through talking and the last thing I said was "I have a new phone number, do you want it?" Her response was quick and direct, "No." I thought that was a little abrupt and weird, but, oh well.

I remember teachers' names, Miss Battle, and Miss Gunn, also, principal Mr. Harold Saxon. He had a son, a playmate named John, who later became a mathematician and wrote a book, well received, for teaching school children math in school. He lived across the street and about 3 houses up, next door to another playmate, Audley Jones.

There wasn't much going on in my life at that time to remember, except just "little boy livin'"—like riding my tricycle, enjoying running around barefooted, stepping on sand spurs, pulling 'em out and getting 'em in my fingers, going with Daddy to take a big sheet load of washing to the washer woman, and playing with her little boys at her house.

She would start a fire under a big kettle of water. When it got hot, she would cut up a big bar of dark yellow soap into the water and stir it up. Then she would put our dirty clothes and sheets and towels in the kettle and stir them all around. She had a long round stick like a hoe or rake handle that she stirred with and picked 'em up and down and washed 'em real good.

Her boys would take me into their house that had wooden floors, and newspapers, thick layers nailed on the wall like wallpaper. She said it kept her warm in the winter. There were a few kerosene lamps around, and a few pictures. I remember liking to go there and playing with her boys because the ground in her yard didn't have anything growing in it. It was all just plain dirt, and no sandspurs, so we could run and play and not step on those things to hurt our feet, or stub our toes. In four or five days Daddy would drive us back to pick up our clothes, all clean and ironed and folded neatly with white paper wrapped around the stack.

On Sunday we went to the Methodist Church Sunday School, and Church, where Mama went. Daddy' father was a Presbyterian minister, so Daddy went to that Church. He would take us there with him once in a while. I didn't see any difference, and I remember wondering why we have so many churches, when they all taught about God the same way.

In 1929 the stock market crashed, I'm told. That was the beginning of the Florida Boom bust. Quitman was having financial trouble. They let Daddy go, because they couldn't pay him. The Mayor's son in law was working in Alabama and lost his job. So the city hired him at a cheaper salary than Daddy as the City Manager. Daddy and Mama decided to go back to Missouri, where Daddy was the County surveyor for Mississippi County, where my mother's family grew up. The job wasn't open at this time, so Daddy got a job with some Engineering firm in Cairo Illinois, just across the Mississippi River east, from Charleston, Missouri. This began the depression of the 1930s.

We moved to Cairo in 1930, I went to school in the 3$^{rd}$ grade. We moved in a private home and rented 2 rooms from a Miller family.

They had a teenager, named Jim Bill Miller. He didn't have much time for kids.

I took on a job of trying to sell Collier's Magazines, and Grit, a weekly newspaper, and The Saturday Evening Post. Every week, I received by mail a stack of magazines to go out and sell. I walked all over Cairo, door to door, carrying my magazines in a white sack that was much too large for me, with the large cloth handle slung over my shoulder. It was heavy and hard to manage. With Terry trailing behind me, I was trying to sell my magazines. I was working for brownie coupons, so I could turn them in for things. Week after week magazines came to our home. Those that weren't sold were stacked in a closet the next week, when the new ones came. Terry was very faithful, wandering along with me. I sold one here, one there, but never had enough to get any brownies. I was a total failure, and lost interest in making it big in sales. We had stacks and stacks of the magazines. It was hard trying to stop them from sending them. They kept on coming, even after we moved back to Charleston. They accumulated in one of grandma's closets behind her kitchen. They finally just stopped coming. I often wondered how many thousands of magazines were scattered over the United States stashed in people's closets that were never sold.

I remember being taken to a clothing store; way down in the poor part of Cairo to get me a pair of shoes, since my feet were growing and my shoes were too short. The old ones hurt my feet. Daddy and the clerk were arguing over the price of the shoes that I wanted; I remember hearing Daddy says "sharpen that damned pencil, and let's get it over with." I was kind of shocked, that was the first time I ever heard my Daddy curse. I never heard it any more. We finally left with the shoes. I remember this happening at several different stores during this time, but I heard no more cursing. Now I recognize that must be what you did during the depression, when you didn't have much money.

In school at this time we were supposed to write a school paper, telling what I wanted to be when I grew up. I wrote, "I want to be a doctor when I grow up." I still have it. My Mama kept almost every thing her children wrote or made in school.

After a year or so, Daddy got his job back in Mississippi County, and we moved back to Charleston. We moved in Grandma's house where my mother grew up. We moved in with Grandma Finley, Mother's mother, and Mother's sister, Alma Barrett, divorced, with her daughter, Rachel. Aunt Alma was the sixth child of Grandma Finley. They were Mattie, Aura, Lela, Eva, Sidney, Alma, Howard, Frankie, Maurine (my Mama), and Josephine. Grandma had another child named Cora, who died at age 13 months. She was Grandma's 3$^{rd}$ child. Another lady I remember there that frequently visited Grandma was named "cousin" Cora. She was extremely deaf, and we had to yell loudly to her so she could hear. I was told she was adopted and raised by Grandma and Grandpa to adulthood, and was educated with the other children. She was very friendly, and was in her late middle life. I never knew what she did or where she lived. I remember being impressed that my grandparents took another child in to raise and educate, with all their own children.

We were raised almost as a family. Upstairs, Grandma lived in the front left bedroom. The four Tanners had the bedroom next to and just behind her. Both of these rooms had doors into a larger room to the left, which had a large coal burning stove for heat, our sitting room, and dressing room in wintertime. From that room, a little hall went back into a long glassed in porch where Aunt Alma and Rachel slept, and Rachel kept her paper dolls and stuff. She was between me and Terry in age. The bathroom entered to the left from the little hall. It was a little cozy living, but we got along fine. I was about 9 years old when we went back there.

Grandma's 2- story home was on a corner lot at 214 South Third Street in Charleston, Missouri. An acre or so next to the house was where Aunt Alma had all of her beautiful flower garden. That was where we kids made our money, working for Aunt Alma pulling weeds from her garden. She paid us10 cents an hour. We had one of those dime banks that you filled and screwed the top screw down to empty the $5 dollars out of the bottom when we filled it up. It took weeks and months to fill it up.

There was a grape orchard with delicious Concord grapes there also. We ate them off the vine, cut a few grape stems and used about 4 inch stems to smoke. They burned like a cigarette, and we thought we were really something—smoking. Once we were out there smoking grape vines and we noted the ground trembled a little and the grape leaves shook and shuddered. We got scared and ran into the house. We found out later there was a small earthquake down in East Prairie, Mo., which is 10-15 miles south. In the late 1800's there was a well known significant quake in a known fault in the earth in that area, called the New Madrid Fault.

Behind our house was about 2 acres, half in cotton, the other half had an old barn and a pig sty attached. Each winter we had a pig that we raised, to butcher and make sausage, and get ribs, loins, and hams. There were men hired that knew how to do all that stuff. They would come early in the morning, shoot the hog in the head, and then stick the hog in the neck to reach the heart so he would bleed out. Then put him in a kettle of really hot water for a while. And then string him up by his feet from a limb on a big pecan tree in the back yard, scrape all the hair off, gut him, cut him up and go about making cracklings from the skin and fat so we could make "crackling corn bread." They cut up all the meat, ground up all the leftovers and made sausage and stuffed the intestines—turned wrong side out—with the sausage. All the meat was hung up in a shed. It was winter and cold all the time, so we ate. I remember one winter after hog killing time, and the meat was all hung, it had snowed, and the next morning all the meat was gone. There were tracks of footsteps in the snow, from the edge of the street to our shed. There were a lot of upset people in our house. They suspected the hired men, but couldn't prove they took it, so we did without our meat.

It snowed often in the winter. Once in a while the snow was pretty deep. Daddy would tie a rope to the back of his car and tie a sled to the rope, then another sled behind that one, and a third sled behind the second one. He drove the car slow around the neighborhood, with me, Terry, and Rachel on the sleds. This was great fun, we thought. There were no hills that we ride down. A couple of times Daddy had to stop the car quick and the sleds didn't stop. We all kind of slid into each other and into the back of the car. We never got hurt because we were going pretty slowly.

The cotton field was another thing I remembered, trying to pick cotton. They were going to pay us something per pound picked. I don't remember how much we were going to be paid, but it was a lot of money to us at the time. We agreed with the deal. So at cotton picking time, they gave us a great big sack with a big strap to go over our shoulder, and drug behind us when we walked. We went to work. Cotton grows, and is picked in hot weather. Cotton grows in cotton bolls, kind of hard to get all of it out of the boll. After a long time, picking and dragging, picking and dragging, we had gone for a long time, but not very far down the first row. We seemed to find out that this was not going to get us rich, and we seemed to get tired, really hot, and real sweaty. Looking down in our heavy sack, there was maybe a double handful of cotton way down in the bottom. We couldn't even feel any weight more than the heavy sack. We therefore resigned our position as cotton pickers. We never thought about ever applying for that position again.

When I was about 9-10years old I was caught doing a very bad thing. Three or four blocks down the street, playing cowboys and Indians, my friend had a beautiful new cap pistol, looking almost like a real six shooter. We were running around, and shooting each other, and we all got tired and sat down, time was getting late. He put the gun down and we had our attention somewhere else. When it came time to go home, I couldn't get that gun off my mind. I just had to have it. I put on my jacket, and snuck the gun into my pocket and took it home. At home I took it to one of grandma's back pantry areas, behind the kitchen, and put it high in a top shelf. I could hardly wait until the morning when I planned to 'discover the gun." Next morning I was fooling around in the pantry "found" the gun and went to grandma and asked her if this old gun I found belonged to grandpa that he used during the Civil War? (He was in the civil war, as a water boy about 16 years old.) She said no, but my mother heard all this and on severe "professional-like questioning," got the truth out of me. I started crying and wanted to run away, but she told me I had to take that gun right back to my friend right now, and apologize to him for STEALING his gun. I was mortified, devastated, and very ashamed to be called a "common thief." I took the gun, and by myself began the "mile"+ journey very slowly walking down the street, not wanting ever to get there, and stood outside the front door during the most miserable time in my whole life. Finally, I couldn't think of any way out of it, so I softly rapped on the door, scared to death, hoping no one heard the knock. His mother came to the door, and I told her I took the gun home yesterday to play with it. She said, "Oh, he wondered what happened to it." I said "I'm sorry." She said "that's all right, he'll be happy it was found." What a tactful women, I don't know if she ever knew I just flat out stole it!

Later that day Daddy came home from work. After a little while, he called me and Terry and said get in the car. In the car Daddy started telling me what a bad boy I was and he didn't want me growing up to be a person that steals and does bad things. He asked me if I knew what happens to that kind of person. I said "they get arrested and go to jail" He said yes, and we're going down to the jail now. I just knew he was going to have to get me arrested for stealing, and I was really worried and crying, ashamed and scared to death. Daddy stopped the car in front of the jail, and just kept on about how I had embarrassed the family, Mama and him and everybody. Finally, he started the car and drove back home. I told them how sorry I was for what I did and wouldn't do anything like that ever again. I was really wrung out over that bad kid episode, and learned never to do anything like that again. I'll never forget the helplessness, lost and alone feeling that I brought on myself.

We had a nice play yard behind the house, so we decided to do more of that. Daddy had brought home a big 55 gallon drum, and later on old hot water heater container made of iron, I think. We learned to walk all over the back yard on those barrels, easy when you're barefooted.

We had some chickens in a fenced in part of the back yard. Every year Daddy would go somewhere and get eggs and put them in a flat 4X4 foot, 6 inch deep box with a top on it and light bulbs inside to heat the eggs. It wasn't long until they started hatching. We had a bunch of cute little yellow biddies. They started growing up and we'd chase them around the yard. It was sad when it would rain and we didn't run out and put them in the chicken house. They would just go in the corner of a fence and huddle up and point their little beaks in the air. Then we would go out and find some dead biddies, drowned. They seemed to be rather stupid. The ones that grew up laid us some nice eggs, and some of them got eaten up, by us. I used to get an egg, stick a hole in both ends with a needle, then blow real hard on one end and force the yolk, and white stuff out in a bowl, to keep the empty egg shell and cook the egg. We sometimes dyed some of the empty shells for Easter, along with the hard boiled eggs. I think I still have a few.

We would play cowboys and Indians, with Rachel. When she would point her finger at one of us to shoot us, she would yell "phew, phew" (sounded like pew, pew. Come to think of it, it did sound like a ricocheting bullet), with each shot she made. I was Tom Mix, or Buck Jones, or Bob Steele, or Ken Maynard, or William Boyd. I loved Tom Mix, the greatest cowboy that ever lived in my estimation. He was the advertisement for Ralston cereal. I became a member of his "straight shooters," and received a membership ring. It was a horseshoe nail bent to be a ring. There was a code, and secret handshake, and books that told the interesting life story of Tom. Each time we started to play, you had to call out who you were going to be before anybody else called out the name. One Christmas Santa brought me a real pair of leather chaps, a plaid shirt, a neckerchief, and two side arms and a belt with 2 holsters for my guns. I was the proudest cowboy around.

We also had a tree house up in a peach tree, and a swing set with a croker-sack filled with old clothes and stuff, knotted at the top with a rope tied and it hung from the swing set. You get it swinging and jump on and straddle the sack and swing.

Rings hung from the other end of the set. There was an old wicker high backed arm chair about worn out. I thought it would be really good to tie that chair to one of the rings and sit in the chair and swing. I tied a rope under the arms and looped it through one of the rings. I called it my "Flying Chair." When I tried to get up into the chair, the weight of my body in the seat kept the rope real tight, and trying to sit down, I found I had to hold the ring it was tied to, away from my struggling body and as I finally sat in the seat the ring slipped from my grasp and forcefully snapped back into my mouth striking my left front, beautiful white tooth. Bad pain! The inside corner of the tooth broke off and was gone. When I ran into the house, crying, to be calmed, and soothed, and mothered, but she was not happy. I got scolded for thinking that was a good idea. This left me with a distinctive, masculine look. I had that chip all of my years, until one of my dentists said he could fix it, in the 1980s. Previous dentists recommended leaving it alone. After the repair, some 20 years later, it became brown and no longer masculine. So, had them all fixed, so now I am masculine appearing again, at least to me, with nice white teeth.

As I got a little older, Christmas came, and with it, presents. Santa brought me my hearts desire, a Red Ryder BB air rifle, with of course, ammunition. I would walk around with my gun, taking pot shots at birds, targets, and I imagined I was a big game hunter like Frank Buck., the noted big game hunter. I would walk all over Charleston, hunting. Sparrows were all over the place. I could never hit one. But doves would sit on wires. You could walk right up under them, and shoot, and shoot, and watch the BB go straight to the target- the dove. It would shudder its feathers, and just keep on sitting. After 4 or 5 hits, the dove would finally fall to the ground, dead. Walking up and down the streets, hunting, finding doves, shooting and finally I got pretty good. Good enough to bring home a few doves. Mama would clean them and cook them. The birds were tough and had a bunch of BB's in the breast and hard to eat and not swallow BB's. So I quit bringing them home. I'd just shoot them.

I have a memory of a near disaster, that I remember when we were kids. Daddy was the civil engineer for Mississippi County and had to ride through the county frequently to check on some of the projects that were current, and he decided to take the family with him late one afternoon. Mama, Terry, me, and mama's mother, Grandma Finley were in the car and we were riding on a wet clay road in the country after a rain. Daddy lost control of the car and the car started skidding sideways down the wet, clay road as we were approaching a bridge that had been damaged. The part over the little creek was guarded on both sides of the road with an iron fence. The end of the left side fence was broken off, exposing three parallel horizontal angle irons, and we were sliding sideways into it. We struck the left side of that bridge and one angle iron penetrated the back door on the left. Our car was a 4 door Ford 1934 sedan. Mama was seated in the back on the left, Grandma in the right rear seat next to Mama. Terry and I were in the front with Daddy.

The upper angle iron went through the back door into the back of the rear seat and was embedded all the way through it. Mama was injured with a couple of fractured ribs, the iron having passed between Mama's left arm and body, grazing and scratching the left side of her chest wall fracturing 2 of her left ribs. A few inches more to the right she would have been impaled on the angle iron through her chest and on into and through the back seat. Grandma wound up crumpled on the right back floor. She suffered a fractured ankle, and was in a lot of pain. There were no seat belts then, which would have kept Grandma in her seat, and probably not broken her ankle. But Mama would have been kept her in her seat and probably had been impaled by that angle iron. We were in the country, no one lived near, but Daddy knew the folks who lived up the road a mile or so, so he took off walking on that wet slippery clay road to get help. It was a while getting a way to take us to the hospital in Cairo, Ill., across the Mississippi River. Mama and Grandma spent several days in the hospital. We boys and Daddy weren't hurt, but we were scared to death, and very thankful we still had a Mama and Grandma.

I'll never forget one night Terry and I were playing in the living room. He was running from one side of the room to the other, and I was trying to catch him before he made it to the other side. I couldn't catch him, so I suddenly said "I'll just shoot you." My BB gun was standing in the corner, so I just ran to it, picked it up and quickly cocked it and immediately aimed it and fired. Terry screamed, put his hand over his right eye and started crying.

I had run out of BBs during the day and put the gun in the corner with no BBs in it. As soon as Terry screamed I remembered finding one BB on the floor, and going to the gun and putting it in the gun. I was so scared I started to cry, because I thought I had hurt him severely. They called Dr. Love, and he came and found the BB in the right side of Terry's forehead, just above the right eyebrow. The doctor was able to use a small instrument to remove it from beneath the skin. I really was worried, think of the BB 2 inches lower into the right eye. There was a very stern lecture about the use of guns, not to play with them, not assuming any gun is unloaded. That bothers me to this day.

In those days, we never locked our doors. We were allowed to go all over town with no worry. On Halloween, we would each take a bar of Ivory soap, and go down town. Most of the stores were closed, so a lot of kids would use the soap to streak up the plate glass windows with, circles, numbers, words, (nice words—we didn't know bad words), just to fill up the windows with soap. I'm sure the merchants were busy the next day, cleaning windows. We always walked to school, only 6-7 blocks away. It seemed like a very long walk, especially winter time with snow. We came home for lunch, then back to school, for afternoon school until 4PM., and walked home. Sometimes, we would walk down the street from our school, to Aunt Lela Crenshaw's home for lunch. I think Mama made the appointment for us to go eat there. She sure cooked good food, and made wonderful pies and cakes. She was my mama's sister, and she had two older, grown boys, Henry, and Bridwell, and one daughter Mary Lela, a little younger than we were, and she came over to play with us sometimes. I thought she was one of the prettiest cousins we had. Henry helped his daddy on the farm, and delivered milk in quart glass bottles to our house early in the morning. In the winter time the milk would freeze and the frozen milk rose up out of the bottle a couple of inches, with the cardboard milk stopper on top.

I remember going out to their farm sometimes and climb up and play on their tall haystacks. Henry had a deformed right hand from an accidental shot gun injury while hunting. I don't know what kind of work Bridwell did.

Another dumb thing I did, on the 4th of July we had some firecrackers, so we would set them off. We would use a tin can, light firecracker, and put it beneath an upside down can to see how high the can would go. I got the bright idea of dropping a lighted firecracker into a glass quart milk bottle, while I was holding the bottle. Terry lit the firecracker and dropped it in the bottle. It went off, the bottle shattered and the palm of my left hand and the inside of my 5th left finger were cut. A small sliver of glass cut a small place on Terry's stomach.

What did I think would happen? I don't know. We got another lecture from Mama, and then from Daddy when he got home.

When I was in the 4$^{th}$ or 5$^{th}$ grade I started taking piano lessons. My teacher was Mrs. Moffitt. Also started on the clarinet and in the last couple of years in school there, joined the band. The band director was Mr. Fish, a larger rather obese gentleman, and a good teacher. I learned to play the clarinet pretty good. I had a hard time with the piano. Seemed I couldn't get my right hand to work separate from the left hand. I would wind up with the same beat with both hands striking the piano at the same time. I did well if I memorized the song. One song I memorized was "Long, Long Ago" I had to play it every time company came. It was the only song I could play. Mama was real proud of me, because she really was a good piano player, and thought I would be one too. It didn't work out.

I remember one time I was walking down town alone, why, I don't know. I was a walking down the street on the side of the hotel in town. As I walked by a side door of the hotel, a man with a hotel uniform stepped out right in front of me and spoke to me. I said "hello." He said "I'll give you a quarter if you let me see your little peanut." I had no peanuts, but I seemed to know something's wrong, so I said "no thank you," and kept on walking. Thank goodness he just went back in the hotel. I never told my parents about that. I still have my little peanut, and it's OK.

The ice man came around daily in his horse drawn wagon to supply us with ice. There was a piece of cardboard about a foot square with numbers for pounds of ice needed along each side-5,10,15,Or 20, placed in a window with the correct number up, for him to see what size block we needed. The horse would stop, the iceman would uncover the big pieces of ice, drag it to the edge of the wagon and saw off the right size and carry it into the house and place it in the ice box. When he sawed the ice we held our hands under the operation to catch the shaved ice and follow him down the street to eat the shavings, and collect more. That was great fun, especially in the hot summer time.

We wandered all over town, during summer. Sometimes as I got a little older and was roller skating pretty good, our friends would go down to a cement street, called Danforth hill, and play hockey. Our street was a dirt street. Mr. Danforth later became a well known U.S. Senator, or Representative. A Pet milk can made a good hockey puck. We stepped on it and crumpled it all up. Then we all had gone to a tree, and cut a limb that had grown off of a little larger limb, leaving part of the larger limb attached, shaped like a hockey stick. We all cherished our stick, and learned to smooth the handle so it wouldn't hurt our hands. We played roller skate hockey for hours at a time. There weren't too many cars running around much, so we just had fun.

We also got our gang together, usually after school, and played tackle football, somewhere in empty lots between people's houses, or fields somewhere. A couple of guys got banged up a little, like skinned knees, and elbows, little cuts on heads, a couple of arms broken, etc., but we all kept doing it. The only thing that I had was broken glasses, or badly bent frames, incidental scratches, or bruises. I had to wear my glasses because I couldn't see if I didn't. Anyway, we always healed up from the scratches and bruises.

Once I was wandering down town and went behind Brewer and Trickey's Drug store, which was an empty lot with a lot of stones and gravel covering it. At the end of the lot was a large advertising billboard. I was walking around, picking up rocks and throwing rocks at the billboard. I had been doing that for a little while, when I picked up a larger one to throw, and noticed it was smooth, and different from the others I had thrown. It looked like a stone hatchet, so I took it home. There was a groove around one end, and the other end was tapered to a flatter end. It was a stone Indian tomahawk head, and I still have it.

Another drug store had a soda fountain. That was Hummel's Drug Store. Occasionally they would have a special on root beer drinks— all you could drink for 5 cents. Terry and I would go down town with our nickel, and drink root beer until we were about to either bust or vomit. Kids were there from all over town, drinking, and drinking. Occasionally, one would run out of the front door and vomit in the street.

Mr. Hummel's son John Vernon Hummel was in our school, a little younger than I, became a Physician. He later married a Miss America winner. I am ashamed I cannot remember the year, or her name. Some time later they came here to Winter Haven, Fla. for some promotional gala, probably for Cypress Gardens, that we attended, and I was happy to run into him again.

Among my friends that I remember in grammar school, at Eugene Field School in Charleston, was a friend who later became Governor of Missouri, Warren Hearnes. Other names I remember were, Virginia (somebody), Pauline Swope, a Wheeler girl, David Lair, Oliver French, Marion and James Wagoner (James became an Army General), Jack Carson, Crawford Lovelace, Fred Dark and Thomas Russell. Teachers I remember at Eugene Field School were Mabel Roberts, Mattie Henry, Mrs. Farris, music teacher Mr. Fish, he started me on clarinet, and I was in the school band.

There was a big pecan tree in the back yard. The pecans were big ones, called paper shelled pecans. All the boys would find the toughest pecan we could find, and called it our "cracker." We carried our "cracker" in our pants pocket. At school, we would challenge another kid to see if our "cracker' would crack his "cracker." We took his "cracker," put it in our hands, together with my "cracker," and squeeze to try to crack the other guy's "cracker." If my pecan won, then, I could eat his pecan. It was hard to find a good cracker. I tried oiling it, shellacking it, even soaking it in salt water. I heard that would really work. It didn't. Somebody always ate my pecan.

During the fall, our family and the Clyde Swank family, friends of our parents, went out in the country where a couple of wild pecan trees grew. They were big trees. Both families took along long cane fishing poles to thrash the limbs of the trees to knock the pecans down A lot already had fallen on the ground. So we picked them up. We kids would climb the tree and get high enough to thrash more, and we had pecans all over the ground. Then we had to pick up more pecans. Both families had plenty of pecans. Still none were hard enough to be really good "crackers."

At school most of us boys played marbles. We always had a pocket full, and played for keeps, if we won. I got to be pretty good and won a lot of marbles. A triangle, with sides about a foot long, would be drawn in the dirt, and everybody that was in the game had to put a marble inside the triangle. Then we'd lag our shooter at a line drawn. Closest to the line got to go 1$^{st}$, next closest lagged next, and so on. The shooter was a bigger marble called a Taw, so the first shooter may hit a marble in the triangle, and it may go out of the triangle. That would be his marble, and he could shoot again from where the Taw stopped, until he missed. Then second shooter took a turn, and so on. Some kids loved to play, but were lousy shots. We knew who they were and always tried to get them in our games. We were bad little boys.

I grew and got older, had a lot of fun with Terry, my cousins, and friends. Daddy was having trouble with his back, the heel of one foot, and a little finger. There came a few times during the summers that Daddy's doctor recommended he go to Hot Springs, Arkansas for heat baths and treatment. He had taken x-rays, and was identified as having arthritis. So daddy would drive us boys and Mama back to Quitman where we had a house, to spend the summer while Daddy went on to Arkansas.

On the way south we'd go through Birmingham and stop over night at Aunt Eva and Uncle Elmer, and cousins Finley, Elmer Guy, Paul, and Henry, lived. Their father was a Pharmacist, owner of his own drug store. We slept on the floor, quilts, etc. to make pallets to sleep on. They lived on a hill, under a famous huge metal statue of Vulcan, far up the mountain. It was visible from all over Birmingham. Their street was on a hill. The cousins were always building "soap box derby cars" and sitting in them, and rolling down the hill. There was a cross street at the bottom of the hill, and some one had to sit down there and tell the rider when it was safe to come down. I don't think any of them ever got hurt, because they all lived to a pretty good age.

In Quitman farmers would ride around through town in their horse drawn wagons with their vegetables to sell. You could hear the horse's hooves striking the pavement, slowly and methodically coming down the street. Mama would send us out to see what he had to sell. Usually they had butter beans, field peas, string beans, collard greens, tomatoes, corn roastin' ears, okra, and maybe watermelon, or cantaloupe. The butter beans, field peas were shelled and 10 cents a quart. Collards were sold by the mess; I don't know what a mess is or what it costs. They sure were good cooked with bacon grease and eaten with corn bread to sop up the pot "likker." For supper many times we had peanut butter and bread covered with cane syrup. This was in the 1930's during the depression. We didn't realize we were poor, because we loved peanut butter and syrup.

During the summer time we would go out in the country and find an elderberry bush and cut a straight limb off, about a foot long. The wood is really hard, and has a pithy center, that we would work on a long time to clean out the pithy center. When you got it all out you have a hollow tubular piece that you can shoot chinaberries through at each other. Chinaberries are hard, solid green berries that grow on chinaberry trees. You need a staff to plunge one berry far down into the tube, the follow it with another berry placed just inside the near end and wait with the staff just inside the near berry, until you want to shoot somebody. Then you aim and fire, by rapidly plunging the staff into the tube to the end. It makes a "POP" when you plunge it in., and the near berry is then positioned for the next shot. You then place the next berry in the near end and wait, ready for the next firing.

The staff is also very hard to make. You need a broom handle, using a piece longer than the tube. You must whittle the wood away, starting with a comfortable 4-5 inch handle left for you to hold during firing. The whittled staff must measure a little shorter than the distance from one end of the tube to the other. You must whittle, and sand the wood down so that the staff is the center of the broom handle and will fit into the tube, nearly to the end. Now you need to make a mop on the end of the staff, so you can push the berry in fully, leaving it just inside the end. You do that by spitting on the sidewalk, or cement, and pound the narrow end of the staff up and down in the spit over and over to finally perfect the moppy end, which will be a little bit bigger than the inside circumference of the tube. It takes nearly all summer to perfect your berry gun. Now you are ready for war, with a pocket full of chinaberries.

We also made sling shots, out of a Y shaped limb or sawed from a board. An old inner tube is cut to get strips of rubber, secure them to the Y with strong cord tied at the notchings on the Y to secure them. Now the tongue of an old shoe is attached to each end of the rubber to hold the rock, or what ever you're going to shoot. You notch each side of the tongue, and slip the end of the rubber through it and fold it back and secure it with a strong string. Now you are ready for war, again. I got real good with my sling shot. We use to shoot at birds, dogs, cats, squirrels but no kids. I shot a lot of blue jays, blackbirds, and one day I hit a poor little humming bird sucking the nectar from one of Mom's flowers. He was so small, he just about disintegrated. He was so pretty, I really felt bad about that, but how did I know I was going to hit the thing?

Daddy spent the summer in Hot Springs getting hot baths, trying to get better and would come back later and take us back to Missouri. During the winter, back in Charleston, Daddy was having a terrible time with his arthritis. He had been advised by one of his good friends, who owned a successful Independent Oil Company that he needed to retire from his job, as county engineer, and not spend the winter outdoors working that was so hard for him. He advised Daddy, to go down south, in the warm weather, and start the same kind of business. Daddy learned a lot from his old friend Mr. "Chilly" Simpson, about building an independent oil company.

That is what he did. In 1937, we moved back to Quitman, I had a new little baby brother named Maurice Baskerville Tanner. Maurice was less than a year old I was 13 years old, Terry about 10years old. This was our second time living in Quitman.

It was the middle of the depression when we moved back. Many times people had no money and men, black and white, came to our back door wanting to work around the yard for a meal. Mama would always fix something for him so he could have a meal. Rarely did she ask him to do any work; if she did it was weeding in the yard around her flowers and shrubs.

I noted during this time back in Quitman, neighbors didn't call on each other at their home very much at all. I think most people had a telephone and just telephoned if they wanted to talk. Another thing I noted that my mother seemed a little put out by the people she used to know, because she thought they may have had something to do with the firing of Daddy. She just kept to herself all those years we grew up until the end of our schooling.

In the town of Quitman there was only Mr. Patton's barber shop with 4 barbers. I remember it cost .35 cents for a hair cut. A couple of miles outside of town on the Thomasville, Ga. highway, beyond West End, where we got hamburgers, went swimming in a big pool, and later went to dance to a juke box for a nickel, Daddy took us to the top of the hill, named McGregor Hill where Mr. McGregor had a one chair barber shop. He only charged .25 cents for a haircut. Daddy said we went there because it was cheaper and the hair was going to grow back anyway. During the Depression you could buy a loaf of bread for a dime. When I was a little older, I remember going to Patton's barber shop and telling the barber I wanted a "Man's" haircut. That's when they put a little shaving cream on the side burns and shaved the hair away. It looked good, like I had shaved, and I was "growing up."

I entered the freshman year of high school. I graduated from Quitman High School in 1941, at the age of 17. I did a lot of learning during that time, and had wonderful friends, and a lot of fun. I entered the freshman year of high school, 8th grade. They had only 11 years of school. I made pretty good grades, joined the brand new band, and played clarinet. I was better than most other members, since most of them had to be taught how to play their chosen instrument, by the new band director, Mr. Chester Morris. It was an uphill battle for most, but we had a great time learning together. Mr. Morris would occasionally get so frustrated he would cuss, like "Good Gravy, Paul, can't you learn to play it right?" Terry played the cornet, and was really good. We used to march as a band in uniforms down town occasionally. Uniforms were white shirt and white pants, with a purple and gold cape, and a band cap. Kathryn Terry was our Drum Majorette, and we all looked good, strutting down town. Later when we were out of high school, Maurice grew and got old enough and played clarinet in the band, after we left high school.

Daddy bought a large empty lot 1 block south of the Brooks County Courthouse, on the east side of South Court Street. This is where he built his 1$^{st}$ gasoline filling station. The company was called Tanner Oil Company. He named the gasoline "Tanoco." He bought gasoline from a wholesaler, and became an Independent Oil Company. He hired the employees, and the business grew, because Independent companies sold gasoline about 2-3 cents cheaper than the Major oil companies. Daddy hired Tom Taylor, and Kinch Kindle to run the station. I worked there on Saturdays, pumping gas, checking oil, cleaning windshields, and learning to fix flat tires. Gasoline cost about 16 cents a gallon at our station, that was about 2 cents less than the major oil company's gasoline. Once in a while prices would go up a few cents, or come down a few cents. Sometimes the big companies would get into a gasoline "price war" and the price would start down, so Daddy's would have to go down below them. That was a time of real worry for him, and his profit was much less if the gas war lasted too long. Daddy expanded his stations to Adel, Georgia, north of Valdosta, then on to Thomasville, Georgia where he built 2 stations.

One time when Terry, my brother, was old enough and working in the Quitman station, in my previous capacity, a man rapidly drove up to the gas tank, stopped the car, got out and dashed to the rest room. Terry noticed a lot of blood and other unknown stuff with an awful odor covering the windshield. Terry waited until the customer, after a long time, came out. He sheepishly told Terry, he had been in the rest room vomiting.

He related that he was driving along, just out of town when a large buzzard flew into his windshield, and was killed, but had apparently just eaten something that had been dead a while, and the blow to the buzzard caused it to regurgitate the foul smelling stuff, all over the hood and windshield of his car. The gentleman said he immediately became very nauseated, nearly vomiting, but was so happy to see the filling station he made himself drive on and into the station. He made it. Then he asked Terry to clean his windshield, and then walked away from the car far enough not to be involved with the procedure. Terry went through the same violent nausea reaction, but since the customer is always right, Terry managed to nearly wash the entire car, to rid it of the catastrophic results of the wayward Buzzard. The driver didn't need any gas, politely thanked Terry, and left. Nobody ever tipped anybody in those days.

Before the gas station work, I had gotten a job down town at a chain grocery store, named Rogers Grocery. I went to work every Saturday at 7 AM. I was paid $1.25, for the day. I stayed until they closed, at 11 PM. After 11, we had to fill the shelves up, with what had been sold during the day. I usually would get home at 12:30 to 1:00 Sunday AM. They also took out the cost of my lunch and supper that I bought there for my meals. I would buy a 10 cent package of cinnamon buns, 6 in a package, and a big RC Cola, for 5 cents. I ate 3 buns and an RC at lunch and the same for supper. I had to buy another 5 cent drink at supper, because I drank the first one at lunch. After restocking all the shelves I got paid $1.05 for the day. I was really tired and my feet were killing me. I always wore flat tennis shoes, high tops with the rubber baseball on the outside of the ankle. And, boy, did they stink sometimes!!!! Sometimes I would have to walk home, only if I didn't ride my bicycle to work. I remember a few times he would give me 75 cents, when I ate more during the day.

My next job was working on Sunday afternoons at Glausier's Drug store. My job was curb-hopping, bringing drinks from the soda fountain out to cars, on a tray and hanging it on the door, with the window open. People would just go for a ride on Sunday and before 5 pm they come by the drug store, park out front, and beep the horn for service. I would run out, take their order, go back in, make it or the other guy would make it, and take the order out to them. Most people would order a plain dope, or vanilla dope, or a cherry dope, or occasionally a chocolate dope. (All coca-colas were called "dopes." That was probably due to the old formula of coke had a small amount of cocaine in the formula. The originator was a pharmacist in Atlanta named Pemberton in mid 1800s, who later sold it to another pharmacist named Chandler.)

When they were through, they would beep the horn again, I'd go get the tray. I don't ever remembering receiving any tip. Nobody tipped, and we never expected any. My pay was 35 cents for the afternoon.

I went to work at another competing drugstore, Terry's Drug Store, down the street. I was a full fledged Soda Jerk, working in afternoons after school, and Saturdays. They had sandwiches made from ham boiled in the back of the store, boiled peanuts, boiled in the back, pimento cheese mixed in the back, with lettuce and tomato. I went to work after school each day and left after closing at 9 PM. All the soda fountain stuff was my specialty, too. On Saturday I worked from 10 am until closing at 11 PM. I was paid $2.50 a week.

I continued working at Terry's Drug Store off and on until I graduated from high school.

I decided to join the football team. The Quitman High "Pirates." Our colors were Purple and Gold. There was a football field behind the high school building, mostly clay, with sparse areas of grass. I went into the dressing room at the beginning of my freshman year to be issued my uniform. There was one coach, Mr. Quarles. He taught math. He told me to \pick out a pair of pants, a long sleeve shirt, shoulder pads, helmet, and some shoes. There were only about 18 players, some of whom had been on the team varying numbers of years. I was one of 4 new members, J.T. McCoy, Julian Lazarus, Eugene Walker, and me. We all wore thick glasses, and didn't see too well if glasses were off.

The record of the school football team was not very impressive in past years. The shoulder pads were old, stiff and were only a little better than nothing. They lay on our shoulders, sticking out in every direction until we put on our jerseys that had PIRATES on some of them. When we put the jerseys on over our shoulder pads and pulled them down hard, and tucked them in our pants, they kind of molded to the shapes of our shoulders—but not much.

My shoe size was, and is, 7. The shoes were much larger, and had been used for years. They were high topped, old, firm hard leather, and not very malleable. The cleats were of tapering strips of leather, piled on each other, tapering from the sole out to the tip, like little pyramids, and they were nailed on the soles. They were scattered over the surface of the soles, and it was obvious they had been replaced many times. We were told if they needed new cleats, we had to take them to Kirby's Shoe Repair, down on 5 Points, in town. I couldn't find any to fit me, so I found the closest to my size, probably about size 10-12. I had to stuff paper wadded up into the toe ends. Not very comfortable, but who said playing football was comfortable? The old shoes were not comfortable at all. Sometimes the leather cleats wore out, or came off, and the nail came through the sole and stuck in our feet, making it hard to keep on running.

Trying to find a helmet that fit was a real chore. They were leather and kind of pliable, with a layer of felt inside. The earflaps were loose and you had to keep the heavy cord from one ear flap to the other ear flap tight under your chin to keep the helmet on your head. Finding football pants was also a problem. They were all old, with hardly any padding. Some had a little padding at the knees, nothing for the hips, and rarely thigh padding. The older and better players got the better uniforms, but none were great anyway. You could just about fold the helmets up and put them in your pocket. We looked like airplane pilots of the 1920s.

There was no such things, as nose or face guards. That made it sort of difficult for me, J.T. McCoy, Julian Lazarus, and Eugene Walker, because we all wore real thick glasses. Many times during a game we all were able to plough through the opponent's line and kind of look around in the backfield to try to find the guy who had the football. We sometimes ran into each other in the opponent's backfield. None of us could see any better than each other.

We played offense and defense, because we didn't have enough players for both. I was a good center, and was used sometimes, to center the ball. The only problem was that my vision was so bad I had to identify the guy that was very fuzzy, that was supposed to receive the football. I was a little off- occasionally. There was an occasion when we kicked the football, as a tackle I was supposed to run fast down the field and tackle the receiver as he ran down against us. I was streaking down where the ball was going. I was trying to see who caught the ball, and was running not knowing who caught it. Suddenly I saw who had the ball—I was only a short distance from him, but he was directly in front of me running fast as I was and straight toward me. I had no time to bend over to tackle him, and ran right into him, both of us standing straight up not knowing he was that close to me. He may have been as blind as I was. I got the tackle, and we both were hurt. We got up slowly and they had to walk me to the proper side of the field. I soon came to my senses. Being one of our football heroes, I returned to the game, ready to get killed again. Too bad we didn't have face guards so we could use our glasses.

We never got into shape, like they do today. Before practice the coach had us make two trips, running around the field. Then we would practice plays. When it was real hot, we stopped early. We thought the coach got tired and decided to quit for the day. We were not allowed to have any water during the game, if we did drink a cup of water they said if you get hit in the stomach you could rupture your stomach. We sure got dry during the game, in South Georgia.

Once on defense, I got the ball carrier in my sight and tackled him, almost misjudged his position, got hold of one leg, and he was dragging me along, when one of our big guys tried to help tackle him, running full speed and put his head down hitting us- especially me with his helmet right directly in my left eye. I thought this was the end of me. After a short game time out, they brought me off of the field. I was apparently a little rattled, because they told me I answered that my name was Zeke when they asked me my name. I didn't remember that. I got OK in a little while, but I noticed I couldn't see out of my left eye. Feeling for it, I found a huge lump covering my left eye, and thought it was my left eyeball. It was only a sudden broken blood vessel, hemorrhaging into my left upper eyelid that kept me from raising the lid, it was so big. I could see if I pulled my lid up with my fingers just enough to see light.

Saw Dr. Smith next day, made a little incision in the lid but no blood came out, because the blood had clotted and wouldn't flow. So I couldn't see out of it for three or four weeks. But I was a football hero.

Another injury was a cleat to my left shin, on the front of the leg. I didn't go to the Dr. for a couple weeks, so it was infected. It was red, sore and draining. He cauterized it, made me soak it, dress it, and cover it while playing football. That thing lasted for months, no antibiotics then, he just had to keep cauterizing it. Finally it healed, after football season. Our team was not very good, because our coach was not terribly knowledgeable about football, but we loved him. We had two or three plays, one was 2x to the right, and another was 2x to the left. No body could pass the ball, but once in a while we tried to run straight ahead. I don't remember what it was called, but that one didn't work too well either. We thought we were good, even though we won rarely.

The school loved us and cheered for us and even came to our games. We tried to be their football heroes. We thought the girls liked us anyway. Once I dislocated the end joint of the 4$^{th}$ finger of the right hand. Next day Dr. Smith pulled it back straight and taped a tongue blade beneath the finger, keeping it straight. I went back in two weeks and he removed the splint. I've never been able to bend that joint since then. It stayed stiff. After Medical School I learned to splint injured fingers in a flexed position, so you can still use the finger even if it winds up stiff.

Blue Springs was a popular swimming place on the Valdosta highway about 7 miles east of Quitman. It was a flowing spring that had been walled off with a cement wall to enclose a clear, cold water swimming pool, with the excess overflow going over the far end into a small creek that ran into a flowing river on south.

When we returned from Charleston and I entered high school, the springs flow after many years, had begun to decrease rather significantly so that it was not more than a trickle of water and swimming ceased. The surrounding old parking area, with tall trees had become a place for fishermen, and campers to park, and was used as camp grounds. The large river ran north and south along the east side and the railroad track ran east and west on the north side of all this property. As the train came along the track it started over a high trestle and went over the river on its way.

While we were camping on several occasions we found it exciting to go back to the tracks, walk down on the trestle to go to the river and look down the 30 or 40 feet to the water in the river. We had no idea when the train was due but we went anyway.

Once we heard it coming but we were too far from the land or water to be able to jump, or run back to where we could get off. So we had to climb down from the tracks onto the large timbers that made the trestle, and hold on tight a few feet below the train as it rumbled over us, with frightening shaking movements and loud train noise moving at lightening speed. This was a dumb thing to do, except very exciting when it was all over. After that we did that several more times hoping the train would come again when we were out there, but it never happened again. Our timing was off. I never mentioned this to my parents that would have been the end of my camping there.

Before we left Missouri one Xmas I received a Remington single shot .22 caliber rifle. I had shot some birds in Charleston in trees and on wires and stuff, and after we came to Quitman I continued to practice shooting things and stuff. Behind our home was a large field. One day I was walking in the field with my rifle and noticed a large bird circling over the field. He came nearer and nearer but stayed higher. I took aim, lead him a little and fired. His wings shuttered and he turned head down and did a rapid decent, nose dive into the ground. I had amazingly hit the thing. I walked over to where he was and found him on his back, staring at me with his claws up in a menacing manner. It was a large hawk. As I started to reach to pick him up he raised his claws, so I shot him again, and then I took him home and cut his feet off, and his beak off for souvenirs. When I had his feet off, the talons would grasp when I pulled the tendons.

Another time with my rifle I was riding around the country roads, in winter time, looking for something to shoot. I spied a hawk high in a tree off the road, so I stopped and tried to shoot him but missed and he flew to safety. On the right side of the road there was swamp, and on the left side there was more swamp. All of a sudden I spied a green head mallard duck flying from my right to my left about 50 feet high and fifty feet in front of me. I aimed, leading him and fired, He crumpled and landed far to my left, deep in the swamp. I tried my best to figure how to go get him to take home for a duck dinner. The swamp was too dense and wet so I gave up. I got nothing but my memory, and nobody was there to see my shooting ability.

Often some of my friends would get together at night, with our guns and go hunting for rabbits. One of us would get the family car and load up with 3 or 4 buddies and our .22 rifles. One night someone else was driving and I was sitting on the right front fender over the tire, while we were going slowly in the cemetery looking for rabbits eyes that glow in the headlights. The rabbit would stop, rise up and stare at the light, we would stop the car and someone would shoot him.

Suddenly there was a rabbit, the car stopped, I slipped off of the right fender ready to take aim and a shot fired behind me and I heard the bullet whiz by my right ear. J.T was off the right running board behind me quicker than I was and fired, barely missing my head, as I slid off the fender. We all got really scared and were shaking and talking about what could have happened and how lucky we were that I wasn't shot in the back of the head. We also decided this was a stupid form of entertainment. I don't remember doing that night hunting anymore. I think it may be illegal to do that anyway.

I played on the tennis team. I thought we were good. I was one of the best of the 4 or 5 tennis players in our school, so obviously I was on the school tennis team.

Our first game was against Albany, Georgia at their school. My opponent was obviously much better, and knew a lot more about tennis than I did. I don't remember winning a game. I do remember him running me back and forth, over and over, until I started having cramps in my calves. I would take time out a few times until I could make my feet stay flat on the ground. The cramps were painful, and almost unbearable until with the calf contractions continuous and shortened so I had to walk on my toes, I finally quit and forfeited the match. That was my tournament tennis. I still played a lot of tennis, but we quit when we'd get tired so we wouldn't get cramps in the legs. It was too bad we didn't have a tennis coach.

One summer, visiting from Missouri, I found an iron rod, 3 feet long that I carried around in the yard, just sticking stuff, like cardboard or paper. It was off of an old baby bed that guided the side up and down. I was walking around one afternoon, swinging it, like a cane—one end had a 90 degree angle for a handle. I suddenly stuck it into the ground to leave it to pick something up. I misjudged its location, and it went right into the top of my left foot, entering in the top between the big toe and second toe, about 2 inches from the web of the two toes. A reflex response pulled it immediately out. It was bleeding so I had to go the doctor. The rod had penetrated from the top of my foot through the foot and came out the bottom. He told me it was going to hurt, but it had to be done. He was right, it hurt. He used forceps, and picked up the end of a long thin iodized gauze strip and stuffed it into the wound, to about the center of the tract, and then from the bottom did it again to meet the one from the top. That was done because it had to heal from the inside out. That was very interesting and fairly painful. Then I had to see him once a week to have both drains pulled out a little, to allow the healing to take place from the inside out, to both entry wounds. It gradually healed fine.

We went to the movies at the Ilex Theater in downtown Quitman almost every Saturday to see the movie, a weekly serial, and cartoons. It cost 10 cents, later 15 cents, finally went up to a quarter. We always had to get a coke for 5 cents, and a bag of boiled peanuts for 5 cents, sometimes they were 2 for a nickel. One of our school mates, Peanut Murray, son of a well known, long standing vegetable vender across the side street from Daddy's new gas station, would peddle boiled peanuts daily forever, up and down the streets of Quitman.

After the station got going pretty good, Daddy would come down town every Saturday night, park his car on his station lot, light up an "Above the Average" cigar (cost was 2 for a nickel) and walk up and down in town, and after a while would go to a Saturday movie. He would make his rounds of all of his friends in their stores all over town, just to speak to them. He was always a real old time Southern Gentleman, tipping his hat with a little bow when he would meet any lady, and very cordial to all the men.

On Saturdays, people would always come into town from the country, in their cars, or maybe in their wagon sitting in a straight chair in the back wagon bed, and park them in the city garage area across the street from our station, or park in the station lot. You could hardly find a parking space on the main Quitman streets, because people from town would come down town and park and never move their car, just sit in them and smoke, or get out and walk, or just watch people walk up and down the streets.

In those days all stores downtown stayed open weekdays until 9 PM, and 11PM on Saturdays. Only drug stores opened on Sunday, from 2 until 6PM. On Saturdays, usually about 9 PM, they would begin to slowly clear out of town and return home. There was no TV and not much on the radio, except about 10 o'clock The Hit Parade came on the radio. They played the top 10 music HITS of the week.

About 8-9 o'clock, Daddy would show up at the station after he'd been down town greeting people, or going to a movie. I noted always, he would move a little differently, smoke his cigar a little differently, and smelled of a little alcohol. We were not supposed to know that he would drink a little, and he handled it quite well, but we could tell he was just a little tipsy. He always made it home OK.

As we got older, we noticed occasionally, he would go the bathroom often in the evening after supper, and after a while noted the same little signs later in the evening. Then we found his stash under a little table cloth that hung down to the floor on a small little table in the bathroom. It was some kind of wine, or brandy, apricot, or something. We never discussed it with him. There was no bar, or place to buy alcohol in Quitman. The only place I knew was a honky-tonk on the road to Valdosta. This is probably why my friends never drank. It wasn't part of our growing up knowledge, or interest. Just smoking was.

When we came back to Quitman, I was getting to the age the people in my age group were allowed to have boy-girl parties. A mother would host a Prom party. Sometimes two or three mothers would give the party, and they would chaperone it. So the friends of the son, or daughter would be invited to attend. They would have sandwiches, cake, cookies, etc. Parents would bring the kids to the party because we were all too young to drive.

When we arrived, girls and boys would be given a Prom Card. Usually there were empty lines, numbered, to write the names of the persons who asked you for the prom time, or you asked them for a prom time. Usually, the boys asked the girls for a prom time and write it down on her card, too. The prom period was usually 10 to 15 minutes long. When they began the proms, a bell would ring, or a whistle would sound to let everybody know its time to start, or time to go to the next name on the list. Some time we would ask the same girl for 2 or 3 prom times in a row,

After a little while, and after eating some of the goodies, the bell would ring, and we would find the person, usually of the opposite sex, that was 1$^{st}$ on the list. We knew we had a specific time to be with the 1$^{st}$ person. The bell signals the end of the prom time, so then we go find the 2$^{nd}$ on the list. We were controlled by the bell, and nosy Mothers walking around being nice vigilant Mothers. So this was the way boys and girls could get together, walk together, get to know each other, and get a little more comfortable being exposed to the opposite sex. We could sit together in the house, or walk around outside, or up and down the street, etc.

One of my first Prom Parties was given by my good friend Randall Garrett, who lived in a big house down in the next block on North Court Street. The street was two paved streets, one into town, the other going away from town, separated by a park in the middle, with bushes and flowers along the way in the park. Our house was on the opposite side from Randall's. I had gotten a prom with a girl I really liked, and we were walking down the street, in the dark. I was excited and a little uneasy, not being used to that kind of situation. When we got even with my house, on the opposite side of the street, I heard, a very loud whisper, "Paul! Paul!" I whispered back "What!" mortified. Then he said, "Who you got?" Terry was too young for prom parties, not in my age group, and not at the party. He had sneaked into the park behind a bush. I said "You go home." My prom date laughed, I was so embarrassed. Terry and I had words when I got home. I told Mama on him.

I went to the Junior-Senior Prom at the Country Club. I was a sophomore in high school. Bill Lay was playing records for the prom. Bill was a disk jockey locally. I loved to dance especially Jitterbug to some of those wonderful swing pieces of the late 1930s, Glenn Miller, Artie Shaw, Tommy Dorsey, Jimmy Dorsey, Woody Herman, and many more. I was a sophomore, and it was a time I wanted to be accepted and recognized as a "Hep" guy, and impress all the girls.

I got my prom card filled out with pretty girls, most were older than me, but they could dance really well. I wanted to stay inside and dance. Some people went outside for their prom time. They would walk around the area, talking, or sit in their cars. One of the girls that I selected was a senior, good dancer, pretty, but overweight. When our time came for the prom, I was going to dance, so we started to dance, it was a slow tune, so we were close. In a minute she said, "Let's don't dance, let's go outside. "I said "OK," and we went outside. We walked out onto the porch and she said "Let's go sit in my car." I said "OK." We did, she got in the drivers seat and I sat in the passenger seat.

She looked stunning in her large, flowing ORGANDY evening gown. The skirt almost took up the entire front seat. She started talking about her new gown, and where she bought it, and what it was made of, and asked didn't I want to feel the material. She picked up the edge of the skirt, covered with a large net material, and said "Feel this." I did, and commented how nice it was, and what a beautiful dress. The next thing I know is that she reached over put her right arm around my neck and pulled me close and KISSED me flat on my mouth, and stuck her tongue IN my mouth. There was something fierce going on in my body IMMEDIATELY. Tingling took over my body. This was my first kiss, and I didn't have any idea what happened to me. But later I figured it out.

Then we heard the bell ring to end my first step into the unknown. She was a senior and I was a sophomore, she seemed a little more "HEP" than I was. We went back to the dance, and I told her I had a good time, she said she did too. So I just kept on dancing. After that, when she was riding in her car and saw me around town she'd just smile a great big smile and wave and wave. I never knew if she expected me to call her, or what.

The Quitman Country Club House was at the tee of the 1$^{st}$ hole. The 9 hole course circled the rather large lake that we fished in, and we often spent Saturdays or Sunday afternoons playing golf. During our summers it was very hot so we would go out to the Quitman Country Club and spend the day swimming in very cold artesian well water pool, then maybe go up to the clubhouse and start on hole #1 and play golf. The 9-hole course went around the large lake where we sometimes fished. On the other side of the lake, at about Hole # 7 we would be very hot and tired. Along the left side of the fairway a wire fence separated the course from a farmer's field, usually growing watermelons—big, green, ripe watermelons. Occasionally, we might climb over the fence, thump a few melons until we recognize the sound of a "ripe" thump, and pick it up and pass it over to another hot tired golfer, who would happen to drop it on the ground and accidentally cause it to rupture.

Then all of a sudden is exposed the cool, juicy, red watermelon heart. Not wanting to waste the perfectly good, beautiful, sweet, red juicy meat, we each would help each other dispose of the delicious, juicy, red morsels of sweetness, removed by the handfuls to the mouthfuls. Soon only a naked, green rind was lying there, so we thought we should put it back where we happened to find it, back on the farmer's side, in the watermelon patch. It was a little easier to complete our game after we had sated out thirst and dehydration. We also always felt bad every time we stole the farmer's watermelon and thought we wouldn't do that again. But we always did, if it was hot. And it was always hot every time we played golf.

One time we were playing golf during the summertime. On the tee for the second hole, I was going to tee off. I put my tee into the ground, placed the golf ball on the tee, took a mighty swing, hit the ball down the fairway and the tee flopped out of the ground. When I picked my tee up there was a small, baby turtle impaled through the middle of its back, through and through. His little feet were attempting to crawl, but he was waving them in the air as I held him up to show everybody. I noted it was a little hard to put my tee into the ground, but I had no idea it was because I murdered the baby turtle. We dug around a little looking for more turtles, but found no more. It must have been where the mama turtle laid her eggs, and this little fellow was probably just about to leave the dirt nest and walk across the road into the lake. He was about the size of a fifty cent piece. If I had been a doctor then I might have taken him home and glued his shell back, and covered the wound with a band aid. I did feel really bad that he never had a chance to get started in his life.

I mentioned Randall Garrett, a real close friend who lived up the street from us. During our junior year, we would often go out to the golf course, on the weekends and swim or play golf. Playing golf on a Sunday afternoon, with Randall and Terry, we were teeing off from the 6$^{th}$ tee that required a drive over the road up a little hill. Terry was waiting for us to tee off, and he noticed some nice juicy, ripe blackberries growing along the dirt road to the right of the tee. When Randal was preparing to tee off, Terry was bending over picking and eating blackberries. He was almost at a 90 degree angle from Randall to his right. With an attempt for a mighty drive off the tee box, Randall swung the wooden driver striking the ball just on the toe of the driver. The glancing blow to the ball sent it flying straight to Randall's right, striking Terry right exactly between his eyes on the right side of the bridge of his nose. Terry screamed, nearly fell and started crying. The country club is a 9 holed golf course, built around a large lake. The road around the lake is a dirt road that people would just spend time riding leisurely around on a Sunday afternoon. We were on the 7$^{th}$ hole, on the opposite side of the lake from our car, and the clubhouse telephone. The nose was bleeding, and was sitting under his left eye where his cheek was supposed to be, and all we had was a dirty golf towel. We started walking back to the clubhouse, trying to console Terry, and calming Randall down, upset that he had hit Terry. Soon a car came around the lake with two ladies who knew us. They took Terry home and we called Dr. Smith, and took Terry to his office. Terry didn't have a nose where it was supposed to be. It was under his left eye. He looked like a freak. Dr. Smith did a fantastic reduction of that severely fractured and displaced nose. Terry turned out to have a perfect, straight nose, with no evidence of a previous fracture.

That episode was a few weeks before Randall, got severely ill. I heard Randall was in the hospital. We had been doing things together during the summer, and I couldn't believe he was sick so quickly. He had cerebral infection, severe meningitis, which developed a few days after he squeezed a pimple on his nose. He had acne and pimples occasionally on the nose, like all teenagers get. The nose is a bad place to squeeze, because of the lymph drainage from the nose. An infection drains along the lymph system. From the nose, it drains directly back into the area just beneath the brain, and if severe can drain up into and cover the brain quickly. Infections on the sides of the face drain down the same side neck, causing lymph nodes to enlarge.

I went to see Randall in the hospital. He was unconscious, and his face was immensely swollen. We were told he had a severe coccal infection, either a staphylococcus or streptococcus. I don't remember which one. There were no antibiotics, but sulfa drug had just become available. This was in 1939. Dr. Smith had ordered it from Atlanta, too late. Randall died right after it came. He was in the hospital only about a week before he died. His infection was massive, and drug came too late. All his friends had a hard time dealing with his loss. He was 16 years old and the only son in his family. He had 2 older sisters, Myra and Janie.

In high school I would usually double date with my friends J.T McCoy, Norman Beverly, Leroy Yates, or Frank Branch and our dates. One night Frank and I were dating, in his grandmother's car, and rode over to Valdosta, Ga., sixteen miles east of Quitman.

Frank lived with his grandmother who was quite elderly, and went to bed nightly, very early. Frank was in the habit of waiting until she was asleep, and then sneak the keys and go out behind the house to the garage on the back street, manually push the car backwards out of the garage, start the car and leave. This night he picked me up at my home. Frank knew two girls and he had set up the dates, and we rode around their town with me and my date in the back seat. Naturally, one couldn't pitch woo with his glasses on, so I had mine off and had placed them on the ledge in the back window. After time dictated they had to go home, and we had stopped for a hamburger, the date was over so then we drove back to Quitman.

Frank dropped me off at my house and went home. As I entered my house I recognized I had left my glasses in his car. I had to have my glasses. I sneaked into my parent's bedroom and slowly picked up Daddy's keys to his Ford, and sneaked back out of their room. As usual, my Mother said in a sleepy voice, "Paul?" I said "Yessum." She said "Are you OK?" I said "Yessum."

I waited a few minutes and sneaked back out of the house, took our car drove to Frank's house barely able to see without my glasses. I drove very slowly due to lousy vision all the way to Frank's back road garage and found it locked. After a few minutes I figured I had to get Frank down here to get into his car. I knew his upstairs window so I set out trying to whisper, or yell with quick muffled "Frank" and throw stones to hit the window to wake him, and I certainly didn't want to wake Mrs. Branch. After a while, he opened the window and came down to help me. I did get my glasses, never woke Mrs. Branch, I drove home sneaked back in my house and didn't wake my Mama. So it all worked out well, but it was scary to me at that time.

During summertime for a couple of years, J.T.'s mother, twins Ann and Fain Thomas's mother, and Norman Beverly's mother, I think, took a group of boys and girls to the Jacksonville Florida beach for a couple of weeks. Me, J.T., Norman, Leroy Yates, Louey Lowery, Ann and Fain, Madda Hubert, Mildred Mabbett, and Carolyn Prance. They rented us a house on the beach and we had a great time. Hot, sunburned, hot, sandy, poor sunscreens in those days, nearly blistered our feet if we didn't move fast enough in and out of the water. Just a lot of good kid fun, with Eagle eye mothers watching too well over their brood. We had a great time anyway. Good, good memories.

My dates were with Ann, or Fain, or Kathryn Terry with J.T., Norman, or Leroy, and their dates. We would drive around with one hand on the wheel, or find a deserted dirt country road, park, pitch a little woo, drive back to West End café for one of the best hamburgers I ever ate, and a coke.

We didn't have lot of money so many times we would take our date's home, and THEN go to West End for our hamburger. I believe those were 10 or 15 cent hamburgers. They grilled the thick, juicy hamburger, put mayonnaise, dill pickle, maybe mustard, big slice of tomato, and lettuce all on these large buns, then put the whole sandwich in a hot sandwich press until it was all mashed down and hot. We would have a Coca Cola in one of those green shaped coke bottles with the name of the town that the coke was bottled in, impressed on the bottom of the bottle. This was in the late 1930's, and I don't remember ever having French fries in those days.

We were in the high school band and I was pretty good on the clarinet and tenor sax, and Terry was really good on his trumpet. We use to play the big band records on the record player and play along with it, and memorize those neat instrumental solos. We bought our records at the Cocroft Music store in Thomasville, Georgia about 28 miles west of Quitman. At the store we met a really good musician from Thomasville that worked there, graduated from their high school and band. His name was Osco Hughes, played alto sax, and had a severe bilateral nystagmus.That is when both eyes uncontrollably, oscillate back and forth laterally; gave him quite a disability when reading. He had accommodated very well and got along fine.

He wanted to start a swing band and asked Terry and me to join. We both were flattered and agreed. There was a good piano player there, Alec Crittenden, he needed us and another sax, and some drums. We knew Donnie Channel, a drummer in our high school that liked to play, and had a set of "traps," so we asked him. J.T. McCoy, my best friend, played a great trombone and was part of our group. We asked Donald Ostereicher, tenor sax man from our band. We thought we were ready, and were excited to get practicing. We did several times and decided we were ready to play for a dance.

We noticed one little problem. Donnie the drummer, seemed to gradually increase the tempo, especially in the slow, dreamy dance numbers that would wind up about the tempo of a march, which makes a slow dreamy number wind up as a fast number. And a fast number to start with, wound up a faster number. We would have to make him try to stay at the same tempo start to finish, during the number. Also Donald, playing tenor sax, read music OK, but he played with no feeling, just blew the horn the same through the entire number, with no expression at all. He would tap his foot with every note he played, not every beat of the music.

Osco had been asked to put on a dance in the Veterans Hall, sponsored by them, in Thomasville. He made all arrangements, put fliers on poles in Thomasville, and was charging 50 cents to come. We got all dressed, and drove to Thomasville, got all set up, and kept waiting for everybody to show up. When time came to start only about 6 couples had come. We played a while and nobody else showed up. The people who sponsored it came over and said they couldn't pay us because nobody came, but he would give us free drinks, coca cola, root beer, or any other soft drinks. We were pretty good, playing music of all the old bands we'd been practicing, but we never got off the ground with our band.

I was old enough to be allowed to drive the car, so as time went by, we would go out on dates, ride around all over town, wind up at West End, get a hamburger and coke and get home between 11 and 12 midnight. We'd go to movies, go dancing, and ride around mostly.

None of my friends drank alcohol, or even beer. We had no conversation about that, or drugs. We were not aware of drugs being taken for recreation by anybody. There was no such thing that was even prescribed by doctors, unless we were just not aware of it. Back then I'm sure they had phenobarbital, and derivatives, but later there were a lot of types of that drug used for different things as time went on. I was aware of some people that would come into the back of the drugstores, and the pharmacist would get a small bottle out of the back of the store where they would compound prescriptions. After questioning some of the employees, they told me these people were buying Paregoric, a derivative of morphine given to infants for colic (stomach aches), that could be bought over the counter without a prescription. The dose was 2-3 drops for infants. The pharmacist knew these individuals, they would buy a 25 cent bottle, it was about one ounce, and they would drink it and apparently get a high feeling.

This was in high school, and some of my friends were experimenting with cigarettes. So I tried it. I really got dizzy at first, but soon I did good, and learned to inhale. The family tried to get me to stop, after catching me over and over. I kept saying OK. But after a few days—caught again. We would get one of our family cars, ride around at night, smoke, put all the windows up, and see how long we could stand filling the car with heavy smoking until someone said ENOUGH. Of course, our clothing was filled with the heavy aroma of cigarette smoke and the family knew. One day in my senior year, Daddy said to me, "I want you to quit smoking. If you will stop until you graduate, I'LL LET YOU SMOKE ALL YOU WANT." So we made a deal, and I didn't smoke until I graduated.

After graduation, Daddy planned to take me on a trip to see colleges, so I could decide where to go. He graduated from Virginia Tech, as his father did, and he really wanted me to go there. I had been looking at a lot of schools and couldn't decide. Before we left I bought Marlboros, Chesterfields, Lucky Strikes, Camels, Home Runs (very, very strong cigarettes), a pipe, Prince Albert, Edgefield, and a couple of other pipe tobaccos. I needed to find out what I liked, since I'm now going to be a smoker.

We left home early one morning. We drove to Valdosta, 16 miles east, and Daddy had to stop down town for some business, so he stopped the car right out in front of a men's clothing store. He walked away, and I got out of the car and, looking in the window, saw a nice looking regular men's straw hat, with a colorful band, above the brim, around the hat. Now that I'm almost a mature, cigarette smoking, or pipe smoking, attractive young man, I need to dress and look the part. I went in the store tried on the hat, and looking extremely sophisticated in it, and bought it. I walked out of the store with it on, and proceeded down the street to be able to be seen, and to see how I looked in the store windows reflection. I lit another cigarette and the new me really impressed me.

I had begun to really try to get grown and be attractive. I kind of liked some of the movie actors that were handsome and debonair, and smoked, and didn't have curly hair. I had curly, wavy hair. Mama would take her fingers and try to make a bigger wave in the front of my hair. I use to buy Brilliantine and try to paste my hair down straight and flat, and get rid of the waves, like George Raft. In the army it was cut short. Now there is not much even to worry about, and I don't.

We left and began the long drive to look at Duke, University Of Virginia, and a few others I've forgotten, and finally Virginia Polytechnic Institute. At the end of a long day driving, and smoking a variety of cigarettes, to decide which had the best taste, and several pipe loads of pipe tobacco, we chose a hotel in Columbia, South Carolina to spend the night. It was a large hotel with a big lobby, and a nice restaurant. We checked in, and had a nice meal. We were tired and Daddy said he wanted to go up and go to bed. I said that I wanted to spend a little time down in the lobby first. He said OK. I had my hat on all day and still had it on and knew I really looked sharp. So I wanted to sit there reading and smoking, to impress whoever there was around there that need impressing. I was really waiting for girls to come through the lobby. I lit my pipe, found some magazine, sat in a soft lounge chair, waiting, holding the magazine as if reading intently, and nobody came through looking. I finally got sleepy and went up and went to bed. I often wondered why I was thinking girls would be walking through the hotel lobby. Only men and families traveling would be in a staid hotel.

The next morning, when I woke up, my tongue was so swollen, and sore, I couldn't eat. I couldn't brush my teeth due to great stinging and burning from the tooth paste. My breakfast was a glass of milk. Daddy said my pain was due to smoking a lot. Imagine!!! We continued our trip, slowly I got better, decided Virginia Polytechnic Institute was my choice. Daddy was elated. We met a couple of Professors Daddy knew there. This was in 1941, Daddy graduated from Tech in 1911, 30 years before, in Civil Engineering.

Some of his classmates were now professors, and taught me when I entered there in Sept. 1941. He was really excited to be back and show me the school.

The school nurse, Miss Hannas, a friend of Daddy's, was still there working in the infirmary when I got there. I was impressed with his friends, and the school, and I was happy to have had the opportunity to be there with him at this reunion time for Daddy.

# 2
# College and World War II

I entered Virginia Polytechnic Institute, a military college in south-western Virginia, Blacksburg, Virginia in Sept. 1941, at age 17, where my father Paul A. Tanner, Sr., graduated 1911 with a degree in Civil Engineering. His father, James Gilbert Tanner, graduated in 1879 with a degree in Mechanical Engineering, later to enter a Seminary and became a Presbyterian Minister. He married and had two sons, Frank, who was the oldest, and a writer and printer at a Dallas, Texas newspaper, Paul, my Daddy, and three daughters. Grace, never married, Eloise, never married, and Edith married 3 times, last time to Mr. Lee, Gen. Robert E. Lee's cousin's son.

I elected to pursue a degree in Biology, so I could qualify to attend medical school. I also chose to join the Regimental Marching Band, name "The HightyTighties," and also the swing, dance band, "The Southern Colonels." I played tenor saxophone and clarinet. I thought I might wind up as a musician. I was pretty good. In high school I had received 1$^{st}$ place in District Music Contests solos. (1$^{st}$ in clarinet and tenor saxophone in Albany Georgia), Georgia State Music contest, (1$^{st}$ in saxophone and 2$^{nd}$ in clarinet in Milledgeville, Georgia) and went to the National Music contest in Richmond, Va. in 1941, (1$^{st}$ in saxophone).

Life was extremely regimented. In the freshman year all cadets had to walk on the extreme right side of all sidewalks in the "Braced position"—walk straight up, chin tucked close to the chest, shoulders back, arms swinging from the shoulders very slightly back and forth as you walk, with thumbs very close to the black stripe down the length of the trouser uniform. You must speak to every upper class cadet you meet with "good morning, SIR." Answer questions with a loud "Yes SIR" or "No SIR." We had to march as a company to all meals, and freshmen (RATS) had to go to our place in the formation and stand in the braced positioning front of our dorms before all other members came to march. This was the time the sophomores in the band, last year "RATS" walked around to each of us inspecting our polished shiny black shoes; our shiny, polished brass belt buckles; clean white belts that all rats wore for the 1$^{st}$ year; clean recent shave; and military haircuts.

The first year, in my room, three freshmen lived together. Roommates were called "ole lady." One of my "ole ladies" was told at inspection to get a haircut. With all the time constraints, he didn't have time to go downtown for a haircut. So the other 'ole lady," Bill Kindle, and I offered to cut his hair for him so he wouldn't get demerits for not doing so. At the next formation for inspection he was surrounded by the sophomores, laughing and yelling at him about his lousy haircut. We had attempted to cut his hair with our scissors, the only thing we had. I started on his right side, the other roommate started on his left side. The terraced levels on my side of his head, didn't match up with the terraces on the other side. No matter what we did to match them up, nothing worked. It looked ratty and terrible. We didn't know it was so hard to cut hair. All three of us were given demerits for "unauthorized haircutting" We had to walk them off, for a couple of hours daily, for several days.

My grades were terrible and embarrassing. In high school at Quitman, in South Georgia I did ok, A's and B's mostly, without too much studying. But I was a poor learner, with no way to remember how to retain all that stuff in college to remember it for tests and exams. Grades were mostly C's and D's, I only failed 2 courses-first quarter Physics, and second quarter Physics. Took them over and made A's in them both. I passed 3$^{rd}$ quarter Physics the first time I took it, with a C.

In one of the failing quarters of Physics, I wrote a poem in class when the paper was returned with my failing grade, marked "34" as my test result. This was it:

On Return of My Physics Test Paper

I wonder why I cannot learn this Physics like the rest?

For instance, take a look at how I fell down on this test.

I studied so hard on so much stuff that I could see no more.

And all I got on the doggone thing was a measly 34.

PAT, Jr. May, 1943

Daddy's friend, and still the school nurse, Miss Hannas was a sponsor of the dance club, named The Cotillion Club. She was instrumental in getting me in as a member of the club. It primarily put on a military dance annually, bring in a Big Band, and cadets would invite their girlfriends to the dance for the week-end. We brought in Fred Waring's band, and another year Tony Pastors band. I didn't have a girl friend within 1000 miles and I couldn't afford a girl. I never was able to stay out past 7:30 at night because of poor grades, so I had no opportunity to meet a local girl friend either. I would go to the dance and dance with my friend's girl once in a while.

There was a contest between all the military companies on campus. The "Eager Squads" made up of the best marching 8 cadets in each company. I was selected as one of the 8 from the band. We carried rifles, and marched through all of the intricate drills, doing tricks with the rifle, while marching to the commands of our Squad leader. The judges were the Commanding Military Officers assigned from the Regular Army to teach Military Sciences at our college. The Eager Squad of the band won $1^{st}$ place. You can imagine how pleased, proud, and happy we were to bring home the 1st Place Award to the HightyTightys.

One of my uncles, Howard Finley, Mama's brother, wrote me a letter during my $1^{st}$ year at Tech expounding how exciting it was where he lived in Nebraska. He worked with an oil company, they were expanding, and seeking new young men to join the company, and probably make his fortune in oil. This would be a ground floor opportunity, if I chose to quit school and join him in Nebraska. I got excited. Here I was making poor grades and therefore no way to become accepted to medical school. I was hoping to get drafted into the army and save face with my family.

My Daddy was writing letters to some of his old college friends, who were high officers in the army, and professors in colleges, or high officers in businesses, trying to get someone to help me not be drafted or to get on into Medical school, now, so I wouldn't be drafted. Poor Daddy, none of it worked, of course. When he sent my grades to the colleges, the return letters suggested I continue and pull my grades up.

Army people told him they had no ability to change draft status, if I was healthy. So when I sent my uncle's letter home and told them I was going to go to Nebraska, I received blistering, angry demands of "Forget that!!!" "You WILL stay in school!!!" I felt so guilty I decided to stay. I didn't have any money anyway, so how could I leave school. So that ended me leaving school at that time. Time came that pending draft was coming, and my grades weren't good enough for a deferment. So that was that. I needed to enlist so I could choose the branch of the service that I would be in...Otherwise, good luck!! Go where they send you!! I chose the Medics, and boy, am I glad I did! I grew up and matured, and finally became a man that I'm pretty proud of.

VPI (Va. Tech.) was a far away place from southern Georgia. You could hardly get there from my home I had to get on a train in Quitman and ride for about 12 hours, change trains in Richmond, Virginia wait for a couple of hours, get on another train to go to Roanoke, Virginia. Then wait until the little train that was called the "Huckleberry" got there. It ran once a day from Roanoke about 40 miles, to Christiansburg, Va. which was about 10 miles to Blacksburg. Usually there were other students arriving at the same time, so we all chipped in for a cab ride to school. It took nearly all of a day and a half to make the trip from home to school, if everything worked out time wise.

Trying to get to Quitman from Blacksburg was worse. Trains didn't run even close to times for each other to be helpful for each others passengers. I hitched hiked home to Ga. several times during the 2 years before the war. That was tough. I'd dress in my VPI uniform, have only 10-20 dollars in my pocket and a very small suitcase and start walking to the edge of Blacksburg. Stand there with my thumb out, smiling, looking out for someone to pick me up. You get lonely quick, when all the cars just ride on by, like nobody is standing there.

I would try to spend the least amount of money to get home. I would live on a 5 cent package of Tom's peanut butter cheese crackers and a coke. Usually the trip would take 18 to 24 hours to get home to Quitman, with no stopping. I would stay awake the entire time. There were no motels, only hotels, so no money no hotel room.

One time a friend in the band, Ben Cullen and I were standing there, and a car kind of old, stopped and picked us up. The driver was accompanied by his girlfriend who he introduced us to. He was a talker and we talked back. Nearly halfway to Christiansburg, the right back tire went flat, and he pulled over to the side of the road. We all got out, and gaped at the tire, like "idiot tire!" I noticed the driver had on bellbottomed trousers with a wide waist band at the top. There were two rows of buttons in front, the first of which were side by side, and the rows of buttons starting at the middle of the waistband, slanted down and outwards to reach the bottom edge of the waist-band, separating the needle-and-thread-sewed in name, "Doyle." That verified that was his name because she said, "Doyle, what are we gonna do?" After a few minutes, he said "well, I ain't got no jack, so I figger I got to walk to git us some help." She said "OK." He told us to wait right there and he'd go. He did. And we did too, after only a short time. He left her there with us, and we thought it was best for us to keep on hitchhiking.

It wasn't long before we got a ride to Christiansburg, where we separated and went away to our homes. Ben went north to Richmond, I went south to Quitman. I often wondered how Doyle and his girl friend got along after we left them.

I had several interesting episodes during the few hitchhiking trips going home. Going south from Christiansburg, the main highway went southwest to Bristol, Tennessee right on the Tenn.—Va. line, then south to Knoxville, Tenn. Another way was to start going down the same highway toward Bristol, but cut left about half way to Bris-tol, and travel through southwest Va. and enter North Carolina and travel through some of the Blue Ridge Mountains. I took this second way one late afternoon going home for Christmas. The weather was clear but cold. A nice gentleman picked me up in one of the small towns we had to go through and I had been let out in that town. It was at a crossroad where the highway that would leave the Bristol high-way and would take me into South Carolina through the country. I was standing there a long time, it was getting a little cold, and a little toward evening time, and I finally got a ride going into North Caro-lina. There were 4 men, southern working men, very nice and talk-ative and jovial sorts. I got to sit between the 2 in the back seat. They were chewing tobacco, offered me some, and I politely refused. It was really close in my seat between two big working men in overall and big coats. We drove until well after dark, and had been driving through small towns, farmlands, forests, and it got real mountainous terrain. I could tell it was mountainous because we went around a lot of curves and in the headlights I could see trees going uphill abruptly from the edge of the cement road.

All of a sudden we came to a crossroad and the driver slowed an said, "Well it's been nice knowin' you, and were goin' to the left here, we just live up this road a little ways—4-5 mile, so you better get out here 'cause this roads gonna take you right on into the next big town." I thanked them profusely, and asked if there was any stores open around here, they said no, not at this hour, and nothing is close by here anyway. It was about 10 o'clock at night.

They left on their way turning left, leaving me recognizing I didn't have a flashlight, and there wasn't a speck of light of any kind. As we drove in the area, I had seen with the car lights no buildings, no barns, no cows, no nothing, except trees all around. I put my hand to my face and couldn't see it. I suddenly realized what it would be like to be totally blind. There was no moon, no stars, and just me, and no traffic. I was 18 years old and scared to death. I don't know what of, because there was nothing there. I didn't hear any animal, or sound of anything. I tried not to think of bad things happening to me, but the more I didn't think of them the worse they got, and the worse the bad things became. I tried humming, and sounded stupid, couldn't whistle because my mouth was so dry, and I had no water. There was no place to sit down, because I couldn't see the snakes, if they were there, or the "cow pies" if they were there. I was really lonely watching that car leave me and slowly, as they left me, I watched the little red tail lights get smaller, then at a curve, gone. Then absolute quiet darkness and fear embraced me, for a long time. I kept telling myself "You're OK, nobody knows you're here, so they can't hurt you." I figured if I couldn't see they couldn't see me either. It didn't help much, but nothing did happen,

It was a couple hours later the first car came by, saw me and stopped. I was so grateful I thanked him and told him how scared I was out there in the pitch black night all alone. He was an older man going far enough to get me back to civilization. He told me I didn't need to be scared, because "there ain't nobody lives in 5 miles of that crossroad, round here nobody'd hurt you noway." That didn't make me feel any better, I was still scared.

From then on I tried to make my hitchhiking trips along the bigger highways. Most of my trips were pretty uneventful, except one I remember, in Chattanooga, Tenn. I had gotten down to Knoxville, Tenn. Late in the afternoon, I was picked up by a traveler going all the way to Chattanooga. We had a nice trip and he let me out as we entered town. I was picked up after a little wait, and taken to the other end of town.

On the other end of town I waited a long time and it had become dark earlier. By the time I got a ride it was near midnight. A very nice gentleman, dressed in a suit, and tie, and spoke as an educated man might, polite conversation, seemed interested in me, and what I was studying. He was driving a nice, rather new car. As we drove along and talking to each other, as we left the lighted areas, as street lights, and buildings, I noticed he didn't seem to be in any hurry to get any where, and suddenly I felt his right hand on my left thigh about half way up my thigh. The hand was placed gently, not grabbing, not caressing. I suddenly grabbed his hand forcefully with my left hand, and forcibly threw it back to him, angrily I yelled, "Stop this car, now. I want out of here." Without a word, he stopped the car I got out and took my suitcase, and left the car without a word. I was left way out on the outskirts of Chattanooga in the middle of the night.

Some of these roads were very desolate then. Now there are people filling in all of these desolate roads with motels, small towns, farming, automobile sales offices way out of town with hundreds of cars all over their big parking area, with big lights all over the place. They wait for the cities to come out to meet them, so they wind up right in town as the town grows. Rides were from people usually going a long way.

It was a very interesting way to travel meeting all sorts of people. Some were easy to talk to others seemed not to want to be bothered by talking. That would always make me a little apprehensive, because I never had any idea what they were thinking, or what they might do next. I guess they wondered the same about me.

The least amount of money I spent going home was $1.75, for a day or more traveling. I always thought I was very lucky not to have had any real problems. Today I wouldn't think of hitchhiking any-where, nor would I pick up a hitch hiker.

Since December 7th 1941, when the war started, as time passed, my grades were barely passing and getting no better. Here I was wan-tin' to be a doctor, with these totally inadequate grades and knowing it would never happen. I wanted to be drafted to get me out of this embarrassing situation. Of course, my mother and father were vehe-mently opposed to that. After the first 2 years, I thought that another quarter of college, would maybe allow me to take some of the chem-istry credits that would improve my chances to enter medical school.

It was this weird thinking that made me decide to enter Vanderbilt University, Nashville, Tennessee for the summer session 1943.

During that summer quarter at Vanderbilt, I was exposed to the freedom at college, not possible at a military college. I became aware of that due to my meeting some students who were a little more experienced and sophisticated than I was.

So now I'm at Vanderbilt, out of structure and control, meeting friends with cars, and money and brains, and I had none. We lived in a dorm, coming and going when and as we pleased. Two of my friends were drinkers, who convinced me it was OK. One night they had been to the store, came back with a bottle of "Southern Comfort" and a cocktail set, consisting of 6 pretty glasses and a tall pretty pitcher that matched. They came into my room with the liquor and cocktail set and invited me to join them. We sat around and talked, and had fun, and I decided this was a good time to see what drinking was about.

I had never drunk any, had just completed 2 years at Virginia Tech., a complete military, and very strictly controlled male student body. We marched to meals, and back. The "Mess" hall was huge. The entire Corps of Cadets marched to meals as companies, and were seated together for each of three meals a day. Tables seated 10 cadets. At each table, a senior sat at the head of the table, a junior sat next to him on both sides, then sophomores next to the juniors, then the rest filled by freshmen, "rats." At meals freshmen had to sit at attention, not speaking, throughout the entire meal, until the upper classmen had served themselves from the plates and dishes as they were passed up and down the table, then the freshmen (rats) could serve themselves, and finish the meal. Thankfully, all empty dishes would be refilled by the cadet waiters.

Occasionally, an upperclassman would require one of us "rats" to eat a "square" meal. This meant while continuing to sit at attention, take a forkful or spoonful of food from the plate, raise it straight up to mouth level out in front of us, and then bring it horizontally to our mouth, follow the same path back to the plate, put the utensil on the plate, sit at attention and chew the food and swallow. Then repeat until the meal had been consumed. Bugle Taps, blown at 11 PM, meant lights out, and bedtime. We had to be in the room by 8:30 PM, if we had a C average or better. During those 2 years, I never had good enough grades to stay out until 8:30, I had to be in my room by7:30 PM.

So back to Vanderbilt period, out of military structure and control, meeting friends with cars, and money, and brains and I had none of any of that. We never had alcohol, not even beer. So, my new friends had the cocktail set, ice, and glasses. After the first drink, it was obvious to me that I didn't get "drunk," so I'd drink another slowly and enjoy my friends. Southern Comfort is sweet and tastes real good and is easy to drink, especially mixed with coca cola, and makes you feel good...AT FIRST!

As time passed and we were having a good time, I felt I need to go to the rest room. I remember saying to myself, after a few drinks, and not feeling it, that it was OK for me to maybe drink with my friends in the future.

So I got up from where I was sitting on my bed, leaning back against the wall, and walked to the door to the hall to walk half way down the hall to the bathroom. I made it to the hall fine, turned to go down to the bathroom, and suddenly noted the hall had become a foreign place—very slanted, slightly moving more to the slanted side, then with each step, the hall slanted back the other way, over and over, tricking me, in how to place my feet to keep me from running into the wall of the other side. After a few short runs from wall to wall, I got to the bathroom, with difficulty I noticed trying to stand in front of the urinal, was difficult, since the urinal kept moving. After a few squirts, many in the wrong area, and clamping it off with one hand, I thought I'd better sit down on the commode. Commodes were in a different area in the large bathroom, than the urinals, which required me to first find them, and then try to go there. Funny thing— the walls of the bathroom moved like the hall wall, only they were a lot further apart, and very hard to reach and hold to, with one hand. I lost a few squirts on the way. It dawned on me this must be what people mean when they say they get "tipsy." On the commode, holding each side of the stall walls, my mission was accomplished, despite of a little extra wetness scattered around here or there. On returning to my room, along the same route having to be coursed, the same difficulty, having to be repeated, I got to my room, and claimed it was time to go to bed. My friends left. Leaving me, having to some way, undress myself, and climb into bed. Then after lying down, a whole new group of miserable feelings came to me. Guilt, extreme dizziness, nausea, gagging, and the necessity to sit up, find my waste basket to vomit into, and repeat most of those undesirable attacks, including, recognizing the stupidity of trying to learn to drink alcohol like a gentleman. I learned also, that "Southern Comfort" is very easy to drink. It is sweet and tastes good. You drink way too much before you know it's too much.

Needless to say, the summer quarter was more of the same, hard courses, studying but not knowing how to study to learn. My grades were more of the same, passing but less than average. Not helping my case in any way, but I did have fun, I thought.

I had been informed that my draft number was coming up in October 1943, by my draft board in Quitman. The only way to get into the branch of service you wanted was to enlist before you were drafted. Otherwise, you had no choice, and may wind up anywhere in the armed forces. My vision was very, very, poor. With glasses, vision 20/20. Without glasses, vision 20/400. Poor vision kept you out of the navy, marines, and air force. But the army took anybody, and most started out in the Infantry. And I wasn't too good at hand to hand combat, or seeing far away, especially if I lost my glasses. So I enlisted so I could choose the medical department, against my family's protective concern and fear.

After enlisting in the army, I chose the medical department, since I wanted to be a doctor. The day came to leave. In October, 1943, my Father drove me to the bus station in Quitman, Georgia, my hometown. My sweet Mother couldn't bear to go with her husband to see her oldest son, 19 years old, go off to a terrible World War, wondering if he would ever return. I understood that and kissed my Mother several times, several days in a row before I left. I was thinking like I thought my mother was thinking—I could get killed in the war and never come home. I left the house with a smiling, supportive, proud, brave, and worried teary eyed Mother waving as the car backed out of the driveway of my home. I heard the words she always said when I'd go any where. "Now Paul, be careful" I had a little wetness in my eyes, too. I understood her worries, as any parent, even more so, during my later life when we had a total of 6 children, 5 which were boys. It's a scary thing for parents to have to send their kids of to war. Mine didn't have to go to war, only we had to send them out into a different world than I grew up in.

At the bus station several people were waiting for the bus. I was apprehensive and worried, and noted Daddy wasn't talking any more. The bus drove up, we shook hands, then he kissed me and I teared up a little, and got on the bus. I waved to Daddy as we drove away, really teary. Probably all the other families were going through the same deep emotions of separation.

There were about 25 draftees on the bus and were taken to a large camp in Macon Georgia, where new soldiers were weighed, examined, and given uniforms and written orders to get on a train and go somewhere. I knew only one of the boys from Brooks County on the bus to Macon. After Macon I never saw him again. He must have been sent in a different direction. I had no idea what direction I was going.

My train was loaded, pulling several cars full of soldiers. After a couple of days we wound up in Camp Barkley, at Abilene, Texas, for Basic Training for three months, then for reassignment somewhere where there was war. At home there was no TV to look at the daily fighting and dying. News was delayed coming back to the families at home. Letters we wrote were censored. Some radio was censored. Gas, auto tires, and most food, were rationed, requiring coupons to be turned in when buying. No coupon, no buying.

We learned how to be soldiers, and take care of ourselves and each other. Marches, calisthenics, classes of all kinds, etc. During the marching, it was noticed by the company commander, that I was well trained and knew how to march, due to my 2 years of military marching at Virginia Tech.

He spoke to me and asked me to become an Acting Corporal, and take over the marching training of one of the 3 platoons of the company, since they were short of corporals to train the new recruits. I of course agreed, however, they never mentioned any increase in pay. My pay continued at the regular pay for privates in the army, of $21 a month. I also was given a GI insurance policy of $10,000.00, just in case I got killed. Big deal!

During basic training in Camp Barkley, I was thrown with men from all over the United States of America, and from all walks of life, and from every job category—laborers, funeral home workers and owners, pharmacists and drug store workers, farmers and farm workers, actors, professional baseball players, college students and other human individuals, and any other field you can name. Any male from 18 years old to 42 years old were all thrown into a mass of people to train to fight the war.

Most everyone was drafted into the army and had to leave their jobs and family. Most had no idea how to be soldiers to fight a war without training. The only people I knew that started with an Officer's Commission were Physicians, and possibly some attorneys. There may have been some I was not aware of. They all had to be trained, where ever they landed in this massive group of citizens, to join together to defeat the enemy of the United States.

It became deeply apparent to me at that time in my life that I had to change my entire attitude about becoming a doctor. If it was going to happen I had to make it happen, and do some things differently. It was obvious that most of the people I was thrown with did not impress me enough to want to be like them, I tried many times to picture myself as whatever job they did in life. None suited me, other than picturing myself as a Physician. That was one of the real hard lessons.

I learned to drive myself to learn how to study properly, and take the time it took to prepare myself to become what I wanted to become. I also learned it wasn't easy to learn to drink alcohol. I had never tasted alcohol of any kind, wine, hard liquor, or beer, until I went to Vanderbilt the previous summer. My friends in high school never indulged to my knowledge. The only bad thing we did was try to learn to smoke, and inhale like the big boys did. In college- very strict Military College- nobody could drink on campus, but we could smoke. I heard of some that drank on weekends when they went to their home. My home was far away and it was hard to get there from where I was.

During our basic training in Texas, the weather was beastly hot most of the time. Our day started at 6-7 o'clock in the AM. We spent the day in from moderate to severe physical activity, until about 4-5 o'clock.

We did a lot of marching 1 mile, 2 miles, 5 miles, 10, 15 mile hikes, slowly increasing up to a final 25 mile hike. This was hard on my feet, and difficult while carrying a full backpack. About every mile or so, we got a 10 minute break. We get to lie down on the ground, mostly clay, sandy, hilly ground with mesquite scrubby, scattered bushes, and really tired, hot and sweaty. Trying to conserve our canteen of water was a problem, taking teeny sips to conserve for later. Biting yellow deer flies hurt whey they bit us frequently.

Some of our hikes were to take us out in the wilds for camping at a place for a few days at a time. Sometimes we camped by a river. Here we were allowed to take a frigid bath, naked, with soap if you remembered to bring it. Soap (this was before detergents) doesn't lather much in cold river water. Without soap you just got wet. I had a problem at first getting naked with a bunch of men. I think most guys had this problem because of the inevitable comparison factor. I found I was worse than some and better than some. (I didn't mention here what is worse, or what is better.) I didn't have enough guts to comment and nobody else did either, at least not to me. I never heard any discussion, but I guess it's only natural to wonder.

We had to pitch our pup tents, using our half shelter with another's half shelter, then both of us sleeping together in that little tent. Some men were assigned to dig a slit trench for a latrine. It was about 8-10 feet long, a foot wide, and 2+ feet deep. I was a little overweight and had a hard time straddling and squatting and waiting long enough for the inevitable to happen, before I would lose my balance and fall over backwards. I never fell, but tended to want to hold out until we got back to the base. That wound up making me constipated, and that was worse. That made you have to squat longer, I found out. I always hoped they dug the thing close to the bushes or trees, so I could hold on to a branch for better balance and control. I also tried to wait for a time when nobody else was there, because I always hated to line up behind somebody, or even in front of somebody. I hated when somebody came in and squatted facing me. I found that was a poor place to strike up a conversation with somebody. I thought that was not the most pleasant part of Army life; however, I never worried about it except when I was out in the boondocks, and had to go.

After being dismissed, hot, thirsty, and really tired we all took off to the PX for cold drinks. The PX was surrounded by a high fence, enclosing a lot of benches and the PX building. Every soldier was allowed 2 bottles of beer–only. No more. They had cold drinks, fruit drinks, colas, etc. The only thing was, they had all the ice on the beer, and "cold" drinks were very lukewarm. I had never tasted beer. So I bought my 2 allotted beers and went out and sat in the sun to drink my 2 beers.

I smelled it and nearly gagged, but I was so thirsty I took a big swig and swallowed it—and immediately, almost puked, not vomit, almost-PUKED. I put the beer down, got up and walked around and around, finally holding it down, not vomiting. I asked a couple of my buddies if they wanted my beer and almost caused a riot. Everybody wanted it, somebody grabbed one, and somebody the other. Everyday I bought my 2 bottles, drinking a little out of one because it was COLD, nearly vomiting, I noticed I was very popular with the guys at the PX, hanging around me to get my beer that I couldn't drink. As time went on, I found the few drinks of beer that I could drink got easier to get down, and keep down. Before I left basic training I was drinking both bottles and enjoying them.

I never really learned how to study to learn the subject, until I was sent, after 3 months of basic training at Camp Barkley Texas, to Medical Technician training school at Fitzsimmons General Hospital in Denver, Colorado for three months. I was so interested in the medical knowledge that I was taught, it was easy for me to make great grades. I learned it is very easy to learn things if they are related to what you really dream of doing in your life. After the 3 month training in Medical Technician School, My grades were exceptional, I was told.

So they kept me there another 3 months in a Surgical Technician training school. Again, I loved the subjects, and working, and assisting in surgery. It was easy to retain knowledge, so, I earned excellent marks at the school.

This proved to me that I really did have sense enough to be a doctor. I just had to change my attitude about some of those ridiculous courses they make you take in college preparation for medical school, that I kept asking "why the hell do I need this to be a doctor?" I had to pass them anyway, no matter if I liked them or not.

After completing my training, I was sent back to Camp Barkley, Texas. I was advised that I would be assigned to the European Theater of War. There were several really good friends that went through basic training, medical technician and surgical technician training with me, who were at Camp Barkley awaiting the same fate of reassignment to Europe. While waiting, it was announced there were openings for candidates in Officer's Candidates School, in the Medical Administrative Corp. I didn't know what that was, only that if I passed, I would become an officer.

I decided to apply as did 5 of my good buddies. Two were Bill Stinson, from Indiana, and Sammy Saras from Idaho, We applied and were chosen as candidates to become 2$^{nd}$ Lt., MAC (Medical Administrative Corp). Physical exams had to be passed. I knew I was physically all ok, except my vision. Vision requirements were known to me, having just finished the technicians training at Fitzsimmons in Denver. I knew the vision had to be no worse than 20/200 in one or both eyes correctable to 20/20 with glasses. I also knew the eye chart used had a big E at the top, which is 20/200, and a second line of smaller C D which is 20/100. I knew my vision was 20/400 in both eyes, correctable to 20/20. So, when I went into the room for vision, I quickly noted the same chart on the wall that we had to read.

The technician examining eyes told me to remove my glasses and cover one eye and read the chart. I did and my right eye couldn't read it, so I said "I can't see it so well, but I think it's an E. I can't read any more." Then covered the other eye, and said "E and below that is CD. I can't read much more than that." Next I had to put my glasses on and go through the same routine. This time I could read 20/20 with each eye. So I passed the physical. Just a little small fib because I knew the U.S army needed me as a bright, young, vigorous 2$^{nd}$ Lt. in the Medics, and certainly would forgive my fib.

After 3 months of study, classes, very arduous daily physical training, early AM calisthenics, hiking, a lot of military stuff, camping, and anything else they could dream up, our class graduated with a promotion to 2$^{nd}$ Lt. MAC.

I was then assigned to Lawson General Hospital, in Atlanta, Ga., working in the Personnel Division of the hospital.

After 30 days working in personnel, I received orders to report to Fort Lewis, Washington, in Tacoma. I was sent on a troop-train which was loaded with soldiers, from Atlanta, across northern America to Tacoma, Washington. Going through South Dakota, there were several small towns that the train slowed, stopped a short few minutes, for mothers in the area standing along the tracks, to hand into our windows sacks of pheasant sandwiches, with happy, smiling, and "good luck wishes" for us all. Those were some of the wonderful, never-to-be forgotten good memories, and really delicious sandwiches. I never ate pheasant before, or since. This wouldn't be allowed today, the sandwiches may be laced with poison, or drugs. This is a very sad commentary about today's society.

I was awaiting assignment overseas, attached to the 21$^{st}$ Medical Service Company. Our company was to serve as administration, supply, food, and basic aid, for 12 or more small medical specialty units. Each unit was composed of a general surgeon, thoracic surgeon, dental surgeon, maxillofacial surgeon, orthopedic surgeon, urological surgeon, plastic surgeon, medical internist, and each surgeon had an assistant surgeon, a surgical nurse, and 3 soldiers, to be nurse aids, truck drivers, and any other help needed in their unit. For each unit a large truck was equipped for surgery, one smaller truck to move equipment, and a jeep for personnel.

The plan was for my company, with the attached units, to be available for the planned invasion of Japan, and be set up behind the front lines, to get to the soldier's injury or problem quickly, manage the injuries quickly and return the soldier to the front lines, or evacuate them back to the next larger facility for more elevated levels of treatment.

At Fort Lewis, during the waiting time, I was assigned to teach new recruits about the army structure, with separate parts, how each fits into the function, what, and where the medics fit in and their responsibility to the whole military picture. I held a 4 hour class each morning for about 25 students. I had to study, and repeat the information in class as the brilliant teacher.

This is when I found out how to study, retain what and why I learned, and teach the student. I should have known in college, so I could properly answer test and exam questions. I remember it was during this time that our President Franklin D. Roosevelt died. We were all really saddened by this news. Vice-President Harry S. Truman became President, Our new Commander-In-Chief.

This is the period in my life where I came to grips with the requirements to become a physician. I had to qualify academically for acceptance and entry into medical school. After the war when I returned to Virginia Polytechnic Institute to complete my pre-med requirements, my grades were high for the remainder of my time before entering med school. And, even in med school my grades were in the upper third of my classes for the 4 years. I finally learned how to study because I had set my goal to become a Doctor, and I love what I was learning. I found out you never quit learning, if you're going to be a competent Doctor.

I remember thinking how fortunate I was to have been able to attend a military college for 2 years before joining the army. Meeting boys and men out of civilian life entering the service allowed me to compare myself to the average person. I had learned discipline for myself and that nobody was going to teach me but me, and I had better get it right if I was going to make anything out of myself. Being with the cadets at Virginia Tech. from freshmen, to seniors who had matured so much compared to us freshmen, taught me to believe in me and make out of me what I want to be. It is difficult to explain the feelings that I had, and have about growing up. I was 17 years old entering college, and came out of the army just before I became 23 years old. Virginia Tech. and the U.S. Army taught me and helped me find myself and mature to a competent and responsible individual that I am proud of. I think it would be a very good idea for a compulsory period of about 2 years after high school to be served in the armed forces for a little time to grow up and mature. They could make a little money, have a roof over their head, be fed good food, have health care, be supplied clothing, and learn some things. Most young people need some discipline and control at about that age. Of course nobody would agree with me about that.

My company received orders to go to the dock, get on the ship, with a boatload of soldiers, and sail the pacific. We had no idea where we were going. We spent 30 days on that ship, stuffed with soldiers. We knew only men in our company, but we made a lot of other friends.

Officers were kept on the rear deck and enlisted personnel kept on the front deck. Officers slept in the rear hold of the ship, enlisted men in the front hold of the ship. In our hold there were 4 bunks vertically, with just enough room between them to horizontally roll yourself into your bunk. There was barely enough room between the vertical bunks to walk down the isle.

All was fine, if the weather was calm. Occasionally storms upset some people- only the ones that got seasick, with the forward and backward, and side to side rolling of the ship with wave action. I was lucky no one near me became sea sick.

During the night there were a few times you would hear someone gagging, then, followed by sounds of a volume of water hitting the floor from above, followed by gagging and groans. I'm pretty sure the soldiers on the bottom bunks knew what was happening and didn't stick their heads out and look up to find out what was going on. At least I didn't hear about it if they did. In the daytime those who were affected by seasickness would run to the rail, "upchuck," hoping they could toss far enough out to sea not to affect those on the rail next deck down.

We sunned ourselves a lot, napped a lot, played a lot of cards on deck, read a lot of books, listened to a lot of '30s and '40s music over the ship loud speaker. We saw Naval Destroyers on the horizon going along for our protection. We never had a time that we felt anxious or scared. Food was good, and nutritious, not terrific, but edible. We had a dining room, with fixed tables and chairs, utensils, heavy plates, heavy coffee cups that wouldn't break easily, and cola type drinks, iced tea and water. In a storm, with heavy seas, things tended to roll or slide around on the table, requiring us to learn to eat one handed, with the other hand rescuing food and drink from falling over the rimmed edge of the table to the floor. Those who tended to get sea sick failed to show up for meals, they were usually meeting with their buddies at the railing.

I remember one episode after a nice relaxing rest time upon the commode, in the large rest room, with a number of commodes, and several other men sitting, during especially rough seas, we all were holding on. The ship was rocking side to side and forward and back- ward. I had just finished my rest time, was standing pulling my cover- alls up, flushed, and was just beginning to walk away. The ship lurched heavily to the left, causing me to grab the stall wall, just then, a very loud profane yell and profane oaths and vile comments, from a few stalls to my left, attracted my attention. I didn't know what some of his words were, or what they meant.

The soldier, unknown to me, was sitting on his commode, arms in the air, coveralls around his ankles, and looking down into his coveralls. The coveralls contained what his bowels had contained only a few minutes before, only somewhat diluted with sea water.

Recognizing that there was no way I could help, I quickly walked out of the door to my right. He must have been from a different part of the country than I was from, because he spoke a different language that I never heard before. I also noted there were several other commodes to my left that had suddenly flooded due to the refluxing sea water, with each roll of the ship to the left, entering the large sewer pipes leaving the latrine to the sea. Only that water was "pure" seawater and nobody was seated on them. I didn't know the poor soldier and never saw him again. Hope he didn't jump overboard.

After about 30 days on the Pacific Ocean and stopping a couple of times at some very small pacific islands to get supplies, we landed during the night on an island. Later of course, the "Enola Gay" B29 bomber took off from this island to drop the first atomic bomb. This was Tinian, one of the Marianas Islands, only 3 miles from Saipan.

We started to disembark. They stopped, and loaded us back on the ship. Then the ship started backing out and put out to sea again. After a short cruise we landed where we found out later that we were supposed to land the first time. It was Saipan, where one of the major battles with the Japanese occurred. The island was captured and secured less than 1 year before our arrival.

This island became my home, waiting with my company for orders, planning to back up our soldiers in the invasion of Japan. We had no idea of when that would happen, only that it would. We were taken by trucks to an area where two very large tents were empty awaiting us.

One tent was the Officers tent about 60 feet long and 20 feet wide. Army cots were lined on both sides, the heads of the cots against the sides of the tent and an aisle down the middle to the other end of the tent. There was enough room between the cots, side by side, to have plenty of room to dress and sit to put on our boots. During our time there we learned more and more about each other. There were two 2nd Lieutenants, one me, the other a young man that carried a pistol on his hip, daily even though the real war was many, many miles north of us. He was pretty sure that he was one of the sharpest, best looking, smartest, army officers in the war, and he walked around with a superiority attitude, even when playing penny poker, and in every thing he did or said with a stern, slow monotone voice, seemed to think he was superlative. He had all the answers.

There were three Captains. One was smart, friendly and helpful to us all, and was second in command to our Colonel. The other was a very friendly dentist. Another was a grumpy, continually upset, hot, sweaty, obese, with a big full red beard, and about 45ish dentist, really unhappy, about having to be in the army. He did not get along well with any of us, so none of us had much to say to him. Our Commanding Officer was affable, likable, helpful and a friend to all of us.

After a few nights in the tent, it became apparent there were foreigners in our tent. RATS. We could hear their little feet pitter- pattering on top of the tent. Playing, or chasing each other.

During one night, we heard a yell from one of our friends in the tent. He jumped up and yelled that a rat fell on him. Then a night or so later, another man yelled during the night. We all decided to get our small pup tents out of our duffle bag and use our half of the tents to string out from the ceiling, with ropes, to cover our cots, while we were sleeping. We all did that. Then it became apparent the rats now had flat ceilings over our beds, so we began to hear them running and jumping from one shelter-half to another. Occasionally a rat would fall between the tent-half onto our beds. What a surprise, and what a sudden fear we had if we're awakened by a big rat landing on our sleeping stomach.

We spent a lot of time reading, talking, writing poetry, and playing penny poker. Not much else to do while waiting to become involved in the war. I did make a mold in wax of my Virginia Tech class ring. We used a manual dental centrifuge, which worked on a spring mechanism, to cast in silver, from a melted fifty-cent coin. Coins were 90% silver then.

Later on Saipan, a friend of mine went with me to a recreation area that had a tennis court. I took my ring off, put it in my pants pocket, folded the pants, and put them in the jeep. After playing tennis in shorts we returned and found out someone stole my ring from my pants pocket. Jeeps are open, no doors, so, no lock. I lost my class ring, but I have a silver replica that I cast. I still have it.

A few weeks passed. Then our company was dissolved, and we were scattered on assignments to various companies, or hospitals on the island. I was ordered to the 369th Station Hospital on the island above where our tents were located.

The island of Saipan was of volcanic origin, about 4 miles wide and 12 miles long situated some 100 miles north of Guam, and three miles from Tinian. Another in the chain was named Rota Island. All these islands are in the Marianas Group.

My duties were to become the Adjutant of the hospital. The hospital received a continuous stream of casualties from the war north of us, still raging on islands such as Iwo Jima. The doctors that had been in our company were scattered among several hospitals on the island, including my new hospital.

Daily about 3-4 PM, the B29 bombers streamed across our bay loaded with bombs, headed for Japan. Our Officers Club was situated high on a cliff over looking Magacene Bay and they took off from our right, the bombers struggled to rise above the surface of the sea to barely reach climbing speed until they gradually went out of our sight.

They returned home the next morning about 10-11AM. Some had one engine not working, noticeable holes in a wing or a tail. Occasionally, there was a smoking engine not working. B29s had 4 engines, 2 on each wing. We never knew how many didn't return the next AM. I often wondered. We prayed for their crew daily.

Among my duties was to write and publish daily orders of our Commanding Officer having to do with the daily functioning of the hospital.

Another duty assigned to me, was to become the Liquor Officer for the officers of the hospital. A large cave in the middle of the island, up in the mountain, previously held Japanese supplies during the fighting for the island. Our troops secured the island just less than 1 year previously. This cave was the depositing area for the liquor as it came to our island aboard ships. The liquor was shared among all Officers stationed on the island.

There were still hold-out Japanese soldiers up in caves scattered through out the mountains, afraid to surrender. They thought they would be killed. Occasionally 1 or 2 enemy soldiers would be caught at night in the mess line for supper served for soldiers after dark. They had stolen the army clothing that had been washed, and hung out to dry. Also, a few were captured at night sitting in the back of audiences watching outdoor movies. They became POWs and were placed in fenced-in areas and guarded by prison guards. They were fed and treated well, and probably happy and thankful to be prisoners, instead of being killed as they were told would happen if they were caught.

At night, occasionally, on the side of the hill, very bright lights were trained up the hill, with very loud public address systems blaring in Japanese language into the lighted area, pleading for Japanese soldiers to come down and surrender, that the war was over and they wouldn't be harmed. I also remember, years after I returned home, finished medical School, married, had several children, some 20 or so years into my years of practice, an article in the newspaper reported on the surrender of an old man on Saipan, a Japanese soldier. He was afraid he would be killed all of these years. He was sent back to Japan. The date was in the 1970's or 1980's, I'm not sure of the exact date.

Some time in our spare time, a buddy of mine and one of the teen aged native boys went up exploring the hills and caves. On one trip up near the top of one of the small mountains in our area, we ran across an area that contained some old leather straps, clothing remnants, bones, and what was probably a leather ammunition case. The bones were white and clean, and seemed to have never been moved. The skeleton was complete. We thought this was a Japanese soldier killed in the battle the year before. I located the area beneath the thigh bone, scratched around in the dirt below it and found some 15–20 Japanese coins, that probably were in the soldier's pocket. I still have them. I'm still unable to read them. I thought I'd bring the complete beautiful skull home with me, since I thought it would be nice to adorn my desk, if and when I became a doctor.

After thinking a little, I wondered if I ever would become a doctor. I thought the bones would be better left where they were, and that soldier wouldn't have been happy to be sitting on my desk.

We were told later, that any bones found were off limits and that they would be found and properly buried, or returned to their homeland. I did however, have my buddy use my camera and take a picture of me with my skull. I still have that, also.

On the west side of the island, very mountainous, was a very high cliff, edges treacherous, and probably several hundred feet straight down, sheer, to the many large rocks, and a crashing sea, called "Suicide Cliff." This was the area that many of the native people, especially mothers and mothers with their babies jumped to their deaths. During the US attack on the island, the heavy fighting, the native women were told by the Japanese soldiers that the Americans would kill the babies, and rape and kill the women, and they must commit suicide at that site. This is documented in the archives of the Battle of Saipan, TV series of World War II. I saw that episode on the History

Channel. One mother threw her baby off, then, jumped. It showed a quick view of the bodies floating in the sea. This was horrible, and very, very, sad.

The Chomoras, native people that I met there were beautiful, and were likable and very cooperative. They had lost their homes and buildings during the war. A few old churches that were half destroyed and not usable were seen around the island. Families were in a large fenced compound, in quanset huts, or tents like the rest of us. During daytime the men were used building roads, or, cleaning areas, or where they were needed. The women were used as house cleaners, in the officer's quarters, and nurses' quarters, or the hospital, and offices where they were needed, or were servers in the mess hall. They all were paid a small amount for their work. They also were provided with food.

The Liquor Officer was the officer in each organization who took orders for alcohol, go to the distribution site and bring it back to their men A ship came to the island once a month, bearing beer and liquor, and other supplies for the island troops. It was unloaded, taken to the large cave I mentioned before, up high in the island. At the cave, soldiers carried cases of liquor to rollers at the mouth of the cave, rolled them far inside on the roller frames, and stored them.

Once a month each company, hospital, or military installation on the island came with their list, picked up their liquor and took it all back to their units, for distribution. Ordinarily available was, scotch, bourbon, blended whiskey, gin, rye, and sometimes red or white wine. Each officer was allowed to order 2 bottles of liquor a month. They were liter bottles, not 5ths. I took their orders, and when we got back with the bottles, sometime what came was unpredictable. We had to distribute what was available. Then sometimes the men would trade around to get what they wanted. Most of the time, the brand names on the bottles were unknown to us. We got it anyway.

They cost $2.50 a bottle. Beer was in the PX, amounts sold to the enlisted men were limited. I liked bourbon. There was one named "Old Methuselum," came in liters, it was good added to a can of cold chocolate milk.

When I went to pick up the liquor, I took 2 of our sergeants, armed with rifles, and .45 hand guns. I also had a side arm. We went in a weapons carrier truck with plenty of room for us and the liquor. My liquor intake gradually increased, so that by now, like everybody else, I went to the Officer's Club every evening after 5PM. We all took our liquor, had our name on it, and had the enlisted man bartender mix drinks for us. I had a hard time learning to drink. The episode at Vanderbilt was about a year before, and I had only 1 other episode, before going overseas.

When I first got to Fort Lewis, Washington, before going overseas, one night I went to the Officer's Club. I met a really nice girl, after talking a while, and dancing a few times, found out she was a daughter of one of the Colonels at the fort. I felt like I should drink, so I could show her what a man I was. She didn't drink. So I ordered the only thing I knew—Southern Comfort mixed with coca-cola—sweet and very easy to drink, without making a frown. Soon it was time to close and leave. She had asked me to join her at her dad's home, a short way away. I was ready to go!! Then she said she had asked some other people, too. What a bummer! But I decided to go along any way. I didn't know any of these other officers. They didn't know me. There were 6 or 7 others. They knew each other, were joking around, laughing, and just having fun. At her house she served cookies and soft drinks. I had only a few cookies and one coke. I was very uncomfortable, felt out of place, so decided to thank her and leave to go to my quarters to retire.

When I left her home, which I found out was one of the many homes that was along side of many other homes, officers quarters, on the edge of the huge, huge drill field at Fort Lewis. I had no idea where my quarters were. I knew they were on the same drill field, but I knew not the direction or location. The night was a beautiful, clear, starry, moonless night, black dark. Lights in homes and buildings were visible far away in all directions. There were no markers that I knew to locate where I was going. I soon became aware that I was staggering pretty badly. I figured out I was in the same "drunk boat" I had been before, after Southern Comfort at Vanderbilt. Only, I didn't know how to get home. I knew also, I had to walk, I had no driver, or car, or anybody with me. So I began walking, and walking, in the direction I thought where my home was, but nothing came closer to me after walking a while. I wandered a while, not in a straight line, I guess, because I found out I was again looking at her house. So I made it a point to pick out a light on the opposite side of this big field, zero in on it, and walk as fast as I could, straight toward it.

The club closed at 11:00 P.M., I went to her house, hung around a little, left about 12:00 and walked, and walked. I got to the other side about 2:30 in the AM. I finally recognized my officer's barracks. There were three buildings, exactly the same for the officers. I chose the middle one and entered it, walked down the hall I thought was mine, chose the room I thought was mine, entered, looked around and recognized my wooden foot locker, with my name on it. Quickly I undressed, unstable, went to bed, tired, happy, and tried to go to sleep. When I turned over on my side, I suddenly became extremely dizzy, and nauseated, starting to gag, I leapt up, ran back down the hall to the latrine, bouncing from one wall to the other all the way there, vomited all alone in the commode, thank goodness. I felt better, eased back to my bed. I sat on the bed a minute and thought I'd lie down very slowly. Same thing happened again, when I got horizontal. I repeated this several more times, and finally was so tired I think I just passed out. I did not feel very good the next day.

On Saipan, my job as Adjutant of the 369$^{th}$ Station Hospital got more comfortable and I felt a little more confident, since I had recently been promoted to 1$^{st}$ Lieutenant, I was now one of the guys.

I had become friends with many of the Officers in my hospital. My office closed at 5 PM daily. It was my usual practice to go immediately to the bar at the Officers club, use one of my bottles of bourbon, and ask the bar tender (an enlisted man) to mix me a bourbon and a canned chocolate milk. I found I could stand drinking that and not throw up.

I got to be a pretty good ping pong player, after being beaten so many times. I became one of the better players in the club. I learned to play bridge after being embarrassed so many times, when I often would trump my partners trick. There would be some fairly vocal outbursts by my partner. I finally learned the game really well, and came home as a good, seasoned bridge player. One of my bridge teachers was a surgeon, Colonel George Archer from Mississippi. He presented me with a bridge book by the master, Ely Culbertson.

The evening became an enjoyable time, a place where over time I increased drinking, and tried drinking more different beverages. I really got to liking DRY martinis, with only an olive added.

The Nurses of the hospital also uses the Officer's Club, and I set out to charm the ladies. I charmed so many of them that none of them zeroed in on me, so we just all became good friends. One nurse I remember well because she always said I looked like a Kewpie doll. After I returned to my home in Quitman, Georgia I received a Kewpie porcelain doll in a package from her, and the head had been broken in the mail. Her name was Miss Kramshuster; that was a nice thought anyway. She didn't put her return address on the package so I was sorry I was unable to thank her.

We sometimes would go the beach for swimming, and sunning, where ruined tanks, and landing crafts were still scattered along our beach. These were remnants of a terrible battle, where so many, many soldiers died less than a year before. I was so glad I wasn't a couple of years older. I could have been here the year before. My life may have been very different. I often thought of that.

I remember doing a lot of thinking about drinking. I remember, daily, along about 3:30 to 4 PM, in my office I would get this real longing, thirsty feeling in my throat yearning for a nice, cold Martini. I wondered if this meant I was now an Alcoholic. And how are my folks going to react to my alcoholism, and my necessity to HAVE to drink. And how am I ever going to get into Medical School, and even function as a Doctor. This worried me a lot, but not enough to change my ways.

I kept on keeping on drinking and socializing. Sometimes after drinking and going to my quarters, I would sit in bed and write poetry, not very good poetry, but an enjoyable pastime. Drinking kind of releases your mind to think weird things, and you think those little poems, weird, and hard to understand, would really make you a famous poet, until you re-read them the next morning. Then they were just really weird.

Some of the doctors would have parties in their rooms, to play poker, and, or shoot craps. I tried joining them, but their game was too fast for me. I couldn't even keep up with what they were saying, and whether it was betting, or just chatter. I never understood fast betting, and what odds were and what side bets in craps was all about. I had to quit. It seems I never won, at least they never told me I did. Everybody was drinking and gambling, laughing, talking loudly and betting all at the same time. It sounded like somebody was going to get killed, then suddenly everybody's laughing and friends again.

I enjoyed the parties and sitting there drinking, until I began noting that when I would drink a while my lower lip would begin to get numb. If I quit then, I didn't get so drunk that I got nauseated and badly dizzy. I from then on, could use that as a signal to change from alcohol to soda, or ginger ale, with a sliver of lemon. Everybody thought I was still drinking with them, and I knew I wasn't going to stagger home. I could get up and not be hung over going to work the next morning.

Some times in the evenings at one of our friend's parties, while the gamblers were gambling, and the drinkers were drinking, and the watchers were watching, the cookers were cooking the steaks our friends had gotten from the kitchen.

With the steaks frying in the butter on the hotplates, occasionally a stray grasshopper would land in the pan, sizzle, die and lay there, buttered and crispy and dead. A bold friend would pick it up, pop it in his mouth and chew it up. He swore it really tasted good. He convinced most of us to try it, and he was right, they were good. So we searched for grasshoppers, enough for everybody to try one. I think the butter and the alcohol was what was good. It's hard to run down a bunch of grasshoppers, when the mood is right for the chase, I think you've got to be kinda drunk to do that.

On one of the holidays, I believe Labor Day; our hospital had planned a big baseball game against another big hospital on the island. We were hosting them and the big game was to start at 1:30 or 2:00 PM. Our kitchen was to prepare a large buffet lunch before the game. Eating was planned for 12:00, on the area next to the baseball field. The cooks had prepared baked ham, all sorts of vegetables, biscuits, gravy, salads, beer and other cold drinks. Long tables, full of food was set up behind home plate. We had no bleachers, just crates and boxes for seats for the fans.

I had been to one of the parties I talked about, the night before. I was in no hurry to get to the game, so I slept in until almost noon. I got up and showered and dressed, and went down to the game. It had just started, and they had just removed all the food to take back to the kitchen. I was able to get a small plate of salad, everything else was gone.

In the first inning, suddenly the shortstop, dropped to the ground holding his stomach, and vomited, then lay down on the ground, rolling around, and groaning. People ran out and picked him up and rushed him back to the emergency room. Soon, a few minutes later, same thing happened to the center fielder. It wasn't 15 minutes later that people in the outfield were one by one, falling to the ground, as well as spectators on the sideline. All of a sudden, there were crying, vomiting, sitting, rolling, groaning people everywhere. I ran back to the emergency room spoke to one of the doctors who said "we've got severe food poisoning on our hands." I asked what from? He said "I don't know yet." He had just finished eating a plate from the buffet right after the first man came in. Within about another 30 minutes he was one of the sick ones, and useless as a doctor. It was apparent that it was the food, but what?

Another doctor came in to work. He, like me, didn't eat any of the meat or vegetables. I never became ill. It turned out to be the baked ham.

Then came the severe cramps and diarrhea. People had been admitted to the hospital, given IV fluids, and I don't know what else. People were wandering around, half dressed, and undressed, dragging their IV poles going to the bathroom, that were already full, so many that couldn't help it just squatted and went on the floor in the showers. Remember this was in 1945 or '46. I wasn't yet a physician, and didn't know what medications were available to use, except Penicillin and Sulfa.

There were scores of really sick, dehydrated, hurting people. They identified a Staphylococcus, resulting in gastritis, causing the symptoms so rapidly after eating. It later became the Enterocolitis, with diarrhea. They also identified the cause was a cook's, draining paronychia (finger nail infection). He had cooked the hams the day before, the evening they were done cooking he sliced all of the hams, with his bare hands. He then left the hams in warm ovens overnight, and served them on the buffet at noon. This gave the inoculated hams almost 18 hours for the bacteria to grow and multiply until there was almost a pure culture of Staphylococcus entering the stomach from the surface of the ham slices eaten.

How fortunate I was not to have gotten out of bed for the game, and lunch. Nobody died, but there were many who had wished for death for a few hours that day, and some that did become severely dehydrated and remained hospitalized for several days.

While on Saipan, I found out one of my cousins, Paul Rockhill, from Birmingham, Alabama was a Navy pilot, stationed on Saipan, the other side of the island. We were able to get together once in a while to remember and talk about our times together as children.

He informed me of his meeting and falling in love with one of our cousins, Maurine Finley. Maurine had joined the Marine Corp; and he told me they had discussed cousins marrying and had consulted with physicians and Geneticists They married in January 1945.They learned that it should be OK if there is no known genetic abnormality in the family. (Long after the war, I found out they had 2 daughters, and 2 sons, all perfectly normal healthy children.) His mother and my Mama were sisters; Maurine's father, Uncle Howard, (the letter writer to me about the oil wells while I was at Virginia Tech) was one of their 2 brothers. Our families would occasionally get together for visits. Our visits gave us a little touch of "closer to home feeling."

One day I received a call from a Signal Corp Sergeant, telling me my brother Terry contacted him on the radio, and asked him to find me and make a date for us both to get on the radio together and talk. I was really excited to be able to talk to Terry. He entered the army about a year before, was put in the infantry, and was in the Philippine Islands calling me. His training, I found out later, was preparing to attack and invade Japan.

We talked on two occasions. Sometimes contacting was difficult, but I really treasured our talks together. He had told me they were going to leave there, but didn't know where he was going, or couldn't say.

We later found out after the atomic bomb was dropped, that they had just gotten orders to get on the ships to leave for the invasion of Japan. Orders were cancelled. Shortly after the second bomb a few days later, they did leave and shipped out for Japan.

Japan had finally surrendered, after the second bomb dropped on Nagasaki.

Terry's ship was in the harbor 2 weeks later, at the time they were signing the papers on another ship. He spent a while in Japan, having entered the island shortly after papers were signed. We were both very lucky boys.

Some weeks after the bombs dropped, my Commanding Officer, called me in his office and informed me that he received a call from the commanding General on the Island telling him that I must come to his office up in the Island Command Office. He didn't know what it was about but I must go.

I was scared to death. I thought, and thought about anything that I did that may have been wrong, or what kind of trouble I was in. I couldn't imagine what I'd done.

I went to the office, his aide walked me into the General's office and left. I saluted smartly, and gave my name, and was given "at ease." The General said that his aide was leaving and my name was given him as a good soldier and he wanted to offer me the appointment as his private aide. I was flabbergasted, never dreaming of such a thing. What a premium job, meaning a promotion and status. I politely advised the general that I was completely surprised, and honored to have been given the opportunity to be considered for this position, but my plans since the war is now over, is to return to college as soon as possible to continue my journey to become a physician. I thanked him profusely, and saluted and left. He told me being a doctor is a noble commitment. I felt very proud of even being asked to fill such a position.

In the army while on Saipan I mentioned I was the liquor officer for our hospital, and I was the Adjutant on the hospital. I had some left over unused liters of whiskey. I was faced with the opportunity to trade a few liters for a few things. I traded 2 liters for a Japanese Samari sword, a dagger I was told was Japanese, but recently found it in a National Rifleman magazine pictured and identified as a Marine dagger. I also traded for some Japanese female platform carved shoes, and some necklaces hand made probably by a soldier, but with beautiful cowrie shells. I traded 2 liters for a Japanese rifle.

During this time I went to the island supply office and signed out a clarinet so I could continue enjoying playing it. I had it in my quarters about a year, then the war ended and I had orders to go to Hawaii before discharge, I took my clarinet back to turn it in and found out that department was closed and had gone home. The officer in charge of it told me to keep it and take it, or send it home if I wanted it. It was not going to be sent back to the U.S. It was considered expendable and like so much other stuff that had been sent overseas was going to stay there, because of the expense to return it to the U.S.

So I packed up all of my treasures and had them sent home. On my arrival home everything was there, except my Japanese rifle. Daddy said he didn't think I should have such a big gun in the house so he gave it to one of his gasoline station attendants when it arrived. I was a little disappointed, but understood Daddy's fear and reassured him it was OK.

It was a few months later that I received my orders to be assigned to Tripler General Hospital, on Oahu Island, in Honolulu, Hawaii. This was a nice way to spend the last 2-3 months in the service in the personnel department of that hospital.

They had just started building a new Tripler General Hospital high up on the island. The old hospital where I was may not be there now, I don't know. It was quite old and most of the beds were in one story, long, side by side buildings. It was not far to town, and the famous Waikiki Beach.

When I went swimming there I was extremely disappointed, having been used to Florida beaches. This was a very narrow, sandy, and short, rather rocky beach, hard to walk on it without shoes. The entire beach, except the widest part, the long horseshoe shaped famous area, where all the swimmers and surfers go, is lined with all the noted hotels lined up very close to the water.

I bought a 1936 used blue rather beat up Ford 2 door sedan from a nurse going home. I paid $500 for the Ford. I had to buy a case of oil, keep it in the car, because it really used a lot of oil. It did however, provide me with transportation on the island, and I was thankful for that. Honolulu was a beautiful city, and the island of Oahu is very beautiful, full of gorgeous trees and flowers and beautiful women.

I found a lot of great restaurants on the island. One of my favorites was Trader Vic's. I seemed not to have needed to drink so much on this stay, no desire to drink, but occasionally did a little, with friends. I got sick there from viral pneumonia, was in the hospital a couple of weeks, and did fine. I liked the rest, and peace that came with the hospital bed. I loved the Seconal, a barbiturate given for sleep, even if I didn't need it. You feel really good and can write poetry like mad. I stayed in the hospital two weeks or so, and was discharged fine.

While in Honolulu I was able to see the wreckage, sunken ships, and damage the Japanese bombers caused on December 7, 1941. One of my high school friends, Paul Bass was in the navy on his ship there that was destroyed, and the men killed. I didn't know which it was.

I met a pretty nurse that was sad, and grieving her Colonel who had been shipped home for discharge. We dated quite a bit but I was unsuccessful in clearing her mind of that other guy. So I wound up supporting her sadness, she came to see me several times while I was in the hospital with my pneumonia.

The time there gave me some good memories, until after about 3 months my orders came for me to get aboard a ship and leave for San Francisco. I was really sick, with another bad cold and cough and fever. I stayed in my bunk the whole trip back, except to go to eat, with difficulty. It took several days for the troop ship to get to San Francisco, landed, then we all went to some fort for bunking, and I stayed right there. I was still sick and I didn't get to see the city or any thing else.

A few days later, got on a troop train to San Antonio, Texas. There we all went through the discharging from the Army, physical exams and a lot of paperwork.

When we finished there, another troop train took me to Quitman, Georgia my wonderful family, and my sweet home. It was wonderful being able to see the town, the homes, and the people I longed to see again, after too long being away from home.

I really am fortunate to have been involved in the war, because it served as a phenomenal educational opportunity and time for me to mature, grow up, and learn how and why I needed to study, and decide to pursue my life.

I learned that where I am in my life is generally due to decisions I've made in the past and the time I spent, obtaining where I ultimately want to be. However, sometimes we have no control over things that disrupt the process. Like a World War.

I am so glad I was able to be involved in trying to protect our country that so many others before me have done throughout the centuries since our beginning. Our country is unique in the world. Our freedom must be protected for our families and the generations that follow us. Everybody can do something for their country, if they love it.

After returning from the war, honorably discharged, in the fall of 1946 I came home and just stayed around home, planning to return to VPI to complete my Pre-Med requirements, hoping and expecting to make good enough grades to be accepted into medical school, my life

Paul A. Tanner Jr., First Lieutenant, Medical Administrative Corps during WWII. (Picture taken in 1946, shortly after being discharged.)

long dream. Too late to enter the fall Quarter, I planned to enter winter quarter beginning in January 1947. While in the army I managed to save about $2500 as I remember. I didn't want to ride trains back and forth to college so I thought about buying a car.

New cars were too expensive and rare in any auto show room, so in looking around, found an advertisement in the paper about a 1941 Buick for sale in Madison, Florida, about 30 miles south of Quitman. I called the man and rode down to see it. It looked good, said to use a little oil, but a good buy at $1200. This was a 4 door sedan, no body damage, seats were in good shape, drove smooth and engine sounded good, tires looked used but still had some tread on them, and I wanted that car. I decided to buy it so we could drive back and forth to Virginia.

Terry had just gotten out, or was to soon get out of the army. I don't remember who got home first. So we spent the time with our buddies. I had told my parents that I occasionally drank a beer. After their shock, and surprise, I promised I wouldn't get drunk and embarrass the family. Terry didn't drink and was not happy with me. I went a few times with some of my old friends from high school, who now drank, so I left Terry at home.

There was a dance hall on the Valdosta highway, 3-4 miles east of town, where beer was served, but none in the city limits. It was a JUKE JOINT named Kokomo that had a reputation for wildness and fights. My buddies took me there, and we all started drinking. I ordered a beer and sat drinking it with my buddies. There wasn't a soul in the place that I knew, or even looked like I wanted to know. There were all sorts of loud talking, some sounded like it might be profane, but I had not heard some of those words, so I wasn't sure. But I had a few doses of profane during the war, here and there. Anyway, I found out that what I knew as old buddies, were now hard living, hard drinking people that had changed a lot. I also found out real quick that I probably won't ever become an alcoholic, like I feared I would, previously. So from then on, I almost always had a good excuse, or at least, a reason, not to be able to make it, when they called inviting me out. I just didn't need the drinking at home. While we were waiting to go back to Virginia Tech, Terry and I would take some time to go the country club, either to swim, and sit by the pool all day, or golf, or go fishing.

When we fished we went out into the lake with some wet flour, and make little dough balls, put them on little teeny hooks, use a short cane pole and catch "shiners," sometimes called "roaches" Most were

6 to 10 inches in length, and we kept them in a bait bucket. They had silvery scales, and tails and fins that were reddish-brown color, hence, their names. Then we had several glass gallon jugs, which we tied a black fishing line, about 10-15 feet long to the handle, tie a bass #4 fishing hook to the line, and row out into the lake. Then pick out a nice shiner and put the hook through the meat in the middle of its back and scatter the bottles around and let them float. You needed to miss the shiner's backbone with the hook, or it couldn't swim. Then we just sit and look at the gallon jugs, and wait for it to start moving in the water. A bass would swallow the bait, get hooked and we had to paddle to catch it. Onetime we caught a very large shiner. We thought it was way too big to use for bait. It was nearly a foot long. We decided to use it anyway. After quite a while late in the afternoon, we got a bite on my rod and reel, using that big shiner and a large cork on the line. The cork began moving away from us then it would stop, then move, then disappear, then surface again. I knew if it was a fish it had to be a big fish, because of the bait. We had been catching turtles, and occasionally a snake, as well as bass. So I waited a few minutes so he could swallow the bait and have a better chance of getting hooked. Finally I sat the hook real hard. I couldn't move it, he just sat, then a slow movement away from us. I was trying to reel him in, but I thought I had been hooked on a log. Suddenly he moved faster, and we had to paddle the boat to follow, with me fighting and pulling, nothing was giving. Slowly I was winning, and he gradually came to the surface with his mouth opened. Huge, opened mouth, the biggest I ever saw. He went down again, and finally came to the surface lying on his side he looked as big as a baby laying there. I grabbed his lower lip and lifted him into the boat. Terry kept saying "He's as big as a baby." We took him home, weighed him at a little less than 10 pounds. Mama was amazed at his size. We cleaned him and ate him.

Around the lake, we would find some tree with branches over hanging about 4-8 feet of water depth. Then, we tied a line with a hook to a limb, and then we baited it with a shiner, so the bait would be a couple of inches under the surface of the water. When he would swim, he made a little ripple or a little splash on top of the water, attracting a bass to strike and eat. We caught some nice bass, a few snakes, and a few large soft shelled turtles. We didn't eat the turtles, or the snakes. We spent many a day during our youth enjoying the pool and the lake.

Eric Williams and I took a wooden boat and launched it in the Okapilco creek, on the Valdosta road one morning. We used cane poles, and earthworms for bait. This creek runs through the country to the Suwannee River, then on to the Gulf of Mexico, His mother would pick us up about 4-5 o'clock in the afternoon, down in Florida some 25 miles at a place the creek goes under one of the highways. Eric went to Virginia Tech. on a track scholarship and was from Quitman. One of us would paddle, or by only steering the boat, keep it straight. The current ran at just the right speed to let the guy in the front slowly pitch the bait out in front of the boat, under the edge of the trees and bushes along the creek bank. Almost every time, before the boat got to the bait a redbelly perch, or a bream, or a stumpknocker (perch), or a warmouth perch, or maybe a small bass would be hooked and caught. We alternated paddling, and fishing. We put the catch on a stringer and tied it on behind the boat dragging in the water. A couple of times we would brush against a limb as we went by and a little water snake would fall from the tree into the boat. It would be fast enough to wiggle and climb out of the boat, or Eric would grab it and toss it. We knew what a water moccasin looked like and only rarely even saw one. When we got almost down to where Mrs. Williams was to meet us, we had a good mess of fish. We decided to pull them up and look at them. To our surprise there were only a few left, some still were not eaten by the two good sized snakes that were hanging on the fish. We wondered how many snakes we fed going down the creek. But we still had enough to eat when we got there.

We spent hours sitting by the pool at the Quitman Country Club. A nice, quiet, serene place snuggled in the pine trees, with water continually running from an artesian well into our pool. The water was very, very cold, and it took real determination to get in the pool. You had to sit and get hot enough in the 90+ temperature weather. We would have to grit our teeth and dive in hoping we would survive the cold water shock.

Mrs. Betty Sheffield, who was the grower of the beautiful camellia that bears her name, "The Betty Sheffield," and her sister, Mrs. Pankoke often came to the pool. They were very nice gentile, cordial friends, that came to the pool, all ready in bathing suits, and caps, and rubber shoes, walked up to the steps and slowly walked down the steps and on onto the freezing water still grinning and talking to us showing no notice of entering the cold, cold water. They began their slow swim, using their sophisticated side stroke, gliding blissfully along. I often thought they must have been on drugs, or something, seeming not to mind the cold water. Mrs. Sheffield's home, surrounded by many camellia bushes, was off of Screven Street, behind the post office. Many of our friends would, at one time or another come to the pool and sit talking to us. Twins Ann and Fain Thomas, Mildred Mabbitt, and her older brother Joe Mabbitt, J.T. McCoy, Norman Beverly, Kathryn Terry, and so many more I tend to forget the names. Mrs. Beth Powers noted journalist of the Quitman Free Press, hometown newspaper, often wrote of those of us who grew up in Quitman. The town paper was edited by owners, Royal Daniels and wife Edna Cain Daniels who had many noted visitors to their home, among whom was the author of "Gone with the Wind," Margaret Mitchell.

We took off in our Buick to go back to Virginia Tech in January 1947. There were several episodes of problems, and situations over the years going back and forth to Virginia Tech, and also Richmond after acceptance to medical school. I will relate a few, but the time is not important

One spring break Terry and I were driving back to VPI (Virginia Tech), taking our friend Eric Williams and one of his friends with us. Eric was the one on a track scholarship at VPI. We were entering North Carolina, going up through the mountains, late in the evening, and we ran into a snow storm. We had these two friends from school with us. The further we went the deeper the snow got. It was dark and we began going up a rather hilly road. Snow plows were out and had been getting a lot of snow off of the road. We were going rather slowly, and as we were coming up to a side road a snow plow came right out of that road in front of us and continued down in front of us, moving slower than we were. We couldn't go around in the deeper snow. I was driving and staying behind the plow, leading a whole bunch of cars right behind us. We suddenly recognized we had a flat tire, and had to stop to change tires.

The snow plow continued, slowly going out of sight. The cars behind couldn't go around in the really deep snow. We had a time in the cold, cold weather, dressed like we had left home that morning, like we were ready for the beach. We changed the tire, freezing to death. We couldn't get the car going again due to slippery snow. But here came back over the hill in front of us the snow plow, who gave us a shovel to use to get dirt under the tires. The ground was frozen, and with great difficulty finally managed to get enough dirt under the tires to get the car moving. People behind us weren't real happy, but we finally got going. We were able to move over and stop, far enough to allow the pile of cars behind us to pass us. When all was clear, we started up the mountain again, and what do you know: icy road and couldn't get going again. Somebody had the idea, since it had been a while since the last rest stop that we should all pee under the back tires, melt the ice and gain traction that way. There wasn't that much pee, and besides, by the time everybody peed, and getting back in the car, it all froze up again. Back to the frozen ground, we struggled with the shovel, to get enough dirt under the back tires to move us on. We all had good memories of that trip.

By morning, snowing stopped, but roads were still icy. Daylight was nice and we came down a long hill and started up a very long hill in front of us. The road was straight, near the top of the hill I could feel the tires slipping and as we neared the top the car couldn't get us on to the top. The wheels just spun and forward motion stopped. I felt the tires slipping, so I yelled "Everybody out and push." Not in time. They just couldn't push us over that hill. So we backed all the way down to the bottom and started faster, to get up the slick hill. Same thing, we couldn't get over the top. This time I turned the car around, and drove back almost to the top of the last hill, turned around and took off really fast, and still couldn't make the top of the slick hill.

A trucker stopped and told us we'd have better traction if we turned around and backed up the hill. It worked and we got over the hill and had a good trip the rest of the way. We were told by the snow-plow man to leave the shovel at a place he designated in the next town. When we got to the town, his directions to the place to leave it were wrong, or we didn't get them straight, because we drove all over the next town, real early in the morning, trying to find the place he designated. Nobody was awake so we brought the shovel all the way back to Quitman, Georgia. I was sorry North Carolina lost a perfectly good shovel.

Terry and I were on our way to VPI another time, driving alone up through North Carolina, into southwest Virginia. We came to the entrance of the Blue Ridge Parkway that runs north. It was very late and we thought we would make better time that way, and stay off of the highway toward Roanoke, Virginia. We got along fine in the mountains on the parkway, until it got dark. We noticed there was a small amount of fog that we ran into and through, without much trouble, until a little later it became constantly foggy, and lights didn't help us much. We came to a place that Terry thought was a shortcut to go to school, so we took the road. Right after we left the main high-way, on our shortcut we saw a dead rabbit on the road. While travel-ing at a rather slow pace for an hour or so, we saw another dead rabbit on the road. Then we recognized it as the same dead rabbit. We recognized then that we had made a circle through the country. We had to move cautiously, slowing down to about 15 to 20 MPH. We could only see the road, not the surrounding land, it was all forest and foggy. We noticed a few dirt roads leading off this road, and many of those roads had big milk containers sitting beside the road, and immediately recognized that we were on a milk route off of the parkway, making a circle through the forest among the farmers, not a road to the regular highway. So, continuing until we reached the parkway, we crept along until the next exit, got on the right road and found our way to Blacksburg by 6-7 o'clock in the morning. A tiring drive but another embedded memory.

We started our studies again after the war. I was very apprehensive about whether or not I could make grades good enough to be accepted to med. school. We both studied hard and made much better grades. I found a little time with friends for some fun, but there was some.

During one of the winters, several of us were invited to someone's cabin out of town, on a lake. The weather was cold, there were beer drinkers there, having fun. The lake was frozen over, and people were ice skating. Some of them were really good skaters, and it looked so easy. I was a good roller skater at home, so I thought I would try it. I had never tried ice skating, never even saw ice skates up close. So they found a pair that clamped on your shoes. They put them on me. The first thing I noticed I couldn't stand on them, without someone holding me. So with the help of friends, they helped me to the edge of the lake, and I stepped on the ice, got the other foot on the ice, got my balance and with a teeny shove I glided about 6 inches, lost my balance, and of course fell. My ankles were not made for that kind of torture. I guess you have to be bred for those kinds of ankles, with very thick ligaments to hold your ankles straight. I never thought ice skating was something I needed to learn how to do.

Later in the spring, after the cold weather was gone we had an occasion to go back to the same cabin, on the same lake. They were cooking hamburgers out side, some were fishing and others went frog gigging. Nobody caught any fish so everybody enjoyed hamburgers, and beer and all the trimmings.

Later after eating, cleaning up, and sitting around, the frog giggers came in. They had gigged a whole lot of frogs. They were all in a big croker sack. They'd been drinking, and were happy as could be with their success. They dumped the frogs in the big sink. It was nearly filled with moving, wiggling, jumping, and occasionally, croaking

frogs. They wanted to clean and fry the frog legs. They started whack-
ing off those poor frog's legs, and nobody knew how to do it any better. So a bunch of frogs got their legs amputated, skinned, and fried.
When they were all done, all the rest of us tried a frog leg or two. And
I'm here to tell you they were good. They weren't just little toad
frogs. These were big bullfrogs. I'd never eaten frog legs before, but
since I've grown up I have ordered them at restaurants, and they are
good.

One time Terry and I left VPI for a drive home, one morning. It
was a break, like Spring Break, and we would plan to drive the entire
way, without stopping except for gas, and get on home because we
didn't have but a few days break. We had done this before, and we
knew it would take about 12-15 hours straight driving. After dusk, it
had become dark and we were in the middle of Georgia going south
on our way to Waycross, Georgia where we would turn west and go
through Valdosta and on to Quitman.

I was driving and was tired, and Terry was dozing in the passenger's seat. The road we had selected was a rural road, few communities on it, and hardly any traffic. It was a very pleasant drive, no stress,
no traffic, but my eyes were getting a little tired, like "puckering up"
that made me blink and stretch my eyelids to try and rest them a little.
I was traveling about 65 miles per hour, when I noticed way down the
road little spots of white that made no sense at all. I said "Terry, look
down the road and tell me what that is." He rose up, and about the
time he said "COWS," I had recognized the herd of cattle, and we
were right with them. They were lying in the road on the left side, and
off the right side of the road all over the grass, not on our road right of
way, and we rode right straight through the herd. No cow required me
to swerve, or change my direction. I had tried to slow but, was still
going fast by those cows. There was no way that I could have stopped
the car. Those little white spots down the road were the markings on
the cows. Of course, I should have slowed sufficiency to be able to
recognize what I was seeing.

We could have either killed a cow or two, or either, or both, of us.
I'll always believe that God had a hand in that clear lane of the road.

It turns out that the rural area of Georgia that we were traveling
through is mostly farming and cattle country, and they had Open
Range laws there. That means the land owners have no obligation,
and no law on the books to require fencing to control animals roam-
ing. I am sure that now there is a law that requires fencing.

After the war the school continued its military cadet corps, but there was no requirement for all students to be in the corps. Veterans of the war, generally had had enough military, and chose civilian life. I was almost a year ahead of Terry, because he left school earlier, and had a little less military time, so he had another year to finish. I received my degree in Biology, in 1947. I stayed in college another year, and took a year of post graduate chemistry. In 1948, Terry received his degree in Biology, we both applied for several Medical Schools. We were amazed to have both of us called to Medical College of Virginia in Richmond, Virginia for interviews. We both went, met with 6 or 8 different professors, separately, administrators, and the Dean of the school.

We were shown around, met a lot of different people, and were very surprised, and grateful to later receive our letter of acceptance for the freshman class, entering September 1949. This was after the war, and they had only 84 places for the freshmen class. We had been told during the interview that they had received 1200 applications for entry. I guess they didn't want us to get our hopes up, because of the many applicants. Terry and I couldn't believe that 2 brothers, from out of state, from a small town in South Georgia, would be given 2 places in that class.

Our grades after returning to VPI were obviously much, much better than before we left. I found out that the Dean of the Biology Department, Dr. I.D. Wilson, who had known Terry and me since before the war at Virginia Tech. and was still teaching us, had given us glowing, exceptional letters of recommendations to the Medical College of Virginia, Richmond, Virginia for our admission. We really appreciated that. We left Virginia Tech, feeling proud to have been educated, and graduated from the same college our father, and grandfather did. We became acquainted with the German professor who taught us the required German classes during our 1$^{st}$ 2 years at tech. He would often after class ask how Daddy was doing. His name was Dr. Miles, a football player, for VPI around Daddy's time there. They called him "Sally" Miles, why I don't know. The football stadium at Tech was named Miles Stadium for years. He wasn't too successful teaching me German, but I did pass the 2 required years. I wasn't too successful in any of the courses I had to take during the 1$^{st}$ 2 years at Virginia Tech. I made up for that my last 2 years there after the war.

# 3

# Medical School, Internship, and Marriage

During the summer before going to Richmond to enter medical school, my Buick had begun having some problems. Daddy thought it would be good to trade it in for another car. We were tickled to agree with him, but there weren't any new cars on the lots and waiting periods for any car delivery was months. However, a new Hudson dealer had a couple on the lot, so Daddy took us down to see them, with my Buick. A deal was made by Daddy, and we traded my Buick in on a new 1949 4-door Hudson sedan. It was a great car—easy riding, grey color. We headed out to Richmond, arrived, and found an apartment house owned by a nice lady who had rented to medical students for years. She lived on the 1st floor, another student lived on the 3$^{rd}$ floor, and Terry and I rented the 2$^{nd}$ floor room. There was another basement room rented by a classmate, Moe Martin and his wife. The house was convenient, only 1 block from the class rooms, and the medical school, and hospital.

The first year in medical school was spent mostly in classrooms, for Gross Anatomy, Neuroanatomy, Histology, Bacteriology, Physiology, all basic sciences. We walked to classes. Out the front door, go left down to the street corner, turn left, go another block, passing the Richmond Juvenile Detention Center Playground, on the left. On the right, across the street was the old building that was the White House of the Confederacy, the old home of Jefferson Davis, President of the Confederacy is now a confederate museum. At the corner, across the street was the building where our classrooms for the basic sciences were. This is where we spent most of the first 2 years. From the corner, up the street to the left is the Valentine Museum which has some walk- in windows designed by Thomas Jefferson, who, incidentally, had the same grandfather as one of my ancestors during that time, as I said before.

One day, late in the afternoon in the first or second year, I had finished working in a classroom and was walking home. I had crossed the street, and was walking alone by the playground at the Detention Center. I noticed two teen aged girls sitting right by the 8 foot high chain-linked fence, on a bench facing me. When I got about 10 feet from them, walking toward them, one of the girls said in a regular voice, "Damn, Look at the balls on that one." Of course, I heard her. I looked away, and immediately tried to keep my legs tightly together, and bent over a little bit wondering if my fly was open, or what. I know I immediately felt the heat in my face, and kept on walking as best I could, on by them. They were laughing and obviously got the biggest kick out of my embarrassment.

Our anatomy lab was a very large room, with tables all throughout the space. The first day each table had a cadaver on it laying its back. Each student was assigned a table, with 4 students to one table. Terry and I had one side of the body, Allan Pirkle and Charles Richardson had the other side. The man we had was an elderly gentleman, of average size. We named him "Dead Earnest," and we came to know him very, and completely well. We spent every morning in detailed dissection of a particular assigned part of his body. I think we started on his upper extremity, on the left side. The other side was for Allan and Charlie. We followed the anatomy book to learn what we were seeing. There seemed to be no labels on our body parts, especially the teeny, minute parts you didn't even know you had, or how important they were.

As we finished one part, and all excessive, unimportant stuff was cut away and discarded, we would cover the worked on areas with cloth soaked in formaldehyde, to keep things pliable. Some mornings on arrival we were told we had a test. The Anatomy Professor had been to every body, and something that had been dissected out was tagged. We had to go each body in the room and identify the tagged structure and record the name of that item. The items were of anatomical importance, such as a nerve, a muscle, a lymph node, a bone, a gland or whatever he had tagged. The real problem was that every student was not as adept as some others in their dissection of their cadaver, and identification was sometimes difficult due to their carelessness. Some of them cut away stuff that was not discarded, but left attached to the tagged item that made it hard to identify. We sometimes had to complete the work a little more to identify what was tagged.

When we were in our first class of any of the subjects, before the hands on stuff, we were lectured to by the professor on the subject. We all took notes rapidly and the best we could. They talked fast, and used not so easy to understand words. The language was unknown to me. Words were foreign. I had a terrible time knowing what words meant, therefore, what they referred to. I tried to write down unknown words the way they sounded like they would be spelled. After a week or so of hunting words in the Medical Dictionary, things seemed to clear up a little, and the more I tried, the better things got. It wasn't long that the foreign language became our language. The nights were filled with study, on and on until the wee hours of the morning. After midnight, we'd take a break, go across the street from the hospital to an all night eatery, named Skull and Bones, and eat a hamburger, or sandwich and milk, then back to work. We'd get to bed when we felt comfortable about our studies. Classes began at 8 o'clock every day. This was our life, if we wanted to get through school. Nobody felt like changing what had to be done. There were a couple of guys in our class that would nod in class and sleep, because they had studied all night. Then at the end of the lecture hour, want to borrow our notes to copy.

Once in Histology lab, we all were looking through our microscopes at tissue, while the Professor was lecturing about what we were looking at. He continued talking, and continued his walking around, finally, stopping in front of one of our friends. Our friend was obviously asleep, but his two hands held his head, with his elbows on the table, and his eye was over the lens of the microscope. The professor silently and carefully slid the microscope from beneath his eye, leaving him with his elbows on the table and his hands supporting his head. As the class slowly became aware of what had been going on, they started some snickering, developing to gentle, then boisterous laughter awakening our friend to an embarrassing moment. He was teased about this for a long time.

After being in school a while, we were told that the class needed to elect a President, Vice-president, and a Secretary-Treasurer. Our class had 3-4 students from VPI. I had gotten to know a lot of our class-mates. For some reason, I was elected as President of our Freshman Class, which I felt was quite an honor.

Terry and I were selected as members of the medical fraternity, Theta Kappa Psi. Their fraternity house was down the street, on the corner, where we turned to go to the basic science building. The big main hospital was diagonally across the corner, and Hunton Hall, dor-mitory for juniors, was directly across the street in front of the Frater-nity House. Hunton Hall is where we moved into during our junior year. We continued living in our apartment house through the second year. The fraternity house had a television in the back downstairs room, adjoining the living room. Some students lived on the floors above. Terry loved to play 10 cent—25 cent poker with another 10-15 people who all just wandered in when possible. There were freshmen to seniors that joined in when there was room for another in the game. They all kept their winnings and losses on a piece of paper, to keep records. The TV was on most of the time day and night, an old sofa sat in front of it, about 3 feet away. The screen was about 6 inches diagonal and a little hard to see. The floor model was about 5 feet tall, with this little bitty screen. But we all loved it when we had time to watch, whatever was on. Comedian, Milton Berle, was one, others I can't remember, and maybe the news.

In the second year I was selected as President of the Fraternity. Another honor for me, I thought. We had meetings, but I can't remember any noted thing we did, just had parties sometimes. Terry and some of the others decided to go on a diet, consisting of milk, and I believe crackers. They had orders for several quarts a day delivered to the fraternity house. It wasn't long until they began to slack off eat-ing their diet and milk started piling up in the refrigerator. Finally, someone stopped the milk and they were trying to get people to drink the milk.

During our 2$^{nd}$ year one of our classmates developed a malignant melanoma on his back during the summer. He died the next year. One of our classmates failed the freshman year, and two had to repeat the first year. So we lost 4 of our 84 first year students. A senior medical student died of colon cancer during our first year in school. We knew him only by name, and I have forgotten it now.

During the first and second years, Terry and I often went over to the emergency room, and hung around to see what was going on and how the patients were treated. Terry and I both had some experience in first aid and suturing wounds, in the service. The doctors soon knew us because we would go often when we had time. They soon asked us if we want to sew up some wounds, and of course we did. Some weird situations came in there sometimes. One Saturday night, a drunk, verbose, angry, man came in with a rather severe laceration on his face. He was ranting and raving about the guy that cut him and what he was going to do to him after he left the ER. They had a time settling him down to carefully suture his face. He just would keep on threatening the other guy. Finally, after carefully repairing his face, bandaging in place, prescriptions given, and instructions for care and written orders for return for follow up, the patient left still very vocal. Some time later that night, loud sirens, hubbub in the ER entrance, a stretcher was rapidly brought into the ER with the same patient, and he was dead of a gunshot wound to the head.

Terry had a patient to sew up on a Saturday night. This was a nicely dressed cooperative, quite obese lady that had a perineal laceration. They put her in a closed room, had her on a table and her legs up in stirrups. There was a circular laceration, on the perineum, around the anus, and the vulva, nearly the entire circle was cut. She said they were having a party in her home with a lot of her friends, and with some drinking. She had to go to the bathroom really bad, and other people were using the one bathroom, and she finally couldn't wait. She said she had a couple of Crisco lard cans in the back room, and as occasionally before, she decided to use it before she wet the entire kitchen. She said she got a Crisco can and put on the floor, and started to sit on it and in an effort to do so, lost her balance, and sat down quite hard on the can cutting her. Terry said he did a good job in his repair of the area. For a long time we all called Terry "The Crisco Kid."

There was a poor man in the middle of winter, who got into a fight, while drunk. They both had knives. His friends brought him to the ER. He was in the back seat lying down in their car, and they needed help getting him into the ER. The man had on a large heavy coat, they brought him in on a stretcher and found him unresponsive. Seems he was dead but his friends said he was talking on the way in. They checked for gunshot wounds, cuts on the body in a quick check, nothing found. They finally took his heavy coat off. There was blood over his body, from a 2 inch cut on the under side of his right arm between the elbow and the armpit. His opponent had swiped at him, probably when he had his knife in the air trying to cut his opponent with his own knife. The opponent probably had a very sharp knife that cut through the coat, into the arm to sever the large brachial artery, and he bled to death getting to the hospital. None of his friends knew he had even been cut.

The Emergency Room at the Medical College of Virginia Hospital, Richmond, Virginia was very active and we saw a lot of weird, yet interesting injuries, and conditions. There was a patient that had come to be a well known, frequent emergency room visitor, because of his condition. He had a long standing diagnosis of syphilis. It was found that he had developed over a long time, untreated, a very large developing aortic arch aneurysm. This is a recognized later complication of untreated syphilis, however now you never see it because early treatment of the disease stops the development of those now rare complications and changes that occurred in the untreated disease. On chest x-ray an enlarged aortic arch was a finding that required testing for Syphilis. In those days there was no vascular surgery that could change the known progress and the inevitable death. The death was predictable, but the time of death was not predictable. This unusual patient had begun to develop an erosion of his left anterior superior chest wall due to the huge size of this aneurysm. X-rays showed the enlarging aneurysm had already eroded through the upper ribs on the left, and the surface of the skin was beginning to become very thin and darken due to losing blood vessels to this area of the skin. It would eventually, suddenly open with the rupture of the large aorta.

The patient would die immediately due to the sudden severe massive bleeding. The hospital provided a special room for this patient to stay in, with a movie camera fixed on the upper wall of the room at the end of the bed, trained on the patient to follow the end of this disease in this patient. We learned a few weeks later that the predicted outcome happened as was expected. The patient was a very cooperative, appreciative individual that understood what he had, was a common complication of years of untreated syphilis. Now, with the prompt diagnosis and treatment of syphilis it is rare to see this well known rare complication.

In our 2nd year we started learning how to take a history and do the physical examination. For the history of the present illness we asked "why he was here." Then starting with the hair, scalp, headaches, head, eyes, ear, nose, throat, neck, skin of the body, cough, chest pain, irregular heart, lumps and you can figure out all the other questions for information down to the toes. You see they included every part of the body. The examination had to start at the head scalp, hair, down over the body, down to and including the toe nails and everything in between, and it all had to be recorded. This was time consuming and often boring. But after we were allowed to go to a clinic for histories and physicals, we learned how patients respond.

I was assigned to an older very nice polite and cooperative gentleman that I was going through the voluminous questions about his symptoms. I came to the gastrointestinal tract, and the question to him was, "Do you have any problem with your stools?" he said "no." I asked "what color are they?' He answered "Well, let's see now, we got some green ones in the kitchen, and some blue ones on the porch." I learned to be a little more specific about my questioning.

We had been separated into groups of 8 students, and were assigned as a group to various hospital floors with different areas of interest, such as surgical, medical, ear nose and throat, etc. Our group was on a medical floor, taking histories and doing exams, on patients who were already in for treatment. I had been on the other side of the ward doing my "H" (history) and "P" (physical). Walking through the ward I passed one in our group sitting in a chair facing the bed, with his left elbow on the bed and his head in his hand. His clipboard with paper was lying on the bed with his right hand holding a pen, over the paper, as if writing. The patient was talking and my friend was asleep. My friend was doing his history and physical on the patient, and was so tired and sleepy; he had just drifted off to sleep during the patient's response. Some of their responses to questions were long and involved, and boring. We really didn't get much sleep at night. Some people had more trouble than others, managing without much sleep. This friend was the same one that had trouble staying awake during class, and would borrow our notes from the class.

During rounds in a medical ward, during a physical diagnosis class, our group, and an intern, and a couple of medical residents were following rounds on patients by our Professor of the class, Dr. Harry Walker. Dr. Walker came to the bedside of a rather large bloated lady that could hardly open her eyes, because she was so swollen. She had just come onto the floor from the Emergency Room where she had been waiting for a bed for several days. She apparently had a heart difficulty and emphysema, and they had placed a nasal catheter into the left side of the nose when she entered the hospital ER to administer oxygen to her. Dr. Walker explained to us that she had become bloated due to a rupture of an alveolus under the pleura of the lung surface, and had dissected along the trachea to the face and neck and over her upper chest wall. This created subcutaneous emphysema, which was palpable under the examining fingers, called 'crepitation.' Everybody had the opportunity to feel the skin of the chest, and experience the feel of subcutaneous emphysema. We heard an extensive dissertation about emphysema in the lungs of smokers and this was an example of the condition resulting.

This sounded like this may not be the case to me, and I wondered if it might be due to the nasal catheter pumping oxygen into the subcutaneous space. The oxygen tank was about a 5 foot tall cylinder, and had been turned on for several days for the delivery of oxygen. I asked one of the residents if he thought if it would be OK if I aspirated some of the air from under the skin on the chest wall and test it for oxygen,. He said fine, go ahead. The group had moved on to other patients. So I got a 50 cc syringe, and a needle, and an alcohol sponge, went to the patient and told her what I was going to do. She agreed. I sponged alcohol in an area on the left upper chest, inserted the needle, filled the syringe with whatever was under the skin, and then carefully left the plunger in the end of the syringe. I went into the nurse's station, lit a cotton swab with a match, and after slowly removing the plunger from the barrel, then I carefully put the lit cotton swab into the barrel of the syringe. The cotton swab suddenly glowed much brighter due to the oxygen. Oxygen makes things burn brighter and easier. It will not explode. The resident had to see it again. He called Dr. Walker over and I showed him again. He was really impressed. He said "We need to give that fellow his degree right now," But they didn't. They made me go through the whole 4 years like everybody else. Now, they understood that this tube in the nose had eroded against the back of the throat, the hole on the side of the tube directed oxygen directly into her subcutaneous tissue. The tube was covered with dried mucus that kept the tube tightly in place on the pharyngeal wall. They tried right then to remove it, but it was too tight in there and they couldn't remove it. So they had to call an Ear, Nose, and Throat specialist in to remove it. It took a little surgery to cut it away. In my senior year, I was told one of the residents wrote an article on this as a complication to using nasal catheters to deliver Oxygen. I never tried to look it up in the literature.

Our group had an assigned time in pediatrics at Dooly Hospital, which was the black hospital, next to the main Medical College of Virginia Hospital. Integration had not yet come about at this time.

I had a female baby assigned to me, to evaluate and diagnose. No diagnosis was made yet. It was a difficult problem. The child was febrile, fretting, about 16 months old, was in a crib, and wouldn't stand. I went to see the child and we decided to do some blood work to help try to figure out what the child had, in order to begin treatment. The child would not stand, and she cried when you picked her up. Examination turned up nothing on my examination. So I had a nurse pick her up and put her on the table so I could draw some blood. Infants are so small, their veins are, too. So we were taught how to draw blood from the femoral vein, which is much larger.

She was on her back, the nurse holding the outside of the right leg flat on the table with the knee flexed. I found the right femoral artery by the pulsation, and knew the vein was next to it. I put the needle straight in where the vein was and put it deep so you could enter the vein. I thought I was in, and aspirated to get the blood in the syringe. What came into the syringe wasn't blood, it was white milky liquid. A little frightened, I called the resident, and ask what this was. She didn't know either, but said take it to the lab. I did. It turned out to be pus from an abscessed hip joint. I had gone through the vein into the joint. The culture came back as Brucellosis hip joint infection, an unusual finding, and the diagnosis was made. That's why she wouldn't stand up. She had so much pain in the hip joint and especially when she tried to bear weight on the leg. And I diagnosed Brucellosis, probably from feeding the baby unpasteurized milk, out in the country.

It seemed to me, I understood some of what I was learning about. This was the time we were learning all about medical illnesses, cancer, bad infectious diseases, and every kind of things that people can get or find wrong with them.

One night I wakened at 3am with my chest hurting, and especially in the middle of my back. I just knew I had suffered a heart attack, or gallbladder disease, or pancreatic cancer, or esophageal cancer, or stomach ulcer, or one or two of these things. I got up and went over to the Emergency Room, which was real busy as usual. I sat there a while and finally an intern took me to a room and asked me all the questions, examined me and concluded I had an esophageal spasm, due to nerves and stress. He made an appointment for me to have a barium swallow x-ray the next morning. I had the test with fluoroscopic exam as ordered. The Radiologist told me I had an esophageal spasm due to nerves, gave me belladonna, an antispasmodic, which relieved my spasm, and my pain. This is an example of uncontrollable stress, frightening students with the fear of the conditions they are learning about, that they might have.

At the end of the 2$^{nd}$ year we had the opportunity to spend the summer at a community hospital as an Extern. This program was started by our college to give the student experience in many different specialties in the community hospital in surrounding states and areas, much as an intern would. I was able to go to Holsteen Valley Community Hospital in Johnson City, Tennessee for the summer. Several instances served as educational for me at this hospital. I became the first surgical assistant for several of the surgeons during major surgical procedures. I had learned a lot while in the army during my surgical technician training in Denver. I got more good experience here.

I was exposed to my first confusing patient in the emergency room. I was on call for emergency room, and a young man came in about 1 o'clock in the morning complaining severely of intense right back pain. The nurse called me to see him. He gave a history of having previous kidney stones. He was yelling loudly, and asking for something for pain. He said pills for pain never relieved him and told me they had to give him shots of Demerol to relieve the pain. I got a urinalysis and the urine had no blood in it. There is usually blood in the urine with the stone trying to pass down to the bladder. I gave him a shot of Demerol. After 30 minutes, no relief. He continued to yell with pain. So, I called the urologist on call. He came and saw the patient, who seemed to be yelling louder with pain after the doctor came. The doctor examined the patient, and talked to him for a few minutes, checked the urinalysis, and then said "Pull the sleeves of your shirt up." Then he looked at the front of both arms at the elbow, and said "Tanner, look at the needle marks." Then he addressed the man, "get up, and get out of here, you're here for a hit, and you ain't gettin' it here." The patient said nothing more. He got up turned and walked out the door. I was embarrassed, and apologized to the doctor for getting him up to come in. He asked me if I learned a lesson. I said, "Yes sir. Thanks."

Another episode was again an emergency room patient. This was a middle aged farmer, who presented to the emergency room with rather severe abdominal pain. He was hurting so bad he couldn't move very easily, because of his pain. He was nauseated, and stated he began having pain sometime after breakfast, and occurred rather suddenly an all over his abdomen. He was on the examining table, and feeling his abdomen I found he was quite tender all over it. It was obvious he had an abdominal rigidity that you might find with a perforated ulcer, or appendix, or other bowel perforation, but these should have been a result of longer onset than his was. I thought of a black widow spider bite and asked if he had been bitten. His story was, after breakfast, he went out to his outdoor toilet and had a bowel movement, but remembered a slight little bite on his scrotum. He inspected it, and found a small red spot, but didn't think of a spider. He thought of a mosquito bite. We suspected he had been bitten by a black widow, because the bite is many times not even recognized by the patient, but the board-like abdominal rigidity, acute onset of pain, and tenderness, occurs some 30-45 minute after the venom is injected at the time of the bite. There had been several reports of males, using outdoor toilets bring bitten while sitting. Also, the rigidity caused by the other things usually is limited to the area over the intra-abdominal infection, or intestinal perforation, not the entire abdominal musculature as in this case. Our complete blood count tests showed no infection, so we started intravenous calcium gluconate, which relieves the muscle spasm rather quickly. We asked his son to go home and carefully inspect the outdoor toilet, especially under the seat, for a black widow spider. He did and reported a black widow spider located and killed.

While I was at this hospital, and was on emergency room call, the emergency room nurse called me in the middle of the night to check out a pregnant young lady she thought might be in labor. So after examining her, she was in labor and about to deliver something. She wasn't under any physicians care. She had thought about going to a doctor, but never had money enough to pay for it. She was in her late teens, and unmarried. On rectal exam I found the baby's buttock midway down the birth canal, and something was going on pretty quickly. I had seen a lot of births, but until now had never delivered any. This was her first, too. There was one other extern at this hospital, between his 2$^{nd}$ and 3$^{rd}$ year also, at Tulane Medical School in New Orleans, Louisiana. We had become friends, and worked together before, I had to have some anesthesia help, and breech delivery support, so I called him. He came promptly to the delivery room, we both examined her again, and she was moving along nicely, but we didn't want her to move along so nicely. Neither of us had ever seen a breech delivery, and I was about to do one. So I asked my friend if he would run up to my room and get the Obstetrics text book and read about how to do this thing. He did, and began to read while he was dripping ether into the gauze covered cone over her nose and mouth. The book warned about the possibility of delivering the body, and the after-coming head being a little too large to easily come out, because there was not enough time for the head to mold before delivery. It went through a lot of stuff about how to recognize a breech, and how to try and turn the baby in the uterus, before frequent violent contractions start, because then it's too late to turn the child. Well, all that information was too late too, because things were happening while he was reading it to me. I was supposed to put my hand up there and flex the babies knees, one at a time, and then with the knees extended and legs coming out, gently grasp the hips, and slowly pull and turn the body so that the back of the head is against the front of the mother, reach your hand up along the child's chest and try to get your finger into the baby's mouth to flex the head down and guide the face and head out the canal, therefore, delivering the breech baby. By the time we got through reading all that stuff, most of that never happened because she was moving right along, there was a short delay getting the head out. I was really worried about compressing the cord against the birth canal by the after coming head after the trunk was delivered, and bringing the head down and out. It seemed like a long time, but the baby cried right after the head was delivered, and all was well. She was in the hospital 10 days, as was the practice then. I visited her and the baby and she did fine, and she was happy. She named the kid "Paul" something, and I felt honored. I often wondered what happened to the kid and the family. I worked in that hospital 3 months, in the summer of 1951. Then we returned for our 3$^{rd}$ year of medical school.

We spent the next two years in a kind of haze, studying about so many different things, and so late at night to try and learn and remember the things we'd never heard of, or seen before, now it's kind of a blur. With time, we became familiar enough with many of these repetitious things that patients had, or were infected with, or did to themselves, that we felt comfortable trying to diagnose, and or treat them. The frequent pop quizzes kept us on our toes, in the classes. The last two years in medical school was primarily patient contact, in clinics, or hospital floor. Nurses were always a big help to us. Medical students also were a big help to the student nurses.

When we became junior medical students, we thought we had "arrived," because we were entitled to, and were told to, wear white coats. Not long white coats, those were for senior medical students, but short white jackets. During the last part of our sophomore year we had to take Virginia State Board Examination. We had to pass that exam, covering all of the Basic Science courses that we had struggled through, before we could take the Clinical Courses part of the State Board Exam, which we had to sit for at the end of our senior year. If we passed that complete exam we were given a life time Virginia License to practice Medicine in Virginia. Everybody passed the basic exam. That was a good thing because if we had to wait 2 years to take the Basic Science board, we would not have remembered all that stuff for the exam. We all passed the clinical exam after our senior year, and were very happy to receive our license at that time.

At the beginning of the junior year we had an additional 20 + students added to our class. These were transfer students from the West Virginia University 2 year medical school. That state had only a 2 year program, and they came into our last 2 years and finished with us. They all were good students and became good friends of us all. I learned later that West Virginia did add the final 2 year program to their medical school.

One quarter during the senior year, several of us had the opportunity to spend the quarter in an outlying hospital in the state. They had made arrangements for a few students to go down in south western Virginia to Abington Hospital, in Abington, Va. acting as externs there. Charlie Richardson, Jack Stanford, and I were among a group from MCV to go down there and work for 3 months. Terry elected to go somewhere in a Suffix, Virginia hospital. I think the name was Louise Obici Hospital, or something close to that name. We both had really good experiences. I met a very pretty, nice nurse there named Jolene, and we dated mostly the full 3 months. She got more serious than I wanted to get. I had no desires to get serious enough to even think about marrying anybody. I made it very plain to her, this was premature for me, because I had no money, no job, and wasn't absolutely sure of my graduating. I still had to finish the intern year, and possibly a residency program for specialty medical career. Anyway we continued a nice period together, and she was very sad to see me leave to go back to Richmond, and I was, too.

During my senior year in med school we had to choose a subject and do library research on the subject and write a paper about it. After a while thinking and thinking about it I came upon the idea of smoking cigarettes and medical results. I was a smoker, and there had been some newspaper articles about lung diseases caused by smoking.

In the library there were several articles on the subject, but they were all by the same writer, a Medical Resident in a New England medical school. This apparently was a new group of articles about the development of chronic obstructive lung disease, (emphysema), chronic bronchitis, arteriosclerosis, and heart diseases. After reading all these new medical scientific articles I felt that I needed to quit smoking my daily pack of Lucky Strike cigarettes. Each time I lit a cigarette I said to my self "that's the last one!" After about another 4 years it finally was. The name of my thesis was "The Affect of Cigarette Smoking on Pulmonary and Cardiac Disease."

Later, in my medical practice, it became quite apparent to me, following the progression of these conditions in smokers, they were all becoming slowly more ill. More and more of my patients were developing lung cancer. I became obnoxious to many of my smoker patients, however, some did quit, and many patients still praise me for making them quit.

I was on the student council a couple of years, as I remember. In my senior year I ran for president of the medical school, and was elected President. The Medical College of Virginia had a student body from students in the nursing school, the dental school, and hospital administration school, as well as our medical school. The presidents of each of these schools had to meet and decide which of us should be the president of the entire student body. We had to vote for the president, a vice-president, and a secretary-treasurer. I had too much to do and I didn't want to be president, so I voted, not for myself but for the president of the dental school to be the president. He did get elected, but I was elected as vice president of the student body. So I was happy about the honors given to me. I was also elected as a member in a leadership fraternity. I cannot remember the Greek letters that identify the fraternity. Anyway, I received another honor. We all felt very proud of ourselves for now knowing we were going to receive our cherished M.D. Degrees.

In the last couple of months there was one more thing that had to be done. We had to decide on what we were going to do with our degree. That meant, where we would intern, and what kind of specialist we wanted to be sort of dictated where we would go for post graduate education. Everybody was reading information from all the intern and resident programs in the United States.

Five members of our group elected to apply to Mound Park Hospital in St. Petersburg, Florida. This was a new hospital and the staff was mostly young talented specialists, graduates of very prestigious residencies. Ours would be their first class of interns. We thought they would be the excellent teachers we needed to give us a good postgrad education. Another positive was the hospital pay for interns was $300 a month, one of the highest in the country. Most interns received nothing, others $21 a month, of course they also gave room and board. Another plus was the wonderful Florida weather. It was not too far from Terry's and my home in Quitman, in southern Georgia, about 250 miles north of St. Petersburg, Florida.

We started our internship on July 1, 1953. We were the first intern group to be trained at the Mound Park Hospital. We met a lot of excited Doctors, Administrator, and Nurses. There were 5 from our hospital in Virginia, and 2 others from Tennessee, Ranell Spence and Elbert Young. From Medical College of Virginia there was me, Terry, Charlie Richardson, Earl Fox, and Jack Stanford. Soon we all became friends, and were assigned to various sections to begin our training. The services were surgery, medicine, obstetrics and gynecology, pediatrics, and urology. Other minor specialties were combined with the others. We spent 1 or 2 months on each service, throughout the year. Doctors on the staff were our teachers. We had dedicated, interesting well trained teachers. They had our interest and our success utmost in their minds to be sure we got an excellent internship. We were taught, and allowed to do things that only residents were doing in larger hospitals. The radiologist was really exceptional, loved teaching, and gave us all an opportunity to sit with him and teach us how to read films. He was Dr. Lennie Freed.

After we had been there about a month he had a dinner at his home for the interns. He was single, but prepared the meal. He invited a number of single ladies for dinner also. They were teachers, technicians, nurses, and business ladies, with some of the intern's wives. The ladies arrived after we were there. I was sitting on the couch in his living room and the front door bell rang.

In walked 2 young ladies, both beautiful but the taller of the two was especially gorgeous. In my beauty book she struck me as #2. #1 was Marilyn Monroe, to me, the top beauty of the day. This new beauty was a stunning blond with a long ponytail hairdo, wearing a red dress, and white shoes. I had dated beautiful girls in my life, but this one was way out of my league, I thought. She looked around the room, and she and her sister were introduced by Lennie, to the group. Her sister was a beauty herself, but I couldn't get my eyes and my mind off of her older sister.

There was a seat next to me, and she floated over and gracefully sat beside me to my thrill and excitement, and astonishment. I wasn't used to this kind of immediately positive activity toward me, especially so quickly, from this kind of beauty. We began a conversation that was calm and fun. I felt like she might even like me, because of her apparent interest in ME. To this day I do not remember another female that was at that party except a couple of the intern's wives, and

Helen her sister. We had a wonderful time at the party, eating, drinking some, talking a lot, and leaving. Terry and I were driving, so we left together. Elizabeth Redcay, home economics teacher of two years in a middle school, and her sister Helen left to drive home in her Henry J automobile.

I was driving our 1953 Buick, Daddy helped us buy, Terry was sitting in the front passenger seat, driving home and we came upon their car, so I drove by and waved. As soon as we went by, it dawned on me I wanted her phone number and didn't ask her for it. I knew she wouldn't give it to me. But I thought it would be easier if I had Terry ask her for it through the window. I slowed the car, with the window open we yelled "what's your phone number?" She yelled it back, we didn't have a pen or paper yet, so we hurriedly got one before she changed her mind, slowed again, she yelled it, Terry copied it down, and I had it!

We began to be very busy in our duties, requirements, and responsibilities, to our studies and to our patients. There was very little time to socialize, even time to study, depending on which service we were on for the month.

There were several very interesting, learning episodes that occurred from time to time. Some I'll try and relate in a sensible manner. We heard of a "Physician" who had a practice, was not on the medical staff of our hospital, but apparently had patients that he cared for. The story was that this man had in his office a tall machine, with lights, gauges, numbers, and sounds attached. He stood the patient in front of the machine, attached straps on the arms, legs, and chest. Then the machine was turned on, and during a period of time, he was recording the severity of, or presence of cancer, infection, colonic inflammation, and a variety of illnesses, that needed treating. The levels of these results were given to the patient. They were treated with elixirs, pills, or massages, or whatever he said they need to treat, or cure the problems. Patients would tell us they were brought back after a month of treatment to compare the results. Were they better, or worse, or had no change? No one ever got well. Always needed longer and more treatment. All treatment resulted from the report that came after again being attached to the machine, and a lot of lights went off and on, then an answer of no change, worse, or better. All of these reports required continuing, or changing medicines until the next future visit. As far as we knew, no one ever was cured or didn't need to return for follow up visit. The medicines were dispensed from the doctor's office. This was some of the quackery going on in the United States during that time.

One of our emergency room patients was brought in with near coma. This patient had diabetes requiring daily insulin injections, was under the care of one of the endocrinologists on the staff. The patient was admitted and they had to work fast and hard to control his diabetic acidosis. The history was that the patient had gone to see a chiropractic doctor, and had been told he didn't need to continue taking his insulin as long as he would come into his office for chiropractic manipulations on his back, to realign his vertebrae and allow the nerves that go to the pancreas to heal, and cure his diabetes.

He had been off of insulin for several weeks and had become quite ill. The treating specialist in the hospital explained all the reasons that the patient had to resume and continue the insulin and follow up care for his lifetime. The patient seemed to understand what he had to do. He was advised that insulin in the body normally responds to chemical reactions in the pancreas resulting from sugar and carbohydrate in the normal diet, if the insulin producing cells, Isles of Langerhan in the pancreas, are normal and producing properly. If not, diabetes can result, and may need insulin regulation. There is no control of the pancreas through nerves coming from the spine, only chemicals in the blood, and the vagus nerve running down the inside of the body to the internal organs.

After discharge, in two to three months he was again brought to the Emergency Room by ambulance, in coma this time. After again emergency and rapid treatment, by the specialist, he responded, was kept until he was controlled and discharged home. He gave the same story, his chiropractic doctor told him he didn't need the insulin. This tragedy was repeated a 3rd time. This time the specialist was unable after several weeks trying to save him, the man died of his diabetic complications.

One night a patient came to the emergency room claiming she was walking across her floor that was carpeted, and she stepped on a needle. Apparently the needle was lying on the floor and she was sort of shuffling across the floor, not picking her feet up very much, and she felt a stick in the front of the foot, just at the beginning of the sole between the great and second toe. It was sore, no needle was showing, but there was a pinpoint entry point visible. The intern on ER call came in to see her about 8 o'clock in the evening. He elected to take an x-ray to identify the needle. The needle was clearly visible on the x-ray, so after injecting anesthesia in the foot, he made an incision over where he thought the needle would be. After searching for the needle for a good 45 minutes to 1 hour, he again took her to the X-ray, to try to better locate the needle under fluoroscopy, and clamp a hemostat on the needle under fluoroscopy, so he could identify and remove it. He was still unable to locate it in the clamp. Another intern came in and knew he could find and remove it. They and even a third intern took their turn to try to locate and remove it. Nobody could succeed, I came by and heard the failure story, and they asked me to try. I politely declined. But I suggested that since it was midnight and the lady was tired, and 3 guys had tried and failed, they should probably call the Staff Surgeon on ER call to come in and find it. By now the bottom of the foot did not look good. After continued, and more and more extension of the incision, and the pulling and tissue exploration in all directions, the entire bottom of the foot is wide open, from the toes the length of the foot, to the heel. Still no one has located the needle. X-ray showed it still to be present. The surgeon, Dr. Garby, came in and listened to the intern's story and what they did to help the lady. He sat down and explained to the lady how hard it is to locate and remove a needle, and he wanted to give her a rest, let some of the healing go about beginning, and he was going to sew it up for now and worry about removing it at a later date. She was happy, so after the suture repair was done and the patient given an office appointment to follow up with Dr. Garby, she left.

Then he called all of us down to the x-ray department, which was closed and dark, and began to quietly lecture us on how not to handle this kind of foreign body, in this location. He began by letting us know that that poor woman may be in for a long road of healing. Pointing out one of the hardest thing to do, is first to find, and then to remove a needle, from the foot. Many times it is much better not to dig around like they all did. Now she can possibly develop more and more scaring from the healing period and the weight bearing on a healing scar may become very painful and create a larger, thicker scar. She may have to stop any weight bearing until complete healing is accomplished. And he added that he was the one who had to follow and try to minimize any complication for the entire healing time, of possibly several months. If the needle is left in place, with time it may migrate to the surface, become locally tender where it can easily be removed from just beneath the surface. That is exactly what happened in my office many years later. A needle in the foot watched for months, finally a tender spot on the side of the foot told me where to nick the skin, and I easily removed the needle.

The rotating intern year served me well. I was trying my best to pick out a specialty that I may want to spend my life practicing. So, if I did decide on one, I would have to go to another part of the country to a different hospital to learn. I found that I couldn't commit myself to just one field, I liked most of them, so I made up my mind I would go into general medicine, and do all of them. Terry and I felt the same way and decided to plan to practice together in general practice.

A specialty required one to finish 2 to 5, or 8 years doing a specialty residency, then to take the board examination to become a Certified Specialist in that specialty. The years required to take the board exams varied, depending on which specialty you chose to pursue. General Practice required only completing the rotating internship year. When we decided our future, we set out to try to learn all we could while at Mound Park Hospital. We became friends with most of the Physicians we worked with. They taught us many things that helped us set up and run our practice. I think we both thought we had learned all there was to know about any thing the progress of medicine had come up with by that time, in the history of medicine. Later we found out that wasn't entirely true, things kept being developed on and on, so we had to keep learning.

We had to take the Florida State Board of Medicine exam before setting up practice. We took the board examination, the basic sciences first. Terry passed it. I failed the pharmacy section and had to take that part over. I did and passed the exam after studying hard. At that time Florida required every applicant to take the board exams, basic and clinical parts separately. Most other states allowed reciprocation, and would accept all other states exam. We had passed the Virginia boards, had our licenses, but Florida required you still to take their Florida State Board examinations.

I learned later when I was in practice and served as a delegate from our county to the state meetings, that Florida required all new physician applicants coming to Florida to practice had to pass the Florida board examination. The reason was that it was a common problem that retiring doctors from all over the country wanted to come here and practice part time, or in an unsupervised atmosphere.

In those days there were much fewer board certified specialists, and the quality of medicine was lower, unless they were able to pass the boards. Older practicing physicians, even board certified physicians, had no requirements to recertify any time after their graduation, or in some way display their medical practice ability later in life.

Later, I don't know when, but Florida finally allowed reciprocity of other state's board examinations.

Our time in St. Petersburg, Florida was really enjoyable. We found time to fish a little, beach a little, boat a little, date and dance a little, and even study and learn a lot of medicine. Different doctors took us to those places and did those things with us. We learned some surgery, how to deliver babies, learned how to set fractures, and learned a lot about medical problems and diseases people get. We obtained quite a diverse and in depth medical education by doing, under expert tutelage.

After our dinner at Dr. Freed's home, I kept thinking about the beautiful young lady I met. I was a little afraid to call her, because I figured she had a boyfriend. She had to, because everybody could see her beauty and by now, 2 years a teacher in Saint Petersburg, Florida somebody already had her hooked. So it was a good 3 or 4 weeks later that I got up enough nerve to call her. I called and she accepted a date to go out to a beach restaurant for dinner on a Saturday night. I was so excited; I could hardly wait to see her.

We went out, had a nice dinner and we danced. I was a good dancer, she was not so good, but I could see she was a quick learner, so I thought of that as a plus. She told me she expected me to call, and asked why it took me so long to call. I took that as a plus also. I of course, told her doctors are always busy and I had to finally get some free time to be able to go on a date. She said I could have called and just talked. I took that as a plus also. I was really impressed with her personality, interests, and down to earth conversations. I was so impressed I even got to thinking, this might be the one. I was now a doctor, 29 years and 10/12 months old, and could make a living. I had not been excited about looking for a wife, yet. I needed to decide if I really wanted her as my wife. I also found out her birthday was October 3, 1930. That made her about 7 years younger than me, so I could teach her everything she needed to know to be my wife, plus she could take care of me when I get old. Yeah, right, how do you think that worked out for me? Remember she was a school teacher.

I needed more time and experience with her, therefore, I had to make more time to be with her. So we spent more time, trying to go out, or most times I would go to her upstairs apartment in somebody's home, talk and listen to some St. Petersburg, Florida radio station that signed off at 12:00 nightly with the "Star Spangled Banner." We decided that would be our theme song, and I knew it was time to go home. Money was scarce, $300 a month as an intern, and she was making $2700 a year as a home economics teacher.

Many times we spent the evening at her apartment, when I could arrange the intern, call night, and the on call limitations weren't too restricted. There were evenings that I had night emergency room call at the Mercy Hospital. We would sit and talk, listen to the radio, and I love to read Pogo comic books. Mercy Hospital was the black hospital that we also used as part of our training and on call services. This was long before integration occurred. It was located in an area between Mound Park Hospital and Elizabeth's apartment.

One night I was on call for Mercy Hospital, and the call came in for me to see a patient that was in acute respiratory distress in the emergency room. I was eating a sandwich with Elizabeth and had to leave. When I got there, this large obese black man was walking the floor breathing forcefully, rapidly, sort of raspy respirations. He told me that there had been a fight, and another man hit him really hard in the front left side of his throat with his fist, and he slowly swelled up in the neck and got so he couldn't get his breath. The left front of his neck was obviously very swollen, and his trachea was off to the right a little. He was so distressed I couldn't get him to sit down and calm down. I felt he had a ruptured blood vessel in the neck, and the developing hematoma was beginning to obstruct his ability to breath and pushing the trachea to the right He needed a tracheotomy to clear the hematoma, and relieve the tracheal obstruction. I called the surgeon on call, Dr. McClanathan about 1:00 o'clock in the AM. He told me to go ahead and do the tracheotomy. I told him, I'd never done one and he had to come in. Please! We argued a few minutes, finally he said "Go ahead and give him a little sedation and I'll come on in." So I gave him a shot of Morphine, to settle him down. I had convinced the man to sit on the table. In a few minutes, before the doctor got there, the man slowed his breathing, quietly began to slip off the table. I yelled at the nurse and assistant to help me lay him down, which we did with difficulty, due to his size. He barely was breathing, so I called for a tracheotomy tray. I knew this man would die if I didn't do it. Of course I'd seen pictures of the procedure, but doing it is a different thing.

I made the midline incision over the trachea in the anterior neck, I then quickly put my clean, but ungloved index finger in the soft tissues of the neck, expecting blood to rush out and relieve the near tracheal obstruction. No blood. So then I had to open the trachea, and place the tracheotomy tube into the trachea and place the oxygen tube into the tracheal tube. Then here comes into the room the doctor I had called.

There wasn't any more that needed to be done, so we reviewed the evening. He pointed out most everything was done correctly, except the morphine. As soon as he mentioned it, I knew what was wrong. Morphine suppresses the normal reflex to breath. That's why he nearly was unconscious, and slowed the breathing. I should have used Demerol. The other thing he mentioned was that I didn't need to use my finger to evacuate the hematoma, that wasn't there anyway, but if it was there, I still needed the tracheotomy, and let the hematoma alone. I could have induced a deep infection in the neck. It didn't happen, so the patient was kept in the hospital several days, until the massive swelling went down enough to remove the tracheotomy tube.

Another interesting Mercy emergency room patient came in that interrupted my wooing evening at Elizabeth's. This was a very well dressed black gentleman, with a preacher's collar. He complained of real, severe pain in his rectal, and buttock area. His history turned up nothing that I could decide what may be going on. So I decided to do a rectal exam and see if he had hemorrhoids, or a fissure or some similar problem. On inserting my gloved finger into the anus, I identified a firm, about 3 inch long, very hard, object, that seemed to be about ∫ inch wide, He vehemently denied inserting anything into his rectum. On further careful examination, I felt the object coursing from one side of the rectal wall close to the anal opening, to the other side higher on the opposite rectal wall. It seemed to be wedged in the terminal rectum. After careful, repeated attempts to identify the foreign body, I noticed I would remove the finger and find blood on it, more with each insertion, and causing more pain. Finally, with more attempts to adjust the position of the object, I was able to get the upper end vertically in the canal and slowly extract the object through the rectum, and out. I recognized it as a rib bone, just about 3 inches long. The patient admitted to eating barbequed ribs at a church dinner several days ago, but said he wasn't aware of swallowing one, but could think of no other way it got there. It was amazing to me that this size rib was able to traverse the entire intestinal tract without pain, or obstruction, until it came down ready for passage. It finally became impacted just above the anus and really painful. That's when he came to the emergency room. And the patient wasn't aware that he may have swallowed it. This wasn't a particularly pleasant job for both of us. However, he was most appreciative of the results, and he thanked me for his relief.

One of our friends, and physician teacher of orthopedics surgery, Dr. Paul Wallace, and wife Dorothy had two little girls. He enjoyed taking his wife out for dinner, and would often ask us to baby sit for the evening. We loved that, because we could get the kids to bed and sit on the couch in the living room and watch TV. TV just got started in this area, and not many people had TVs at that time.

The first time we were at Dr. Wallace's was several days before the first baby-sitting, when he invited the two of us to his home on Lake Maggiore to learn to water ski, which was a sort of new water sport. We really enjoyed learning, and were getting to be pretty good on 2 skies. No body was using one ski. We also noticed in riding on the skies behind his boat, we occasionally would glide right by a floating alligator in the lake. In fact, they were all over the lake. By the end of the day, most of them would wind up on the opposite shore, which was all swamp, and no homes. We were told they wouldn't bother us at all, so we didn't worry about it. When we fell, and the boat had to make a big circle we worried a little, but nothing happened. After dark we sometimes fished, and our spotlight would pick up the alligator's glowing eyes all on our side and not far away. We even caught an occasional big snook, a salt water fish, and this was a fresh water lake. I was told it used to be connected to a creek from the bay, but was cut off, and dammed up. I suppose the salt water fish learned to tolerate fresh water.

I was really getting serious with Elizabeth, and she knew how I felt. I was really upset when one evening we were having dinner at Dr. Wallace's home. They were entertaining a visiting French physician, who was charming, handsome, unmarried gentleman with a heavy French accent.

He seemed to be showing an awful lot of interest in my date, Elizabeth. I also noticed Elizabeth was showing a little interest in him, and was often coyly cutting her smiling eyes in his direction, and he was responding with more interest. I was sitting at the table eating, drinking, and began to seethe a little more and more at what was going on. It seemed to me she was paying a little more attention to him, than to me when we first met. I think I'll call it jealousy. Jealous bad! I went through the night being very polite, very jealous, and quite angry, still quietly seething really bad.

This was the first time I had really felt like she may not care for me as much as I really thought. I also felt hurt and figured I would just let her be, and not see her a while, and see how I felt later about all this rejection of me.

When we got to her home I took her to her door, politely told her how disappointed and hurt I was to watch her reaction to that Frenchman. I told her I would not see her again, and for her to go ahead and date him. She seemed quite surprised and seemed to want to talk. I didn't.

I took leave of her. I went home very sad and upset. I can't remember how long it was before she called me. I think it was the next night she invited me over for a nice roast beef, carrots, and potatoes dinner. After my refusal and her continual pleading, I finally agreed to see her again, especially for a superb sounding dinner that she would cook. She, being a graduate home economics teacher, I thought this would be a fabulous evening.

Well, when I got there we had a really good down to earth talk, she didn't know how bad I felt, and she apologized. So I thought all was really good, and we sat down to a great meal. After struggling to cut the beef, and chewing the first bite, I kind of wondered if she would serve this ultra tough beef to get back at me. I even wonder that to this day. Anyway, we did eat most of the beef, with an excellent taste, just tough. The potatoes and carrots were really good. I did remember that good beef was quite expensive for a struggling teacher.

We made up, and I forgave her. She maintained she was just being nice to him, with nothing more in mind. The guy left and went on back to France, I guess. Anyway, he was out of my hair. We continued seeing each other, feeling more and, more in love, and feeling more and more comfortable with each other. Any other woman that I had dated and thought a little about marrying, seemed to have some big problem, or even a small problem that was not suitable as a wife for me. So I had never gotten anywhere close to giving serious thought about marrying anybody. I was pretty picky in my mind for the perfect woman for my wife.

I felt very strongly that this was my future wife, so 3 weeks after we started dating I asked her to marry me. She agreed and we then wanted to meet our parents. We even didn't know if we should set up a wedding time, or just elope. In Florida there was a blood test requirement, and a 3 day waiting period. We found out that there was a town in South Georgia where you could just go and get the test and get married. Time of getting there meant me getting off from my training, and for her, out of school. There seemed to be just too many complicated problems, so we made plans to go to each other's homes to meet our parents. I called my parents and told them the good news.

They were excited but I was the first of their children to surprise them with marriage.

We drove to Quitman, Georgia, my home, to visit my parents. We took Terry and Helen, Elizabeth's sister, along for the weekend. We exposed the Pennsylvania girls to southern Georgia, and my northern fiancé to my Victorian, quite southern Mama and Daddy. I took them to the Quitman country club, and all the sites any traveler to the area would want to see. It wasn't much, except our beautiful, small southern town. Mama and Daddy were pleasant and nice to our visitors, had good conversations, and all seemed to go quite well, and Mama fed us all well. I was really pleased to show off my new fiancé. Helen had a good time too. After a whirlwind visit we headed back to Saint Petersburg, Florida to continue our internship.

After we had been back to work a few days I got a letter from Mama, and I think Daddy. I remember Mama's letter as a real shocker, and a blow to me. She politely told me she thought Elizabeth was a real nice pretty girl, but she thought she may not be the girl for me, being from the north, and educated in the north. She wondered if I ought to wait a while before I went ahead and married.

I was so upset by that letter, also very angry, and disappointed that I couldn't help but breakdown and just bawl. Terry came in my room, found me crying and really upset. He tried to comfort me and calm me down, but I was so despondent I couldn't stop crying. I was extremely disappointed, angry, and worried if I could have been wrong about my assessment and love of Elizabeth. I knew I was deeply in love with her, and I knew I still was going to marry her. I called Mama a couple of days later, and told my mother, that I knew I was right, I loved her deeply and I was still going to marry her. Mom said well, "I just hope you know what you're doing." I said I know I do know what I'm doing. (Here we are right now, 3 months short of 55 years of marriage, and I still love her more than I did then.) I found out later that Terry wrote Mama a letter and told her that Elizabeth was a really nice, hard working, religious and conscientious school teacher and we both loved each other. That was a big help to me.

It was a few weeks later that we flew to Pennsylvania to meet her parents. They lived in a two story, old home, on the Susquehanna River in Selinsgrove, Pennsylvania. They had been there when Elizabeth grew up, and they were interested and well versed in antique furniture. They had collected early American furniture from country, and home auctions, and refinished them all themselves. The household furnishing were beautiful. I got educated by her father Luther about what was good and how to refinish it. We attended several auctions, and I got hooked on beginning to collect for our home when we get married.

I thought her parents were wonderful people, and had raised 2 beautiful and proper young ladies, and I thought this was another plus and I was going to get one of their daughters. I didn't know what they thought of me as a son-in-law, but I assumed all was well, because Elizabeth and her mother were reading, and talking about what to do and how to go about getting married, in a church, with a lot of people, maid of honor, bridesmaids, and ushers, and all the stuff I didn't really want to go through. I didn't say anything because I was afraid they wouldn't let us marry if they couldn't do it their way.

They read in a book the groom had to polish the bottoms of his shoes, so they would look nice for the congregation to see during the service when we knelt at the altar. Then all the flowers, and the kind and colors of gowns; and what the groom, best man and ushers had to wear. They spent a lot of time figuring out the date of the wedding, and where it would be. We were visiting there in October, and they were planning the affair for far away in the summer. The more they talked and planned the worse it sounded, so they set a date for June of 1954, when her school was out, and my internship was over. I heard later that Helen had to reassure her parents that I was a nice guy, acceptable to her, and loved their daughter.

When our weekend was over we flew back to Saint Petersburg, Florida. We went back to our work, and continued to date and talk. We got tired of waiting, and told the families we were going to go ahead, and plan our wedding on November 25, 1953, the night before Thanksgiving in Elizabeth's Lutheran Church in Saint Petersburg for just the immediate families. Then afterwards we would share a family Thanksgiving Dinner in a nice restaurant in town. And we did.

It went off without a hitch, with our parents, and Elizabeth's sister Helen, her aunt Helen, they called Aunt Honey, and my brother Terry. My brother Maurice was in college and couldn't come. Everything went really well, and after the nice evening wedding dinner my wife and I left the party, and drove to Lido Beach Resort out of Sarasota, Florida. We arrived late, checked in, and began our wonderful honeymoon weekend.

On returning to her teaching and my internship, we started our life in a small room that the hospital provided for us. We had left our wedding dinner on Thursday night Nov. 25th, 1953, returned Sunday Nov. 28, late in the evening. Sometime after we were married, still during

1953: My intern year, here with my beautiful bride.

my internship, Elizabeth informed me she had been voted "Miss Saint Petersburg Saints." The Saints were a semi-pro baseball team in Saint Petersburg, Florida. A photographer had apparently learned about this beauty teaching school, and did some pictures for the newspaper. The publication got her noticed, and she was elected the team's "Miss." Then she rode on a float in the parade through town representing the team. She also told me about her being in the Miss America pageant for Pennsylvania in 1950, and was 1st runner up in the state contest. Amazing she didn't let me know about this before we were married. I could have told her I played football in high school for Quitman High AND played sax and clarinet in the high school band.

A little later the hospital made available a small house on the hospital property, furnished, except for the television that we later added. We had no air conditioner in those days and our little house was bordering the parking lot of the hospital. We had our bedroom windows up to keep cool and almost every day one of the interns would stick their head next to the window and say "Good Morning." We learned to be happy and very quiet in the morning.

This was our home until internship was over in June of 1954. I had decided I was going into general practice and I wanted to have another year of surgical training, so I stayed there as a surgical resident. I was appointed chief resident. I helped the new intern class when I was needed. One of the new interns was Rudy Garber, in the class behind us at Medical College of Virginia, an old friend of ours. Terry was ready to leave, so he took a Locum Tenum position in a doctor's office in Wausau, Wisconsin for about 4 months.

I learned a lot of surgery, mostly office type. This is so I could expand my ability in the office practice. I scrubbed in many, many surgical procedures, as 1st assistant to most of the surgeons on staff for every type of major procedure that was done in that hospital, neurosurgery, general surgery, pulmonary surgery, urological surgery, gynecological surgery, and orthopedic surgery. I loved it all and learned it well, but I didn't want to spend another 3 to 6 years in a residency program for the specialty of only one type of surgery. Then I would have to take the board exams and pass them to have the board certification. I loved all medicine disciplines and tried to learn all that would present in my office in the future. I found out rather quickly that a good doctor knows what he doesn't know and gets that patient into the hands of someone who does.

Terry came home from Wisconsin in October and we decided we would like to find a place in Florida, and go into a partnership general practice. We traveled through the central part of Florida, looking for a place to practice. We thought the prettiest and best place was a small town between Lakeland and Winter Haven, Auburndale, Florida. This little town of about 5000 people was full of friendly, cooperative people, and situated in almost the exact center of Fla. north and south, and east and west.

There were a lot of local lakes in the county and a lot of orange groves. We loved fishing for bass and Terry and I agreed this was a place made for us. Auburndale was just about equal distance to the Atlantic Ocean as to the Gulf of Mexico, about 50 miles west of Orlando, and about 50 miles east of Tampa, so big city shopping was not too far away. We talked to the chamber of commerce, and to a couple of pharmacists, and realtors. We were encouraged by all of them. So we explored the surrounding area, mostly groves. There were a few large orange juice companies, and other companies in town, Adams Packing Co., Minute Maid Corp., Continental Can Co., Eger Cement Block Co., and Florida All Bound Box Co.

There was a physician in general practice who had built a two doctor building and moved his general practice from Orlando to Auburndale, Florida 2-3 years before this, in about 1952. His name was Dr. Clinton Whitehurst. Terry and I went in to meet him and introduce ourselves and soon found out he had been thinking about leaving and moving to Tampa to semi-retire from practice. He said he would sell his building, and help us start our practice, if we would like. He offered us both a salary of $300 a month, for 6 months then he would leave Auburndale after we had worked into his active and busy practice.

We thought it over and decided this was a good move for us. There were two other medical doctors in town, both were rather elderly, Dr. Simmons, and Dr. Morland. Neither was doing hospital work. Dr. Whitehurst was the only MD from Auburndale on the Winter Haven Hospital staff, which was only about 4-5 miles east of Auburndale.

Terry was free, and I was still in my surgical residency. I talked to the administrator of Mound Park Hospital, and he wanted me to stay at least until 6 months of my planned 12 months residency was done. It was late October, or November and my 6 months would have ended in January. I agreed, so Terry went on to Auburndale and began working with Dr. Whitehurst. I planned to come over in January 1955, which I did.

# 4

# A Family Doctor at Last: The Golden Age of Medicine

Terry came over to practice with Dr. Whitehurst in October or November of 1954. I finished 6 months of my planned 12 month surgical residency at Mound Park Hospital in St. Petersburg, Fla. and Elizabeth and I moved to Auburndale in January 1955. It was an exciting time in our life, coming to a new place, new people and life ahead of us. Elizabeth and I bought a five passenger, 2 door yellow Chevrolet and were so proud of it.

We found an apartment to rent on Lake Ariana from Mrs. Dudley. It was a little square two story building. There was an apartment upstairs and one downstairs. We rented the downstairs, 2 bedrooms behind 2 rooms in front, open kitchen left and family room right. There was a little hall leading to the bathroom separating the bedrooms. We owned two wicker chairs and a floor model Capehart TV, and a Collie dog, named Bonnie that the Dr. Paul Wallaces gave us for a wedding present, and what clothes we each had. Mrs. Dudley lived in her home directly to our right, on the lake, as we face the lake. To our left, lived the Episcopal Minister and his wife, Cyril and Kay Stone. Right behind us was Mr. Dudley's large grapefruit grove. Above us lived, for only a shot time a divorced insurance salesman.

After Dr. Whitehurst left, we changed our office name and put a sign out front of the building, Tanner Medical Offices, painted in letters 4-5 inches high After about a month we got a letter from the Polk County Medical Association, warning us that it was against the associations rules, and unethical to advertise with letters over 2inches high. There was no advertising in those days, for either physicians or attorneys, as I remember. It was frowned upon, and considered unethical to do so. We changed the size as required. Later, after Terry left, a metal worker patient, from Polk City, a small community 10 miles north of us, brought me a black metal sign made with individual metal letters, cut out and mounted on a black metal base, of my name to attach to the building right by the entrance door. I appreciated that gift. It was 2 inches high and couldn't be read very easily from the road. I didn't care because I was very busy and everybody in town knew who I was and where my office was.

I loved the location of our home, because I could go right down to the lake and fish for bass, any time I wanted. I went to the office at 8AM worked until noon, came home for an hour, back to the office at 1PM, after fishing for a 15-20 minute period. I worked until 6 PM, came home for an hour, back to the office at 7 PM and tried to leave at 9 PM. Sometimes I did, and sometimes I couldn't.

One afternoon, during my supper hour, a quick sandwich and glass of milk, gave me a little time to run down and throw a plug off of the minister's dock. Suddenly, next to the weeds jerking a top-water bait I got a strike and hooked a nice bass. Playing it a little, suddenly another big hit again, then a little battle and after a few short minutes I pulled in and landed two bass at the same time. The first was about twelve inches long hooked on the front treble hook of the plug, and the second, some 15 inches and heavier, was hooked on the rear treble hook. Apparently the second bass was striking the first fish, thinking (if fish think) that "here is a little fish moving around slowly and erratically and would make a nice easy meal." Well, they both made a nice easy meal for us. That episode occurred within the first few weeks of living there, and I had dreams of frequent fishing and a leisurely living, and catching a lot of fish. I knew we had picked the right place to start our medical practice. That dream didn't last very long because we got so busy my fishing became few and far between. I still enjoyed driving around the lake to and from work every day, looking and dreaming for the next almost 50 years.

On Saturdays we opened at 9AM tried to leave for the day at 12. Office call fees were $3, house calls were $5. These were Dr. Whitehurst's fees and we were working for a salary for 6 months. We were getting busier and busier, and when he left we continued the same fee schedules, and we had an active and very busy medical practice. For a year or two the fees stayed the same.

When we came to Auburndale we applied to the hospital staff of the Winter Haven Hospital for membership, and were accepted. The Administrator at that time was Melvin Arnold, a friendly gentleman who welcomed me. I remember the head of nursing was a delightful, capable, friendly nurse Mrs. Elswick. She was a big help to this new frightened young Doctor. She was always ready to answer my dumb, significant questions that I was sometimes afraid to let anybody know I didn't know. She answered with understanding and never questioned why I didn't know some of the usually known things that I asked. She helped me for years to get comfortable and become absorbed into the staff. Another nurse I remember on the floor was Miss Ertle. She also made me comfortable during my learning years of being involved as a new staff member. They both were of great comfort and help for me during the neophyte years. Mel Arnold retired and the next Administrator was Barney Johnson. A few years later came Lance Anastazio, who continues to be the capable, forward thinking leader and Administrator who has brought this hospital through some tough times to what it is now, one of the top hospitals in Central Florida.

There were so many doctors and nurses that have come and gone, I hesitate to try to remember them all, even though I have such wonderful memories of them. A few I'll try to name: Dr. Bond, Dr. Keramedis, Dr. Bill Steele, Dr. Rita Marrotti, Dr. George Dorman, Dr. Bill Cottrell, Dr. Perry Keith, Dr. Sam Garrett, Dr. Simpson, Dr. Ivan Gessler, Dr. Charlie Parks, Dr. Robert Jahn, Dr. McCullough, Dr. Pat Sullivan, Dr. Paul Mahan, Dr. Art Moseley, Dr. Howard Lucas, and his brother Dr. Roy Lucas. Our Pediatrician, Dr. Raymond LaRue, and others are mentioned later in this book of my memories.

A lady came in one time to see Terry, saying she heard he was "real good on arthritis." We had being giving a shot of a salicylate for arthritis, and it worked quite well. She was from another town, Wauchula 30 or 40 miles south of us I think, and said she heard about him "Being real good on arthritis." She was happy with his treatment.

Dr. Whitehurst had been buying a lot of intramuscular injectable drugs for most of whatever you had wrong with you. He had been using them quite a long time. We had to continue for a while, because of the patients returning for their shots. We tended to change them to oral medication, as we slowly ran out of the injectables. This was slowing our income down, not continuing the money charged for shots and drugs. Patients commented how happy they were, "not having to take them ole shots and doing jest as well on pills."

We felt like we weren't making any money, so we hired a Practice Consultant to evaluate if we needed to change something. We just wanted to see and treat patients.

He came and did an evaluation. He told us it was costing us $4.62 to see a patient in our office, and we were charging $3.00, and $5.00 for house calls and hospital calls. He advised changing to $5 for office and $7 for house calls and hospital calls.

As usual, changes in medicine and laws, found me having to have a Professional Management company send a person into my office on a monthly basis to keep us up with county, state, city changes in fees and requirements to slowly increase office fees to overcome necessary increases in employee salaries, insurance fee, etc. They were a big help to me. We were never taught in medical school how to manage a growing, busy medical practice business.

When Terry was with me we had some interesting challenges. One day in the office we started seeing a lot of patients, when we talked to each other we found out that most had severe diarrhea and vomiting, and most were children and some adults. We saw over 100 patients over the next 2 days, most sick the same, and it seemed they had all eaten the same food at school. We were worn out with this many really sick and miserable patients. They all got over it, and the health department was notified.

Another time we were called to the Emergency Room when one of our patients was brought in. Terry was still with me, and one of us went over and called the other, so we both were there.

This cement block layer was laying cement blocks, and was on top of the wall, about 8 feet high. He was standing up, lost his balance, jumped, landed on his feet, and wound up breaking both heels. The arch of both feet was reversed, and x-rays revealed both heels were comminuted, fractured into multiple little pieces. We knew we had to reduce the fractures and put both feet into casts. We moved him to the operating room, because we knew he couldn't stand for us to reduce them and cast them, without anesthesia. All was ready, he was anesthetized, and we couldn't manipulate the heels, so we couldn't reduce the fractures. We didn't have an orthopedic doctor here so we decided to call Dr. Paul Wallace, in St, Petersburg, Florida where we had interned. We got him on the phone, explained what we had, and asked if we should send him over there. He told us no, and to go ahead and fix it. He told us all we have to do is loosen the impacted bones in the heels, by wrapping a towel around the heel, then striking it with a mallet to separate and loosen the fragments, so we can mold the heel bone to its usual shape, and cast it. We said thanks and hung up. We asked the nurse if they had a mallet, and if so get it, please. She called the hospital maintenance department; they had one and brought it up to the operating room. We had the patient asleep, lying on the left side, with the outside of the left ankle down flat on the table wrapped in a towel. I told Terry to go ahead and hit it. He took the wooden mallet and tapped the heel. Nothing changed. He tried again with a little firmer blow, nothing changed.

I said let me have the mallet. I drew back and struck a rather severe blow or two, heard it crack, and then we were able to manipulate all the fragments and fashion a really normal appearing heel and foot. I turned the patient over on his right side, repeated the rather forceful blow to the heel with the same result. When we finished with our molding by our hands, both looked like normal feet with nice arches once again. X-rays looked really good, just like normal feet, but heels made of many pieces of bone. We had never heard of such a thing in our previous "years of practice." We put casts on both feet, kept the patient in the hospital for several days, to keep him off his feet and control his rather significant pain. He was in a wheel chair for some 4-6 weeks, then crutches, and finally walking fine. When he healed, he was back to his usual occupation, and had two good looking and functional feet and was very thankful for his painless and useful feet.

One of the interesting things that Doctor Whitehurst taught us was how to treat impetigo quickly and completely. He suggested injecting intravenously 500 milligrams of Vitamin C, using a very small needle and inject slowly into the vein. We didn't get that information in medical school. We did that on several occasions when the kids had multiple lesions on the face and hands and extremities. Most lesions melted away in 24 to 48 hours. We found that miraculous.

The office we purchased had a large x-ray machine and a fluoroscopy capability. Dr. Whitehurst used to do Gastrointestinal Series, Barium Enemas etc., but neither Terry nor I wanted to take a chance doing that, so we called our teacher and friend, Radiologist Dr. Lennie Freed in Saint Petersburg, and talked, he said "why don't you set up a day a week and schedule several fluoroscopy patients and I'll come over and do them for you." We did that, and got a lot of good help from him, and even learned how to take, and read the x-rays ourselves. We also had a small laboratory for blood and urine tests. For a while we had a technician that did both lab, and x-rays. We used those facilities to good advantage. The hospital had a radiologist, a very old and feeble gentleman, doing the work, but I found a few flaws in some of his reports, that had to be re-done. That was one of the reasons Dr. Freed was so helpful to us. The hospital radiologist soon retired and we had a new and competent replacement, board certified radiologist, Dr. Ed Burns, who soon brought in a partner, Dr. Arnold Spanjers and as time went on, expanded to a wonderful group. I had to learn how to take x-rays, and this gave me the opportunity to position the target in varying projections to show fractures that sometimes didn't show up on the prescribed routine view.

I would take my office x-rays to the hospital radiology department early every AM, before my rounds, and sit with the radiologist while he read and dictated the report for my office He taught me an awful lot about reading x-rays, but for my legal protection, I needed a Board Certified Radiologist reports in my records. I expected to pay for their service so I received a bill from them for reading and dictating my office x-rays monthly.

Terry and I both made a lot of house calls. After a while it became apparent, that Terry was getting more house calls than I was. He was single, and was not finding any one to his liking, to date. He was not a drinker, and didn't like to go out to honky-tonks, or dinner or night life of any kind. We both were very busy making calls, seeing patients and trying to make the payments on our office, which we were doing, but it was rather hard. Some body told us they generally called Terry for the house calls, because I was married and they didn't want to bother me as much. I don't know if that was true or not.

Anyway, after about a year and a half, Terry decided he had enough of general practice, so he left to return to Saint Petersburg, Florida and he went into Insurance Medicine there. There were a lot of insurance companies that needed physical exams done quickly and competently. He became very busy in that practice, and had several insurance companies send their clients to be insured to his office for a complete physical exam. He slowly cut the numbers of companies down, and wound up being the Medical Director of Minneapolis Honeywell Company.

He went on to become the founder of a very successful medical product company, Concept, Inc. Concept later was bought by the medical company giant Bristol-Myers Squibb Corporation, and Terry was able to retire.

I really didn't want him to go because he helped me a lot, and I occasionally helped him. I really missed Terry for quite a long time.

He was my support many times, when we could talk over a situation, and it was nice to talk about a little uneasy situation, or a questionable diagnosis.

I remember the first patient I saw when I first was in the office was Helen James, wife of Wynn James, Comptroller for Adams Packing Company in Auburndale. This was in 1955, January 15th. When I retired from my office practice, the last patient I saw on that day December 31, 1995, was the same Helen James. We treated her off and on all those years.

I did continue working after retiring from office practice, for another 7 years as an employee of the Winter Haven Hospital as a part time Emergency Room physician, and also rotated around their outlying clinics in Auburndale, Bartow, Lakeland, and Winter Haven. This was a way for me to slow down my activity, yet continue practicing in this new capacity, no more hospital work or night call, but able to continue seeing many of my patients who would call my wife, or the hospital, to find out where I would be, and what day. They found me to have me treat them. Quite a complement, I thought. An hourly salary, malpractice and family insurance, retirement benefits and no night calls and no hospital admissions to handle, was a perfect way for a Family Practitioner to gradually slow down as he approached retirement years. Clinic hours were 8 or 9 to 5 PM.

After Terry left to return to Saint Petersburg, we began to have gradually, new board certified doctors coming into the area, and joining the staff. I became active in the Florida Medical Association, Polk County Medical Association, and active on our hospital staff.

After months of waiting for the stork to arrive, one finally came and dropped off a healthy baby boy. I asked him his name and he said, "Paul Alexander Tanner III." I told Elizabeth about the new baby and she was thrilled, and agreed to accept him with great fanfare, because she'd never had a baby before, and everybody thought we were unique. We were, because we had a BABY!!! Paul III was born 3-30-1956.

We still lived in the little apartment with our dog Bonnie. The dog would run around in the neighborhood, and sleep in the house at night. She was a wonderful dog; however, she also brought us a whole bunch of her friends. Ticks. We noticed them in the mornings climbing up the walls, and a search of our cement block and plank bookcase revealed hundreds of the little fellows- thin- fat- big-little ticks under the shelves. We finally were able to protect our baby, and get rid of them. Bonnie appreciated that too.

I should have been aware that we probably were going to have some kind of baby, because Elizabeth got so sick and nauseated most of the time 6 to seven months before Paul 3rd came. But being a neophyte physician, in the early months I thought she just got hold of some food she couldn't tolerate and she apparently kept eating it to continue the miserable state of affairs. It was because of my uneasy feeling that she wouldn't quit eating the offending food, I sent her out of the state to her mother hoping she could fix her own daughter. It worked, because about 5 months after she got to her Pennsylvania home in Selinsgrove, she began to improve and she came back here. It was after that, that Paul 3$^{rd}$ surprised us. We were really happy that he got here, after what his vehicle had to go through to bring him here.

When we began practicing in 1955, hardly anybody had medical insurance; in fact it was not common at all for people to have it. Most of the people in the area worked hard, either picking fruit, or sectionizing fruit in the plants, for canning. Some of the companies had medical insurance available, but the employee had to choose it, and pay for most of the charge for it. Most of my patients elected not to spend the money for it. We always saw patients that came in. Nobody was refused treatment for lack of money. They were not asked if they had the money, only asked them what was wrong that needed treating. They were all billed every month, and some came in and paid their bill or paid on the bill, a little at a time. I never had a bill collector. I have no idea how much I never collected.

Sometimes we'd have a mess of fish brought in for me, or turnips, or tomatoes, or oranges, or avocados, or mangoes, or a mess of sweet corn roastin' ears. There were some really good large avocados that came from Jere Stambaugh's tree, or the Walter Kersey tree that was in the yard of Kersey Funeral Home. A delicious mango that Fred Jones's Mama brought in for me from her tree. Fred became a Florida State Representative and was re-elected for years. After a few years most of those good old bearing trees got frozen out, and few are around now.

When I first started practice, I began delivering babies, as part of my practice. We were on the Winter Haven Hospital staff. There were about 15 doctors on the staff when we came. Nobody was a board certified specialist. Several general practitioners did obstetrics. One doctor limited her practice to pediatrics, Doctor Rita Marrotti, 2 others limited their practice to obstetrics. There was one eye, ear, nose, and throat specialist, not sure about his board certification. There was no other ophthalmologist, or neurologist, or neurosurgeon. One orthopedic surgeon came shortly after we came, Dr. Robert Jahn. One general practitioner in Winter Haven, Dr. Roy Lucas, a good friend of mine, was financially helping his brother Howard finish a medical specialty in ophthalmology. When Howard finished his specialty training he returned to Winter Haven to practice, Roy returned to specialty training in Radiology with financial help from Howard, and returned to Winter Haven to practice radiology on completion of his residency. I thought quite noble things to do for each other. They continue today to be our friends.

There were several of the older general practice doctors on the Winter Haven Hospital staff that did surgery. The usual thing done was a three month training period at a medical school, to learn 1 or 2 operative procedures, come home and practice awhile doing them, and go back to learn another surgical procedure. I continued delivering babies for about 2 years. The doctors doing obstetrics were charging $150. I was charging $75. I got paid for 4 of 16 deliveries. One lady had insurance, and the bill wasn't paid so I call her insurance company. They told me they had paid the bill, but the money was paid to the patient, and it was her responsibility to pay her doctor.

I called the patient, and she said she had been paid but she thought that money was for her. I told her she was supposed to pay my bill with that money. She said she was sorry, but nobody was working right then, and "they didn't have no money, they already spent that money for a new washin' machine." She said she'd pay me when they get the money. I don't remember ever getting paid for that baby.

The big trouble with OB in a General Practice is women go into labor anytime. With an office full of patients, a call from the hospital labor room means I gotta go. The waiting room patients were quiet but real unhappy when you tell them you gotta go, they frown, mouth draws down, and they get up and stomp out.

Mrs. Dudley told us we had to move, because her son was moving back to town and had to have a place to stay. We had to start looking around for a place to move. The Dudleys were also building a new home right in front of our apartment.

Jack and Trish Summers moved to Winter Haven first, and joined the People's Bank of Auburndale. After a few months, he decided to move to Auburndale where his new job was. By that time the Dudleys moved into their new home and the Summers moved into the home the Dudleys had lived in, next door to us. They had a pretty little baby girl named Nina. They became our friends, and our friendship has continued through the years.

Our new house, at 2032 Ariana Boulevard, was a $2^{nd}$ hand house, nice and another lakefront, built for Sam and Barbara Killebrew, who had 2 kids, Sammy and Bert. Sam started to benefit from his new kind of 18 wheeler trucks for hauling bulk stuff, and could be emptied from 4 individual V-shaped containers at separate times. He had formed Killebrew Manufacturing Company and was making and selling his invention. He bought a bigger home on the other side of the lake. The family became our friends and my patients.

One weekend, Elizabeth and I had planned a nice Saturday night party with 15 -20 docs and their wives at our new home after we moved from the Dudley's to 2032 Ariana Boulevard. I had babies due for a couple of months. I had all the chicken, had a hot fire in the grill, every body was imbibing our liquor, beer, and wine, and about ready to put the chickens on the grill, phone call, my patient in labor. I gotta go. I left after my humble apology, and told them to finish cooking and go ahead and eat.

It was at that Saturday night grilling party, my good friend and surgeon, Frank Zeller came in late. Everybody was on our covered porch, drinking, eating olives, and peanuts, when Frank got his drink, walked over to the table that had black olives in a dish, picked up a handful and was talking away, and suddenly stopped, spit the olives back in his hand, out of his mouth then back in the dish and said, "Damn, nearly broke my teeth." He had picked up a handful of olive seeds from the "used" dish, thinking he had a handful of peanuts, until he chomped down on them.

I came in much later, found out from my wonderful wife they wound up pretty tipsy, and ate raw, and or, burnt chicken, of those pieces of chicken which weren't dropped upon the ground. Some of the guests, trying to cook the chicken apparently didn't know much about grilling chicken, or got so tipsy they didn't care. Anyway Elizabeth said it seemed like everybody had a good time. So I did no more OB after the 2 years of rarely sleeping, and dozing in my office next day after an all night delivery, free babies, mostly. I was just trying to be a good general practitioner.

I tried also, to be a good pediatrician, since I was delivering babies. I had learned how to carefully circumcise little boys, and take care of infants who were vomiting with diarrhea, and became dehydrated, until one little child brought to my office one morning dehydrated with those symptoms. I admitted the child, ordered fluids by clysis (fluids administered into both anterior thigh areas beneath the skin. when unable to find a vein.). When I came in later in the afternoon to check on the baby, I was really scared because the baby was severely ill. A new young pediatrician had started practice in Lakeland a month or so before. I called him, described my patient and my fear, and he said send him right over.

It would take too long to call a funeral home for an ambulance, so I told the mother to pick the baby up and go to my car, and we were going to Lakeland's Morrell Hospital emergency room to meet the pediatrician who will take care of her baby. She did, and I did. (Now days it would take half a day to get the kid discharged from the hospital. I just told the nurse to let them know I was taking the baby to Lakeland, they could worry about the paperwork later.) We flew in my car the 15 or so miles to the emergency room in Lakeland and the pediatrician was there to take over the care of the child. The mother was happy, and I was really happy. The baby survived and did well.

I learned I was pretty stupid thinking I was proficient in every damned thing a person or a kid could have wrong with him, or her. I concluded I needed to concentrate on what I knew and not on what I thought I knew. That was the end of my trying to take care of kids under 2 years old. I found out they can't talk and tell you where they hurt. They just cry.

During our evening hours, from 7 to 9 PM, one night a nice lady came in to see me because of a rather severely bleeding gum. There was an obvious rather large, torn, jagged laceration to the bottom gum on the right, where a tooth was supposed to be. I didn't know how to handle it, so I called one of the dentists in town and asked him to come to his office and please sew up this lady's bleeding gum. What had happened was that she had an abscessed very painful tooth, so her husband was going to pull it. He got a strong piece of fishing line, tied it around the tooth, sat her in a chair a couple of feet from an opened door and tied the string to the doorknob. The string was shorter than the distance to the door. He then, with all of his might stood next to the door and suddenly slammed the door closed with his full force, jerking the tooth out, and severely lacerating the gum.

I hadn't met Dr. Ken Roberts yet, but he graciously agreed to see and care for my patient. Before he hung up, he said they noted in the local newspaper, that I came from Quitman, Georgia. I said yes then he told me he married one of my high school classmates, Marie Lovett. She had moved to Clearwater, Florida and they met and married several years before and had 2 or 3 kids, I don't remember how many. I really appreciated Ken helping my patient. He came down, sewed her up nicely and we had a nice conversation about Marie and their family, and bringing me up to date about her family. He became our family dentist until he retired several years ago.

It was at this point I had learned a valuable lesson. Don't think you can handle ALL of mankind's illnesses, and treat only the stuff you know you know well. You may know how, but every individual doesn't respond the same to the same treatment. From then on, I stopped seeing any child under 2 years old, and never did learn, nor wanted to learn how to sew up gums.

Not long after I came to Auburndale we met our Postman, who had married a nice French lady he'd met in France during World War II. He was a happy and friendly gentleman. She had a delightful French accent, and they had 3 boys of grade school age. They were all my patients. One day I receive a phone call from our Dentist Dr. Roberts, telling me he wanted me to see Mr. (Postman), my patient, for the cancer in his left mandible. Seems as he had a painful left lower molar, and Dr. Roberts removed the obviously infected tooth. It continued to bleed, hurt, and was not healing. A biopsy was done and sent to the Winter Haven Hospital Pathology Department for diagnosis. The diagnosis was cancer of the gum.

I saw Mr. (Postman), with his report from Dr. Cox, Pathologist at Winter Haven Hospital, and one of my doctor friends. I called Dr. David Cox and was told he was certain that the diagnosis was correct, because he had sent some slides to a couple of places for conformation of his opinion, and they both agreed with him. One was a University in a New England Medical School, and also the U.S. Department of Pathology in the Us Army Hospital in Bethesda, Maryland. Dr. Cox told me these were the places pathologists over the country send some difficult cases for confirmation, or diagnosis, and stated gum cancer was extremely difficult to sometimes really tell cancer from a severe infection. I referred the patient to Dr. Zeller for probable surgery. After he called me, he set up a conference with Dr. Cox, Dr. Ed Burns Radiologist, and himself with the patient and his wife. They went over the problem, and advised the family that he needed removal of the left jaw, and a radical neck surgery to remove all of the lymph nodes on the left side of the neck, as soon as possible. This was a shock to them and the decided to go home and decide.

I heard nothing more, but the wife was in my office a couple weeks later with one of the children and I asked about her husband and what had they decided. She told me one of the families that he delivered mail to, was told about the problem, and she told Mr. (Postman) to go immediately to her doctor at Duke University where she had had her breast cancer surgery, so they were going to Duke, in North Carolina. They already had their appointment.

About 3 to 4 weeks later I was making rounds at the hospital and happened to see Dr, Ivan Gessler, who started the Gessler Clinic in Winter Haven and is a large clinic, stopped me and said "I want to talk to you." He told me that a few days ago he was returning from a conference in North Carolina and happened to be seated by Mr. (Postman) flying home from Duke. He related to Dr. Gessler that he had just completed an examination and another biopsy on his gum and the results were completely normal, and these doctors here wanted to cut him all up. He said the biopsy showed only a little infection but no cancer. He also told Dr. Gessler that the doctor at Duke told him that those LMDs in small towns were not competent to diagnose cancer and shouldn't be trying to treat that kind of stuff there. LMD stands for "Local Medical Doctor." We had heard that kind of characterizations in medical school and commonly used by students writing history and physicals done on new patients sent to the hospital by the LMDs. It kind of gave the impression that the LMDs weren't quite up to diagnosing anything beyond the usual simple things that show up in his office. Dr. Gessler and I knew better.

Several months passed and I had not seen any of the family again, and they had moved to Winter Haven to live. Sometime after that I was told that Mr. (Postman) went back to Duke when a larger lump developed in the gum. They biopsied it again, found cancer, and he wound up with half of the jaw gone, and a radical neck operation was done. I lost track of my patient. One morning I was in the X-ray department to sit with the radiologist while he dictated my office films for my office charts. As I entered the office there was somebody's chest X-ray on the view box with an obvious orange sized tumor in the left chest. Looking on the name on the film, this was my patient, he had come home from the Veterans Hospital in Saint Petersburg, Florida, developed a cough, came in the Emergency Room and had this X-ray done. This was a large metastatic lesion from his gum cancer. He later went back to the Veteran's Hospital and later came home for Xmas and developed a severe cough, began to cough up blood, and his wife hurried and began the drive back to that hospital but he bled enough that he never made it back there and he bled to death on the way. This was a sad story of my good patient friend. He never told us that he wanted to go to Duke. Maybe with some records and tissue in a formal referral, they may have agreed with these LMDs' diagnosis.

The citrus companies had employees, mostly women that section-ized the grapefruit and oranges for canning. One AM very early there was a car with 5 ladies in it driving to work to sectionize fruit. They had to go over the railroad tracks in the center of town and the car was hit by the train going through town. The car was demolished and all five of the ladies were killed. Three of the ladies were my patients. It had been the custom, since there were no ambulance service avail-able, the funeral homes had ambulances, and were called for automo-bile and any other type of accident. Somebody had to pronounce them dead, so Mr. Kersey called me to come down and do that.

I had never experienced the terrible results of such a horrible inci-dent. I had a hard time identifying my patients because of the man-gled bodies. They were pretty dead, so I had no problem pronouncing them all dead. I felt so terribly sorry for their husbands and children. I don't think I'll ever forget that. I had a terrible time coping with my emotional reaction that night with the most mangled humans I ever saw, and some of these ladies were my patients.

Grove workers trimmed trees, weeded or hoed weeds in the groves, or sprayed chemicals on fruit and trees. Work was seasonal, summer was hot, nobody had air conditioners, and Polk County was "dry"-no alcohol. To get alcohol we had to drive to Hillsboro County, west of Lakeland, to an alcohol outlet just on the on the other side of the county line, about 30 miles, nearly to Plant City. We still had alcohol-ics, and plenty of social drinkers who would get a list of what their friends wanted, make a run to the county line and bring it back. With no alcohol to be obtained locally, when one would go out to a restau-rant to have dinner, and if one wanted a highball, one would order a mixer at dinner, bring one's own bottle, mix it at the table and imbibe with no problem, unless one would get unusually rowdy. Most every-body that went out to dinner drank before or with their meal. Occa-sionally, the driver would drink a little too much, and get stopped by the police on the way home. They police knew everybody in town, and more often than not, would give a warning, no ticket, but tell the driver, "I'll follow you home to make sure you can make it safely."

Pete Franks was one of our social friends that I had suspected was an alcoholic. He was about 30 years old and loved drinking. When he attended parties with us, he was a happy go-lucky very friendly sort that everybody liked, but he would invariably wind up drunk at every party. He began to come to my office frequently to try to get some-thing to help him stop drinking. After months of failure with my ther-apy, once he came in complaining of seeing things, snakes, bad frightening things, and wanted something. I talked him into being admitted to the hospital for treatment. In those days there were no places for these people to go except jail, or heavily sedated in the hospital to try to control the withdrawal. He agreed to being admitted, and he was. I called some orders in. After office hours, I went to the hospital for rounds. When I got up to the floor, the nurse stopped me and said, "Dr. Tanner, Pete died a few minutes ago." I couldn't believe it. The story was, he was admitted, and shortly thereafter became extremely loud, profane, still seeing things and making such a ruckus, they put him in bed and tied him in, controlling his feet, and arms and lying flat on his back. He, after a short while, vomited, and aspirated his vomit. The nurses called, and Dr. Gessler was in the hospital and responded, but before anything like "Crash Carts" or emergency ways of handling these things were available they just did the best they could do, but it was too late. We all felt terrible, and I made up my mind I would never try to handle this kind of problem again.

Appointments didn't work in my office. We tried a while but soon learned the patient with an appointment became upset if somebody walked in with a cut or some other more acute emergency. There seemed there were always unpredictable injuries, or happenings that required being seen out of sequence, so we went back to just signing in order of arrival, still didn't always work but seemed better overall. I never was able to make everybody happy, but rarely did a patient quit coming to me because of that problem.

Our office was open to any patient I saw whoever came in, or called, and wanted to be seen. A rare patient had insurance, they were seen in the order they came in. Segregation was still the usual way things were done at that time. The waiting room was usually full; the black waiting room was too. We had a black waiting room, seating 5 people at one end of the long hall running through the building, entering from an outside door, and one black adjoining examining room with an adjacent black restroom. When a patient came in there was a bell they rang, the nurse went back to get their name, and they were added to the list and seen in order. There was just one list for all my patients.

We developed a very busy practice, both black and white. Many times patients had no money, so we put it on their bill. Many of them came in weekly and paid on their bill, 25 cents, 50 cents, 1 or 2 dollars, whatever. Most patients felt a responsibility to their doctor. Many families had several children and something was always happening that they had to come in. Their bills would slowly climb. If that family was making a conscious effort to slowly and consistently try to pay their bill, at Christmas we would pick out those families and send a Christmas card stating "As of January 1, your bill is considered paid. Thank you."

I remember one man would come in every Saturday, ask for a penicillin shot because he knew he was going out that night and drink, and look for a woman who might have "a disease he didn't want again." He would save up and have the 50 cents for the shot, and we didn't charge the office call fee. Now today, if I would do that, and he developed a penicillin reaction, and died, I'd be sued, or lose my license.

When I came to Auburndale, there were 2 Pharmacies. An older, very nice gentleman, Jim Anderson owned Jim's Pharmacy, Mel Taylor owned the Rexall Pharmacy, and a little later Cecil Christian who worked with Jim Anderson, bought that Pharmacy and named it Christian's Pharmacy. Mel Taylor's store was the only one with a soda fountain. They cooked the best hamburgers in town. There were no hamburger national chains yet. Taylor's was the place everybody hung out for lunch, and after school. All the pharmacies served me as a physician, well, with any information of drugs I needed to know.

When we started our practice we were advised to have Malpractice Insurance. We did and ordered it from one of the few writers of that kind of insurance, named Medical Protective, I think. It cost us $75 APIECE, annually.

To continue that subject at this point, I'll change to the insurance item for a short diversion. As time went on, the malpractice insurance bill gradually increased. By 1975, the year I was President of Polk County Medical Association, the previous year, my malpractice premium was $750. My agent was a good friend Earnest Gutteridge, and he sent me the year's new premium. When I opened it, the fee was $12,500 for the year. I knew this had to be a joke, so I called him. He said he was expecting a call from me, but that was the proper charge. I couldn't believe it.

He informed me that my charge was the same as a surgeon, because I had been taking out tonsils and adenoids and that is major surgery, and also, I was first assistant to surgeons during their major surgery procedure, and I would be held responsible, if for any reason the surgeon couldn't continue in a procedure, then I am responsible to continue and finish that major surgical procedure. Therefore, this changed the way I was going to continue my practice. I was not doing enough of these procedures that charges could pay for the insurance fee, much less profit my practice. My fees for tonsils and adenoids removal was $75, and surgical assisting fee was $50. So, no more hospital surgery, I became mostly an office and hospital general practice doctor.

I made up my mind to try and educate myself more in internal medicine, dermatology, office surgery, and diagnosis. I really enjoyed assisting in major surgery, and I missed doing it. The malpractice problem had just been slowly increasing, since the automobile no-fault insurance came into being. Some attorneys had been using automobile accidents to get insurance cases with back injuries, and whiplash injuries. The no-fault law stopped that. Doctors were beginning to get threatening letters from attorneys, wanting records of a patient who had surgery, or compensation job injuries, etc. It was scary for doctors, to get their name in the paper associated with being sued for malpractice. Doctors wanted their insurance to settle every claim, regardless of their innocence, and did not want to go to court, or have their name in the newspaper. It was bad for their reputation. Insurance companies found it was cheaper to write a check to settle the cases, rather than go to court and fight them. Slowly, the premiums were getting outlandish, and this increased the cost for office visits in every specialty, especially obstetrics, and neurosurgery, and other surgery. Some of the specialists moved to other states with lower malpractice fees. I was continuing to use the hospital for my patient admissions. The insurance bill for a general practitioner was $1200.00 for that year, 1975. It is way up now, but I don't know what the cost of their coverage is now.

Many of my patients were indigent and had to be admitted to the Polk General Hospital in Bartow, county seat for Polk County. This was Polk's indigent hospital and they received excellent care. In my early years I volunteered my Wednesday afternoons off to go help the physicians at the County Hospital care for some of their patients. Having that facility was a big help for the general care for many of our Polk county indigents. It was funded by county taxes, and maybe state help, also. It has been closed now since 1995 due to increasing expense. This resulted in a marked increase in other hospital emergency room visits, which continues to be a mounting, increasing, patient numbers in hospitals emergency rooms.

As a Winter Haven hospital staff physician, we had to take a 24 hour shift covering the emergency room, from 7 AM until & 7AM the next day. My home was 8 miles to the emergency room. Many nights I would be over there for hours, and occasionally thought of just sleeping on a gurney. I never did, but I spent a lot of the nights going back and forth to the emergency room. There was no emergency room physician other than staff physicians taking their turns on call.

This is where I continued to learn that I was wrong when I mentioned that I thought we, as medical students, were taught everything that had ever happened in the history of medicine. I found out people came to the emergency room with things I had to look up and read how to treat it. That's why they have a variety of books in the emergency room to help us. That also is why they call it "Practicing Medicine." You can't learn it all, and you're continually practicing the art, reading, trying to learn new stuff, asking a colleague and trying to remember what you read about less common things that come up once or twice a year. I doubt if any doctor gets it all correct. If he sees enough of one thing, he gets good at that one thing, not at everything. I have told others, I think one thing that makes a good doctor, is one that knows what he doesn't know, and knows when to get the patient to a more knowledgeable physician to care for that patient. Dr. Harry Walker, one of our professors at Medical College Of Virginia of Physical Diagnosis, told the class one day "All you need to be a good doctor, is be bald headed for that look of distinction, and have a good case of hemorrhoids for that look of concern."

I learned what "creeping eruption" was. It is a very small larval stage of the dog and cat hook worm. The medical name is Larval Migrans. Mostly kids came in with it from running around in the summertime, barefoot after a good rain. On the ground, after the animal has deposited his feces on the ground, a rain spreads it out, and children walk, or sit in the area of former deposits. The eggs in the stool hatch, and the larva is picked up by another animal eating something, or snooping and sniffing in the area. Then there is another infected animal.

If an individual walks barefoot in that area, the larva gets on the skin, and within a few hours, there is the area of penetration into the skin. It begins the intense itching, and the larva travels just beneath the skin and makes a red track of his migration. It never gets deep, only superficial, causing redness and intense itching, and the trail will show where it's been. When I came to town, I had no idea what I was seeing when the kids were brought in for me to freeze the area. I asked the mom "freeze what?" The first one was referred to a doctor friend, who told me what to do and how to freeze it.

You have to get Ethyl Chloride in a spray bottle with a very fine spray, and then find the end of the inflamed tract where the larva would be. But he may be already out of the area, so you must spray an area of about a quarter size circle to kill him. You must spray the area long enough to make the frozen area feel like the thickness of a nickel in the skin. It frosts up and gets white and very firm like a nickel under the skin. If you spray too long, the tissue will die, and a large ulcer will form when the tissue dies. Then you have a mess. It was an over the counter medication when I came to town, and some mothers would go get it from the druggist, and treat their kid. I saw a couple of disasters, from mom's treatment, of trying to freeze the areas and not know how, other than just freeze. Two kids came in with large areas of sloughed away skin over the top of their foot, the size of a silver dollar, exposing the tendons. They had to have tissue transplanted over the exposed tendons, from another part of their body. The law finally made Ethel Chloride a prescription item.

It is very tricky when the kids, especially little girls, come in after sitting playing in the sand. They do not like to have their little perineums frozen to kill the larvae. Most of these were on feet or bottoms, or the forearms.

I had a few truckers that noticed these larval tracts on their hand, or arm, and while in a northern town stop to see a doctor. The doctor didn't know for sure, what they were due to, and usually gave a cream of some kind for treatment. When the trucker returned home and came in, we could treat their Larval Migrans. The southern truckers knew what it was, but the northern truck drivers didn't.

The worst I had with this miserable diagnosis was 2 brothers, about 30+ years old. They were plumbers, and were under a house doing their work, with their shirts off, and the ground was wet. I saw them the next day and they were covered with hundreds of the red, inflamed tracks over their body and the itching was intense. Cats, dogs, possum, or raccoons must have slept under the house. And while there, defecated. I gave the affected patients antihistamines, codeine, or Phenobarbital to try to allow them to sleep. I couldn't freeze the entire body, so we decided to draw a circle, and freeze just those at one time, and to return tomorrow to continue the same ritual. One came back several times; finally we were able to help him get over it. The other went to Lakeland ER. I never knew how he was treated.

Now there is an oral tablet, or liquid form, named Mintizol, given for several days will kill the larva. Almost everybody got nauseated, and many vomited with it. We found out that applying the liquid to the skin over the ends of the tracks, several times a day, kills the larva rather quickly within a couple of days use. No more miserable freezing of the skin or patient nausea from the oral medication is necessary now.

The transmission of human hookworm is the same, except it's the human that deposits the eggs in the feces. And the skin itches, usually the foot, and is called "ground itch" but in a few days, the itching disappears, and the larva travels into the body, winding up in the human intestines the same as in the animal. It is not common now because most kids wear shoes, and outdoor toilets are rare today, and outdoor use is not very common now.

Living here in this citrus growing area, growers have to spray chemicals to kill bugs, increase production and all sorts of stuff. Parathion spray gets on the skin, and is absorbed into the system of the tractor driver of the spray machine; if the wind is blowing it is much worse. They get a severe poisoning, needing admission, and I needed to read chemical and toxicology books to learn how to treat it. Fatal results occur if not treated properly. When the patient arrives sick it was due to exposure during the day, and doesn't know what chemical he was spraying. He just did what the boss told him to do, to "go up and down these rows and spray the trees." All the physicians had to learn these things, and the doctors that had been here a while all had been exposed to many of what was new to me. I often had to call one or another to help me treat some of these weird and new difficulties.

One time in my early 4 or 5 years of practice, one of my male patients in his 50s came in for a routine recheck of blood pressure, which was well controlled on medication. I was examining him and had him on the table and was palpating his abdomen. In the middle of the abdomen I felt a mass which I thought was an enlarged abdominal aorta. An X-ray seemed to show an enlarged aorta in width. We had no surgeons around to fix that kind of thing, but I had read about a new surgeon in Texas, at Baylor, I think, that was doing that kind of surgery. I called Dr. Michael DeBakey and asked him if he would accept a referral for an enlarged aorta. He said he would so I referred my patient. He went, was operated, and returned to Auburndale singing my praises. He lived several more years here then they move back to Michigan, I received a nice letter from Dr. DeBakey outlining what he did and had set up a return appointment in one year or as needed for follow up. Dr. DeBakey was very grateful and thanked me for sending my patient to him.

I must admit the staff physicians were very, very cordial and helpful to me in some of these earlier years. And I was also quick to help any who asked me to help them, after I got to be an old hand at this stuff. This is what is called the "art of medicine'—-learning and teaching other physicians what you've learned, for the good of the patient. Our physicians had a tremendous respect and a cordial feeling for each other. I was extremely proud to be associated with them and considered each of them my good friends.

We had made a lot of friends at the Presbyterian Church, and I had been invited to join the Auburndale Rotary club. The hospital staff members included us in their social activities. We attended many Saturday night at either a local friend's home or a doctor's home for a party, or a dinner.

The football coach at the high school occasionally brought a team member to my office for treatment, and one day asked me to be the "Football Doctor" and take care of the team injuries, also do football physicals at the beginning of each season. The coach was Tom Terry and been quite successful as their coach for a few years. I agreed, I would pack my black bag for the game each Friday night, and go sit on the field for each game at home or away, if I could arrange it. We had no football stadium at the high school. The home games were played on a baseball stadium, named Connie Mack Field. The seats were along $1^{st}$ base line and $3^{rd}$ base line. The football field was laid out and the lines were from home plate to the grassy outfield. The infield had very little grass, mostly sand and clay ground, and hard. The weather was always very hot from August until mid October or early November. Playing football was very hot and very hard on this field. A few years later they built a gym and stadium at the high school. Jack Turner, a local Architect drew the plans and supervised the construction. I was on that committee for the stadium.

In 1956, I noticed the players were not allowed to have any appreciable amounts of water during the game, and only a small amount at halftime During the game at a time out, a water boy would run on the field with a dripping wet towel to wash their faces, and some of the kids would suck some water out of the towel. I also noted how terribly fatigued, and dehydrated they were after the game. I discussed this with the coach, and he told me the same stuff my high school coach told us. No water, because if you get hit in the stomach after you drink you may rupture your stomach. I argued with him and told him how important it was to stay reasonably hydrated, else some day, somebody is going to die of severe dehydration.

I asked if I could try a little experiment to prove to him the importance of allowing fluids during the game. He agreed. So I took my lab

technician, Bill Masters and a bunch of test tubes with labels for identification, and needles and syringes to the next game. I divided the
team players, allowed half of them to have all the prepared fluid they
wanted at any time during the game, as long as no one drank more
than 8 ounce cup at a time, with at least 15 minutes between drinks.
The other half of the team had to continue the way they had been
coached before I came here, no fluids during the game, a limit of 1
cup at the half.

I told the kids what they had to do, (1) allow us to weigh and
record each player before the game and immediately after the game,
naked, (2) allow us to take blood from their arm before the game, at
the half, and at the end of the game, (3) know which group they were
in, take fluids, or restrict fluids. They all understood and agreed to our
little experiment. I knew they needed salt, potassium, sugar and fluids. I also knew orange juice has sugar, and a good amount of potassium, and water. So I also knew that it is a little difficult to drink a lot
of orange juice at one time, unless we could dilute it almost half with
water. Then we had to add salt. I elected to add about a level teaspoon
of salt per liter. It was a little saltier to most people but they did it fine.
I never thought for a minute I needed to get parents permission,
signed for me to do that to their kids. Today no doctor would dare do
what I did without papers signed. The parents trusted me not to harm
their kids.

I had made arrangements with the lab technicians at the hospital to
meet us after the game and do the lab work that I wanted. I wanted a
hemoglobin, hematocrit, blood urea nitrogen, sodium, potassium, and
chloride. One of the technicians is still living and has recently retired.
He is Tommy Dryden, a good friend. Later he served as the director
of lab services at the hospital. They stayed up that night until about 2
AM completing all those nearly 35 persons lab work. I really appreciate those friends. The results of the two groups were different enough
to convince Coach Terry that I was right, and he then allowed the fluids to be in use in every game from then on.

The weights were really impressive. Water weighs a little less than
8 pounds per gallon, so the amount of fluids these boys sweated out,
in the group without fluids was impressive. I remember one very large
boy, off of fluids, weighed 16 pounds less than he started. The fatigue
was so much less in the high fluid intake group, and it was really
noticeable to compare how each group felt after the game. I congratu-
lated the team for their cooperation, and allowing us to take blood,

and deprive some of them of fluids. They were very supportive of what we did, and what was accomplished.

After I got these reports and because I wanted to share this with other schools, I knew the football doctors at each school. I called Dr. George Dorman, Winter Haven team doctor, then I called Dr. David Green, football doctor of Haines City high school and told them what I'd done and advised them to do the same, if they didn't want a death due to acute dehydration. They both thanked me, and agreed that that should be done and that it makes a lot of sense. So we had them all covered, and each team began using fluids. The teams of each school were playing with more energy longer through the games. Our team had many good successful seasons.

Some of these teams had players that were recruited and attended the University of Florida on football scholarships over the next several years. I've often wondered if there was some conversation or information passed to the coaches, or trainers, or somebody at the university that triggered some interest to get Dr. Cade's interest to create what was called Gatorade, which was developed in 1965, some 8-9years after we started our local schools drinking fluids on the football teams. I did my "research" and we used our drink every year since we started in 1956. The orange juice we used was donated to the football team from Adams Packing Company and /or Minute Maid Corporation, both in Auburndale, Florida every Friday night for years.

Here I sat in the middle of the juice world, making our concoction for the teams to keep them healthy and play football better, and never once thought of getting one of the plants to make us a drink we could market. I wonder where I would have been, if I had done that. If I had, I would have probably retired a rich man. But I would have missed being a dedicated, hard working physician fascinated by the practice of medicine, and loving all my contacts with groups of families, and people in this warm, wonderful small town and community.

Of recent interest, regarding the use of my orange juice concoction, beginning in 1957, and during all football games during my 44 years as football doctor for the Auburndale Bloodhounds football, was a new gentleman I met. I was speaking to a man in Cardiologist Dr. Richard Guiste's waiting room recently, 2008. Mr. Price and I were talking and a friend of his came up and sat down. I was reciting my "research" of fluids for our football team. The new gentleman, Mr. Vic Story, said he was on that football team at the University of Florida, during the mid 1960's, when they began the testing of fluids during the developing of Gatorade. He said each player was given pint bottles of either water, or a mixture of electrolytes, and sugar, and he didn't know what else. Nobody had any idea why all this new use of fluids was being done, but they were really happy to be able to drink fluids, when it was so hot and exhausting, and fluids had been so limited prior to this. This was their research developing Gatorade, he later learned. I was excited to meet someone that was active in the era of the Gatorade development. He was impressed that I had used my fluids almost 8 years earlier. He had played football in High School in Lake Wales, 20 or so miles south of us. I never thought to call Dr. Barranco, team physician at Lake Wales, Florida. They were also among our opponents. Dr. Barranco was the father of Dr. Sam Barranco, Winter Haven Otolaryngologist a good friend of mine, who died suddenly and unexpectedly in recent years.

I appreciated the community's acceptance of me and my family, and their confidence in my ability to treat, and council them in their hours of need. In those days there were no ambulances at the game, and no requirement that a doctor be present at the game. I enjoyed the game of football, and wanted our team to do well, so I began coming and staying on the field during every game. If the opposing team didn't have a doctor, I ran out on the field, like I did for our injured player, to assist, and assess the best I could, what was wrong. Their coach always told me they really appreciated my help.

No parent ever mentioned not wanting me to stick needles in their kid's arms, for blood before the game, at halftime, and at the end of the game. Or set their kids broken, displaced bone in an arm, on the football field, right after he got it broken. Doesn't hurt so badly if you set'em right after the injury, but it sure does tomorrow, if you wait. Or stick a little Novocain in a tendon strain on the foot, when he can't run as the star halfback when it wears off, again. I always had alcohol with me, to clean the skin well before any injection. Fortunately, I never got any infection or complication from my "on the field treatments." Or sew up a bleeding laceration, quickly, so he can get back on the field. Or take the kid with a dislocated right elbow to my office downtown, for x-rays, with his mother, at halftime. X-rays negative for fracture, but verified the dislocation, Mom holds upper arm real tight, I take off my shoe and put the foot above the elbow with force, and carefully and forcibly pull the forearm down and relocate the ulna anteriorly, around the distal humerus, re-x-ray to see if I fractured it, reducing the dislocation. X-rays negative, then take'em both back to the field to see the rest of the game, with an immobilized arm and he will not play ball for weeks. I'll say when.

Early in foot ball season I would go down to the gym, gather all the players and give a lecture to them about how to take care of and manage all the little injuries and problems that occur. Abrasions, cuts, bruises, and things happened, but the kids didn't pay attention or bother to treat them. We were trying to educate them what to do as soon as the injury occurred, or as soon as they could after the injury. They were to scrub the areas hard and completely as soon as possible with soap and water, cover with band-aids, or dressings. It hurts some, but not as bad as a day later. We learned this would keep a lot of little things from becoming big things, keeping them out of the games with bad infections, fever, or increased pain. They seemed to learn and remember that, and it cut down the numbers of skin infections from the inevitable abrasions. Most occurred from playing on that hard football field that they played on before a new one was built at the high school.

We tried another little experiment again, trying to increase their stamina and strength. After a football game, they were tired and spent. We requested they not eat or drink anything with carbohydrates or sugar, after the Friday night football game, until the following Tuesday afternoon. Protein and fats were OK until late Tuesday afternoon. Then Wednesday, Thursday, and Friday they could really put away a high intake of carbohydrates and sugar. This is supposed to deplete the carbohydrate stores in your body (glycogen), especially muscles, by not eating them, and by really exercising, which further depletes the stores of glycogen from the muscles. Then load up on high intake of carbohydrates and sugar until the game Friday night. This allows increased storage of glycogen in the muscles for more energy exertion for the intense activity of football. This really works, but not many kids liked doing that. They got very tired and hungry and cheated, in the early time of sacrificing the foods they liked to eat. But the few that did stated they had a great increase of energy that lasted the entire game.

Another thing I tried, to get them to understand how to increase their stamina, I got about 6 guys, timed their ability to stand upright, and hold the left arm horizontal with a 5 pound dumbbell weight in the hand with the palm down. We timed them until the deltoid muscle began to fatigue and drop. Then when they were given 2-3 days of high sugar and carbohydrate, then repeat the same weight timing to compare with their original time. All were able to increase the time significantly, usually more than twice the time. I thought this was significant, but we had poor luck in getting them to carry this out for football. This again showed them they could increase their energy for the game by rearranging their intake of specific foods during the week before.

A few years after our fluid use began Coach Tom Terry moved to Melbourne, Florida, I think, to coach football. Some years later out of the blue, after Gatorade came out, he wrote me a long, nice, letter praising me for starting the local team on fluids, and recognizing I might have been the stimulus for the development of Gatorade. I really appreciated that letter, but I'll never know if that was true.

For years I was doing all of the Auburndale football player's pre-practice physical exams for free at the beginning of each school year. As time passed, we found some players from other high schools around, came for physicals. We had to stop that by asking where they went to school. Also, the junior varsity, and track teams expected the physicals, then the junior high football players, then the female basketball, male basketball players, track, then Little League, then Cheer Leaders High School, and Junior High cheer leaders. This took up a lot of time, and added a lot of potential legal risk for me, because many of these students were not my patients, so I had no past history or knowledge about those students. Soon there began to be newspaper articles about a student that had been examined to play football and passed the physical exam, had a heart attack, and the examining doctor was sued for missing a heart problem.

It got so worrisome, that I decided to limit my free physicals to Auburndale High football players. I got so much static; I decided that each player needs to see his own Physician for his own exam and I would charge a small fee, for my patients only. Sometimes when we had 10-15 players in the waiting room for the physicals while I was doing the exams on a couple in the exam rooms, a little horseplay happened. When I was through, and I went to the waiting room to lock the door for the day, I would find all of the waiting room pictures off the walls, and propped against the wall. We just had to re-hang them.

For the physicals, we needed a urine specimen on each player, and the nurse would hand them the urine cup and point them to the restroom and say, "Go to the restroom and get us a specimen and put it on this table, then go into this exam room and wait." One young man took forever to come out of the restroom, and when he did, he had gotten a stool specimen, not knowing to get a urine specimen, into that little cup. I still don't know how he managed that. He was quite embarrassed. The nurse figured out we must always specify what specimen we must ask for.

As I said before, when I joined the Winter Haven Hospital staff each physician was obligated to take call as the Emergency Room Physician for a 24 hour shift, from 7 AM until & 7 AM the next day, on a rotating basis. There were about 15 doctors on the staff, so that meant for me, about every 15 days. I lived about 13 miles from the hospital. Many times I would have to make 4-5 trips to the hospital when patients came in. We didn't have too many severely injured patients, usually minor injuries, like lacerations, sprained or fractured ankles, arms, colds, coughs, earaches, nosebleeds, and rarely had to admit patients to their doctors, or to me.

We had to manage whatever came in. I remember one patient had an auto accident and suffered a lacerated eyeball from a shattered windshield. I carefully removed a sliver of glass, and to stop the further loss of vitreous and using a very small needle and very fine silk material, carefully closed the eyeball. I started him on Penicillin and made arrangements to send him to a Lakeland Ophthalmologist in follow up. I later received a letter from the eye doctor saying I did a good job and probably saved the eye, but vision would probably be impaired. I never knew what happened to that patient, but hoped he wound up OK.

As a member of the staff we had to try to get a signed authorization for an autopsy on each death in the hospital, by an authorized next of kin. I think it was a requirement for a certain percentage of autopsies to maintain hospital certification. It was a difficult situation to approach a family member, especially if the death was not anticipated. We had to approach the subject slowly, and let them know we all learn from each autopsy. We sometimes learn some things unexpected for the benefit of the family and the doctor.

Occasionally, family members become upset that I wanted to do such a thing to their mother or father, or baby. Most people were tolerable and receptive to the discussion, but not always willing to allow it.

We had monthly CPC's, Clinical Pathological Conferences, for the physicians. A doctor would present the history, physical and pathological symptoms, discuss his case and winding up with his diagnosis. Then the Pathologist would give his findings at autopsy, and his final diagnosis. We all learned from the conferences.

One of my patients was in the hospital, quite ill for a long time. Our consultants agreed with me that she probably had a malignancy but didn't know where. She continued to deteriorate and finally died. I got an authorization for an autopsy. I received a call stating that our Pathologist, Dr. Cox was out of town and we would have to wait for about week for his return. The family didn't want to wait to have the funeral, so I decided to perform the autopsy myself.

Dr. Cox's laboratory assistant set the morgue up for me, and all the knives, saws, and specimen bottles for tissue were ready. I did not do the head, only the thorax and the abdomen. I did a good job entering the body, removing tissue specimens for later microscopic examination, identifying what turned out to be a small lung cancer that had spread to her many organs, and hadn't been picked up on chest x-ray. After I finished I carefully sutured her thorax and abdomen.

On his return, Dr. Cox called me and told me I had done a good job for him and that I was one of the rare doctors that would do an autopsy on his own patient. I needed that patient's diagnosis for my own satisfaction. I would have always wondered what was wrong with her. Her family was also satisfied to know what she had wrong.

As time went on it dawned on me there were no more demands for autopsy authorizations. I cannot remember when it all changed, but later in my practice years, I had an elderly patient that died unexpectedly following a sudden massive gastrointestinal bleed. I had obtained several consultants. The family was very upset and worried about whether something wasn't done that could have been done, and demanded an autopsy.

The family was informed by the hospital that the cost would be $2500 for the hospital pathologist to do it. They didn't have the money, so somebody suggested to them to have the county Coroner do it. They were informed that a free autopsy is done by the Coroner only if a felony was proved to have occurred, otherwise there would be a significant charge and the family would have to pay to have it done. I never heard the charge fee, and that was the last I ever heard of it. I don't know what the status of autopsies is now.

In the emergency room, once a man came in very agitated, couldn't be still, walking, unable to sit, he was almost crying. He had been sleeping and was suddenly awakened with something in his ear canal. Looking in the ear, I saw the rear end of a roach trying to go deeper. He couldn't turn around and get out. His clawing was driving my patient crazy. I enticed him to lie down so I could flood his ear canal with alcohol, which I did and soon the roach was not moving anymore. Now to remove it was going to be difficult. With the patient's cooperation, being very still and able to stand a hemostat in the ear to grasp it and not rip the roach apart, I was able to slowly pull it out intact. Even pulling the roach out, I drug its body along the wall of the very tender ear canal. This was one grateful patient.

Another thing I learned to do is to be aware of the person I'm talking to, by observing them for the possible visible so called minor abnormalities that most people and many physicians ignore. Things like thyroid nodules for instance, also suspicious skin lesions. I just suggest they get these things looked at.

I noticed an apparent nodule in the thyroid of a pharmaceutical detail man in my office while he was standing before my desk while I was sitting listening to him tell me about a new drug. When he finished, I asked if I could feel his thyroid gland. He consented. I palpated a rather small nodule, rather firm, that was noticeable to me when his head was turned a certain way, and it was rather apparent. I advised him to please have it checked when he got home in Tampa. Several weeks later he was again in my office and shared with me the fact that the nodule was indeed malignant, and was removed. He was very grateful and I was happy that he got taken care of. I was frequently palpating thyroids that I was suspicious of, both in my patients and other people, by simple observation. There were many cysts, a few nodules, mostly benign adenomas, only rarely malignant.

On one occasion I was aware of a possible nodule on one of the female television reporters on a Tampa television station. I called the station, asked to speak to her, we talked. I advised her to get her doctor to check her thyroid gland for a nodule. I heard nothing from her, and a few months I called again. She told me her doctor checked with an ultrasound, and found a cyst. She forgot to call me back. She did thank me. I'm glad she didn't have a cancerous nodule in the thyroid gland.

Soon after I came to town, there had been a group of doctors that were auto racing fans that had been for several years going to Daytona Speedway for some of their big races. I was invited to pay my share of a large greyhound-type bus they rented for 30 to 40 men, mostly doctors and their friends, and food and drinks. We got on the bus, rode to Daytona from Winter Haven, had our seat tickets, and reserved areas high-up in the stands just before the finish line. The seats were marked off as maybe big enough for a thin 100 pound female butt to fit on. With men sitting next to each other, with their butts and wide shoulders, you had to shift and twist all the time to be able to see the huge oval racetrack. The sun was hot and sweating was miserable. I kept wondering who the hell enjoys this stuff. I never had seen a race, and never care to repeat it anytime in this lifetime. The cars zoom around this big oval track, going like a rocket in front of you, and then looks like an ant as far as you can see it until it zooms by you again. I had no idea who was racing and who even cared. All around us, late comers would come to their seat and ask "Anybody crashed yet?" Somebody would answer, "Nah." So that's what they are there for—to see somebody wreck. Not much fun to me. I thanked them profusely for inviting me. I always had a good excuse in the future.

Another trip I was invited on was for a football weekend. There was a large group of Winter Haven and Auburndale businessmen, and others from central Florida, would rent a train to go to some big college game. It was planned well in the future, select the game and figure the cost and get informed and go. I was asked to go by Tom Keator, a good friend. Many patients and other friends went. We all paid our share, for the Pullman train, with diner car and a club car. We went to New Orleans to some game, and I've even forgotten what teams were playing. We all had our seats, and beds, and ate in the diner, drank in the club car and walked up and down through the moving train to find where our friends were, and met new friends.

I remember a good friend, Andy Ireland, before he ran and won a U.S Senate seat was on the train and we kind of stayed with each other, being as we weren't drinking or gambling like so many of the other people were doing. There was some significant boozing on the train, many of whom were unable to get off the train to attend the game. And many were unable to walk the streets of New Orleans, especially Bourbon Street, because of the massive crowds, and their inability to negotiate the other drunks. There were already enough drunks walking and staggering up and down Bourbon Street.

Andy and I sat in one of the bars at a table, and just talked over a beer, listening to, and enjoying the jazz and, neither of us was interested in keeping up with the majority. One time of that jaunt was enough for me. I had heard of a later trip or two, but lost interest and haven't heard of any train trips in years.

I would much more enjoy a weekend fishing trip to Homosassa River, at Homosassa, Florida, get a boat out of Duncan McRae's fishing camp and go fishing or just ride up and down that beautiful clear water river. I wonder if McRae's is even still there. It was a quaint, congenial fishing dock with good folks and good friends running it.

I became good friends with Dr. Arnie Spanjers, radiologist, among other hunters, like radiologist Ed Burns from Lake Wales, and surgeon Frank Zeller. They invited me to go with them duck hunting. I had never been and didn't have a shotgun. They told me to buy a 12 gauge shot gun for the best hunting. So I went to Sears and bought a 12 gauge automatic Browning shotgun. It was a beautiful gun, so I was ready to go on my first duck hunting trip.

Every year for duck season they would rent cabins on Lake Kissimmee east of Lake Wales, at the Oasis. That was a small café that had boat rentals, and cabins available for hunting season or fishing jaunts. It was situated at the southernmost end of the huge lake beginning the Kissimmee River that flowed all the way south to the large Lake Okeechobee. The Oasis was on route U.S 60 going east from Lake Wales to Yeehaw Junction, and on to the east Florida coast. The reservations were made for the first day of duck season, in November I think, and we would bring steaks, dry onion soup mix, new potatoes, bread, butter, and grilling stuff and things, like a big skillet to cook the chopped up new potatoes mixed with the dry onion soup mix, in butter, in the skillet. And Boy! That was good stuff!

Something to eat, and things to drink and big grilling the night before, get to sleep as best we could, then arise way before morning to dress in our waders and heavy clothes because it was usually really cold and black dark. If we had time we ate breakfast at the restaurant before we got in the boats to journey the few miles up into the lake using flash lights to pick our way to where they would put us out in the lake, one at a time and move on for the next guy to get out and stand in the water. It was cold, windy, moonless, and maybe cloudy to await the flight of multitudes of duck coveys to fly in over you to be shot.

We stood in water almost up to our nipples, and the waders covered to just above our nipples, with shoulder straps like overalls. I found if I moved too fast water would slosh too high and get me wet. I tried my best to move slowly and deliberately. I found it was to my advantage to try to stay dry and move very slowly. When the wind came up, I needed to walk a little closer to the shore, however you couldn't see the holes you just stepped in, that sometimes was a little too deep. Also, carrying around a heavy shotgun shoulder high, made me quickly aware of the water depth. It was really hard to keep the gun out of the lake, therefore; I found shallower water was a plus.

Now, the dawn is showing, and I'm keeping my eyes peeled for all the ducks. Suddenly, off to my right I can see through the breaking day about 6 or 8 ducks feeding diving, back up, diving, back up. So I carefully raised my gun, took a bead on one, fired my gun, and quickly fired again, and again. They all flew off except the three I luckily was able to bag. I eased over and brought my game together. I really felt proud to have been the first of the group to be successful. I also felt the blast on my shoulder when I fired that 12 gauge without firmly holding it against my shoulder. It hurt! I had to learn to prepare for a big hard shotgun kick, unexpected unless you remember what kind of gun you're firing. A little blueness developed on my shoulder a few days later. And the sore shoulder stayed a while.

I had heard no other shots. A little while later, not far away behind me, was another group that I was lucky to bag three more out of. My chest just grew a little more. After a while, I heard the motor start up, and soon Arnie came up and said, "We probably need to get back, I heard you shooting. Did you get any? I said "Yes, six." He said "SIX? Where are they?" I pointed back over my shoulder where I had put them, floating dead in nearby weeds. He stood up in the boat- looked and started laughing and said "COOTS"! He said, "That's not what were after, nobody eats them." I said "What is a coot?" Well, I learned not to shoot them. They're not game fowl and not what we were after. Although Arnie said they had big gizzards and they're good and he likes them, so he took the gizzards home and I guess he ate them. I was the only one on that trip to successfully down ducks. Although I learned you are not supposed to shoot any thing sitting, it ain't sportin.' They're supposed to be flying.

A couple of weeks later we planned another duck hunting trip at Lake Kissimmee. I thought it would be good to call my brother Terry, in St. Petersburg, Florida, and invite him to come over and go duck hunting with us. He said he'd never been duck hunting and had no gun. I told him that's OK, just come on over and go with us and see how much fun it is. I felt like he would find it as much fun as I did and then he could buy himself a gun and go with us sometime. He finally decided to come over the night before and stay with us in the cabins, with our group, and have a steak cookout the night before and ride along up into the lake early the next morning with us hunters.

The next morning it was really cold, wind blowing, cloudy and the lake was rough. I woke Terry, helped him put on his layers of clothes, and get into his waders. After breakfast we waddled over to the boats, struggled to get in and ride, huddled over in the cold, cold wind and black night, with only the flashlight leading our boats, in line up into the lake. One by one we all got out, and Terry got out with me, and the boat went on to drop the other hunters off into the water to stand, wait and peer for ducks, as daylight slowly met us. In the dark Terry commented how cold and windy it was. I had also noticed that, and of course, agreed with him. He asked why we did this kind of stupid thing. I said that it's fun to shoot ducks. He commented how dark it was, and asked how you can see the ducks. I told him we had to wait until morning when the sun comes up and all the ducks come flying into where we are. He wondered why we didn't wait 'til morning to come out here. Finally, I just quit talking and told him we had to be quiet, or the ducks will hear us and won't come where we are.

Finally, after several hours of freezing and no ducks coming our way we all got back in the boat and went back to the Oasis. On the way back, Terry kept commenting about what a bunch of stupid grown-up men to get all dressed up in uncomfortable loads of clothes, topped by a pair of rubber overalls in freezing windy weather, black night, and stand for hours in waist higher deep water, unable to see in the dark, waiting for dawn for some stupid duck to come flying in to be shot at. He said this was the stupidest thing he ever heard about. I told him there was one thing stupider, a duck hunter Watcher! Terry thanked me for the experience, but decided he didn't need to buy a shotgun.

I was so excited about learning to duck hunt, I wanted my wife to be part of the fun. She had never been duck hunting, and she needed to learn and enjoy this sport. She happened to be pregnant and she still had terrible nausea. She agreed to go with me to the Oasis, just the two of us. We stayed in one of the cabins and got up in the dark cold windy weather, got in the boat and with flash lights, found our way up into Lake Kissimmee. We got to a location that, with my experience, I selected as a choice place for ducks to fly over. This is where we should get in the water, stand and wait, and we did. As dawn came we were both standing side by side, waiting with our shotguns. We had finished breakfast at the café and we are now ready. Elizabeth suddenly got nauseated and vomited in the lake. Where else? Since we were standing in it. After a lengthy while, with some repeated vomiting, I see four big ducks flying directly toward us. I was giving instructions about when to aim and fire. They were beautiful real ducks. I said get ready—FIRE. We both blasted away. I kept waiting for one to fall. None fell, BUT, she did vomit again. She continued to be very nauseated, so we decided to give up this safari and take her home to go to bed and try to get by this pregnancy. We did, and she did deliver a beautiful boy, Paul Alexander Tanner 3rd, several months later, March 30, 1956, the same one who surprised us with his appearance, I already told you about.

I was included in their duck hunting trips for many years, and enjoyed them all and learned what to shoot, and was fairly successful occasionally in feeding my family duck once in a while, the same about dove when we occasionally went for them.

Once with Arnie dove hunting, we were walking through a field, came to a fence and we were together. I placed my gun, stock down with the barrel propped against the wire fence. Arnie was somewhere to my right. As I climbed over the wire fence, the gun fell to the ground and fired when it struck the ground. Arnie said "OUCH" and put his hand to his head over his right ear. A #8 bird shot hit him just behind his right temple and was palpable under the skin where the very small skin-hole was. I was petrified; Arnie was calm and reassuring to me. I can't remember if the safety was on or not. But what a stupid thing to do prop the gun up loaded and try to go over the fence it's propped on. This is the closest thing that I ever did that could have been tragic.

Fred Baugh had a shoe repair business in the middle of town. He was an avid deer hunter and with a group of friends had a hunting camp in the Ocala National Forest, near Ocala, Florida. Before deer season, one of his men would go to the camp and take their hunting dogs and get the camp ready for the weekend hunts that they had almost every weekend. Fred asked me to go on one of those weekend hunting trip. I had never been deer hunting, so I was excited to go. I had a Browning 12 gauge shotgun and they told me to get some 00 buckshot for deer, so I bought a box. We left for Ocala really early on a Friday AM, stopped somewhere for breakfast, and got to the camp just after daybreak. Everybody was excited and in a hurry to get to the stand. The forest is cut up in 1 mile squares, as I remember, and each square is surrounded by a dirt road. They take the hunters along one side and put one out about each 100 yards. Then the dog handlers take the dogs to the opposite side and release them to flush the deer toward us hunters. It was quite cold and my usual clothes (a heavy coat and a wool cap and heavy high top shoes) weren't quite enough, but that was my hunting clothes. They took 5 of us in a car down somewhere on a road and put one of us out every 100 or so yards. They said the dogs would be released soon and to listen for them baying, or barking or what ever they do. I was supposed to look in the woods toward the barking and watch for a deer coming toward me, and shoot when you see the deer, careful not to shoot the next hunter down the road. After a while, I was excited when I began to hear barking dogs. I kept an eye in the woods and all I could see was trees and bushes and they weren't very far away. Seemed as though I could only see about 20 or 30 feet into the woods. Barking got closer and closer and I kept looking, suddenly out of the corner of my eye a deer bounded out of the woods 30 or so yards to my right into the road and 2 more bounds he was in the next square of woods, just flying. He looked about as big as a large skinny hunting dog. I didn't even get a good look at him, much less get my gun up and aim. Dogs got closer and finally crossed the road about where the deer did and kept running and yelping on into the next square of woods. Their barking soon faded away and I was all alone in the serene, quiet Ocala woods.

After about 4 hours the car came and picked me up with no news of anybody killing a deer. The guy next to me didn't even see the deer. He just heard the dogs and saw nothing. Back at camp we had bologna sandwiches, made by the dog handler, and cokes and beer. After a while the others got in their cars and had to go find their dogs. We just sat around and heard tales of previous trips and kills, and one of a black bear kill and the taste of the bear meat sandwich.

Later they returned with most of the dogs and said usually it takes a few days to round up all the dogs. Sometimes they never find them all. Sometimes they'll just wander back into camp a few days later. That was the way it was most of the weekends. Nobody killed a deer that trip but it was a trip I'll always remember and don't think I'll be interested in more deer hunting treks. They asked me several other times through the years to go, but I always found some reason I couldn't make that specific weekend.

Our first son, Paul 3rd, was born in 1956. We were looking to have more children, but it wasn't happening. Elizabeth got pregnant again, but soon spontaneously miscarried. So we began checking into adoption. After all the things you have to go through, we were approved for adoption. It was planned for us to go to Jacksonville, where a child was to be born in 2-3 months. Suddenly she announced she was pregnant. Happy, happy time! We canceled the adoption. Happy time, but she again became very nauseated, and could barely get out of bed, and she had a 2 year old to care for. I made arrangements to send them back home to her mother for a period of time so she could get over the terrible nausea. She was gone for 3-4 months, for the second time. After she was better and came home, we had our second son John Matthew Tanner, on Labor Day, Monday Sept.7 1959.

We had gone to Dunnellon to meet a realtor, Joe Cobb, and look at a cabin on Rainbow River, a clear beautiful river, and maybe purchase it. We were there Sunday, with Elizabeth due on Labor Day, the next day. While there Elizabeth walked out on the dock to enjoy the clear river, when all of a sudden the dock gave way and she went right into the water. We borrowed a shirt and shorts for her from the realtor there, and came home. She went in labor the next day, and delivered on time. I don't remember if I ever gave Mr. Joe Cobb his shirt and shorts. We probably did. I do know I thanked him, and we later did buy the property.

In those days at the head of Rainbow River, Rainbow Springs, just outside of Dunnellon, Florida, there was a public area that people could go. For a fee you could swim in a roped off area, or take a ride down the river a way, on a boat that had an area below the waterline, down 4-5 steps, and 8-10 seats on both sides. Each seat had a glass porthole that we could see everything under the beautiful blue absolutely clear water. A driver sat at the rear, on deck, steering the motor boat and reciting in sing-song fashion all the different fish, especially 15 to 20 pound bass that stayed around their specific little areas, and underwater plants, and other sites. No fishing was allowed. In later years the springs became a state park.

In 1959 I had been elected President of the Winter Haven Hospital medical staff. Paul 3rd was three and a half years old, and John was about six weeks old. About the end of October 1959, on a Saturday AM, I was making rounds, trying to finish in time to stop by our church to pick up about two dozen folding chairs, and take them to Lynn Kirkland's house, next to our house with a grove on the lake between us. Lynn, a friend and local attorney, had planned a grilling dinner party for 7 PM with a lot of our friends and their wives, and he needed more chairs. I had also planned to mow our yard in the afternoon.

While I was walking fast in the hospital seeing my patients, I noticed a little aching in the middle of my chest. I thought it was a little esophageal spasm like I had during medical school, a few times. So I drank a lot of water and kept on seeing patients. Then I continued to the church, carried about 4 chairs at a time to the trunk of my car. I then proceeded around Lake Ariana to Lynns's house, and unloaded the chairs, and went home. Half way to Lynn's I wondered if I was having a heart attack, so I stopped the car, got a nitroglycerine sublingual tablet from my medical bag and put it under my tongue, and sat there waiting to see if I got better. It didn't help, so I wanted to

MY WHOLE LIFE 145

believe it wasn't a heart attack, or I would have been better. After I got home I got on the lawn mower and mowed a short while, still hurting, so I stopped, went in, took a shower, dressed, lay on the bed a few minutes and noticed a little improvement. So I thought I'd go on over to Lynn's and help him, and have a drink and I'd be better. I told Elizabeth for her to come on over, after the baby sitter came. She said OK. She didn't know I was hurting.

At Lynn's, who was already drinking and beginning to cook hamburgers, and pork chops, I was greeted, told to get a drink and sit. I made a bourbon and water. After a few sips, I began to note increased pain but now it was radiating down both arms to my elbows. Being the brilliant diagnostician that I was, I said to myself, "You idiot, your having a heart attack, go to the ER and get an EKG and find out." I called Elizabeth and said "I'm having a little chest pain, and I'm going to the ER to get an EKG. You come over here to Lynn's and I'll call you after I get my EKG done." She yelled at me, "NO, NO! Wait!!! I'm coming over now and drive you." I said OK.

She came immediately, drove us to the ER, so slow I thought I wouldn't make it. It's 13 miles to the hospital, and what is now Havendale Boulevard, was then a two lane rather country road. Around 7 PM, on a Saturday night a lot of people leisurely driving, going both ways, negated passing and fast driving. Finally, we got there, Dr. George Graff was on call for his partner Dr, Arthur Mosley, internist. He gave me an injection of Morphine and I loved it because of the relief.

We had no coronary enzymes, or any other diagnostic lab studies, that are available today, except CBC, sedimentation rate, and EKG, and clinical symptoms. CBC was slightly elevated, sedimentation rate slightly elevated, EKG very slight changes compatible with a mild coronary.

I was admitted and placed in an oxygen tent, common at that time. I don't remember having much more pain. They told me I would be in the hospital at least 3 weeks, depending on how I did. And I wouldn't be able to go to my office for 3 months. That was a great deal different than today. This was a terrible blow to me and a very worrisome 3 months. Income stops, except for my disability insurance, $300 a month. I had a wife, 2 kids, and continuing expenses of the practice. It was tough, but Terry, my brother came over one afternoon a week, Dr. Frank Zeller, my surgeon friend I operated with frequently and another surgeon friend, Dr. Bill Read came over other afternoons. They were able to help get my practice through the 3 months. I'll be forever grateful to those good friends. I couldn't understand why me. They just told me to be thankful everything got along well, and I was. This was a scary time for me, just starting a family, and growing my medical practice, and dreaming up all the bad stuff I could think of that could happen. I teared up almost daily while lying in that oxygen tent for three weeks. This was a confusing and sad time for me. The same mental stuff continued while I was sitting at home for the next 3 months, after I was discharged from the hospital. If a Doctor can't work, there seems to be no income for whatever you need money for. It is also very frustrating when you feel fine and the doctors won't let you work.

It wasn't long until Christmas and my mother and father were coming. They came down from their home in Quitman Georgia. While they were here, a few days before Christmas Daddy got sick with abdominal pain. We went to the hospital and Dr. Frank Zeller saw him in the ER, found he had acute appendicitis, and took him to the operating room and took his appendix out.

When Daddy was in the hospital in Winter Haven my 2 brothers, Terry, and Maurice came to visit their daddy. We had company to take care of at home, and Elizabeth did, and did a marvelous hostess job, until all settled down to just normal daily rat race. They took care of me, and so did my friends. A whole lot of them chipped in and the went out to a furniture store, and bought, and brought to me a really nice easy chair and ottoman, which was my place until the doctors let me go back to work.

After the first of the year, my 3 months were up and they allowed me to return to work. My patients seemed happy to see me back, so things went well, but I was still worried and waited for my next heart attack. It was impossible to get the possibility of another one out of my mind, so I felt I was walking on eggshells, and tried to take care of myself. A victim of cardiac heart disease can't buy life or disability insurance for about 10 years, unless you're wealthy.

# 5

# I Fell off the Roof

One of our friend's wives came to my office, and was sitting in the examining room. I was questioning her about her visit. She said she had a back ache. I asked her how long she'd had the pain. She said "Since last Thursday when I fell of the roof." I was stunned and asked "What the hell were you doing on the roof?" She looked at me strangely, and said "Don't you know what that is?" I said "No, what. She said "That's when I started my period." I said "Oh" Then I said "I must have missed that day in medical school. I never heard that before." She laughed then I laughed sheepishly. Somebody should have told me that was what that is, somewhere along the line. I never heard it before and never heard it since until recently when my wife read this, she told me they used to use this in Pennsylvania. But I never told my wife stuff from my office patients, so she never knew of this little morsel and my lack of knowledge of this information, until she read this episode I'm writing. I had two brothers, no females. She had a sister, and she already had heard of that in Pennsylvania. I don't know if Quitman, Georgia females knew of that, if they did nobody told me about it. I don't ever remember that my wife ever told me when she fell off the roof.

In 1960, spring, she didn't fall off the roof, so she soon became nauseated, and being the astute diagnostician I was, I immediately thought we were in the beginning of the "nausea months." It turned out that I was right, so another train trip to Grandmother and Grandfather Redcay for several months. As the months rolled along she got better and came home again. Helen, Elizabeth's sister was pregnant with her first child, husband Jim, and Jim's mother and father Hulda and James Glass, came to our Christmas Eve dinner. Elizabeth's water had broken the day before so she cooked the Christmas Dinner, on Christmas Eve, expecting her baby any time.

Our third child delivered December 25, and her name, we found out was Mary Elizabeth Tanner. What a joy, a female little girl, beautiful as her mother, and I was so proud of my little daughter. I found out after Elizabeth returned from visiting her parents during "the Nausea Months," that people in Auburndale had assumed my wife had left me. Nobody told me, or even questioned me until she returned. Then we set them straight.

When my daughter was 7 days old, I had to omit shaving because January 1st 1961 was the beginning of the Centennial Year of the founding of Auburndale, Florida and Polk County. The city fathers had declared a last shaving required on Dec.31$^{st}$, and then no more shaving until the Centennial celebration was over. If you did, you'd be put in jail, which would demand quite a fine to get out.

So I entered the beard contest, it grew black, full, and large with a handle-bar mustache, by the 6 week contest finals. Elizabeth took my grey suit, turned the collar and lapels up and a gold waist belt around the jacket that hung down on one side. I looked just like Confederate General Robert E. Lee, with my grey brimmed hat, a borrowed sword, and a little gold trim around the collar. Some of the other entries were Dwayne Glasscock, tall, lean with a stove pipe hat looking just like Lincoln, City Manager Bruce Canova, Bennie Poole, red bearded State Representative Fred Jones, and Buddy Corneal. Several others I have forgotten. The judges I don't remember, but they chose me as the best beard.

A few weeks later the Polk County contest was held in Bartow, our county seat. Judging was by some local dignitaries. I was declared winner as the Polk County Best Beard. I just went around my usual activity and work, seeing patients, making house calls, and making my twice daily hospital rounds. During the time my beard was large, black and luxuriant; we were at a Polk County Medical meeting dinner at Lake Region Yacht and Country Club, eating a steak dinner at a large table with our doctor friends and their wives. I was at the head of our table, Elizabeth on my left, and Dr. Beach Brooks' wife, Nancy on my right. A baked potato and vegetables accompanied our good steaks. In the middle of my charming ways, and talking to Nancy

Brooks, my wife touched me and whispered in my ear—"Get the potato out of your beard." There happened to be about a half forkful of potato and sour cream in the front bottom of my beard, like a bird in a nest. A new large beard takes a little time to learn how to gracefully manipulate through any kind of fancy meal. A sophisticated Lady like Nancy Brooks would never have interrupted my meal to tell me about my inability to eat carefully.

I received a call from Bruce Canova, city manager, that he received a call from Sarasota County and they wanted to challenge my beard superiority. They had an annual beard contest, and festival honoring the Conquistadors having something to do with their history. They had set a date, and wanted me to go to Bartow, and meet their Beard winner in a "Beard-off." I went and their judges were Tennessee Ernie's country music group that played each morning over one of Tampa's television stations. They chose me as having the Best Beard.

After that, I felt as the Prize Bull, which should never be castrated, therefore, I should never shave my beard. I still wear the beard, though now my full beard is no longer black, but a beautiful Grey, and now I notice a little white in it. Over the years the beard has become my "trade mark," throughout Polk County.

In mid 1961 Terry came to see us, after we moved to 2032 Ariana Blvd. and we had enclosed the carport, and used it as a play room, and for parties. We had a record player out there and often played some old big band music, and jitterbugged. I had danced and learned to jitterbug in high school, and love it. Terry brought his new girl-friend, Lynn Houser, a nurse in St. Petersburg, Florida some years younger than him, to meet us. While the music was playing and we were talking, I was swaying to the music, Lynn got up and came over to me and said, "Let's dance." I said "I don't know how" so she said "come on, I'll teach you." She took my hand and pulled me up, and proceeded to try to help me learn how to jitter bug. I was feigning not knowing, walking rather stiffly, and stumbling a little as she was counting and showing me the steps. After a little bit I seemed to be getting it and got better and better, while she continued to encourage me and saying "that's it now your doing better," Then I held her tighter and began to lead and really swinging, and leaving her not able to keep up with me. I began to doing a lot of my steps and movements, with Elizabeth and Terry beginning to laugh, and laugh, Lynn finally caught on and stopped and was really put out with me for leading her on. Then we did go ahead and dance, and she was a pretty good dancer.

It wasn't too long that, for some reason, another attack of "nausea months" hit us. After Mary was born in 1960 we had an opportunity to hire a wonderful person as a helper for Elizabeth and the kids. Her name was Johnny Ruth Green, a mother of 5 boys and one girl. Her youngest was 6 months old, being taken care of by Johnny Ruth's mother in law who lived 2 doors away from her. Johnny Ruth was not working since the birth of her youngest, so she was able to work for us. So Elizabeth went through this pregnancy without having to go to Pa. Elizabeth's nausea was mostly after lunch this time, so she could nap some in the afternoon. April 30, 1962, another beautiful little boy, looking like a brother to all the other beautiful little Tanners. He wound up being named James Henry Tanner, named after my two grandfathers, using their first names.

At our house at 2032 Ariana Blvd. we had a lemon pointer bird dog, named Sue. I was in my office talking to one of my friends, a drug representative there to show me some new drug. The nurse rang me to answer the phone. It was my wife, telling me about Sue getting raped by some traveling stranger-dog. I was on the phone answering and repeating her words in amazement—"Caught who? Sue? Hit him with a broom? Who? You what? Gave her a douche? Who? Sue? With a garden hose? You didn't! You did? How? By holding her tail up? With a garden hose? I don't believe you! You did? The detail man finally caught on and was laughing so hard he couldn't talk much. He heard only my conversation which did seem unbelievable, but it was true. Sue didn't get pregnant. I called Dr, Daniels, our Veterinarian to tell him the story, and he said, if it happens again bring her in right away for a shot to abort any pregnancy.

It happened again months later so we took Sue over and got her a shot. A few months later Sue delivered 12 puppies. James was just 3 months old when all this happened. Elizabeth had to supplement the too many puppies' milk, and was glad she had left over baby formula in bottles with nipples. I called Dr. Daniels and thanked him for giving Sue that shot, because she only had 12 puppies. I wondered how many she would have had if we hadn't given her that shot. He just laughed like hell. We kept one of those pups and named him Frisky.

It was about this time that Elizabeth's father was talking about retiring, and wanting to buy a place on Anna Maria Island, Florida because one of their neighbors in Selinsgrove, Pennsylvania had a place there and they wanted to be close to them here in Florida. He asked us to go and search for something. Their friend Mrs. Bergstresser, had a little place on a corner in Anna Maria Island and a daughter had a place two doors away. One weekend, we went over and spoke to the daughter, who knew an old gentleman who had a little cabin 2 doors from her, on the next corner, same street. He lived in New Jersey, I think, and since his wife had recently died, had expressed to her, he wanted to sell. There was an empty lot between her and him. We were able to contact him, and he wanted to sell his cottage for $7500.00, and wanted $3500.00 for the empty lot. The cabin was nice and quaint, we thought a good buy, Luther, Elizabeth's dad bought it, but didn't want the lot.

We thought about buying the lot, but didn't have the money, and didn't see the investment opportunity because this was before I really knew all about investments. As you will find out I became quite amazingly, and increasingly knowledgeable about investments.

Luther retired about 1963 and they spent the winters in Anna Maria, and summers in Selinsgrove. Granny, Betty Redcay, Elizabeth's mother, wanted Luther to sell the home in Selinsgrove, but he didn't, and wouldn't. It was a wonderful cottage on Anna Maria, and our kids loved it, and had many great times there on the beach, just across the street. Luther had been a heavy smoker and a pretty good evening drinker and developed heart trouble.

He had also dreamed of taking Betty on a cruise ship to Europe. He finally had it all planned and arranged it for 1969. They left on the ship, landed in France and took trips with their group into Germany and Austria, and I don't know where else, but he got ill and was hospitalized in a couple of countries. He got back on the ship to return home, got quite ill coming home. At the landing in New York he was admitted directly into a hospital, and within 12 hours had died.

After his death, Granny sold her home in Pennsylvania and moved to Florida and lived with us in our big home, while building a home behind our big house I'll talk about next.

In 1963 we thought we needed a bigger home, at least my wife did. We had gotten excited about some of our antiques, and wanted more, and she had been associated in Pennsylvania with old early American homes, and thought it would be really good to have one to put all our antiques in. There was an old home built in about 1915 on Lake Ariana at 1700 Ariana Blvd. that was on the market. It had been the winter home of the Gerald Work family. Mr. Work was dead, Mrs. Work died shortly after we came here, leaving only one daughter, Virginia. The home had been sold by Virginia to Jack Trawick and family a couple of years before. They were in the process of a divorce.

Elizabeth had gone through the house and saw the promise of a large beautiful home, but some changes had to be made. I saw an old dilapidated, run down, two storied, asbestos shingled house, with a porch on the front, running around to include the right side of the house, looking at it. There was a single upstairs room in the center, with a gable on it, set out in front of one room on the right and one room on the left. It was situated on 165 ft. wide lakefront, corner lot at Tecumseh and Ariana Blvd. and about 200 ft. deep, with a small narrow asphalt road behind the house running through our block and the 2 adjacent blocks.

She kept on and on about what a wonderful home it would be, until I finally said I'd talk to Jack Trawick. Jack said they had just put pink carpet in the whole house and he wanted $2000 for the carpet, and take over the $200 dollar monthly payment, to Virginia, with no interest. I could do the deal, so we did. Elizabeth was ecstatic. I was nauseated.

We took over the payments to Virginia in 1963 and continued for several months, until Elizabeth had all her plans for remodeling on graph paper, showing every antique furniture placement, and nook and cranny that was platted out by the inch, so every thing would fit where she wanted it placed. Everything was working out really good for her, but we had no money.

She pretty well figured out how much it would cost. So she took a trip to Lakeland to a female banker in one of the banks, laid out all her plans, and the banker said OK, but you have to OWN the house.

So one Sunday afternoon, I called Virginia, and asked her if I could pay her off, and give her $15000 cash for the house. I owed about $18000. She said, "Oh, no, I don't think so, but let me talk to my lawyer, and I'll call you." I thought it would take her a couple of weeks to go see her Lawyer. But she called me about 30 minutes later, and said, "My lawyer said we couldn't take 15 thousand but we could take $16,000 cash." I called banker, Jack Summers at home, and asked if I could borrow 16 thousand dollars. He said to come to the bank tomorrow and sign the papers. So we all of a sudden owned two houses, one nice, the other a piece of junk. So after we owned the house, Elizabeth went back to the bank lady, got her loan, she hired a well known local carpenter Tommy Harrison and his friend and carpenter James Cato, to re-do our new old house.

She stayed there watching and continually planning while the men were working tearing out the old plaster walls, carefully taking all the old moldings off from each door and window, and saving the molding to put it back up when finished. An electrician was removing all the old wiring, and replacing it with new stuff. Between each room in the house she made them put insulation, as well as in the attic flooring, and under the new roof that covered the entire whole old house. The front of the house was built forward to the edge of the porch then built up to the level of the roof, and that added a room on each side of what use to be the gable, and brought the entire $2^{nd}$ floor forward to the edge of the porch. She had drawn a roof on her plans, but when she stood on the road, down the hill at the lake, looking up at the house, you couldn't see her roof. So she had Mr. Harrison go up to the attic, nail 2 long 2X4's together, put one end at the edge of the roof, then elevate the other end until it looked right from the road. She kept yelling "HIGHER-HIGHER" until it was right, then she yelled "NAIL IT DOWN." That is how the pitch of the roof was done. That roof covered the whole old roof and old house. The old roof is still there with about 12 layers of roof still on it, with 2 copper roofs covered with old asphalt shingles.

New plumbing replaced the old stuff with all copper pipes by master plumber Lynn Green. All the old electric wires were removed and replaced by master electrician Don Jessup and his son in law, Bob Reiter who later took over the electric company with one of his boys. Then the walls of the whole inside of the house had to be replastered. This was done perfectly by a master plasterer, who went to work at Disney World building and plastering the beautiful buildings there after he finished our home. His name was Mr. Arnold Greatens.

The carpenters struggled to scrape and clean all of the old paint from the moldings, to replace them around each door and window. The old fireplaces were not safe or usable, so Mr. Chauncey, master fireplace builder came and started the fireplace in the family room where Elizabeth wanted it. The old one was covered up and left behind the walls. The new one was going up, and where it was going to come out up on the roof was going to look bad for her aesthetic taste, so she made him gradually shift the blocks and bricks as he elevated the fireplace through the house to come out on the roof in the place that was appropriate to her for the house style. Or something like that. In the attic you can see the changes of the fireplace blocks moving in a different direction as the walls of the fireplace go higher and higher so it could come out of the roof in the place she wanted it to. At the same time he built a new fireplace in the living room. This fireplace was to be surrounded by a beautiful hand carved Federal mantle with columns we found from an old mansion in Georgia.

The mantle over the family room fireplace was part of a large old heart pine thick board that was removed from the floor joists beneath the kitchen. Mr. Harrison and Mr. Cato broke a few circular saws trying to cut it. They finally had a 3 inch thick and about 8 inch wide and about 8 feet long, mantle supported by two curved pieces of the same board. Elizabeth refinished that very hard old heart pine board and it looked beautiful over the fireplace. The carpenters broke several drills trying to make holes for nails in that hard wood to mount the it over the fireplace.

When we were in Pennsylvania, during the building phase of our project, we saw several homes with beautiful unusual fireplaces with surrounding pottery scenes telling a story. These were made in Doylestown, Pa. at an old factory named The Moravian Tile Works. These artists were a group of very old potters who started this company in late 1800s. We selected the story of the Arkansas Traveler. It was a group of panels about 1 foot square surrounding the fireplace opening. In each panel were figures, hand formed, painted, and glazed of a man, a traveler on a horse, an old man at his house with an area of the roof missing, a boy, a dog, and the old man's wife. All the pieces were separate like a puzzle.

The story starts in the left lower corner of the fireplace, and then panels with the characters in each, moved up the left side, then across the top, then down the right side. The story depicted, by the figures showing the actions at different points of the story, the tale of The Arkansas Traveler. We contracted to buy that decoration for our fireplace. Each was to be made, painted, and glazed and shipped to our home when the pieces were finished. They were to be shipped in a large barrel, full of saw dust to separate each piece, and we were to put them up ourselves. A few months later we received a letter informing us that the company had been bought by the county for a museum, and they could not finish our order. They also stated the figures were completed but they could not paint or glaze them. If we wanted them like that, they would be cheaper.

We got really upset, so I called the office, spoke to the president, and pleaded with him to PLEASE complete our order. We needed them for our beautiful fireplace that was already completed. He said he'd try. A few days later he called and said the men (the artists) agreed to come in on their time off at their new jobs, and complete their work, if we allowed them the time it took for them to complete. We had also ordered a lot of 3x3 unglazed red tiles, and a lot of individual tiles impressed with hand painted and glazed birds, fish, crabs, and letters for our name etc., to be placed in the foyer area.

We got a letter agreeing with all of the above and stating that this would be the last of these fireplaces that they would ever make. We were very happy and proud to have the last. However, since then I see on the internet they, as a museum, do continue some of these things, on order.

The tiles finally arrived and Elizabeth called a tile man, Hurley Whidden to come. The two of them put up a large cut out piece of marine plywood the size and shape of the place around the fireplace, then a wire background on the plywood, where the tiles would be placed. On the wire, cement was placed, a little at a time with the specific few tiles that go in that panel, placed on the cement. Then they had to hold a hand on the placed tiles for the underlying cement for those few tiles to set. It took about 10 minutes or so for the cement set, and they could add more tiles to the panel. Or go to the next panel. It took all day to get all of the tiles placed and set, all the way around the fireplace. Elizabeth sat up all night using a wet paint brush to continue moistening the cement so it wouldn't dry too quickly and the tiles fall off. That was truly a labor of love, and I was so proud of her doing what she had to do to make her home like she wanted it.

Mr. Harrison and Mr. Cato built the front of the house all the way up as directed, but Elizabeth had them cover the entire wood with black tar paper so she could quit awhile and have another baby. It was the biggest tar paper house in town for about a year until she was feeling up to more construction.

She had been real pregnant, and nauseated, and went to work anyway with the men. She got more nauseated, gradually worse and decided to put it all off until we had our next baby, Mark Andrew Tanner, on June 7th, 1964. Elizabeth's nausea with that pregnancy seemed to be managed a little easier with Johnny Ruth's wonderful help. Another perfect baby boy, we thought we were so good at getting perfect kids we ought to continue populating the world.

It took about 2 years to complete all of the details, and replacing and painting of the wood work. Where we didn't have enough old woodwork, Elizabeth used a few old solid, 5 paneled doors. She laid one complete old 5 paneled door on its side over the mantle of the fireplace in the dining room. After it had been scraped, cleaned, and repainted it looked beautiful, and like all the other paneling in the house.

We had bought an old, large heavy safe over 3 feet wide and about 6 feet high, on rollers. It was delivered before we finished my study, and it was placed in a closet in the study and built in. Because of the weight of the safe we had cement blocks placed under the house under the floor where the safe was sitting for support. The combination was a little complicated, so I put it on the back of a small drawer in my 1800 period Hepplewhite slant top desk, in case I forgot it. Mary now has the desk in California. Elizabeth needed about 10 cupboard doors in my study, so she cut two more 5 paneled doors for the needed 10 cupboards. The same panels, from other solid doors were placed as little doors between all the rooms upstairs to use as escape routes in case of fire in the house. She stacked molding around the ceilings, and did other things to make the house an authentic, early 1800's Georgian Colonial Home. Hardwood floors were there already throughout the house, and even the window panes were authentic size. Then we picked out a nice colored brick and bricked the entire house. We were extremely excited and proud of what we (I mean Elizabeth) designed, planned, and built.

We were happy to move into it in 1965. The house had 18 rooms, some of which were 7 bedrooms, and 4 bathrooms, a study, large dining room, large living room, large family room, large eat in kitchen, and a huge floored attic with the large new roof enclosing the old roof.

Before we moved to our big home on Lake Ariana, we lived at 2032 Lake Ariana Blvd. It was next to "Tuffy" and Ethel Griffin's house, which was next door to Hannah and Jere Stambaugh's house. "Tuffy" was a citrus fruit buyer here for Winn Dixie stores, and summertime went to the Carolinas to buy peaches for Winn Dixie food stores. Our kids became good friends with the Stambaugh kids, Bill, Carol, and twins Jere and Steve, and Bob. The kids were all raised about together as one family. Living on the lake and enjoying all the wonderful advantages of southern lake living swimming, boating, fishing, skiing, and just soaking in the sun and water.

On weekends early Saturday, and Sunday sometimes, "Tuffy," Jere, and I would get up dark-early and go to one of the lakes, long before any of the home development started and walk in the sand on the edge in the lake and throw our casting lures out in the lake and retrieve it and catch bass, some very large, but all were good eating. This was a great time for us because of our love for bass fishing. Once in a while one of us would lose our lure, to a monster fish, by not being able to haul it in, or the line might break. We could only dream of the size of "that" bass, or maybe it was a gator, or maybe a "mud-fish."

There were times when we would plan a trip for a long weekend of fishing, just for men, at Homosassa River house that the group would rent, at Homosassa, Florida. There was "Tuffy," Jere, me, Fred Bair, Kelly Holtsclaw, Hannah Stambaugh's father Mr. Ralph Walker, Eddie Keefer, and another or two I can't remember. We would take steaks to grill, eggs, bacon, and stuff for breakfast. Plenty of beer, some liked a little bourbon, etc. We would get up way too early, and go to the boats, get on the river and get to fishing. We caught red fish, speckled trout, sheephead, and whatever else would bite. These were wonderful trips with a bunch of wonderful guys. We tried to go on these trips 2-3 times a year, a great chance to relax. If we didn't catch a thing it was just fine anyway.

During the daily ride to the hospital in Winter Haven I would drive on a couple of back roads, through planted, growing, and bearing citrus trees. There had been a great interest in the increasing lack of labor for picking citrus, so a lot was being said about developing citrus harvesting machines. While driving through bearing groves laden with fruit I naturally began trying to figure a way for a machine to harvest the oranges. After a few years of thinking about it, and reading Citrus Magazine articles about the pros and cons of the many ideas for pickers that had been written about, I dreamed up one I thought was the best of any, so far. There were always difficulties that made none the acceptable answer.

So in about 1966 I contacted a Patent Attorney office in Washington, D.C., talked to a gentleman who made arrangements for one of their attorneys to fly to Auburndale to go over and help me put together my idea for a patent for a Citrus Picking Machine. Mechanical devices have to be drawn in a specific manner, as if the light on the drawing must come into the drawing from the right upper corner of the drawing, I think it was. This is to conform to all of the patent applications for ease of reading by the examiner.

He was very thorough and concise, and knew all the requirements I had to add, and anything near my idea that could be added to protect any variation of my basic idea. After spending all of one very hot, miserable and sweaty day, he had complete understanding of my idea. He took all of information back to his office to give to the people who do all of the final drawings. It was so hot in our house because we had only recently moved into the big completed home, but we couldn't afford air conditioning. It was a couple of years before that was accomplished. After several months, I received the final drawings and attached explanations of my idea. They were acceptable to me so I returned them for the examination by the U.S Patent Office in Washington, D.C.

It took a few more years, and in 1969, I was issued a patent for the Citrus Harvesting Machine, I suddenly became an Inventor. The Patent was dated 12-16- 69, my birthday coincidently.

Next came a long period of frustration, disappointment, worry and sometimes anger because I couldn't control the acceptance of my patent. I had made appointments and presented my patent to several citrus machine and farm machine manufacturers from Tampa to the Orlando area.

All were very cordial, but I got the same suggestion—"You build it and bring it in so we can see how well it works." This machine as I visualized it would cost many thousands of dollars to build, more that any huge farm machinery out there.

So as the years went by, and my patent protection slowly faded away, no one called wanting to buy my patent. My Patent is in a drawer somewhere, and what money I had was spent instead on all my wonderful family that I am extremely proud of, and not on a fruit picking machine that may, or may not work. Oh, well.

In the mid or late 1960s, Dr. Wiley Koon came to see me. He was a recent graduate of University of Miami Medical school, was from Lakeland, Florida, was married to Clovis and they had 3 or 4 children, Wiley, Jr., Beth, and James. We talked about him joining me in practice. I asked him if he minded doing house calls. He said "no I would love to do house calls." So I wrote that statement on a piece of paper, and told him I was going to keep that paper, and sooner or later, when he started complaining about them he would have to eat those words. He agreed. So a few years later, he had some complaints about a house call. I got the paper out of my desk, and gave it to him. He said he forgot all about that. I did not make him eat those words. We worked together well, and I thought he was an excellent, caring, affable, and competent physician. The patients liked him very much, and I hated to see him leave. He wanted to move to a larger town and have his own office. He moved to Winter Haven and built an attractive office designed by Architect Gene Leedy, a local well known Winter Haven, Florida gentleman, and friend of mine. Wiley and I continue to be good friends. We both taught each other as we practiced together.

Auburndale was the home of Adam's Packing Company, long a citrus packing and juice company, owned by the Adam's family. The president before I came to town was Mr. Mac Morrow, his wife was Marie. They lived in a beautiful home on Lake Ariana, across the lake from us. Mr. Morrow died either just before I came to town, or shortly after. I never had the opportunity to meet him. I had met Mrs. Morrow.

On a day of Rotary Club dinner meeting, in late 1959, or early 1960, one of our common friends was in Rotary with me and on the way out to my car, he stopped me. He told me Mrs. Morrow was going to call me to come see her about building a hospital in Auburndale. She wanted me to give her some input into how to do it.

After a little discussion, I told him I'd be glad to go and talk to her, but I thought it would not be a great idea. I thought it would be much better to give money for a Morrow wing added to the Winter Haven Hospital, that didn't have to duplicate all things that are necessary to operate and run a hospital. I felt most of the money could be used in patient care with beds, and nurses, and not have to duplicate the kitchen, lab, x-ray, etc.

I didn't think Auburndale could support a hospital. I was the only Dr. in town that used a hospital. There wasn't a terribly affluent population around, most people worked in citrus, and many had to use the indigent county hospital located in Bartow, Florida. Very few people had medical insurance. This new hospital would duplicate Winter Haven Hospital's food preparation, laboratory facilities, X-ray facilities, operating room facilities, housekeeping, etc. If I admitted very sick people, I would have to have specialists available for consultation. Lakeland had a large hospital 12 miles west of town, and Winter Haven Hospital was only 4-5 miles east of us. We would have to have emergency facilities, and I wasn't about to man an emergency facility day and night by myself.

I told him I would be happy to meet with her anytime. I wondered how many of the staff of Winter Haven Hospital would use it, or even come for consultation for my patients when needed. It seemed to me the money could benefit more people by increasing the number of beds and be benefited by the food, service, labs, and X-rays already there. She could have had a Morrow Wing of the Winter Haven Hospital.

I never heard from Mrs. Morrow, and was told she got a little upset at me for my attitude. Within a couple of years Mrs. Morrow died. I was told she was at the Lake Region Yacht and Country club dancing, and dropped dead. It was later announced that money was set aside for the hospital, if the Catholic Church would build it and run it. Money was given to the Knights of Columbus, and Boy Scouts, and Girl Scouts, I believe, and maybe others.

If the Catholic Church didn't build the hospital, it was to be divided between the others. A committee, designated by her will, made up of her attorney, Catholic Church representatives, and Everett Allen, investment banker, Jack Summers, local banker, and others I can't remember, evaluated, and they decided to build the hospital. It was to be a 35 bed hospital, I believe. The home she lived in was razed, and the hospital was built on her large lakefront lot. The amount of money was spent and with some left over. That extra money was designated not to be used to run the hospital, but to be used for expansion only.

Medicare came into being in 1965 or '66. I was on the staff, and I enticed most of the Winter Haven staff to apply and become Morrow Hospital staff members. Being the only local doctor on the staff, naturally they voted me Chief of Staff. And naturally they continued me as Chief of Staff for around 10 to 12 years.

Hardly any other doctor admitted a patient to our hospital. It was a little out of their way to make rounds on two hospitals. I continued my privileges on the Winter Haven staff and spent many years going back and forth to both hospitals to attend my patients. Some wanted to be admitted to one, and others wanted to be admitted to the other.

As time went on we had a few new physicians come to our town to practice. Dr. Cano was one and Dr. Salazar was another. They stayed a few years, and then moved on to other places. The hospital didn't open an emergency room because we had only me to come for emergencies, and I told them at the beginning I wouldn't be the emergency room doctor. It turns out, if you open an emergency room, then legally you must staff it and accept patients. If you don't start with an emergency room, you're not obligated to have one.

I put all the patients I could into our hospital; however, I was not comfortable putting very ill, especially acute cardiac patients in our hospital. It was very risky to have a heart attack patient, and suddenly have complications. We had to call an ambulance, I had to get the patient to Winter Haven coronary unit and consultants had to be called. Besides I was a wreck worrying about any acute severe changes occurring in the patient's condition and some care givers not recognizing and calling me quickly so we could make decisions to treat or transfer to cardiology. Some of the nurses were not trained to read electrocardiograms; even if they were I wasn't comfortable hoping they could. So after a while, to ease my mind, my patients with cardiac symptoms were admitted directly to Winter Haven Hospital and referred directly to a cardiologist. Most of my admissions at Morrow Hospital were medical illnesses or injuries, or for diagnostic tests, that I felt comfortable treating.

In the early years of the hospital in town the hospital would have rummage and auction sales in the city park downtown. Many people would set up booths for items to sell. Maybe occasionally to start these events, an organization, like Rotary Club, would set up a charcoal grill, cook pancakes and syrup, scrambled eggs, and grits to sell for breakfast. Then I would get up in the Gazebo and auction off any thing people brought in to sell. All these moneys went to our local hospital for whatever they needed. We did this several times over the years. This was fun and everybody in town usually showed up one time or another. I knew just about everybody in this wonderful town. Our population was about 5000 people when I came in 1955. It has grown so the population is about 12,000 -14000 in city limits, now many more in surrounding developments.

I never did have a completely satisfactory experience because even though I was trying to support the hospital, my ill patients would be sent to Winter Haven Hospital, and the patient referred to another physician for their hospitalization. I just didn't want to be running back and forth to 2 hospitals. I continued like this until late 1970s, when I resigned from Morrow Hospital, and went back completely to admitting at Winter Haven Hospital. By that time a few other doctors had come to town and were using the hospital. Two brothers, practicing together in the Winter Haven area, joined the staff. Dr. Earnest Dilorenzo did General Practice and was older. Dr. Jim Dilorenzo did general surgery. They both were on the Winter Haven Hospital staff. They continued admitting to the hospitals.

Elizabeth was again, attacked by the "nausea months" and was aided by our wonderful house and home helper, Johnny Ruth Green. She was helping immensely, and Elizabeth was doing nicely, and about the 5$^{th}$ month she developed a severe strep throat with pain and a high fever, and started having abdominal cramps. I called our obstetrician Dr. Perry Keith, in the Bond Clinic, we then admitted her to the new Morrow Hospital. She was losing fluid, so Perry took her to the delivery room that hadn't been used yet. The Morrow Hospital opened 1966, and the delivery table hadn't been set up yet, so Elizabeth had to wait until they put the table together. She was finally put up, and shortly she delivered her spontaneously aborted 5 month old dead baby boy. A week or so before, she had had a short period of vaginal bleeding. So she probably had a small placenta previa, and her severe strep throat infection was enough to cause the babies demise. We all were very sad about the situation.

I kept telling people we were trying to get a good one, but it never worked out, so we wouldn't just give up now. The last one was David Michael Tanner, born January 3, 1968, another perfect, beautiful boy. We are really proud of our family. We are so lucky to have them love us and each other. We have always been a very loving and proud family. Johnny Ruth made our life so much easier, and we were so fortunate to have found her to help us raise our family. Her family mirrored ours so much, and she and Aaron raised great wonderful kids that loved their family as much, she also had 5 boys and 1 girl.

Morrow Hospital opened for patients in about 1966, about the time Medicare came into being. When Medicare inspectors came to examine the hospital, some of their requirements lead to changes in the halls, fire doors, the number of Registered Nurses that had to be on each floor, the number of LPN"S (licensed practical nurses) that had to be on the floor. How many cleaning personnel were necessary on each floor, and many other things, I can't remember, that had to be done.

The first administrator was Bob Jones. He was competent, friendly, and became a personal friend, and still is. After 5-6 years another administrator, Dyrk Kyper came. This was about 1970. This became an era that the town and I, were trying to bring other physicians into town. The older doctors in town had begun to or were about to stop practicing.

One afternoon a doctor presented himself in my office wanting to meet me, and was thinking about coming to town. He was brought back to my office and we had a nice conversation. He told me he had talked around town and people told him I was real busy and was a real good Dr. so he decided to come and join me. He was retiring from his many years of practice in Wisconsin, as a General Practitioner.

He needed a shave and wore a rather old wrinkled suit with a couple of stains on the lapels. He told me he was a very good Dr. and didn't want to do any more house calls, and never did any hospital work and wondered if I could let him practice with me. I asked why he wanted to leave his practice and come to Florida. He said medicine in Wisconsin had gotten too complicated and he wanted a simpler life. I told him I wanted a younger associate, and didn't think he could be of any benefit to my practice. He thanked me and left.

A surprise one day, a Thoracic Surgeon came to my office. He was a physician Terry and I had met and known during Internship in Saint Petersburg. He was one of our teachers in Surgery. He was a huge man, a former college football player, became a Thoracic Surgeon. In the operating room one day he became irate, yelling, cursing, and uncontrollable. The police had to be called to remove him forcibly from the operating room. We heard he wound up in a psychiatric hospital and was there when we left our internship in Saint Petersburg. We never heard what the outcome was, but here he was at my office wanting me to help him get on the staff of our hospital.

My receptionist brought him back to my office. He stopped at the door, in the hall and stood there, greeting me as Paul, talking rather fast telling me of his incredible surgical ability, and the fact he could perform surgery better than anyone on our staff with one hand tied behind his back. He came because he had heard about me here and what a good doctor I had become so he came over here to help me in my practice. I greeted him warmly, half scared to death he would rip me apart if I turned him down, and told him that he was probably right about his ability because I remembered what a great surgeon he was during our internship.

However, this is only a small hospital, and he needed to get into a much larger hospital where his ability would really be needed. His kind of surgery is not able to be performed here due to inadequate surgical assistance and nurses untrained to aid in his major surgery, also the postoperative care would be inadequate here. He sort of stopped, and then said "yes, I never thought of it like that, I need to go to a big hospital." We shook hands never entering my office, just standing in the hall, and me just waiting for a big angry man to take me apart. He politely thanked me and left.

It was a few weeks later I saw his name in the Lakeland Ledger as a new surgeon on the Lakeland Hospital staff. I never saw his name again and never knew what ever happened to him. I was very active in the Polk County Medical Association, and never saw his name, so I don't think he stayed around too long.

Sometime in the later 1960's or early 1970's I received a phone call in the middle of office hours from Sarasota, on the Gulf coast about 90 miles away. A nice gentleman on the phone asked if I was Dr. Tanner, I said yes. He proceeded to tell me he was sending his 17 year old daughter over to me for me to take care of. I said "Are you from Auburndale?" He said "No." I said, "What's wrong with your daughter?" He said, "You know, that's why I'm sending her over for you to take care of." I hesitated, then I said, "Sir, I don't understand what I'm supposed to take care of.' He seemed a little short and said, "Are you in Auburndale?" I said "Yes sir" He said "I understand there is a doctor in town that takes care of girls with problems." Then it dawned on me he must think I'm a doctor in Polk County that was reputed to interrupt early pregnancies. I had heard that soon after I came here. He asked how long I'd been here. I told him "only a few years" Then he said "I heard the doctor was an old doctor." I said "I don't do that and don't know who you're talking about" and hung up the phone. I had never had a query like that before of after that. I had heard of a doctor who performed abortions, was caught and the State Board of Medicine took his license. I understood later and attorney went to court and a judge allowed the license to be reinstated "by court order" until some hearing was held, sometime. That was the last I ever heard of it. It probably happened sometime before I came here. Abortions at that time were illegal.

Sometime in the late 1960s a high school home economic teacher came up to my office to ask me if I would come up to her class and talk to her female class about some questions they want answered, about sexual diseases and such. I thought a little and thought it would be good, but I felt like no one would ask me any questions, because they might feel stupid, or ashamed, and didn't want their friends to know what they didn't know, or be teased by her friends.

So I told her I thought it would be better if she told them I'll come, but for the teacher to tell the students to write down their questions, and turn them in to the teacher. The teacher to take the questions, rearrange them so that I would get a list of the questions, with the most frequently asked questions from the top down. This gives them the chance to ask their embarrassing questions and no one would know who asked the questions.

So I did that and had a very good answer session. The questions were very good, and obviously some of the girls had no clue about much in the way of female anatomy, female physiology, and boy-girl relationships or sexual diseases. Anyway, it went well, and exposed me to the fact that they knew very little and I thought we answered the most commonly asked questions truthfully and completely. The teachers gave me all of each student's questions. It was pretty obvious the students were really in the dark about things I thought they would have known. I got really good feedback from their teachers, and they and the students were pleased with it all. Then I got a call from the boys football coaches to do the same for the boys, which also went well.

In a few months, I got a call from the county school superintendent stating that he had heard that I was at the school teaching sex, and they thought I need to stop that and not do it any more. I said OK. Then I heard the rabblerousing came from a preacher in one of the lesser denominations.

A few years later the same preacher came in as a patient with a bad cough. He had lost weight, and feeling bad. I admitted him to Auburndale's Morrow Hospital. An X-ray revealed a rather large lung lesion, described as probable carcinoma of the lung.

On discussing the treatment with the patient, he was not interested in pursuing any treatment. He stated he had faith and knew the Lord would heal and care for him. He did not want to be referred for surgery, or cancer treatment of any kind. He wanted me to discharge him, which I did. I never saw him again, and I never mentioned my "sex teachin' " to him or anybody else. I was very sad, and sorry for this man, that I could not help him at all. A few months later I saw his obituary in the paper. I can only assume that one of the students in the female class told the preacher or, he found out someway, that I was "teachin' bad things to high school kids" He was the one that called the county school system very upset that I was doing that, so they decided not to allow it to continue.

Several years later the school did develop a course for the girls given by an Obstetrician-Gynecologist. That was probably better, but I think it was long overdue.

Some of my interesting patients in my early years will be reviewed. One was a little 5 year old whose mother brought him in for a runny nose and fever. He had a red, sore throat, and was quite cross-eyed. As I was about to send them out after I finished, I asked the mother if she had taken her son to an eye specialist for his eyes. She said no but Dr. Dakin had been seeing him, and was adjusting his neck, putting heat to it and rubbing it once a week, and since they started a few months ago her son's eyes have gotten a lot better. She said I should have seen him a year ago. I gave her the name of an eye doctor. I never saw her or her child again so I don't know if she took my advice or not.

When I first came to town I met a lot of people, one was a store owner in town. One day his wife came in complaining of a headache, for a week. This was her first visit to me so I decided I needed to do a rather complete visit and take some sort of history. There was nothing on the history or her head exam, lungs were clear and heart sounds were normal so I laid her on the table to feel her abdomen, for liver, kidney, and spleen. She had a huge left abdominal mass, about grapefruit size. It was not moveable and wasn't tender. I felt it was a kidney tumor. I asked if she was aware of it, and she said yes, but she forgot to tell me that Dr. Dakin knew about it, and for the past year she had seen him weekly for heat and massage treatments to her abdomen. I asked her what he thought it was. She said, a few months ago her asked her if it bothered her, and she told him no, so he told her," if it's not bothering you, then we don't need to do any thing, because it didn't seem to have changed, and it's not bothering you."

I admitted her that day, got a kidney specialist, Dr. Dan Griffith, to see her, after the intravenous pyelogram identified a large kidney, probably malignant hypernephroma. We operated her next day or so and removed it. It was malignant, and had already spread to abdominal lymph system and liver. I wanted to send her to a cancer specialist in Tampa, or Orlando. She and her family refused, and took the advice of a neighbor to go to Texas to the cancer hospital, Hoxey Cancer Clinic, a noted quack physician that gave her medication to take and return for more, if necessary. The physician and hospital wound up later being run out of Texas into Mexico. My patient never returned to me, but did not last very many months. I was not happy about the results.

On a Sunday afternoon, I received a phone call from an unknown patient needing a house call for rather severe cramping abdominal pain. The address was in Lake Alfred, Florida a small town a few miles northeast of Auburndale. I found the address in a rental mobile home. The older couple was visiting for the winter. I found a miserable older, thin man, pale, and writhing with waxing and waning pain in his distended abdomen. He was nauseated, and had vomited a time or two. Examining him, I found a very distended, tense, tender abdomen. He stated he had seen a naturopath physician in Winter Haven a few months ago for some abdominal pain, off and on. The doctor performed a barium enema on him in his office, showed him a "lump" on the x-ray in his lower intestine, and told him he had to have colonic irrigations to wash it out, and needed to flush the colon, once a week to remove the "lump." He told him the cost was $300. The patient stated the doctor told him he would have to pay the entire amount before treatment, because sometimes a patient gets good relief after a couple of colonic irrigations, and wouldn't return for the entire 3 months required treatment period necessary to remove the entire lump. So they did pay and start treatment.

The patient stated the third week irrigation had been done two days ago, and he wasn't able to expel all the treatment fluid and his pain persisted and has gotten a lot worse. He obviously had a lower bowel obstruction, probably sigmoid lesion, and had to have surgery right away. He preferred Lakeland's Morrell Hospital, so I was able to get one of the General Surgeons of Watson Clinic to accept him for emergency surgery. I was notified later that this patient did well, but had a sigmoid colon obstructing malignant lesion, already spread to liver. This is another example of waiting too long for treatment.

I had seen a few patients with warts on hands, arms hands, and feet. When in medical school I began looking for and ordering some of the many free monthly medical information journals, many from pharmaceutical companies. One was, a small journal named Medical Tribune, later became a larger journal. One of the things they did was review world literature of recent medical literature, and gave a concise short account of the article reviewed.

One that I found interesting, was an Italian article written by a physician that noted warts being removed by an amino acid, Methionine taken orally. He reported on one of his patients with liver disease, that he treated with the usual lipotropic amino acids methionine, choline, and inositol. They help remove fat from the liver. This patient had warts on his body. While being treated with these drugs, the patient's warts went away. The doctor then spent several months treating patients with warts using each of these drugs separately. He found that only the patients that took methionine had their warts go away. I put this in my notes and waited until patients came in with warts that wanted them off. Most of them did not want them cut, or burned off, so many agreed to give it a try.

I tried what the article said, 500mgm tablet three times a day. It was a large white uncoated tablet that smelled awful, like rotten eggs, probably due to the sulfur in the molecule. Most people took it anyway, and believe it or not it worked on the vast majority of those that took it like I prescribed. I learned that it takes a good month, or more, depending on how big the wart is. Normally it takes about a month to replace the outer layer of skin, so apparently the Methionine must be in the system at least for that long.

The first thing that happens is the base of the wart seems to turn black, like the underlying tissue circulation to the wart clots, and then the circulation doesn't feed the wart, so it dies and falls off. That is my guess of what happens. One of my good friends, Kelly Holtsclaw, came in one day with a large quarter-size wart on the top of one of his great toes. He wanted me to cut it off. There is very little tissue on top of the big toe, and to cut that off, he would have to have a tissue graft to cover the area. You couldn't suture the edges together without a graft. He agreed to try the medicine for a month. He did return about a month later, and we saw no change at all. He wanted a referral, and I agreed. It took about 3 weeks to get Kelly's time available to coincide with the surgeon's time. About the time for his appointment, he came into my office and said he wanted to cancel the appointment because the wart went away, and looked all ok. We both were amazed. It probably took that long because of the size of \the wart. Another thing I found out is that every wart does not respond. The Verruca Vulgaris seems to be the one that responds, especially ones that are tender.

After a while, the price got so expensive for methionine that people didn't want to try it, also it smelled really bad, like rotten eggs, and some rebelled against taking it. I had also been trying another drug, Flagyl (metronidazole), on other things, like viral infections. The drug came out as an antiparasitic drug, primarily for flagellated parasites, like endomoeba histolytica, the cause of amoebic dysentery, and another that causes trichomoniasis.

There was also some information in the literature that another imidazole, called clotrimazole I believe, used in treating horses parasitic intestinal infections in Europe, was being used in female breast cancer to try to prolong life after the surgery, in people with tumors that had already metastasized. At this time, with new chemotherapy for breast cancer, I have no idea if clotrimazole is still being used. At any rate, they were using the imidazole, as a pulsing treatment; treating for a week, then off a week, repeating, and reporting good results of prolonging life, but no cure.

So I thought I'd try treating people for their warts with Flagyl the same way, which might do the same. They were both imidazoles, and were safe for most people to use. I had been using the Flagyl with success on most people with fever blisters (Herpes Simplex) if I could start treating them early enough with the beginning of the little stinging at the site of the formation of the fever blister on their lips. I figured that the drug was performing as an immune system stimulant to bolster their response, and stop the development of the blister. Some patients, once they start having fever blisters, they can repeat over and over for life. So I gave these people a prescription for Flagyl to keep

on hand so they can start the pill immediately at their onset of symptoms, and continue for at least a week to abort the episode. This was
before the antiviral drugs came out for herpes.

One of my patients went to University of South Florida, in Tampa,
to college. I received a call from the school physician stating my
patient was in his office, pleading for him to give her a prescription
for Flagyl, for the fever blister that she knew was coming on. He saw
no lesion, and besides that he never heard of such a thing—Flagyl for
a fever blister. I told him the story and after explaining it works really
well for my patient, and to please give her the drug. He did and we
both were happy.

Now there are available several antiviral drugs to try to control
Herpes Simplex and Herpes Genitalis, and Herpes Zoster (shingles).

I figured if Flagyl was safe enough for people with amoebic dysentery and trichomoniasis, then my healthy patients would do fine. All
of them did, with no symptoms of complications or side affects from
the drug. I advised my medical colleagues of my success treating
patients with methionine, and Flagyl. They kind of looked at me
weirdly, at times, about using these drugs for these reasons, but with
time many of them called me for dosages so they could try it. Some
reported success to me, others never mentioned it at all so I don't
know if they got results, or didn't, and I don't know what they were
trying to treat.

It works out that Flagyl did work very well. I tried it on many
warts, but there were some that didn't go away, especially those on
the bottom of the feet. It may be that I didn't treat them long enough.
The skin on the soles of the feet are so thick, it may need to be given
for several months. However, I have no idea if some of those that
didn't lose their warts just didn't come back to follow up, or didn't
call to let me know that it didn't work. I always thought some derma-
tologist could do some good research to see if this could be another
way of treating warts. I guess it is much easier, quicker and more
lucrative to make a surgical procedure the treatment of warts, but it
may be that this drug might stimulate the patient's immune system for
many other situations, or even malignant ones. I had a teen age boy
with Infectious Mononucleosis, which is treated mostly with rest. He
was told all the rules, and not to do any physical activity. He began to
feel better, went back to school and started being physical at Physical
Education class again. He came back to see me, had a fever, and an
enlarged liver and spleen. A test revealed he had developed hepatitis
from the Infectious Mononucleosis, with elevated liver enzymes. I

hospitalized him, and started him on Flagyl 250 milligrams three times a day. Within 3 days symptoms were gone and liver enzymes had dropped to almost normal levels. I sent him home and he recovered completely rather quickly, unusual for a hepatitis.

A truck driver from Melbourne, Florida came in for a driver's physical. I noticed on his nose, on the end of skin of the septum, there was small, but long wart growing, some $1/4^{th}$ inch long. I asked if he wanted me to remove it. He said no, so I asked if he wanted to take a pill and see if it would go away. He said yes. I gave a prescription for Methionine to him. He was to call me in a month to report. I heard nothing. About 3 months later I received a phone call from his wife asking me to call in a prescription for "that medicine" that took her husbands wart off his nose. She said her 10 year old daughter has some warts and she wanted them off. I declined, and told her I couldn't do that since she is not my patient and I can't write prescriptions for her on the phone. At least I know his wart went away.

I do remember one patient that came in for a cold, and had warts on all fingers, around each fingernail, on the back of each finger. He said he had gone to other doctors and none wanted to freeze, or remove them, because they were afraid to injure the nail beds. I discussed him taking Flagyl, and asked him to take a picture of his fingers before we started the medicine. He agreed to take the pictures. I gave him Flagyl prescriptions to take one pill, 250milligrams, three times a day for one week, stay off the medicine the next week, then start again the third week. He was to come in every week to let me see him. He also had a wart on the heel of the palm of the left hand, and also a wart on the right cheek, low and forward near the chin. He said he picked the one in the palm of the left, with his right index finger, and picked a pimple on the right cheek with the same finger, no doubt spreading them from place to place.

The first visit back I saw no change, the next week back, the one on the right cheek was loosening at the bottom of the wart edges, the following week the one on the cheek was gone, and the one on the left palm nearly gone, some discoloration at the base of some of the smaller ones on the fingers. In a little over a month they all were gone.

I asked about the pictures, he swore he took them along the process, and when finished, but they were on a roll that had other pictures on it, and he said he sent the roll to his sister in Jacksonville for the other pictures, but he'd get them back and would bring them in when he got them. All I know is the warts were gone. I never saw those pictures, if he even took them. This patient was the son of the father that didn't like me, the preacher that stopped my "sex lessons."

One young worker for a home builder using an automatic stapling gun that fired 2 inch staples came to my office with the butt end of the staple against the skin on the thumb side of the left wrist. He was unable to move the wrist in any way. An X-ray showed the 2 inch staple coursing entirely through each of the 7 carpal wrist bones, pinning them all together perfectly. It couldn't have been done better surgically by a surgeon. He stated he was working and his right hand slipped in some way and as he tried to catch and correct the stapler, and he accidentally fired it and this was the result.

There was no blood, and very little pain. I called an orthopedic surgeon in Winter Haven so he could take him to the operating room to carefully remove this staple. The surgeon told me he had never seen this kind of injury, pinning all the carpal bones like this. He had no difficult removing it, and it healed without incident.

A 32 year old new patient came to my office because of a bad upper respiratory infection. On the examination table without his shirt on I noticed a gauze pad taped on the upper outer left arm about midway from the elbow and the shoulder. I asked what was wrong with his arm, and he said it had been broken as a kid. I asked him to let me see it, expecting to see an infected unhealed wound.

There was a 2 inch brown dead piece of bone protruding through the skin with the skin normal and well healed tight against the bone, not draining, red or infected. I had never seen anything like it, and asked if I could take an X-ray of it. He agreed to allow it. The picture showed the humerus having been long ago broken in two pieces, with the upper fourth of the bone protruding from the skin and the bottom part of the shaft well grown into the upper part about 4 inches from the end of the break, with a very large bone callus growth tying the 2 together, and the arm a little shorter than the other.

He gave me the story of how they lived out in the country and he was 6 or 7 years old playing in an orange tree and fell out of it. He landed on the left elbow and broke the arm and the piece of the upper part came out through the skin. They didn't go to a doctor, but his grandma tied a kerosene soaked rag around it and wrapped it up for a long time and it finally got OK.

He said it never kept him from working, and he never had trouble with it. He just kept it covered to keep people from seeing it and asking about it. I took the X-ray films to show to my orthopedic doctor

friend who was astounded like I was. I don't understand how he
didn't wind up with osteomyelitis (bad bone infection).

A carpenter worker, using a nail staple gun building pallets to load
items into trucks, etc., hobbled into my office with the inability to
straighten his right knee. His story was, while nailing the pallet
boards together he was squatting down, and lost the handle on the
gun, fumbled and it accidentally fired. He was suddenly unable to
stand because the 3 inch nail had entered his flexed right knee, just to
the right of the patella and deeply embedded into the top of the tibia
through the meniscus of the knee joint. The nail head was visible
pressing into the skin.

X-ray revealed the nail entering the knee-end of the top of the tibia,
the large bone in the lower leg. He had very little pain, but he couldn't
stand on the right flexed leg. I called Dr. Robert Jahn, orthopedic surgeon, Winter Haven, and sent the patient over to him He was taken to
the operating room and with some little difficulty was able to carefully remove it. There was a little time before the patient was able to
get off of his crutches and bear weight on the leg without pain.

In 1969 I had taken time to go to the University of Florida College
of Medicine, in Gainesville, Florida and spend a week in an intense
program to review medicine to prepare to take the examinations for
the Boards to become a certified Family Practitioner. I had qualified
to take the boards by having been a member of the American Academy of General Practice for at least 9 years. An Academy member
had to accumulate 300 hours of Certified Medical Education (CME)
every 3 year period. This had to be repeated 3 consecutive times for
those of us who had been in practice a long time, and didn't require us
to return to school another 2 years of residency. This made us eligible
to sit for that new examination.

This was a new Board for Family Practitioners. They would now
be able after intern year to go to a certified program at a Medical
School for two more years, and then could sit for the exam. If you
passed the boards, you become a Board Certified Family Practitioner,
a recognized specialist. If you took the exam the first year it became
available, and passed, you would be named a Charter Member in the
new specialty. The first year it was given was in 1970, and I wanted to
be one. I was accepted to take it, but they had too many applicants so
they chose the first group by alphabetical order, and me being Tanner,
I was put in the next year's group. They did, however consider those
of us who had to wait were still considered as Charter members.

I took the board examinations in 1971, and passed. I was tickled but had not revealed to anyone that I took them because I thought I might fail them. Then I told everybody that would listen that I passed them. Dr. Charley Parks, of the Gessler Clinic in Winter Haven had also passed them. In 1972, at the Madison Square Garden, in New York City, with several hundred other Family Physicians I became a Fellow Charter Diplomate of American Academy of Family Physicians. I continued my required recertification exams every 6 years, and was a Board Certified Family Physician throughout my practice years, until retirement.

At the University of Florida our classes began at 8 AM, out at 12 noon for an hour, back from 1PM until 5 PM, out 1 hour, back at 6 until 9 PM. Every subject was covered by Specialty Professors in depth. One class in particular was Orthopedics, having to do with Osgood-Schlatter's Syndrome. This is a condition that occurs in early adolescence, mostly males, and especially physically active students. It is manifested by physical exertion and complaints of marked tenderness in the front of the upper leg just below the knee on the front of the tibia at the insertion of the strong patellar tendon on the tibial tubercle. In young kids the tibial tubercle doesn't grow firmly into the tibia until nearly the total bone growth maturity, about age 19- 20 years. Until then, activity and the force of their activity causes pain, due to the quadriceps muscle pulling on the floating patella and on the extended tendon to the insertion on the tubercle. Continued forceful activity continues pain, swelling and inflammation of the unfused tibial tubercle on the tibia bone and limiting activity. We were taught in that class that the treatment was decrease activity by diminishing, and stopping sports such a track, football and weight lifting. We were always concerned about the quad muscle force pulling off the tibial tubercle. During this class the professor reassured us that it could never happen.

A year or so after this class, one of the football players 15 years old, I believe his name was Wendy Anglin my patient, was having rather intense pain in the tibial tubercle. It was very tender and swollen, and was in walking with a limp. He had been working out with weights and running, trying to get into shape for the football season. I had diagnosed his problem as Osgood-Schlatter's Syndrome and had taken him out of any practice and other strenuous activity so the condition would calm down. He was following orders and stopped all the heavy stuff. He was very muscular and had large quadriceps muscles.

His symptoms had quieted down a good bit, and he was having no more pain.

One day some of the football boys came in carrying the boy with his left leg unable to function at the knee. When I felt his left knee it was obvious the patella was not there but there was a palpable lump above where the patella should be. He could not extend the leg. X-ray of the left knee revealed the tibial tubercle pulled to above the knee and the patella was located further up above the tubercle. Then I could palpate the much retracted quadraceps muscle and the misplaced patella and tibial tubercle way up in the middle portion where the middle of the quadraceps should be. Now I knew I had a situation that the Orthopedic Surgeon at U of Fla. said wouldn't ever happen, a pulled off tibial tubercle in an active Osgood-Schlatter's patient, but it did to one of my patients.

At football practice he was playing catch with another boy, neither was on the team. He was just passing the time of day throwing the football. The ball was thrown to my patient, it was a little long so he ran to try and catch it, but his left toe caught in some high grass that kept him from being able to get his foot far enough forward to support his weight on a well planted foot. His full weight was supported by his fall onto a partially flexed knee, with a big mature, strong quadriceps muscle, causing a severe forceful pull of the quadraceps, snatching the tibial tubercle off it's place on the tibia, and pulling the patella on up into the mid thigh. I called an orthopedic physician in Winter Haven, and admitted him for surgical repair of the most unusual and very rare condition. He was operated and he healed well. I don't remember if he played any football after this episode.

A man was lying on the floor in one of my examination rooms one afternoon, on his left side, pale and weak when I walked in the room. In getting a history rapidly, he told me he came in because of nagging left abdominal pain for a few days. He said today he parked in my parking lot to come in about it. He opened the car door to get out, put his left leg out of the car to stand up and with that effort had a severe pain in the left lower abdomen. He was in the waiting room a few minutes, was called by the nurse to came in to put him in the exam room. He said after she left him, and waiting for me he became very dizzy, weak and light headed and felt he had to lie down and the pain was bad. On the floor, I laid him out and got down and examined him noting a rather large somewhat firm mass in the lower left abdomen that was quite tender. I immediately thought he had ruptured an abdominal aneurysm and was bleeding in the abdomen. I ran to the phone, called Dr. Zeller, told him what I had and told him to call the Operating Room and get the people there ready for emergency abdominal surgery. He said OK and did. I then called the ambulance, they came quickly, we put him in it and they left as a severe emergency. I quickly explained to my waiting room patients that I had to follow the ambulance and assist in his emergency surgery. Again the patients understood this kind of occasional happening in my office. By the time I got there, the patient was in the operating room, Dr, Zeller was scrubbing, I changed, scrubbed, went in about the time he opened the abdomen. The belly was full of blood, rather dark, and by the time we suctioned most of the blood and identified the bleeder, transfusions were being given. The bleeding site was really unusual. It was not from an aortic aneurysm, or any other artery, it was from a spontaneous rupture of his left iliac vein in the pelvis. The venous blood was the reason it was dark, instead of arterial bright red bleeding. Neither Dr. Zeller the surgeon, nor I had ever heard of a spontaneous rupture of a large vein like this. Anyway, the few transfusions and quick cooperative action between me and my surgeon friend, who had learned to trust me when I thought I had a severe emergency situation, served to save this man's life. I hate to relate this, but some three to four weeks after a couple of weeks in the hospital, he suddenly died of a heart attack at his home.

During these years there began some drug uses in high school. They were stealing some of the drugs that their parents were taking, taking them to school and selling or sharing them with their friends. In our church the teens had a class and I took the opportunity to speak to them about drugs that I thought was quite clever.

The drug representatives would come to my office and bring new drugs, or even old drugs, and inform me about their uses and usually leave samples. I would put a few of the loose pills in an old large apothecary jar. Over several years I had the jar nearly full of multiple, varying shapes, sizes and colors of tablets and capsules.

To one of the Sunday Schools classes I went and took my jar full of all the drugs. I had no idea even what they were or what they were used for, but they were pretty. I passed the jar around to the kids and told them to each take 1 pill or capsule, which they all did. Then I told them to put it in their mouth and swallow it.

Mouths dropped open in amazing surprise and nobody took the pills. I continued to encourage them to do that. Still nobody did. I asked "Why Not?" Several piped up "I don't know what it is." I asked, "Then why, at school would you buy, or take a pill someone wants to give you that he may have brought from home? Kids do that at school and they don't know what they're taking. Isn't that stupid?" They all agreed to the stupidity, and danger of the possibility of becoming addicted to some unknown drug, or take a drug that may kill someone. This seemed to impress them about drugs. I hope they learned from that demonstration.

During the same years I was seeing families that seemed not to be able to control kids and kids seemed to be more and more unruly both at home and at school. I felt parents were not able to manage the discipline part of parenthood. I decided to maybe get the attention of kids and parents. I went to the high school principal and told him I wanted each English teacher to require a paper be written for the English class. I wanted the title to be "MY PARENT'S RESPONSIBILITY TO ME, AND MY RESPONSIBILITY TO MY PARENTS"

He thought it was a great idea, and I told him also that the winner in each class would win a $50 Government Savings Bond and I wanted to be anonymous. I wanted him to tell the English teacher to grade the papers and pick what she /he thought was the top 5 papers, and give them to me to select the winner from each class. It happened like I wanted it to happen, and the winners were presented by the principal at the end of the school year at the awards program. I was also given all of the papers, and it was an education to read some of those papers, showing no family respect at all, some unappreciative, and seeming to want more from their families. Most were quite good and it was difficult to choose the best, but I did.

# 6

# You Are Dead in the Morning

One day I was notified by the Hospital Administrator, Dyrk Kyper, that in a day or so 2 doctors would be coming to town to meet him and check out our hospital and town, to decide if they wanted to move to the area. He said they were in practice in Boca Raton general practice, and decided to move to a smaller town. I asked him if I could meet with him and the new doctors when they come, because I felt that if possible, we could join and practice together. He agreed and I was notified when they came, and I went to the hospital where they were, so we had a very good talk.

I was impressed with both of them. One was a retired obstetrician-gynecologist physician who had practiced in Indiana for some years; the other was in general practice in Boca Raton, when the first doctor came there to retire. They met and joined together, then joined a practicing general practitioner there.

They left and Elizabeth and I talked at home about the possibility of a three man practice. We thought we needed to have them come back and talk more. One of them had one child about 16 years old, and the other had one child about 5 years old. We decided to invite them up, with their families, to stay in our big house for the weekend. So I called them and invited them, they accepted, and they came. We took them out to dinner at Lake Region Yacht and Country Club, then back to Christy's Sundown Restaurant for dancing. We had a great evening, and then sat up until wee hours after we came home, dis-

177

cussing the partnership. They left for home on Sunday. We were really excited, planning 2 new competent general practitioners in practice with me, for Auburndale.

Monday morning I called the Professional Management (PM) representative that did our books monthly, and told him what we were excited about, and wanted to get together in a partnership. He asked for their names so he could call a PM representative in that area to find out a little about them. In about 30 minutes he called me back, and asked if I was sitting down. I said yes. He proceeded to tell me about the problems both of them have in their area. They had been given the opportunity to resign from the hospital staff. More information is not necessary here.

This really burst my bubble. So I called them and informed them of the fact we learned of some problems, and we would not be able to join in a practice. I also advised them to please get their problems solved before they get here, because they may have some difficulty getting admitting privileges on the hospital staff. He said OK. That was our last conversation.

I later heard that they had decided to come anyway. I also learned that a town committee to find new doctors had been appointed, and that was the group that found these two. I knew them, and called one of them, and asked to meet with them so I could let them know there may be a little problem with the new doctors getting on the staff. We met, I could only warn them, with no specific information because of my worry of a liability slander suit. I advise them to please send a member of their committee to Boca Raton, Florida to find out the information they needed. They did, but they were told by the hospital administrator the doctors resigned "in good standing" from their staff. The hospital was no doubt fearful of being sued, obviously, because the committee could get no more information. No staff action had been taken before they were allowed to resign.

I was Chief of Staff, and I knew hospital rules and regulations that controlled admissions to our, and Winter Haven Hospital. After they came, I ran into one of them, at Rotary Club dinner, they attended as a guest, and advised him against applying for Hospital Staff privileges until their problems were solved. He thanked me, and said they had already applied. Later I understood that they had retracted their applications.

I was then aware of a few letters to the editor of our local newspaper taking me to task for stopping new doctors from getting on the local hospital staff because "I didn't want the competition in town." I wrote a response stating it would be impossible for me, as Chief of Staff to control the vote. I have no vote except in a tie, also quoted some of the rules of admission to the staff. And besides, I had been looking for a partner, because we needed more doctors in town.

They did open their office, but within the first few weeks, they had a falling out. I understood they had a fist fight in their office one morning, and separated. One built an office, the other rented an office. They both practiced for some 2-3 years, I'm not sure exactly how long, but apparently one day one of them just didn't show up any more. He had been brought up before the Florida State Board of Medicine that controls state licensing. There was some police involvement in a Tampa nightclub and was arrested. Specifics were not clear to me, I wouldn't relate them if I knew.

I understand his office staff had no idea what happened, other than that the family moved out, where to I don't know, and the staff didn't know either. The other doctor stayed quite a while longer, later his wife died, and later I heard he was charged with selling narcotic prescriptions, lost his license, and wound up in jail, and later died.

That was a bad time for me and the hospital. I tried, but failed to control the situation. I had met with the Florida State Board of Medicine at one of their meetings in Tampa before they came here to practice, questioning if the board had any control over doctors that had bad actions in one part of the state, to keep them from moving around to other parts of the state until their problems were solved. They sadly informed me that they didn't, since each doctor practicing in Florida had a Florida license, which allowed them to move anywhere within the state. The board was aware that these two had many reports of charges and delinquencies in their files, but could not stop them from coming, or moving to any place within the state.

Since physicians have to purchase a city license, as well as a county license, I approached both the city of Auburndale, and Polk County licensing board, asking them the same question. Why can't some licensing body control physicians moving into new communities, if they are doing some questionable medical practice in the area they are presently practicing? A plumber or a carpenter has to sit for a test of their ability in their trade, given by the city, or county if they want a license, and they must pass it. But not doctors, who hold peoples lives in their hands. It's always been weird to me.

A year or two after the first one left, I received a phone call about midnight one night, I answered, and a voice I thought I recognized as one of the doctors, and he said, "Dr. Tanner?" I said "Yes," he said "You are dead in the morning" and immediately hung up.

This was a sudden, frightening, electrifying sentence—I'll never forget my sudden cold chill. The anger in the voice was obvious. This was in the winter, and the next morning was dark when I got up the go to the hospital for rounds, I was alone when I walked out to my car afraid to open the car door. Finally, after trying to inspect it for a bomb or some other surprise, I closed my eyes said a little prayer and opened the door cautiously. Nothing happened, and then I had to start the car. I opened the hood and looked for wires or something abnormal about the engine. I wouldn't know anything that shouldn't be there, anyway, but it looked like it always looked to me. So, I gritted my teeth and started the car and all was well. After rounds at the hospital I went through the same nervousness and anxiety getting back to my office, noting every car I passed or that passed me. After office hours, evenings were dark early, before I would leave my office, for hospital rounds, I turned all the lights out, cracked open the door slowly and peeked out looking for an unfamiliar car parked near the back door, it was always OK, so I dashed to my car, looked around and got in and left for the hospital for evening rounds. I spent several weeks very frightened to leave home in the morning, or my office late in the evening, or to start my car anytime.

I went to the Chief of Police, and told him about this and that I was going to carry my little .22 cal. pistol in my pocket he said he wasn't worried, but he wasn't the one threatened. He said OK. But be careful. I was VERY careful for several weeks. But so far I'm fine.

It took me many months of anxiety to finally, so far, realize that "I wasn't dead in the morning," and gradually tired of carrying my little .22 pistol when I went anywhere. This all happened in the middle of 1970's and time and patients kept me busy.

When Elizabeth and I came to Auburndale we began looking around for a church to join. We attended several locally. Elizabeth had grown up in the Lutheran church. Her parents were very active in their church. Her father's brother and their father were Lutheran Ministers. I went to church with mother at her Methodist, and Daddy's father was a Presbyterian Minister, so Daddy went there. We kids went to both. After attending churches here, we decided on Presbyterian in 1955, mainly because our beliefs seemed to be satisfied a little better there, at that time. Dr. Wherry, the minister preached a good understandable sermon every Sunday. One thing I loved about his good sermons was he finished with a prayer, then, he dismissed us, without any more hymns. I liked that because I didn't get interrupted while I thought about what he preached, and I had an opportunity to think more about what he said. I never had any other preacher do that before or since. We both later became Elders and active in all the children things, with our children. Elizabeth is presently a Deacon and very busy with Deacon stuff, choir, and bell choir.

When the kids were young, we had tried to spend family time doing stuff. 3 or 4 times a year we would drive to Quitman, Georgia to see my parents, and we had good family times there, especially when both my brothers and their families were there. There were 2 or 3 trips to Pennsylvania to visit Elizabeth's parents.

On our trips the kids were always excited and active and verbal, teasing or fighting with each other. We had a 9 passenger Pontiac and they were very close together for a many hour trip. Many times Elizabeth would make me take a side road in the country for a short distance, make me stop the car, make the kids get out, and then make me drive on down the road about 2-300 yards. Then the kids had to run to the car. This calmed them down, and tired them out, so they did pretty good the rest of the way. She carried a fly swatter along in the car. She has a long arm and could reach most of the six during the drive if they didn't listen to the leader. After the day or weekend was over, they all were put in pajamas. Back seats were put down, and the kids laid down in the back like cord wood in the back floor with their pillows, and blankets. We finally had a quiet, pleasant trip back home after good times. When we got home, I had to carry the littler ones to bed, the older ones staggered, sleepily to their beds. I've often thought those were dangerous times, driving home late at night with all my family sleeping laying all over each other with no seat belts or any other protection. Luckily, no accidents ever occurred.

With these kids, 5 boys and 1 little girl, after their busy rat-race of their days, Elizabeth piled all 6 of them in a big bathtub in the bathroom next to the kitchen while she cooked supper. After supper, and tooth brushing, they could watch TV until 7:00 when they had to go to their rooms to read or sleep. Bed time was 7:00. They began to rebel and cry that they "are not tired yet." She would yell out "But I am." She would come down stairs, have a beer, and wait for me to come home. It was usually dark when I got home after hospital rounds. I walked in the house and washed my face and hands to get the people germs off of them. Then went into the family room and sat down with Elizabeth to enjoy a beer together before our supper. As we sat in our family room enjoying our beer, we could hear the pitter patter of running little feet in our upstairs. They would run from one of their bedrooms to another, back and forth. Then she or I would yell "GO TO BED" then a whole lot of running back to their rooms, then all quiet. A little later one running then two, then maybe a yell "MAMA, MAKE JOHN QUIT!!!." Again "GO TO BED!!!!" All quiet. Hear more running. One of us would get up and go up the steps, run, all quiet. Everybody is now in bed wide awake, so I would say each kid's prayers with them. "Now I lay me …Amen." Then we would bless all the grandparents, parents, brothers and sister, all the cats (eleven of them: Brownie, Orangie, Whitey, Pinky, Ethel, Myrtle, Blackie, Blue, Bluette, Maxine, and Rudy.) Most were strays, a couple of the cats were Siamese.

One night, saying John's prayers, when he was 5 or 6 years old. I was kneeling on his bed with one knee on the bed. When we were through, John said "Daddy, how much do you weigh?" I said "about 180 pounds, why?" He said "I thought so, you got my jammies caught and I can't move a thing!" Then another time after prayers, John, about the same age said," Daddy, do you ever pray to God? I said "Sure, John, every night when I go to bed,—do you?" He said "Yeah, when I throw something down the commode and flush it, I pray to God it'll go WHOOSH (with swooping hand gestures), and go on down and not stop it up!"

Along these years when the kids were still little, when I went to bed each night I would go to each sleeping kid's room and get them up to go to the bathroom to try to cut down on the bed wetting, which they all did at one time or another. The boys were the worse, and many times I was too late, they were already asleep in a wet bed. I would get them on their feet and march them to the bathroom while they were still asleep. When I got them to the commode, I'd turn them facing me to pull the diapers, or pajama pants down, and more times than I like to admit, they would start their stream, still asleep, all over my pant leg, leg, shoes or feet, before I could get them turned around. It took a while to learn not to pull their pants down before they were facing the commode, because that apparently was the signal for them to cut loose. Mary was the best because she would sit down, and she never peed on me. When the youngest got old enough to get himself up and trek to the bathroom that part of my life was behind me. HOORAY!

One day with all of the kids in the car Elizabeth took all the cats to the veterinarian for their shots. When they loaded all the 11 cats in the car with all the kids, she came on home. When they arrived home the kids took all the cats in the house. When they got in, there was no Whitey. They looked all over and never found her, they went back to the vet and looked all over the vicinity, in the clinic, on the way over and all the way back, but they never found Whitey. We never had any idea where she went or what happened to her. They thought she was put in the car with all the rest. We had to get over losing Whitey.

Then we had to bless the dogs. We had a Collie when we were married, Bonnie, who didn't like it when we had a baby. She obviously became very jealous of our son, so we had to make a decision,—our dog or our son. One of them had to go, so we took our aging good friend to our vet to decide what to do. He took care of the sad occasion for us. Then we had Sue, (the 12 puppies Sue), and Blackie who just wandered up, and Frisky, one of Sue's pups. Old age took care of Sue; cars took care of Blackie and Frisky.

We had decided we needed a dog, so we went to a dog show, tried to learn about what we wanted. We met a lot of dog people and asked a lot of questions, and met a nice lady, Wendy, breeder of Rhodesian Ridgebacks. We liked what she said about the breed and their temperament and habits. They are a large breed, they lay quietly except when necessary, do not shed their short hair, do not slobber all over, great with children, easily trainable, and the only dog that will bay a lion. Now how important is that?

She had some puppies at her Ocala Kennels. We went up to see them. They were all really cute, have a streak of reversed hair down their back from shoulders down to above the tail, generally the body is like a Mastiff, but a little smaller, and are of brown color. We selected one 3-4 months old called Perky, took her home and everybody loved her. During the first week, at our lake front home the kids were going swimming with her, running down to the lake, Perky running behind them, they crossed the road, a truck came along Perky darted out behind the truck, and didn't see the trailer, and was struck by the back wheel and run over the middle of her back. She obviously was paralyzed in the back legs. I picked her up, took her immediately to Dr. Daniels, Lakeland Veterinarian, who confirmed the problem, and we had to euthanize our wonderful Perky.

Because of our devastation, we had to go back and select another dog. This time we chose two dogs, Prudence and Patience. We took them home, after a week or so we noticed a strong odor of their skin and hair that no one liked. I called Wendy and she had a new litter that we selected replacements from. A female and a male puppy, from different liters and were really cute. We raised them, named them Porky and Bess. After Bess also got hit by a car, we replaced her with another female Ridgeback, named Rosie. It was apparent we needed a fence around our home. Elizabeth and the kids dug a trench around our property, filled it with cement so the dogs couldn't dig under it and a fence company put a six foot fence up all the way around our property. It wasn't too long before these dogs learned how to jump on the top rail with front feet on top of the fence and use their back feet to climb on up and over it. It was decided to put an electric rail around our yard on top of the fence. It was quite a shock to the dogs when they first leaped up and hit the wire, and yelped and immediately fell backward. A couple of tries, and they were happy to just stay in the yard. David, our youngest son said all his friends called our home "FORT TANNER."

It also wasn't too long before the Dog–Stork brought us little Rhodesian Ridgebacks. We gave some away sold one or two and kept two, Big Foot, and King. Sam was a really good friendly dog that just came up and stayed at our house. Sam, favoring a German Shepherd, became one of our favorites, a very friendly and humble dog.

Porky and Rosie were from two different litters. We had planned for them to be parents and our first litter was mostly given away to friends, I think we sold one to one of my anesthesia doctor friends. As time went on, Rosie, the mama dog apparently didn't like Elizabeth because every time Mom left the house, and the dogs were left in the house, Rosie proceeded to sit on the stair landing and chew on the carpet until it was kind of ripped apart. A huge hole was slowly growing in the rug. Porky, the large male generally just lay around and slept. One morning Elizabeth was all dressed up to go to Bartow for the annual County Fair where she was usually one of the judges for sewing contests by the high school students. I, and the kids had gone-me to the hospital, the kids to school. When she came down the stairs, Porky was sitting half up and half down with his abdomen extremely obviously swollen. About the time Mom entered the room from the stairs, Porky suddenly vomited, a couple of times and had a loose diarrheal stool all over the braided rug and floor. The vomited material was dark, chocolate-appearing with pieces of cardboard and aluminum foil all mixed in. It so happened, John and Mary, in the Junior High School Band brought home 2 large cartons of Band Candy to sell, and they had left it on the kitchen table the night before.

Elizabeth, like all good wives would do, put Porky outside and "calmly" proceeded to clean up the mess, before she took off for Bartow and the Polk County Fair. And I had to come up with all the money for the delicious candy, that none of us got to eat. We called Dr. Daniels, our Veterinarian, who told us to just watch for any signs of intestinal obstruction in the dog. None developed.

During the next few years, Porky began to have a chronic ulceration on a hind leg. Dr. Daniels had retired, and a new vet had come to town and was treating Porky. In 1977, during the Christmas Holidays, when the kids were out of school, Elizabeth had planned to drive to New York City for a week, with our kids, to expose them to big cities, the subway rides, a play or two, museums, and then stopping for a week in Washington, D.C. seeing all the sights. We had a nine passenger Pontiac. I was going to stay home because I was the only doctor in town and had no way to cover my practice. (I was tickled to death to have a good excuse, and besides Granny and John's girlfriend were going along- which took up all the sitting space, and I didn't need all the hubbub of all those kids, trapped in that car for 2 weeks.)

A few days before they came home, one morning I went downstairs and put the dogs out, and had breakfast. I opened the door for the dogs to come back in. They all came in except Porky. I went outside, called, whistled, and looked around. I found Porky up under a large Gardenia bush dead. I couldn't believe he suddenly died.

I called our Auburndale veterinarian, Dr. Kerry Chatham, who asked if he could do an autopsy on Porky. Of course, I agreed to permit him to examine Porky. I had called my good friend Jere Stambaugh and asked if he could have some of his grove workers come and dig a hole in our little grove behind our house to bury Porky in. He said he would. The Doctor said he would come and examine the dog if we left him at the side of the hole, so he could come after I had gone, perform his examination, then push Porky on into the hole. We could later fill in the hole. I got out the kid's little red pull wagon and wheeled it up to Porky's body, turned the wagon on the side and had great difficulty rolling him into the wagon. He weighed about 155 pounds. I then drug the wagon out from under the gardenia bush and out of the yard and over to where they were going to dig a hole, and carefully put our old friend on the ground where he would be buried. This was a sad day for me all alone with the sudden death of a good faithful pet. I had to go continue my daily routine of hospital rounds, and office visits, leaving Porky for Dr. Chatham to finish, and me a little teary with wonderful memories.

After the autopsy, we found Porky had a rather severe intestinal infection. I really appreciated my friends who helped me with the details of our loss. Needless to say when the family came home and I had to tell the story, there was a lot of sadness in the Tanner household. They all had a marvelous time on their trip and talked a lot about their experiences. I was really a little sad because I didn't get to enjoy with them their experiences.

After we moved into our big house in 1965 and the kids were still little, we decided to buy a pontoon boat. We bought one from Dr. David Taxdal, our friend and local Neurosurgeon that I occasionally assisted in some of my back patient's surgery. His kids were gone from home and he wanted to sell it. So we obliged him.

We had a lot of fun with that boat. Most weekends we anchored out in the center of the lake, and the kids spent all afternoon diving and swimming in the lake. We then would grill hamburgers on the boat, still out in the center of the lake. It was so peaceful. The kids became excellent swimmers. The only problem was that patients began to know that I had a pontoon boat and tried to spend many hours on weekends on it. So many times a car horn would sound, and sound, and sound to get my attention. There would be someone waving, waving, and motioning for us to come in. When we went in they wanted me to meet them at the office to see a kid, or sew up a cut, or see somebody sick, or something, which I always did.

Sometimes patients would come to the house, knock on the door, and ask if I would see somebody they had brought along for some problem. They thought they were doing me a favor, bringing the patient to my home. I politely refused, explaining all my tools were all at the office. I didn't want to contaminate my family or home with their germs, or blood if they were cut. I always sent them back to my office, and followed them there to see them. I didn't want to start making an office out of my home.

The kids wanted to learn to water ski, so we purchased an old, old inboard sleek looking Chris Craft good looking boat from a son of one of an older ladies living in Auburndale. It was moored in a Winter Haven lake and we had him bring it to our lake. It ran good and used a lot of gas. It was one of those wooden hull boats made with many strips of wood called a "lapstroke" that after a while became a problem because of slowly leaking. Every time we had time to go boating we had to bail the water out, because the battery would be down and the automatic bilge pump quit bailing. All the water in and around the engine made the engine so it wouldn't work and we had a hard time finding somebody to come out and try to get the engine to run. We had no way to take the boat to a mechanic. Finally the engine rusted to the point of being totally frozen up. All the kids never got old enough to ski, except Paul, while we had this boat. So after a while we had to let the boat just sit in the lake, with water in it and resting on our shore on the bottom of our beach in the sand. An ad in the paper finally sold it "as is," for not much money. This was not a very good investment. Everybody was rather happy to see our lakefront free of that boat.

We needed a ski boat, so Mom took all the kids to a boat builder in Clearwater, Florida they picked out the color and style they liked, and came home and ordered one from Osborne Marine in Winter Haven. A blue Deep V bottom outboard with 125 Johnson motor came and all were very happy. We went to the Gulf, fishing, swimming and catching scallops; to the Florida Keys, fishing, swimming and catching delicious lobsters; Crystal River, swimming in the beautiful clear springs and playing with the Manatees; Homosassa River fishing and exploring; and everybody learned and excelled in skiing, fishing, and boating. This was a wonderful period of our life. We even got to like each other pretty good.

We needed an easier way to launch and remove our boat from the lake. Otherwise we had to go to the other side of the lake to launch or remove a boat. We talked about building our own boat ramp, and Elizabeth said she wanted to build it herself and save money. So she got the kids down on the lakefront, measured the area, and put stakes up and got plywood sheets to place vertically inside the stakes on both sides, from the road to the waters edge, a distance of about 30 feet, and 12 feet wide. Then she called the cement truck to come and dump the amount of cement it took to fill up the site about 2 feet deep.

As the cement came and started filling the area, it got nearly completely full when all of a sudden, the plywood and stakes began to slowly started bowing out and nearly pushing her wooden, flimsy side walls flat. So with everybody yelling to get on the sides and hold the cement in place, and even the cement men on the sides helping, it held long enough to set and gradually became the biggest, and deepest cement boat launcher in town.

Among the kids involvement in all their activities, at their individual age groups, such as tennis, little league baseball, piano lessons, scouts, and band, Mary had auditioned and been selected to dance in The Nutcracker Suite ballet in Tampa, and had to be taken to Tampa for practice 4 times a week. My poor wife got really good at driving all over creation to make everybody happy. Once in while their Doctors made them come in for checkups, and immunization shots. She had to sometimes take time out to have her babies.

Boy Scouts came into play when Tom Montoya became a very active leader, planning all this stuff for the kids to do and go, to advance by reaching new ranks, and Merit Badges to continue advancing. Elizabeth had to fit that in between her wifely home duties, feed the kids, talk to me at night, helping with kids home work, and our social duties, and church duties. All I had to do was go to work and see nice, sick, complaining patients, and trying to figure out their problem, after early morning rounds at the hospitals, and repeating for evening rounds.

Tom Montoya had a big trip planned for the scouts when Paul 3rd was in the troop. They planned a 2 week float down the Suwannee River. They constricted rafts, with empty 55 gal drums on each corner, with corner poles and a large tarp suspended over the craft to block the sun. They felled pine trees, skinned the logs, lashed the logs together with rope that the kids made themselves. They put plywood on top of the logs for a floor. Paddles and long poles propelled the raft, and migrated through some rapids going down the river. The kids had an ingenious and fun trip.

Tom got an old parachute, cut the seams of the canopy, making a wide end at the edge of the chute, narrowing to the center of the chute, making a long thin strong hammock tied between one tree from the bottom, and two trees from the wide end at the top. Elizabeth and other mothers, made all the hammocks and sleeping bags. They also sewed mosquito netting around the hammocks, and saved us from millions of mosquito bites.

There were 4 rafts, an adult- father- on each raft and 5-6 boys on each raft. Jack Summers went the first week, and I met them half way down to finish the last week of the trip. My son, Paul 3rd, and Jack's son Jackie went along. Other fathers and sons enjoyed this wonderful escapade. The first night, for me was rough. Trying to sleep in that hammock was like trying to sleep in an ice cream cone. I like to sleep on my side or my stomach. That was impossible in that sagging triangle. After a couple of miserable nights, I finally was so tired it was no problem, but I was tickled to death to reach the end of this slow, slow mode of travel. We did have a wonderful time and the kids had a journey they'll never forget. The forests and the river, with some interesting rapids, were beautiful. Good pictures and indelible memories still remain.

When the kids were starting band and John and Mary needed instruments, Elizabeth and I took a trip in our Pontiac station wagon to a music store in St. Petersburg, Florida. We bought John a new bass clarinet, and Mary a new oboe. It was just about dark coming home driving on Interstate 4, and just going over highway 98 in Lakeland, Florida coming down the overpass I noticed a car entering the lane to come onto our east bound traffic, when all of a sudden his auto lights turned onto our inside lane coming the wrong way back up the overpass toward us. Only Elizabeth was with me, and the driver was coming straight up the overpass the wrong way. I tried to avoid him but he ran right into the right front of my car with the right front of his vehicle hitting head on. His vehicle was turned around and stopped in the right lane. We were able to get into the median. I had to climb out the back and went to his vehicle. It was an elderly gentleman, bent over the steering wheel, and his wife was unconscious over the dashboard. Fortunately, a trucker was behind me, able to stop, and quickly get flares out to stop east bound traffic coming up over the overpass. He was yelling to me to get off the road. I had totally not thought about people coming behind me. I was trying to find out about the other people in their car. Police were there quickly and we were removed quickly. I heard the two older people were trying to go back home to Plant City, west of Lakeland. He must have forgotten this was a big interstate highway, and not a 2 lane road. They were in the hospital a good length of time. We were very fortunate and the kid's instruments were fine.

All of our kids took music in the form of piano from Mrs. Lochmiller, and all of them played in the middle and high school bands. In Junior high school, Mr. Agrella, music teacher in middle school, taught them all as they came through his school. They entered high school and had several really good music teachers and band directors through the years.

Paul played piano, trumpet, then French horn, and arranged some of the music for the high school stage band, then took piano from Mr. MacDonald, Artist in Residence, at University of South Florida in Lakeland, and Paul is very accomplished in classical piano.

Sometimes Elizabeth and I would go out for an evening for dinner and some of the nicer restaurants had live entertainment, like a little band with a good set of music easy and enjoyable to dance to. One of our favorite bands was Bruce Canova and his band. Bruce was our long time City Manager and a good friend. He had several good local musicians in his band, and he also had a string bass made out of a wash tub. There was a strong cord coming from the center of the upside down wash tub going up to the end of a 4-5 foot long, 1 by 2 inch board attached to the side of the tub. The player would put one foot on the tub edge, hold the end of the board with the string attached. By forcefully tightening or loosening the string, while strumming the cord, a deep sound mimicked quite well an upright bass, varying the tone produced. I would often go up and 'sit in' with the band and play the string bass. It sounded great and we got a lot of approval of our music playing with Bruce.

Bruce had 3 children; Patty, beautiful daughter married to Hunter McNeer, citrus grower, one of our good friends. Buddy Canova, also an accomplished musician who often played with family, and sometimes headlines in other places. Joni Canova, beautiful daughter, another excellent musician who played with her father sometimes, and continues playing at many places through out Florida. Joni and Buddy often play places together and are well known. Bruce was a cousin to the famous musician, actress, and singer Judy Canova. We had all the Canovas as cordial, wonderful friends and patients. We still see the kids frequently.

Another of my patients and friends that grew up in Auburndale was Bobby Braddock, son of Paul and Lavonia Braddock, and brother to Paul Braddock. Bobby became a nationally known musician and song writer, and recently an author. He was nationally recognized and lauded recently for Country Music Association's Song of the Year Award two consecutive years for, "He Stopped Loving Her Today." Another favorite of his was "D.I.V.O.R.C.E" among several others.

Bobby recently wrote a book of his Rock and Roll early life around Auburndale and Florida, "Down in Orburndale." Bobby's book mentions me in a couple of places referring to his visiting me as a patient. He has been living in Nashville, Tennessee202 for years, coming home to visit his parents and brother. His parents have been gone for several years, but he still visits Paul. I am proud of my copy of his book he autographed for me.

Another of my early families was the Dudeks. Mr. Dudek was a former sailor in the Navy in WWII, married to a lovely wife, named Alma who later became one of my favorite ladies. She was so animated and lively all the time, she was always laughing during her visits with me. Her husband died shortly after we met. They had two children, one a beautiful daughter, who out of high school went to California and got into something to do with placing actors and actresses in movies, I think. A son Les Dudek, was a great musician, a

tremendous guitar player who wound up playing in several famous
Rock and Roll bands. Later he became quite a performer and was a
very good friend of Cher, of Sonny and Cher, for some time and was
in one of her movies "Mask," I think. After his mother died several
years ago, Les moved back to the area, and works out of Orlando. I
think.

Another Auburndale musical family was the Chambers, several
well known brothers that played with some of the famous bands. Carl,
Jessie, and a couple or three more I forgot their names, all great musicians and song writers.

Buddy Corneal, WWII, air force fighter pilot, and good friend, had
sons, Chuck and Jon, and a daughter Ann, who was a singer, piano
player, band member and song writer. Jon, a rock and roll and country
musician, played drums and guitar with bands in Nashville, Tennessee. He continues with his music and song writing, and is an important active member in our church. Ann had an untimely death a short
time ago from an acute severe asthma attack, and we really miss her
in our church. Chuck is in real estate. They are church members and
we see them frequently. This family is one of our close friends, and
all patients at one time or another.

One day we noticed in a citrus tree across the back street from out
big house there was a huge honey comb hanging, some 2 feet long
and 1 foot wide and 8 to 10 inches deep with "zillions" of busy bees
buzzing around. We were afraid one of the kids would get badly
stung, so we called one of my patients, Mr. Russ, who was a long
standing beekeeper and honey- giver- to- me almost every office visit,
a quart jar of orange blossom honey. He was delighted to have the
bees and came with his smoker, calmed the bees, he said, and calmly
sawed the limb and dropped the huge comb full of honey and bees
into a huge plastic bag. He took them home and transferred the new
hive into one of his "bee boxes." He was happy to get some more
bees. We were happy to have him happy.

I noticed off and on when I came to my office and entered from the
Palmetto Street entrance, several buzzing bees flying around the door
area but a little higher. Some days I forgot, and other days I noticed
quite a few bees. I stood by my door one day and watched bee after
bee flying around, then land on the wooden sill just beneath the roof,
on the brick wall just beneath the sill, crawl up the brick beneath the
sill in the little space between the bricks and sill and disappear. There
were a lot more going in than coming out. I figured there was a large
hive in the wall.

Several years before that we had bricked the entire building over the previous cement block building, because we had several drug seekers break in our building through windows, or doors. They never got my drugs, but did succeed in messing some stuff up, and stole needles and syringes. We never had another break in. I figured my bee keeper patient Mr. Russ could handle this bee-job, so I called him.

He came and watched, and said there had to be a huge hive with a big amount of honey in there behind that wall. He said there was no way to tear down that wall and get to the hive and honey. He recommended using an insecticide to destroy them. That's what he did for us, so no one could get stung and no one could get the honey. I guess when the building is torn down someday the honey will be discovered. I don't know how long honey stays good enough to eat. I read somewhere one time that the only food that doesn't spoil is honey.

A family came into my office, having just arrived back home after an all day trip to the Atlantic coast in Melbourne, Florida. They were a father, a mother, a 9-10 year old daughter, and the husband's father and mother. They were all complaining of nausea, vomiting, and diarrhea and the drive back home took about three hours. The worst of the bunch was the mother and the daughter. The others had been worse earlier than they were when they finally got home. The mother and daughter were obviously ill and dehydrated so I immediately admitted them to Morrow Memorial Hospital here in town. The others denied being sick enough to want to go into the hospital, so they elected to go home.

The mother and daughter were both complaining of severe abdominal cramping, mother was worse. History revealed at noon they bought a large smoked Amberjack fish on the beach for their lunch. Mother and daughter ate the larger amount, the others ate only small amounts, and their symptoms began to subside on the drive home. Mother's symptoms started and the daughter's symptoms followed about an hour later. In the hospital, we began intravenous fluids and medication to relieve the cramping and diarrhea. They slowly resolved, but in the morning the mother complained of burning and stinging of her legs, so I ordered warm tub baths for her to sit in which relieved the symptoms. A few hours later the daughter, who was in the next bed started complaining of the same symptoms so I put her in warm water tub baths which relieved her pains also. I was thinking the daughter was copying her mother's symptoms so she could get the same care and attention.

I had asked the husband for the fish so I could send it to the Polk County Health Department for Toxicology evaluation, suspecting some bacteriological cause from the fish. The next morning the mother had developed a rash over her lower extremities where the burning and stinging had occurred the day before. Lo and behold the daughter also developed the same rash over her legs, too. This proved to me both these patients had a real problem and the daughter wasn't feigning her symptoms, and copying her mother. We slowly controlled the systemic symptoms, and the leg symptoms continued, but could be controlled by the warm water baths.

After a few days I received a phone call from one of the Florida Health Department Physicians in Jacksonville, where the fish had been sent by our County Health Department. He informed me that 100 mice had been injected with a small amount of material and 98 of them had died within 24 hours, and this verified that the fish was toxic and is one of the fish poisoning, or Ciguetera. I had never heard of it. It is a toxin, and is found in large fish that feed on smaller contaminated fish near the reefs. Most of the time it is self limited, and gets better with time, but sometime much more serious. The patients were sent home to follow up, and after continuing the warm water baths for several weeks, they both got along fine.

The Health Department Doctor wanted us to write an article for the Florida Medical Journal about my patients. I did, and he wrote about the history and medical symptoms of Ciguetera, in the same article which was published sometime in the early1970s. I received a couple of phone calls from attorneys in south Florida after the publication of the article wanting me to testify, as a specialist in their cases of patients suing the restaurants where they had eaten contaminated fish. I refused, telling them I knew only about my patients, and there are no tests to identify what fish has the toxin.

In the '70s, the other doctors who had kids, most a little older that ours, were buying them new autos and I was dreading that day when mine began needing cars. It so happened, one of my older lady patients, who lived across the lake went back up north during the summer and came back during the winter. She had a 1949 Dodge that she left down here while she went back north. Her mechanic would keep the car for her, put it up on blocks, drain the oil and protect it for her until she returned. Someone told me about her not planning to return here because she was now older and planned to stay there with her daughter. She had things in her home for sale before she left. We were interested in antiques, so I called to see what she had for sale.

She was delighted that I would like to look around. I made an appointment to go to her house. When I got there and after looking around we bought a few nice antiques, so when we were about to leave I noticed her '49 Dodge in her yard. I asked, "Will you be selling your car?" My kids would soon be needing cars. She said yes, she said she wanted $250 for it. There were very few miles on it because she only drove while here, to the grocer, and to church. So I bought it thinking one of my kids would like it later because they weren't going to get a new car. I was pleased the way it ran, so I decide to keep it for me. I decided to go to Sears and get an air condition put in it, and seat belts, then went to Lakeland, to a patient, Leonard Combee who put upholstery in cars.

Leonard did a great job, putting a leatherette pleated, well-padded upholstery in the front and in the back. I drove this car for a few years, and then I saw a 1947 Chrysler 5 passenger Highlander coupe on a lot, received from an older Auburndale lady. I bought it for $250, drove it, also.

I was the doctor at the hospital from Auburndale with all those old cars. Next somebody came to my office with a 1949, blue, 4-door Chevrolet, and wanted $500 for it. I drove it and had my mechanic, Mr. John Denman, check it and he said it was in good shape. I offered him $400, he agreed so I bought it, too. Elizabeth's father had a 1949 blue, 4 door Packard, he was going to trade in so we bought that, too. All these cars were in good running shape. I changed from one to another going on calls, and to the hospital for some years. As each kid got old enough to drive they were able to use them, and I was saving a lot of money not having to buy them new cars. They didn't complain too much, some of their friends thought it was really neat riding in those cars. At the hospital someone would ask "Well, what are you driving today?" I suspected there was a certain amount of jealousy because they spent a lot of money on new cars, and I obviously didn't. Or, they just might have been feeling sorry for me. I didn't care.

After office hours one day during summer I got in my car to drive to the hospital and noticed someone had placed a plant about 3 feet high with a root ball wrapped, sitting on my back seat. I thought a nice patient had given me a flower or small fruit tree or some kind of gift so I proceeded during the late after noon to the hospital for evening rounds. I parked in the hospital parking lot, went on in and made my rounds and after dark went on back home. I removed the plant and took it into my house. Elizabeth and the teen age kids were in the kitchen. They immediately announced "A POT PLANT!" I couldn't believe it, but they verified it was. They were really excited, but not me. As far as I knew nobody in my family ever did try this stuff, but they wanted to try smoking it so they pulled some leaves off and said they had to dry them in the oven. A couple of them made a couple of cigarettes and tried to smoke it. Elizabeth wanted to try it. I argued, but as many times before, I lost the argument, so she did take a couple of draws. Elizabeth had never smoked in her life, so nobody else had either, except me—cigarettes. She said she felt nothing, but I think she had already had a beer or two by then. It wound up in the garbage and was hauled off. The next day my good friend, and neighbor who was in the grove caretaking business, Jere Stambaugh called and asked how I enjoyed my plant. He said he found it growing in our 30 acres amid some groves, and he pulled it up and put it into my car as a joke. I felt very lucky that I wasn't stopped by a policeman for something, or one of the doctors didn't report me for trafficking in drugs.

Once in a while something would go wrong mechanically with a motor of one of my old cars, and John Denman could find what he needed to fix it. He would give me the name of the engine part that was needed. Occasionally, I had to go to some of these old car shows and auctions, where a lot of collectors had a flea market with pieces of the bodies, like fenders or doors, and buckets of parts, some new, but many old car necessities. I was able to kept most of them running with John Denman's help. I don't know if they have any of those kinds of shows any more. He came to see me one day as a patient. He was pale, jaundiced, and weak. Lab studies revealed an acute Leukemia, advanced. I sent him to a Tampa Cancer center. They tried to control the progressive illness but were unable to do much. After he died I had a hard time finding somebody who knew anything about these old vintage autos. I did find a couple of older men, but they were in Winter Haven and they got so feeble they quit working. I was left with only one running old car; the others needed more than I could provide—mechanical knowledge. They sat out in our back yard in the edge of our little grove.

One day Paul Braddock, a patient, and son of Lavonia and Paul Braddock, and brother of Bobby Braddock, noted country music musician, and song writer, came to me and wanted to buy all of my cars. I was delighted to give him the opportunity to own them all, for about $2500.00, as is.

I think in 1973 Dr. Bill Augspurger came by my office, we needed another physician in town, he and Diane and their 4 children wanted

to move to our town. They lived in Medina, Ohio and Diane's parents
lived in Lakeland. They were very nice people, and Bill was a good
family practitioner, so we decided that he would join me, we would
work together. I was in a 2 man office so there was plenty of room.
We worked together until about 1978, when Bill decided he wanted to
practice alone. He then moved his office over near Morrow Hospital
in Auburndale. Diane is a wonderful mother, a registered nurse, and a
great aid to him, his family, and his practice. We have remained close
friends all these years. He is retired now, also.

In 1976 for our country's bicentennial, we had planned a long road
trip for the kids with a motor home to go out west and see all the
national parks, for a month or so. We thought we needed to see how
we could handle a motor home for a week or so first. So in the summer of 1975, we rented a large motor home called a Condor, and
towed our boat, so we went to the Florida Keys to fish, swim and
catch lobsters and see how this kind of living would be. We had a
wonderful time going all the way down to Key West, sightseeing,
Hemingway's home, and all the things we should see. We started
back home on the old two lane 7 mile bridge. We lost power and the
Condor stopped in the north bound lane of the two lane bridge. The
door to the electrical stuff was on the right back side of the vehicle,
which when we stopped, was nearly against the wall of the bridge,
and the door couldn't be opened. We singularly and vehicularly
stopped traffic on that 2 lane road both toward the north and toward
the south until police were able to get out there and control traffic
both ways, alternating automobile lane movements. Then we had to
wait until a wrecker came, hooked us up and towed us to the first key
north that could help us get our vehicle on the road. It took all day.
We finally made it and concluded we could do this for long term trip
with the six kids, and two adult's determinations.

With this behind us, Elizabeth planned a trip that moment by
moment, if we could do it, could accomplish our goal within 4 weeks,
what nobody else could accomplish in 8 weeks. Her plans were so
precise and detailed that by 2 o'clock on 3 days from now we could
be driving up to the site she had planned for us to see at that time, on
that date.

You might think that the experience of getting stuck on a 7 mile
bridge on a 2 lane busy highway in a huge motor home, with 6 kids
for hours in hot steamy weather with no air conditioner would deter
most reasonably thinking people from attempting another even bigger
exciting experience. BUT NO-O-O-o-o! We continued to plan. My

wife obtained from AAA a library of all states, all maps for all states, and all sights and interesting places, and National Parks, and ways to connect the roads to get there, along with driving times and put all together, with maps, and marks on them to follow. This conglomeration wound up being the most comprehensive excursion, with time-tables, food planning, sleeping planning, and driving planning anybody ever put together for a leisurely vacation trip for a family of 8. A mama, a daddy, 5 boys, from 8 to 20 years old, and one 15 year old girl (who of course didn't want to be along anyway) with one of the boys bringing along his French Horn to be able to continue practicing his tone, 4 hours a day, using his 30 odd French horn mouth pieces, trying to find the perfect one for him. Another kid brought along his guitar. The daughter brought about a hundred books with her so she didn't have to engage with the family. General Dwight Eisenhower had less information for the invasion of Europe than we had for our trip.

We got away early one morning in August 1976, going north. We did fine until about 2 hours into the trip, the air conditioner quit. We stopped in Gainesville, Florida, they worked on it a while, told us the part we needed had to be ordered, and would be here tomorrow. We decided to forget it and go on. In Alabama the motor that ran the refrigerator quit late in the afternoon- we went on. No time to stop for frivolous stuff. We had deadlines to make! Find camp grounds—horn practicing. I would get up real early, start driving with everybody still sleeping. Stopping at several places, the mechanics thought they had fixed our problems. Off we went, happy all was fine, but before long the air and refrigerator both quit working again. This went on the next few days, so we finally gave up trying to get them fixed.

We went into Missouri to Charleston where I was born and lived in my early childhood. We went to my old house. Somebody else lived there! But they did agree for us to walk through the house. It had been changed a little, but I enjoyed old memories.

We went to St. Louis, then west to Kansas City where my cousin Rachel lived. We saw her and stayed a couple of days while we tried again to get our motor home fixed. They had it the whole time said the air conditioning and refrigerator were fixed, but after another attempt at having a nice trip, they quit working again. We had to go on, we were way behind! We went to the top of Pike's Peak. David 8 years old, and I got altitude sickness-weak, nausea-and felt bad. Mom and the other kids hopped around the stony top, shrieking with delight at the snow. We left the area, took off on our trip again and we got better down at a lower altitude.

We went to the Grand Canyon, got out and looked at the magnificence of it all. When we were there Mary stayed in the back of the vehicle reading. Mom went in and MADE her get out and look at the canyon. Mary walked up to the rim of the canyon—took one look and said "Very Nice!" turned and went back inside to continue her reading. She now has a daughter- we will remind Mary of that when HER daughter is 15years old!

We toured all the National Parks in the west, and ended up at Mount Rainier. I was driving, so I would set my clock for 4 o'clock AM, and get the motor home going before anybody got up so we could make better time. While driving up the mountain to the end of the road where the Lodge at Mt. Rainier is, they yelled to stop so they could see things. I pulled over to the side of the road and everybody got up to get out to look at the scenery. I turned the motor off, started to get up and the huge Condor motor home started to drift back a little, so I jammed the gearshift into "Park" and there was a loud POP, and it continued to drift. I quickly used my foot brake, and found out I didn't have a "park" gear anymore! I guess I broke it jamming it into park gear while the vehicle was moving. We had no working hand brake when we left on the trip. The only way we had to park the thing is stop the engine and put the gear into reverse, or we had to drift into something to park. It could have popped out of gear and drifted, but never did.

We continued up the mountain, and our speed was quite slow, because of the incline and the traffic on that 2 lane road up to the top. We of course accumulated a line of cars behind this big motor home, and we finally reached the top area. There was a large parking lot for the Lodge, and sightseers, looking at Mt. Rainier. We pulled up in the middle of the large lot and the car behind me stopped right behind me. An older gentleman got out of that car and marched right up to our door, and I went to the door and greeted a very upset citizen, fuming and very angry. He said "We traveled all the way up this mountain behind your vehicle and my wife and I do not appreciate your children mooning us all the way up here! You need to control them better than that!" I had no idea—- but I profusely apologized to him and told him how sorry I was that had happened. He stalked off and we had some words with the culprits, but also a good laugh.

We had to find a chock to put in front of, or behind our wheels. A Ranger helped us secure the vehicle for the night. We checked into the Lodge and everyone had a good nights sleep. We were allowed to keep our vehicle in the lot overnight. Everyone else had to move the cars out of the big lot. The next morning the sun was up and the weather was clear, and there was Mount Rainier in all it's glory. Mom and the kids climbed up the snowy trail as far as they felt safe. And I watched. They were thrilled. Looking south, they could see Mount Saint Helens, Mount Adams, and Mount Hood. The kids built their first snowman by the motor home.

From here on we were very careful driving, because of our brake problem and hoped we would make it home across the U.S. We went east from here to Yellowstone National Park, through the Bad Lands of the Dakotas, and saw Mount Rushmore, the Devil's Tower, and went on to Chicago, Illinois.

We stopped at the Field Museum of Natural History. They have a huge parking lot and while we were in the museum enjoying all of their marvelous items, we had a burglary of our Condor. A window was easily jimmied open, and some one entered and stole my Browning 12 gauge shotgun, and my little small .22 pistol. John lost a diver's watch, and Mom lost a long distance photo lens. When we returned to our vehicle and recognized we'd been robbed we called the police. They came and took detailed information, and told us they weren't criminals, only opportunists. We were shocked at their attitude. They told us we had very little chance of ever recovering anything we lost. Up until now, they were right.

We started home meandering south, through a lot of states until we finally reached our Home Sweet Home. We did have an educational, exciting and wonderful time of family closeness, and learned a lot about each other and it brought us even closer together as a family. Even Mary has fond memories of that trip now at the age of 47.

In 1977, September 30, Friday night we had a football game. My brother Maurice called and told me Daddy died that afternoon.

We had been to Quitman the weekend before this. Daddy was pretty weak and was under the care of his doctor for chronic heart failure. I felt like he needed to be in the hospital then so I called his Dr. and he admitted him that afternoon, Sunday, before we left to come back home.

I asked Daddy if he and Mama had cemetery lots there in Quitman. He said, "Well, we used to have those years ago, but your mother made me sell them, because she thought we'd never need them, but it's probably time to get them again." I said I was going down the street to "Bummy" Maxwell's funeral home who was in charge of selling the lots for the city, and buy some. Mama piped up and said, "Now, Paul, your Daddy is not going to need them, just don't bother." I politely told her I was going to do it anyway, so she wouldn't have to worry about it when the time comes. She just grunted.

I asked Daddy if he had any place in the cemetery that he would like to be, when the time comes. He said, "Oh, it doesn't matter, just so it's a dry place, and there are friends and decent folks around." So I went 3 doors down the street where the funeral home is, took "Bummy" out to the cemetery, and we found 4 lots side by side, with several of Daddy's friends, Mr. and Mrs. Glausier whom I worked for years ago in his drug store, Bill McMichael, one of Daddy's old golfing buddies, and several other old friends close by. Daddy seemed happy when I listed his friends and acquaintances that would be around him. (Mother lived another 12 years and died after a broken hip, that wasn't operable, at the age of 90 in 1989).The day Daddy died day was his 89th birthday, Terry's birthday, and Terry's son, Terry, Jr's birthday.

I told Elizabeth we need to go to my home in Quitman, Georgia now and not go to the game. She hemmed and hawed around trying to get me to go to the game. I kept refusing. And she finally told me I was to be honored at the halftime of the game by the State High School Athletic Association as a surprise, for being the Auburndale football physician for the last 20+ years, or so. So we decided to stay for this honor.

The president of that association made a little speech, at halftime, gave me a plaque, and I thanked them and made up a little speech thanking them for this unexpected honor, and everybody yelled and hollered, and they were happy and I was happy. I continued as the football doctor until I retired from office practice on December 31, 1995, 40 wonderful, exciting years. At games away, I either drove my car or tried to get to the school before the team left in their school buses, so I could ride to the game and back with the boys. I attended almost all of the away games, and almost all of the home games. For the home games I couldn't attend, I would ask one of my doctor friends to come over and be on the field. It was expected the home team have a doctor on the field in case the visiting team didn't bring their doctor with them.

After Daddy died and we were going through some things we found old X-rays of Daddy's spine that had diagnosed his arthritis back in Charleston in the early 1930s. Maurice, my brother who had become a Radiologist, looked at the films and announced that the changes that had been thought to be arthritic were in fact due to tuber-culosis of the spine. I mentioned Daddy's father had died of TB in his 50s. Terry and I both had to have TB skin tests, as every entering medical student had to take at the beginning, and again after finishing school. We both were negative before entering, and we both were positive at the end of our 4$^{th}$ year. We had been exposed to TB, during school but never contracted active disease. Daddy never had pulmo-nary TB, so we kids never contracted it, Daddy contracted systemic TB that settled in his spine, left little finger, and his right heel, which made him symptomatic, and was thought to be due to arthritis by his doctor who read the films in the 1930's. The tuberculosis spinal arthritis appearing changes is extra-pulmonary tubercular disease, which is now known as Pott's Disease. Probably this condition has been identified and named after the 1930's. His disease over many years was no longer active.

Elizabeth's father died in1969, and after Granny sold her home she moved in with us in our new big home. There was grove behind our home belonging to Jere Stambaugh, Senior. We talked to him about selling us a strip of his grove behind our new home so we could pro-tect our back from new homes that someone might want to build. He agreed to sell us a strip about 160 feet deep running from Tecumseh down to the back line of the home facing Osceola Ave. This gave us about 300 feet on our back road and about 160 feet deep. Granny decided she wanted to build herself a new home, so we sold her a lot and Elizabeth drew plans, and had a carpenter contract and build her new home. It was beautiful and well planned, and she was really happy. She spent summers in her cottage on Anna Maria Island, on the corner of Gulf Boulevard and Sycamore Drive, and rented it through a realtor during the winter. As the years went by, the kids would go visit her, and we all really enjoyed the quiet, solitude, and peaceful visits at Granny's cottage. She had so many friends there, people loved Granny. She was such a sweet, gregarious, helpful indi-vidual. Her neighbors all came to her home visiting her.

In Auburndale, every Sunday night we had dinner at our house, grilling, or Mom's cooking, and Granny would always bring a beauti-ful, delicious pie, or cake, or cookies for dessert. Everybody was always waiting for Granny's dessert.

Our next door neighbor Leon and Verle Wamsley, were especially good to her. She was always calling Leon to come to her house to fix something, which he always was happy to do. One time she called him to come over to help her with her vacuum cleaner. When he arrived, he found the vacuum in pieces all over the floor. She had laboriously dissembled it trying to fix it. Believe it or not he fixed it and got it all back together and working. Each time he came over to help her she would bake him one of her wonderful apple pies. She was the champion pie-maker.

She went to Realtor School, and became a realtor in her late 60's on into her late 80's. She was hired by a real estate company in Winter Haven, and made a whole set of new business friends, like Wilma and Greg Gregory, and sold several homes. Granny was quite an accomplished artist; she studied art at Bucknell University in Lewisburg, Pennsylvania, and an art school in Sarasota, Florida. Her beautiful oil paintings grace our home and her grandchildren's homes. Granny lived a full life, very involved in our and our children's lives. She died in 2002 at the age of 95. We continue to really miss her.

Elizabeth's sister, Helen married James Glass, son of Hulda and James Glass, of Winter Haven, Florida. Jim is an attorney in Miami. Florida. They had 2 boys Clinton, and Gregory.

My brother Terry and wife Lynn had three children, Terry, Jr., Gregory, who died at age about 3 with a Wilm's renal tumor, and daughter Rebecca. My brother Terry was born on Daddy's birthday, and his son Terry, Jr. was also born on the same day, September 30, and our Daddy died on the same day.

My other brother Maurice and wife Peggy had 3 children, Jennifer, Christopher, and Kathryn (Katie). He practiced Radiology in Tallahassee, Florida and later in Thomasville, Georgia.

General James Van Fleet, grew up in this area, attended West Point, and became a well known hero of World War II. He was part of the European D-day Invasion in France, and later active in the Korean War. After his retirement, he had a large home 6-7 miles north of Polk City, Fla. a small town some 10 miles north of Auburndale, on a very large amount of country acreage. His sister Mattie Dickey, a former school teacher, lived in Auburndale. She was my patient, and a member of our church. She was a delightful, sweet elderly lady. She died some time before the general came back and stayed here much of the time.

I saw Four Star General Van Fleet several times in my office over the years for checkups after his retirement, and before he would go to Walter Reed Hospital, where the Army Retired Officers had their regular Doctors, for their annual checkups. I think he wanted them to know he was taking care of himself, and wanted a pat on the head from me that he had been a good patient before he returned. He was in his late 80s and into his 90s when I was seeing him. He was generally a very active and healthy man. On his return he would usually bring a letter from his military doctor to me. It would just thank me for following him and taking such good care of him while he was in Florida.

Mrs. Van Fleet, the general's wife, was a very feeble, cooperative, wheel-chair bound lady, overweight and had chronic congestive heart failure, and for the most part we were able to keep it under pretty good control. She stayed in their home about 17 miles north of my town. The General would occasionally call and ask me to ride up there and check her over for one thing after another, mostly to regulate her cardiac medicines. On those visits, I had the opportunity to go with him through the separate house he had built to keep his war mementoes and gifts from some of the world leaders at that time. Much of it was from Korea's leader. I don't know who that was, but the General told me. I should have written it all down. It was a real museum. He would always give me a story about where these things came from, and the people who gave it to him. I'm sorry I didn't pay more attention and make some notes.

He was hell-bent to take his wife on another cruise to the Bahamas Islands. She had enjoyed that so much some time ago. She was at that time in her 80s, and she had asked him several times to take her again on a cruise. He contacted all of his family and their families, got the reservations, took them all to Fort Lauderdale, and they all boarded, and sailed to the Bahamas. They were gone about week or so. On the trip back home Mrs. Van Fleet became ill, and on the last day she died on the ship.

Later he told me that was the best thing he could have done for her. She was so happy on that trip. He mentioned it to me several times over the next few years how glad he was that he did that for her.

After a year or so he remarried, a former secretary, she was in her 70s, and he was in his early 90s. He brought her in to see me for a check up, and we found a small marble size nodule in her breast. I immediately told them I thought it was malignant, and got a mammogram, the report which agreed that it probably was cancerous. I sent her to Dr. Zeller, who recommended radical surgery, and I agreed with him and told the General and his wife. They decided to go back to her home. I think Philadelphia, where they might find it only needed less radical treatment.

They went, they got less radical surgery, a "lumpectomy" and after her healing came back here. It was diagnosed as malignant. A year or so later, she got up in the middle of the night, was going down stairs, in the home out in the country, and collapsed on the top step and fell down 12-15 steps to the bottom. The General called me, I called an ambulance, admitted her to the hospital, got neurological consults and she apparently had a rather massive stroke with no cerebral surgery possible. She had also fractured an ankle. She came into the hospital in a coma, and days later absolutely no change occurred in her condition.

We then were faced with a vegetative state and set about giving her intravenous feedings, later a gastric tube to feed her as best we could. The General was very upset about her condition, but gave us no suggestions as to her future care. I think he was allowing her daughter to call the shots.

Her daughter came down to see her mother; we had a consultation with her about future care, deciding to continue what we were doing. When nothing was changing, the body wasting was becoming apparent, the daughter decided she would like to slowly diminish the intake and allow her mother to die peacefully. I agreed, and began slowly cutting back on all therapy, which was only supportive, fluids, amino acids, vitamins, minerals and oxygen.

After her mother began to look obviously more dehydrated, and less tissue mass she suddenly said she couldn't stand to see her mother like that, and wanted to start more fluids, and vitamin intake. We did as she wished. As days moved into weeks, no neurological change, good or bad, she finally wanted us to repeat the decreasing of fluids and support. This time was the last, and she died peacefully.

The daughter thanked me, and understood what doctors' and patients' families go through with this kind of tragedy. I had a few of these kinds of unmanageable situations, mostly managed with me and with the involvement of their family in agreement the entire way, with slow and methodical decisions.

The General died several years later at 100 years old. I really appreciated my contact and getting to really know this wonderful gentleman. I feel honored and proud that he allowed me to treat him and his family. I'll never forget the 17 mile trip to go on house calls to his home. About 7 miles north of Polk City, a road goes off to the right. Down that road some 2-3 miles is a farm house on the left. The farm is surrounded by fencing, with a gate, closed, at the house. This was the home of the General's farm manager. They had to open the gate to allow me in.

Then riding down into the farm on a winding small dirt road, through pine forests, then through orange groves, and sand dunes, and cattle, I came to a wide open vast scrub open area with a view of several buildings and a large 2 story home, beside a small, but beautiful lake, the General's home, about 2 miles from the gate. Once riding along in the pine forest, at a corner I had to follow the road to the right. That corner was covered with wild turkeys, probably 30-40 of them. Hens and gobblers were unconcerned about me riding slowly by. I never saw that many beautiful turkeys in my life. I saw a few coveys of quail, and doves flying. The general protected the game on his property of some few thousand acres up there in the country.

He had several groves in Auburndale, most of which were on or close to a lake. Before he died he began to develop one not far from, and behind our home, on Lake Arietta, the next lake just north of us. I talked to him about a lot on that lake, but he had quite a price on the lake front lots. He offered me one at a little less, and offered to finance it. Trying to finance college for 6 kids left no room to handle big time real estate. However, the prices did soar, but who's going to know?

I want to tell you about my wonderful office employees. Dr. Whitehurst left after 6 months of allowing Terry and me to get involved in our practices with him. We had one receptionist working, Lou Ellen Headley, a senior high school student who was quite competent, and a middle-aged male lab technician, whose name I have forgotten.

We hired a lady to help us with patients, Mrs. Eldine Reddick, married with two boys in our local school. She had some office experience learned in a Clearwater, Florida doctor's office before moving to Auburndale. She was very competent in helping us with whatever we needed help with, shots, suturing, casting fractures, and etc. I had learned how to take x-rays and we were ready to continue on our own. She worked with me about 7 years and was marvelous help.

My charts in the early days were quick and to the point. A large yellow firm page with lines on it would come in with the patient with their name, address, phone number if they had one, and what they had wrong. In the beginning I would do my history and physical exam like I was taught in medical school. They were long drawn out and complete. Chief Complaint, Family History, Past Medical History, Present History, Physical Examination, etc.

It was obvious after a lot of these time consuming patient encounters, that I couldn't spend that much time with every patient. I was writing it all down at the interview, so gradually it became shorter and shorter. It got to be ridiculous at the brevity that I was charting. I wound up–like—"Johnny Jones (address-phone number) Sore throat. Red throat. Penicillin. Return 1 week." I went through a pretty good exam of head and neck, lungs, heart, abdomen, but didn't write it all down. I was comfortable with my evaluation and conclusion and treatment but I wasn't happy not having it all down.

I decided to buy a dictation machine and I used that after hours and dictated with the charts for the day in front of me. The next morning Mrs. Reddick would come in early, and listen to the dictation and hand write it down on each chart. That went on a while until she couldn't finish all the dictation before new patients came in for the day. So I hired a new person to do the typing. She had to know and how to spell medical terms.

Then I went to hand held new fangled dictation equipment and dictated on the way to the hospital looking at my charts I had with me in the car. The next day they put the little tape in the machine and it was typed in the chart. It wasn't long that the hospital and office records had to be complete, and all the positive information and findings, and negative information and findings had to be included in the patient's charts, both in the hospital and in the office. That was the only way that legal protection could be complete. Charts have become voluminous now, and must be extremely accurate.

Terry had gone after 18 months or so, and I was really busy. Betsy, another student came to work for me, after a while married Clayton Grant, and left. She became an registered nurse and they moved to Louisiana, I think. Our first lab technician left and Bill Masters came in as our new technician. He helped me draw blood from the football players to prove to Coach Tom Terry that they needed my concoction during the games to keep from becoming dehydrated. Diluted orange juice and some salt, and they were told to drink it during the game. Bill's wife Norma Masters, a registered nurse, came to work for several years. Another high school student, Carol who later married Tullie Stokes, was a very good helper in my office who later went to work at a large trucking company Comcar, started by Mr. Guy Bostick not long before we came to town. She continued working there for years, and continues to be a good friend.

In early 1960's Joyce Deese, married to Otis, a Police officer for Auburndale, became a licensed practical nurse working in my office. She was a wonderful, competent, smart, personable and helpful nurse for me in my office. My patients loved her and complimented me on her work. She helped me in every facet of my practice. She was eager to learn anything I asked her to learn, even to take x-rays, and assist in any office surgery I performed, or application of casts for fractures.

During her 24 years in my office one evening after we closed and all my employees were gone I received a phone call. It was from a person who knew Otis and they said he had died of a heart attack. I immediately locked the office, and went to Kersey Funeral Home where the body was supposed to be. It was dark, some 7-8 o'clock. At the large 2 story late 1800 Victorian home no lights were on, so I walked up to the side porch intending to go in the side door where the bodies were taken. There was a large, about 6 feet long, 1 foot square cement step placed beside the porch to step onto the porch, and I was going to go up and knock on the side door where I thought Walter Kersey was no doubt in there preparing Otis's body. I placed my left foot on the foot high step and placed my right foot in the air on the way to the porch, and my left foot plunged to the ground forcefully turning my left ankle as I was moving forward to land on my belly on Walter's porch.

I had apparently placed my left foot on the edge of the end of the cement step. There was immediate left ankle severe pain requiring conversations with the gods, and whoever else was listening, because the thud of my body landing on my belly on the wooden floor of the porch and me flopping around, and my writhing and wiggling and other sounds should have been heard around the neighborhood, especially after I called out for Walter several times, and beat on the porch floor to raise somebody. There was no response, and I was aware of no other sound in the quiet neighborhood, so in my embarrassment I elected to suffer quietly and prolonged, until finally I decided to diagnose my left ankle fracture. I carefully sat up, slowly ran my hand over my rapidly swelling left ankle and palpated for the crepitation, indicating the fractured fragments in the injured area. To my amazement I felt no crepitation, only the rapidly developing swelling. I surmised that there was no fracture and I had to get to my car and get home. Otis could wait until tomorrow. I slowly and painfully limped to my car, and drove my huge throbbing left ankle back to my office, struggled in and got an ace bandage and wrapped the ankle, got back in the car and went home, a little later than I usually got home. With difficulty I got in the house and related to my wife, who had already yelled "where have you been, help me get these kids to bed and say their prayers." Anyway, the next morning I found out that the death was not Otis's, somebody had made a mistake in the identification. I spent a week or so on crutches, and then another couple of weeks with a cane.

However, it wasn't too much longer that Otis did die of a coronary occlusion. He had suffered with heart disease and a few heart attacks for some time before he died. A few years later Joyce remarried, to Jerry Prochaska. I continue to have a place in my heart for Joyce.

During the 24 great years Joyce was with me we had several wonderful ladies who worked in my office. I will name these ladies because I loved, and still do love them all, for their assistance and support in managing my practice. Mrs. Evelyn Jordon worked in the office, and then her daughter Gail came in. They were wonderful patients, and I believe I treated Evelyn's grandmother, mother and father, her daughter and two sons, then her grandchildren, and maybe a great grandchild, just wonderful good people. Marci Kirkland worked in my laboratory, and was a fine, helpful, competent technician.

I cannot place dates or times of their employment, but I need to recognize all I can remember: Betty O'Neal a nurse, Carolyn Merritt a receptionist, wife of Joe Merritt whose mother and father were my patients from my beginning in Auburndale; Jenny Merritt, nurse, no kin to Carolyn and Joe; Jo Ann Hope, who lost a husband due to advanced emphysema, had 4 boys; Donna Warren, nurse; and receptionist Betty Ashby, a middle aged, hard working, conscientious single mother with an unforgettable nasal "sing-songy" voice, recognized all over town.

In 1986 the Bond Clinic bought my office and practice. From then on I had nothing to do with operating the office, hiring and firing, or anything except practice my love- Family Medicine. There were new nurses and typists and office workers that were sent over to work and some of my former employees were sent over to the big clinic. I can't remember the names of those that came over because some were there 1 day, some off and on, but they were very competent and helpful and seemed to enjoy working with me. The Bond Clinic had been recruiting Family Doctors for the Clinic, and shortly after they purchased my office and practice they brought in another new family physician, Dr. Lucy Ertenburg to join me in my 2 doctor office. She was a wonderful, pleasant, and extremely capable physician and my patients loved her. She was married with a family and we got along fine together. They moved her to the big clinic in Winter Haven some time later, and I was alone again. We remain good friends at the present time.

There was only two times I ever fired anybody. One of my office workers was young and came to me and said she had to go out of town for a week to another state on a family matter. I gave her permission but at the time it put us in a bind to have the necessary people. During the week she was out of town, one of my office girls saw here at a night club in town with a man. I was informed, and fired her for lying to me. She applied for unemployment pay and I rejected it and wrote a letter to dispute her claim. She did not get paid. The other was a young female lab technician who did the lab exam, a urinalysis on a patient I was seeing for acute cystitis. She reported the urine as clear and negative. I had the patient get another specimen, and ran it myself. It was obviously full of leucocytes (pus) under the microscope, because her problem was acute cystitis, a urinary tract infection. The technician had obviously not even looked at it under the microscope. I sent the tech home. There's no way I could rely on her laboratory reports.

One day one of my patients came in and talked to me about a sound she had been hearing in her head for several months. She localized the area in the left temple and parietal area of her head. I put my stethoscope to the area and could hear a bruit as the blood ran through the vessels. I was worried about the sound possibly indicating some narrowing in a vessel in her brain and waiting for an atherosclerotic plaque in a cerebral vessel breaking off and occluding the vessel and causing a stroke. I sent her to one of the neurological surgeons in Winter Haven. After her appointment and his evaluation, he apparently made arrangements to send her to a neurosurgeon at the medical school at the University of Florida in Gainesville, Florida. She went and was scheduled for surgery. It so happened that Elizabeth and I had some reason to be in the Gainesville area so we went to see her in the hospital that weekend. She was scheduled for surgery the next week.

During our visit with her I asked about the surgery and she said the doctor said he would have to find the source at surgery. I had my stethoscope with me so I listened again, located the bruit again and noticed when I had her turn her head one way the bruit seemed almost to disappear, and turning another way it was more evident. I thought maybe it is outside the skull, not intracranial. I occluded the facial artery at the notch right in front of the angle of the mandible and the bruit disappeared completely, no matter what position her head was turned. That artery continues up in front of the ear to form the temporal artery and probably a branch back into the parietal scalp area. At any rate, this proved to me that this was external to the brain and in the scalp probably, and the doctor needed to know that before surgery. Maybe it isn't necessary to operate at all. So I called the nurse, and told her that she needed to notify the surgeon before surgery. She apparently did and my patient was sent home and no surgery was done. I probably should have been a little more specific in my original evaluation, rather than jump to conclusions before referral. I thought this was a cut and dried neurosurgical problem at the time I referred her. I understand she is still around and never had a stroke, so far. I wish her continued good health.

One Sunday during this time period I receive a call at home from a distraught individual wanting me to go up to a lake several miles north of Polk City in the country, where a family was having a cook out and swimming party. Apparently a child had drowned and they wanted me to come up and see what I could do to save him. He was in the water only 10 minutes or so when they found him. The lake was foreign to me but I had directions, so I took off to get there as fast as I could. Polk City is 10 miles north of Auburndale and the lake is 3-4 miles further and off the highway a couple of miles. It took me about 45 minutes of rather fast driving, with some good directions, to finally make it there. There were 15 to 20 people there on the sandy side of a rather small lake, a burning grill, ice chests, beer bottles, cookies, candy wrappers, cokes, everybody just quiet, standing, arms folded, some comforting others, waiting to hear what they all knew.

People all around the poor little boy, 7 to 8 years old, people fanning him, shaking his head, pushing on his back, and he was lying on his stomach like they used to do to get water out of their lungs. I turned him over, looked at his dilated fixed pupils, listened to his heart and lungs, needlessly but doing what I thought they wanted to see, before I gave them the inevitable news. "He's gone—I'm sorry." The mother and father were of course taking all of this very hard, and words don't really help a lot at times like this. I just hugged them both and didn't say much. They knew that I knew how they felt, and they knew how I felt. Many of these people were my patients.

One of the football coaches came in worried about being bitten by a rattlesnake. He said he was hunting dove that morning, and the group had just come to the field, and was spreading out to find their spots to sit and wait for the doves to fly in. He was walking, stepping over clods of dirt and large bunches of grass. As he stepped over one a large rattlesnake struck his booted heel and got his large mouth stuck on the boot with the fangs into the leather boot. The coach lost his

balance and fell to the ground with the writhing large snake attached
to his heel. He positioned his foot so he could shoot the snake behind
its head and killed it. He felt stinging on his heel, so he quickly
removed the boot and noticed two scratches on the heel from the
fangs. There was no penetration of his skin, only scratches. He said
he poured about a tablespoonful of the venom from inside the boot.
He had already washed the area, but I repeated it. He was a very lucky
young man.

Another time a patient, Mel Taylor one of our local pharmacists
who was hunting south of here in the area of Frostproof, Florida,
called on the phone very excited and upset stating he was in a field
walking, hunting quail, and was struck by what he said was a rattlesnake, on his right knee above his knee- high boots. He wanted me to
arrange to admit him to Morrow Memorial Hospital and met him
there with snake venom. He was leaving the filling station he called
from and would be there as soon as he could. It took him about and
hour to get to the hospital. When we checked him, we found only a
superficial scratch on the knee, no fang penetration marks. No anti-
venom was necessary, but he insisted on staying overnight in the hospital. We scrubbed it and dressed his little scratch. He was fine the
next morning and was discharged. I was very happy neither of my
snakebites turned out to be serious problems.

Another sprained ankle episode happened to me behind our big
house one dark night, when I came home late from the hospital. I
parked my car got out and was walking to the house, there is a paved
road and the side of the road is sandy and soft and the pavement is 3
to 4 inches higher than the sand. With the same left foot stepping on
the pavement in the dark, and slipping off the pavement with my
weight on the foot as it hit the ground turning my ankle. I was suddenly on the ground, writhing in pain, yelling for a family member,
into a big house with lights in every window, music and television on,
and nobody listening for me. As I lay there in pain and misery the
sand, I thought I would write for help in the sand. I wrote with my finger in the sand a big word—H-E-L-P!! No body came so I finally got
up, hobbled into the house and took my wife out to show her my sign,
and told her she needed to pay attention. Again I was several weeks
on a cane.

1983: Our beautiful children at Anna Maria, Florida. From left to right: Paul Alexander III, 27; Mark Andrew, 19; Mary Elizabeth, 22; James Henry, 21; John Matthew, 23; David Michael, 15.

# 7

# Every Parent's Worst Nightmare

In 1974 our first child, Paul 3$^{rd}$, graduated from high school and left home to go to college. David Michael Tanner our last child was in the first grade, age 6 years old. He went to Elizabeth stating he was very sad to be the youngest child and told her he was going to be really lonely when all of his brothers and sister go off to college leaving him all alone at home. This was Paul's first year in college at University of Florida. David was very perceptive about that future time. He grew up, as all his siblings did, loving their brothers and sisters and it continues today.

As David grew and through his time in school he excelled in academics, school plays and band. He was one of the outstanding students in high school and all the other students became his friend. He was an A student, earned the First Chair Trumpet in the band, standing in front of the marching band playing the solos needed, at the football games. A number of his friends were older, and in classes ahead of him.

In the spring of 1984, at age 16, he was in the school production of "Grease." He played a couple of parts in the play. One was that of "Teen Angel." He was 6 feet, blond, good physique, dressed in only white dancer's tights, and no shirt but 3 or 4 long gold colored chains around his neck. He was lowered slowly from the ceiling standing on a swing, onto the stage while singing the song "Teen Angel." He was quite a sight, among all the cheers of his boy and girl friends.

On the first weekend in November, 1984, there was no football game for the Auburndale Bloodhounds, so the band didn't have to play, and most of them went to the home of a friend on Friday night in Lake Alfred, Florida, some 3-4 miles east of Auburndale to have a party. The parents were not at home. We were not aware of these plans. Lake Alfred high school students come to school in Auburndale, and that was one of their classmate's homes. David was supposed to be home at 11:00 PM. As I laid my head on my pillow, about 12:00AM, to go to sleep, the phone rang. A male voice said "Dr. Tanner?" I said "Yes." He said "This is State Patrolman (somebody), I'm at the Winter Haven Hospital Emergency Room and there's been an accident. You need to come over here right now, but drive carefully." I said "David," he said "Yes." I said "is he hurt"? He said "I know you're a doctor, but I can't tell you any more, just come on over now." I said "OK."

I told Elizabeth it was David, an accident, and I know he's dead because I knew the officer would tell me if he was injured. We both got in the car with Paul, our oldest son back home again, and went to the Winter Haven Hospital Emergency Room. David died immediately driving home, trying to get away from the boys and girls that had to wake him from a drunken sleep when his wrist watch alarm went off at 11 PM, and tried to stop him from getting in his car and driving home.

This was probably the most devastating thing that we ever had happen to us. How can a person deal with such a blow, to lose a child due to such bad decisions that you think are impossible for a bright kid to make. After the fact we were able to talk to some of his friends who told us about the night at the party.

When David was awakened from sleeping on the living room sofa because his wrist watch alarm went off, he jumped up and found Larry, the friend he had picked up in his car and brought to the party and they both got in his car to leave. Several boys tried to stop him, but David rolled the window up on the fingers of a boy trying to get his keys so he jerked his hand away. That boy told me he was so devastated because he could have jerked that window out if he tried, and gotten the keys. They drove away with three or four people getting in their cars, trying to catch David. The road to Auburndale was straight for a mile or so and then a 90 degree right turn, to go over railroad tracks. At the turn there is a large old oak tree at the end of the straight road. Many of his friends were right behind David when he crashed into that tree. They were extremely upset to have seen all of this. David had to have passed out because his car never braked. He drove straight into that tree, dying instantly. Larry suffered a head injury and a severe hip fracture. Larry fortunately recovered and later entered a military service band.

The coroner was a doctor friend of mine. David's autopsy revealed the fatal injuries to his brain, heart and lungs, liver, a compound fracture of the left leg. Externally to his face, the only visible injury was a rather severe abrasion to his left forehead. In the emergency room, he reeked of alcohol, we both bent over to kiss David goodbye, and Elizabeth jumped back and said "You're not in there, are you!" He wasn't anymore.

His blood alcohol was reported as 0.34. This is nearly a fatal blood level. Later we found a fake ID card, identifying him as a college student at Florida Southern College, in Lakeland, Florida, and grain alcohol that he had purchased before the party in the car.

I will now deviate from David's death and relate some after the fact episodes that convinces us that God had plans to help us deal with this part of our life.

First: About 2-3 years before this, my good friend Jack Summers and I were talking about a couple of our friend's deaths, Harlan Sutton and Jere Stambaugh. We felt like we needed to go to the city and buy our cemetery lots, and try to be as close to our friends graves as possible. So in time I made arrangements to meet with the manager of the lots in the cemetery. Jack had already gotten his for him and his wife Trish near Harlan. We went there and found a square of 8 lots together, near Harlan, Jere, and Jack. So I told the manager to mark them for me, and have the city clerk send me a bill. He said OK. I needed 8 because none of my 6 children were married. I could always sell if necessary.

I never thought of the grave sites again until the spring of 1984. I suddenly thought about the lots, and remembered I never got a bill from the city for the lots. I called, he verified they were still there and it was an oversight that I hadn't gotten a bill. I went right down to the city hall and paid for them.

Second: in 1981 Elizabeth and I became Amway distributors, sponsored by Jack and Karen Turner. Jack was an Auburndale Architect, who had planned and supervised the building of the football stadium at the high school among many other fine structures locally and state wide. I was on the building committee with Jack. We elected to become Distributors because I had had a heart attack, and it was obvious that with no practice there is no income. There was a possibility I could build a significant independent source of income with time

In early September of 1984 there was a big Amway meeting at the Omni in Atlanta. Prior to the large meeting we were able, by sales volume for a few months, to have our names put in a huge drawing for a trip to Kauai Island, one of the beautiful Hawaiian Islands. At that meeting there were about 15,000 distributors present. When the time came for the drawing, I asked Elizabeth if she wanted to go to Hawaii, she said "Of course" I said, "OK, were going to win these 2 weeks there."

Tom Payne pulled a card from those thousands of cards, and announced "Paul and Elizabeth Tanner." We had to go up on stage, and I was so excited, flabbergasted, and happy, I could not speak—only stutter and mumble "Thanks." Elizabeth talked a little for us. What a tremendous surprise. A couple of weeks later we had to select a time to go and tell them, so reservations could be made. We chose the last 2 weeks in November to include our wedding anniversary date, November 25.

Third: Jaap Wheelhower, our Presbyterian minister had a sermon on "Unbelieving," in late September 1984. I was really moved by that sermon, and asked Don Flentke, the young man that took care of taping the sermons for "shut ins," to please make an extra tape of the sermon for me, and he said "Sure" Two or three weeks later I asked him about the tape. He said he would find a copy for me. A few weeks more he was still looking for the tape. So I went to Jaap and asked him, he said "I'll give you a copy of my notes, I keep them all together in my notebook." In his study he pulled down the notebook from his shelves that my wife Elizabeth built for his library, and he looked all through it and couldn't find those notes. He was upset and didn't know where they were. He apologized and said he'd keep looking. I considered the tape lost and forgot about it.

Fourth: The weekend before he died, the last weekend in October David and his friend, Larry the friend in the accident, drove up to Jacksonville, Florida to see one of our sons, David's brother, John, and to attend a jazz concert with Woody Herman's big band. John was working there, and David and Larry stayed with him for the weekend. They really enjoyed the concert and had a wonderful weekend with John.

On Sunday when they were leaving John's house to come home, John stopped him on his porch and said "David, wait a minute let me take your picture so I can get this roll developed. I have only one picture left on the roll." That was the last picture of David ever taken and it was superb. David had on one of my golf shirts. We buried him in that shirt, and that picture is on his gravestone.

Fifth: On Thursday afternoon, the day before David died; he came to my office, and was in one of the back record rooms on one of our office typewriters. One of my nurses told me he was back there. When I got a minute I went back to see him, and ask what he was doing, he said "typing my English assignment." I asked what it was. He said "a story about a teenager driving without a seat belt. He lost control of his car and ran into a telephone pole and was killed. We had to write about seat belts." I said "Oh." I read it over his shoulder and noted one word misspelled. I corrected him and he fixed it and said "Thanks, Dad" I said "OK," see you later, and went back to work. He turned the paper in the next morning in English class. His teacher gave us that paper later.

Sixth: When we got home from the hospital, the night David died, and after greeting and trying to console the friends who had followed the ambulance to the hospital after the accident, we had to try to get into contact with his brothers and sister, and others who needed to know.

Our minister Jaap, wife Janet, 14 year old twin daughters Janet and Jean Wheelhower had gone to Tampa Bay area to spend the weekend on their boat. The boat had bunks for the family, and they docked there. Our good friend Jack Summers knew the telephone number of the place the boat was kept. He knew they would be up early to go out into Tampa Bay fishing. We called Jack, and told him of our tragedy, Jack said he would get Jaap. Jack found out no phone available at this early hour some one to two AM. So Jack called early next AM, found that Jaap had already gone out into Tampa Bay. The manager left the message on the dock for Jaap when he returned.

About 10AM Jaap called. He said they got up early, left the dock and went into Tampa Bay. Suddenly the wind started blowing, clouds came up. And they returned to the dock because of the bad weather and saw the note, and will be home tonight and will come over then. He did come over. He related that during the night before they went into Tampa Bay, the night David died, Jean awakened crying and terribly upset at a horrible dream she had. "David Tanner had died, cooking hamburgers, and burned up" They all had a hard time consoling Jean during the night.

Seventh: I could not talk, I was so distraught, my throat would tighten, and words wouldn't come out so you could understand me. I have never found the proper word to explain how I felt about the death of my youngest son. So many questions: So many whys, hows, "My son?" "Whose decisions?" "Drinking?" "What?" I just couldn't fathom or believe what happened. My last, my youngest son... I even thought I didn't want to or need to practice medicine anymore. He won't be needing us anymore. This was not the kind of thing my son of 16 would ever do. When Mark got home, he told his mother, Elizabeth, that when the brothers were 16, they too felt they were invincible.

Elizabeth had great stamina, and had great control and talked evenly and rationally. She called until early in the morning, and spoke to many people getting our kids home. She called John in Jacksonville, Florida. He was shocked, but was coming home. Mary was in college at the University of Colorado at Boulder, Colorado. Mary was advised to go to the airport in Denver, where Elizabeth had made arrangements for the kids to fly home. Mark was in Leadville, Colorado a student in college, living with a couple of guys and they had no phone. She called the local Police gave them Marks address to have him call home, that there was death in the family. The nearest phone was on a street several blocks away, and the snow was about a foot deep. Mark had to walk to the phone, Mom told him the sad news and to get to Denver to fly home.

James was in Glenwood Springs, Colorado seeing a college teacher girlfriend for the weekend. We had her name, but not her phone. We had the operator get the number. It turned out to be a lady, same name, wrong one; she didn't know the right one. Elizabeth called the local Chief of Police in Glenwood Springs; we knew where she taught, so the Police called the President of the college, got her address, then the Chief went to the address, met James and his girl friend coming down the porch steps to get in the car and go skiing early that morning, to be gone all day.

They all got to the Denver Airport on time and flew on the same plane home, and we picked them up at Tampa airport, came home, and met Jaap around our kitchen table near midnight Saturday night. He was of great comfort to us all. As you can notice, all the pieces had to fall in place for all these people to get here. My wonderful wife's calmness and tenacity arranged, with God's helping hand, for everything to work out perfectly to bring our family back together again. I was useless. Jaap had lost a small son due to being run over by a car in front of their home some years ago. He told us losing a child, or loved one is like an amputation. The healing occurs but part of you is always gone. That was comforting to us.

When we finished getting the kids lined up to come home, about 2 o'clock in the morning I called our good, good, friends Hank and Sandee Sytsma in Plant City, Florida, about 40 miles to our west. They were up-line distributers building and Independent Amway business, and we had become very close friends over the previous 3 years. Our living room and family rooms were filled with antique rugs, chests and tables, and other items we had collected. They were shocked like all of our friends about David's death, and insisted coming over to help move the stuff to other rooms and clean the rooms so visitors that we expected to be coming to our home in the morning could at least sit down. They got up out of bed, drove to our home 40 miles, came in and moved all of the excess collections to other areas of our home, making our home presentable for all of David's and our friends. We can never express the love and support Hank and Sandee gave us during that miserable, trying and unpredictable time. They are still among our best friends and we will continue to love them.

Eighth: Saturday, the morning after the accident, I was in my bed crying, Elizabeth was trying to consol me, I was talking about losing a child and the grief, so hard to bear. She mentioned that we have lost only one son. God lost his ONLY son. I don't know why but that was some kind of relief of my feelings. I opened the Good News Bible by my bed, and it fell open at the 18th Psalm. I couldn't believe the title, "David's Song of Victory." David has to be in Heaven now.

Ninth: Saturday AM, people started coming to our home, I had a terrible time greeting, grinning, responding to people asking questions, trying to get me to talk, and I couldn't. I learned the ones that just hugged me tight, no questions or talk, made me feel better without me feeling like I needed to entertain them. I knew their hurt for me was real, and I knew they knew. I appreciated them coming. Now when I go to other grieving people, I need to just hug them. If they want to talk, they'll talk.

The band was supposed to go to Fort Myers, Florida for a Marching Band Contest with a lot of bands that Saturday. The band director Jimmy Parker, the School Principal whose name I forgot, and Polk County School Superintendent, John Stewart, a former Auburndale High School Principal and a friend of mine, came to our home, and mentioned it to us. They had planned to cancel the bands trip. We insisted that they continue their plans, go ahead and do what had been planned. Go to the contest, and don't disappoint the grieving band members. David's and Larry's planned solos where handled by other members, and the Band succeeded in winning first place. They had gone, and dedicated their performance to David and Larry, and were extremely proud, despite the night of tremendous sadness and grieving. None of the other bands were aware of the stress that the Bloodhound Imperial Band members were performing under.

David's accident occurred sometime after 11PM. It took time to get the ambulance there, cut him out of the wrecked car, and take him to Winter Haven Hospital. I think he was pronounced dead by the doctor after 12 midnight, which was Nov. 3$^{rd}$, exactly 2 months before his 17$^{th}$ birthday, Jan. 3$^{rd}$. Our planning was for the funeral to be the next Tuesday, in our Presbyterian Church, after school was out.

The burial was to follow in the Auburndale Memorial Cemetery in the grave we had purchased a few years before. Following the burial we were planning a time of Celebration of David's life in the fellowship hall in the basement of our church and the high school friends of David's were in charge of that, because it was their idea and we thought that would be wonderful.

We got word that the high school students didn't get much work done those two days that week. The entire school was mourning his death. It was a terrible shock to everybody. Our church was completely full with the aisles full of standing friends. The fellowship hall in the basement and the area outside the church was also packed with friends during the service listening with benefit of loud speakers. The stream of cars to the cemetery was incredible; it seemed that every body also went to the burial. When we returned to the basement, it was also full of people standing and milling around. I was greeting many of our out of town family and friends, patients, doctors, students and local friends.

Tenth: Downstairs was crammed, and through all of those people Don Flentke, came up to me and handed me the tape of the "Unbelieving" sermon I'd wanted so bad, but had forgotten about it. He said "I found it." I hugged him and thanked him, I couldn't speak. I put it in my pocket and was so grateful to Don for not forgetting I wanted it.

The student friends were welcomed by me, and I thanked them all for being such good, loyal, friends to our son, and asked them to relax, enjoy this celebration and tell us about their friendship and remembrances of David. People there in the basement were standing, no place to sit. But it wasn't long that more and more of his friends became a little bolder to get up and tell little stories about things that he did with them, sometimes to them, but they all really did seem to love and respect David. We were so proud of our son, after hearing so many things they cherished about David. This was a wonderful time for us despite the terrible sadness.

Eleventh: Our children stayed with us for another week or so. The week was taken up with some of their friends, and some of David's friends that seemed they just didn't want to let go. They all came over during the week to help our kids and support them during their grief.

The following Sunday we all went to Sunday school then to church. The Sunday school class was following the planned printed lessons in the calendar for Sunday Schools. That day the printed subject for discussion was for a member to discuss the loss of a family member, and their feelings and thoughts. We were amazed at the significance of this subject, at the perfect time when we all were able to let out our feelings and tell how this had affected each of us. This was a very significant subject to allow us to ventilate what we felt. We all enjoyed the opportunity to talk, and certainly received a lot of therapy from each other.

Twelve: We had about 2 weeks until Elizabeth and I were to leave to go to Hawaii for two weeks on the vacation we won from the drawing back in September. The trip was perfect, pre-planned, and gave us a quiet, healing time, and new environment for us to get away, enjoy each other, and enjoy our anniversary.

The tragedy was terrible, but as Jaap, our minister who had lost a young son told us, "it's like an amputation—a part of you is gone, but it heals with time, but it's always gone and you'll always miss it." The other children slowly went back to their colleges and work. All of our kids were just as accomplished as David was, and we are so proud of each of them.

I'll always believe that God knew what was about to happen to us, and tried to make it as easy as a thing like this could be. We failed to recognize the significance of these 12 things until after the fact, but now it is very clear.

John and his girlfriend, Patti Rogers, decided after David died to get married. They chose to be married in our Presbyterian Church in Auburndale, on New Years Eve December 31, 1984, about 2 months after David died. John had finished his Geology degree at Florida State University. They were planning to go to Colorado for John to pursue his future in Geology.

I want to write a little about our wonderful, beautiful family, so you may understand me a little better. We had six children, 5 boys and

1 girl. You can imagine who would have to teach, help, drive to get them on time wherever they had to go, feed them, see that they get to their doctors, help with school work, make them practice piano and instruments, get them to Sunday school and church, and take care of her husband which she did very well, like all the other stuff. I was of little help to my wife, my hero, family manager, and architect, and the $2^{nd}$ most beautiful lady I ever saw, ($2^{nd}$ to Marilyn).

Paul Alexander Tanner III, born March 30, 1956, in Lakeland Morrell Memorial Hospital made us very happy, because we very much wanted a family. Paul grew up as a bright intelligent individual. Paul was in Little League Baseball, as a left handed pitcher, and he's not left handed. He was very athletic, excelled in water sports and tennis, as did all the other kids growing up.

In grade school for a science assignment he chose to make a chicken skeleton. Paul and his mother went to an egg farm where they usually have dead chickens in the garbage. Cause of death, unknown, they have a few die daily. They picked one out, took it home, picked it, cleaned it and boiled it until all the meat came off of the bones. Then they had a pot full of bones. Then they had to soak them in lye water to remove all of the last vestiges of any meat, and then Clorox to control the smell. Then after repeating all the above, because of all the bones of the first chicken disintegrating, due to too long Clorox soaking, the second pot of bones were fine.

Paul set out to build that skeleton from the feet up. He glued the feet on a board and proceeded to glue bone onto bone until there was a chicken, with his head bent over a little glass bowl with corn kernels in it, like he/she was eating. I was never part of his chicken-skeleton-making. He had a picture of a skeleton and followed it. He was entered in the Polk County Science Fair and won the First Prize. His mother should have received a first prize, also. The next year I took him to a slaughter house in Polk City and got a cow heart, for him to dissect. He learned a lot, and I reviewed cardiac anatomy. Paul was active in Boy Scouts, and earned Eagle Scout level. He attended Philmont Scout Ranch in New Mexico, one year, and the national scout jamboree in the state of Washington.

Paul had been taking piano from Mrs. Lochmiller, like all the other kids as they grew up, and he showed a lot of talent and later was a student of one of the professors at Florida Southern College in Lakeland, Artist in Residence Dr. Robert McDonald. He continues his love and still plays his classical music. In high school he played French horn in the orchestra and marching band and piano in the stage band, and arranged some of their music. He graduated from University of South Florida, in Tampa, in mathematics. While there he wrote a paper that was accepted and published in an international journal of mathematics, without any accompanying author. I don't understand a word about it, or of it, nor do I recognize any of the mathematical signs or symbols. I might as well be reading an article from a scientist living in outer space. His was the first paper written and published without faculty co-author, by an undergraduate at University of South Florida.

John Matthew was born Labor Day, September 7$^{th,}$ 1959. While in high school, was asked by the coach to come out for football, because he noted John had a lot of speed in physical education class. He did and on one of the early practice days, John was running and was hit rather hard by one of the bigger more experienced team mates. John said he saw stars and felt this was not in his best interest, so he didn't attend practice anymore, electing to concentrate on band. He played piano, another of Mrs. Lochmiller's pupils, bass clarinet, and latter guitar. He started in the Junior High School band, they were taught their instruments by the wonderful band director Bill Agrella. He was able to teach any musical instrument a student wanted to learn. They all continued their music through high school. He was active in Boy Scouts and earned Eagle Scout level, also.

John wanted to be a doctor but thought he didn't have the brains to do that. He became an Emergency Medical Technician, worked for Polk County a while, then went to Florida State University, Tallahassee. He graduated with a degree in Geology. He moved to Jacksonville, where his girlfriend Patty Rogers was from, and worked as a Ship's Chandler, the one who is notified of an approaching ship, planning to dock in Jacksonville, needing supplies. He takes the order, accumulates the supplies, gets it all on a boat and takes it out to the ship. This was where David our 6$^{th}$ child visited to hear Woody Herman's Big Band, the weekend before he died.

John and Patty married, Dec. 31 1984, almost 2 months after David's death, and moved to Denver to pursue his Geology interest. At that time, Geologists were being laid off, and no jobs were available. John became a waiter, later with a friend started a Head Hunting Company, had a mild success, but with time he and Patty divorced and she came back to her home in Jacksonville, Florida. Mary was in college at University of Colorado, in Boulder; John met a friend of Mary's, a lovely girl Billie Grassmuck, a candidate for her PHD at the university. She really encouraged John to re-enter college and get the requirements to be eligible to apply for medical school. She convinced John that he did have the intelligence to become a doctor. He made great grades and did apply for medical school, and was accepted to Eastern Virginia Medical School in Norfolk, Virginia. John and Billie married; he graduated and went to the University of Texas in San Antonio, Texas for a residency in Neurology. John joined a neurology-neurosurgical group in Winter Haven and after 4-5 years decided to move to Tampa, where he continues practicing Neurology with a wonderful reputation.

Mary Elizabeth was born Dec. 25, 1960 and was our only girl. She was a beautiful child, grew to be a pretty little blond beauty, and was very smart. She took ballet lessons, grew to love it and while in 7th grade was selected to join the Tampa Ballet Company and dance in The Nutcracker Suite in Tampa. She was in the girl scouts, joined the band in middle school and played the oboe well, all through high school. She was the first female Senior Class President. Graduating 1978, and went to Belgium with the Student Exchange Program, and lived with a wonderful Belgium family with children at similar ages. She repeated another senior year in their high school, learning Flemish, becoming fluent in the language, and became good friends with that family. Three of their children were able to come to visit us during the next few years after Mary came home.

On Mary's return home she was hired by a fine Disney World restaurant as an interpreter for some of the foreign visitors. She entered the University of Colorado, in Boulder in January1980. After her graduation in 1985 she joined the Peace Corps and was sent to Sri Lanka. She became quite ill with Ameobiasis and was hospitalized, was treated well, got OK enough to come home in Jan. 1986. With the continual war in that country, and her illness, she decided to return to school in Boulder Colorado at the university. She received her degree, and master's degree, in English Literature. Then she went to Los Angeles to teach and pursue her PHD at University of Southern California and completed every requirement except her thesis. During that period she met Maurizio Grimaldi, a movie producer, son of noted Italian producer Alberto Grimaldi, of Clint Eastwood's early western movies. The last film Maurizio co-produced was "Gangs of New York".

After several years they decided to get married and did so in March 1999. They have a very bright, beautiful daughter, Isabella Jane, 6 years old now, fluent in Italian, English, and Spanish. They have a wonderful Mexican live in house-helper, Lulu, who knows Spanish, but not Italian or English. Maurizio has spoken only Italian to that child, purposely, since she was born, Mary, English, and Lulu, Spanish.

James Henry, our 4$^{th}$ child, born April 30, 1962, was the longest baby, and grew to be the tallest of our children. He was named after my 2 grandfather's first names. He was thrown in the mix of 3 siblings, and had a hard time managing their playful activity until he grew a little so he could take care of himself better. Elizabeth was the referee. James also, took piano from Mrs. Lochmiller, in middle school started French horn, and did well, and later the banjo. He continued all through high school in the concert and marching band. He was a Boy Scout and reached Eagle Scout level, also. How could any Daddy not be proud of three sons reaching Eagle Scout level? James was very fun loving in school, acted in several school plays, and was a singer in the vocal group. After graduation, he took off for Colorado where Mary was in college and lived with her in Boulder. While there he took jobs with a carpet cleaning company, and later in a restaurant he waited tables and worked in the kitchen learning to cook. He left Boulder and went to work at Keystone Ski Resort as a cook, to wait for Mark to finish high school. When Mark graduated from high school he joined James at Keystone, then they both entered college at Colorado Mountain College in Leadville, Colorado, the highest town in the U.S., and has a colorful western and silver mining history and cold, cold, snowy weather. They both graduated with an associate degree in Outdoor Recreation. James worked as a courier for the school system transporting things between schools in the county. He learned to drive really well in the winter snows over very treacherous, small, winding, and icy roads through out that severely mountainous area. He learned to fly while he was in Leadville, became instrument rated and received a commercial license. James moved to Grand Junction Colorado with his bride Karen Waters, whom he met at college, and married in Leadville. They had a beautiful baby boy Garrick Alexander Tanner, in Grand Junction. It turned out that Garrick had a congenital severely abnormal heart that required a complete heart transplant at about age 6 weeks. It was the 66th infant cardiac transplant done at Loma Linda University, California, by the infant transplant pioneer Dr. Leonard Bailey. A year or so after the operation, Garrick was doing well and James and Karen divorced and Karen and her new husband moved to Karen's home in Georgia with Garrick. James was in college, at Mesa State University in Grand Junction, Colorado and graduated with a BS and Masters degree in Education and Recreational Therapy. After his divorce, he met and married

Andrea Heath the wonderful mother of 3 children. They have a beautiful daughter, Fiona Elizabeth, 10 years old and smart. James is a great father to that whole family, and they love him. James works at St. Mary's Hospital as a specialist in Recreation Therapy and teaches at the hospital and Mesa State University.

Every 3-4 months James finds time to fly to Georgia and pick up Garrick, and drive down to Central Florida to visit us. We really appreciate James planning the time to be a great father to his son, and share his time with him at our home. At the age of ten, Garrick had a rejection problem with his first heart, had to have a second transplant at Emory University. He did quite well until he began to develop vascular disease that caused his renal function to deteriorate, and he had to go on dialysis, and subsequently, his mother was a match and she gave Garrick one of her kidneys, about 2 years ago. So far he has been doing fine. These complications are usual with transplant surgery. We hope and pray he will continue to do well. He will be 18 years old January 18, 2008.

Mark Andrew, our 5$^{th}$ child was born June 7$^{th}$ 1964, was also thrown into the mix of older vigorous children, but he quickly was able to hold his own, with his mother's protection and control. She had a fly-swatter for the flies and a different fly-swatter for the kids. Mark grew up as a comedian with the other kids. He took piano like the others, from Mrs. Lochmiller. In middle school started on trumpet, learned quickly and well, became the 1$^{st}$ chair trumpet in middle school and high school stage band and concert and marching bands. He was in scouting and reached Life Scout level, one below Eagle. I might mention here that David was also in scouting and working hard, but the leadership changed and he lost interest. Mark was known as a comic among his school friends through high school. He, like James sang in the vocal groups, and acted in school plays. He could hardly wait to graduate so he could head to Colorado to be with his brother, James and sister, Mary.

From high school Mark went with James to Leadville, Colorado, and entered Colorado Mountain College there. After graduating, Mark went to Copper Mountain Ski Resort, was in charge of transportation vehicles, became an Emergency Medical Technician and certified fire fighter. He met a pretty, wonderful girl, Kathleen Mangus from Denver, Colorado. They fell in love, and moved to Denver where they married. He became a firefighter and EMT in Denver. After a short time they moved back to his home in Auburndale, Florida. He worked as an emergency medical technician, and firefighter for the city of Lake Alfred, Florida, about 4 miles east of Auburndale. A year later he became a fire fighter and emergency medical technician for Disney World, Reedy Creek, in Orlando, Florida. He was very adept at driving the big, long fire truck there. They started their family while here and ten years later they had four fine, beautiful, smart boys. Their ages now are David Vincent 17, Anthony Andrew 16, Luke William 12, and Charlie Martin, 8.

Mark received his degree in business administration from The University of Phoenix, and became a certified Lotus Notes Administrator. After 10 years at Disney and reaching a partial retirement level, they decided to move back to Denver, Colorado where Kathy's family lives and the boys have cousins. Mark went to work for Data Corporation as a Lotus Notes Administrator.

David Michael born January 3$^{rd}$, 1968, was our last child and I have already written about him and our tragedy. David died November 2, 1984.

After David died, Elizabeth found a metal company and helped them design a large 6 foot high, brass Celtic cross. We had it hung from the ceiling of our First Presbyterian Church with wires over the altar dedicated to the Glory of God and in Loving Memory of David, from his family. It is beautiful and imposing with lights trained on it from three different overhead directions. It is a hanging cross over our altar. It gives me a sense of gratitude and wonderful memories of our son each Sunday.

I talked previously about purchasing our eight grave sites awhile before David died. We proceeded to choose our grave stones when we had to choose David's. We engraved on ours, and also David's.

The words on David's stone are: his name, his birth date and the date he died, followed by:

BELOVED DAVID, A JOY AMONG US

SO BLESSED WITH MANY TALENTS

THE LORD HAD NEED OF HIM

"WE KNOW THAT IN EVERYTHING

GOD WORKS FOR GOOD WITH THOSE WHO LOVE HIM,

WHO ARE CALLED ACCORDING TO HIS PURPOSE"

ROMANS 8: 26—30

In the late 1970's the kids began to leave home, to go to college so we had less and less kids around. All evenings seemed to remain the same, with David, Mark and James still home, and Elizabeth still had the responsibilities of Mom, and the kids having to be mothered and taken where they had to be. All evenings became the same when I got home. I was met with "DO YOU WANT A BEER?" I noticed she was pretty much drinking more and more, to ease her day and stress. I began to complain more and more when it was obvious she was imbibing way too much. We had a few very harsh words to each other, and finally, I had had enough of worrying about her and the kids. I gave her an ultimatum. She would stop drinking or I would move out. It would be her choice.

Finally she agreed to stop drinking. For about a year and a half we didn't drink a bit. When we went out to cocktail parties or to the country club for dinner, we had no alcohol, only soda with a twist of lime, or lemon.

Before that we would put a six pack in the car on the way over to the club. We would drink it on the way over. I would have a hard time getting my 3 beers down before we got there, or she would say, "Can I have your last beer? I don't have any more." When we got there she would really get upset if the waitress was slow getting to our table for drinks order. She would make me get up and go to the bar and get her a beer. I was really getting to the point I didn't know what to do, so I just got fed up, after going through all this, worrying about her, hating what she was doing, trying to hate her but I loved her too much. I just wanted her to stop drinking, and I thought that would solve everything.

There had been several episodes of embarrassing and worrisome moments, like out to dinner with friends and she had to go to the bathroom, got up from the table, dizzy, lost her balance and sat right down on the floor. She couldn't get up without my help. She thought this was a riot in the nice Sundown Restaurant, with Jack and Trish, our best friends, and many of their, and our, other friends from Winter Haven having a nice meal. Everybody except me thought it was hilarious. I had to help her stagger to the bathroom, wait out side, Forever!—and help her back to the table. And on the way home she tried politely, to vomit out the back window of Jack's car. She succeeded, but not politely. It drooled down the outside of Jack's back door.

Another night at Tom and Laura Keator's home, back down Osceola Avenue on Lake Arietta, about a half mile from our house, and after a wonderful dinner and evening of drinking, she had a snootful and was very angry when I wanted to go home. She wasn't ready even though most of the other couples had left. After much arguing and fussing she got in the car with some difficulty, and we started back down to our house, maybe a half mile away. She was still ranting about not ready to go home, and about half way home she demanded to get out of the car and walk the rest of the way home, which may have been 2-300 yards. I finally just stopped the car; she got out and proceeded to stagger right off of the road and into the grove, 4 or 5 trees deep into the grove. I turned the engine off, walked out into the grove to get her, and she just sat right down on the ground and said she needed to rest. Here we are Dr. Tanner, an Auburndale doctor, pleading and demanding for his drunken wife, who was sitting in General Van Fleet's grove, to get up and get in the car and go home. This was about 12:30 to 1:00 on an early Sunday morning, after a wonderful Saturday night friendly dinner party with our friends. Finally, she agreed to receive my help, and with a struggle, got her up and walked her to the car and went home.

At home, with difficulty I was able to help her out of the car. I staggered with her into the house, removed her coat, pushed, tugged and encouraged her to try to help me get her up those stairs and into the bedroom. Finally, I got her clothes off and into bed. Now you know, that had to be a labor of REALLY COMMITTED LOVE!

Several others episodes, like once the two of us went to Crystal River one weekend to stay in one of our units at Paradise Point. We had brought a bunch of beer, and when we got there found some boat docked at the dock selling fresh live shrimp. We bought a bunch, boiled them and ate them ALL, with nothing but beer, for our supper. We did shell them, you know. It was another actively drinking weekend.

Some of the other episodes need not be included. Maybe you will understand why I had been trying to treat my alcoholic wife and was unsuccessful with all of my alcoholic knowledge. Something had to give, and she agreed to stop drinking.

By the early 1980's we were getting along very well drinking a plain soda with a twist of lemon. Everybody thought we were drinking right along with them.

One evening, as we arrived at the Lake Region Yacht and Country Club for dinner, I thought after about 2 years of no alcohol, she was probably over HAVING to drink, so I mentioned to her maybe we could have a small glass of wine with our dinner and would she like one? She said, "Yes, that would be nice." So we did. Then she said, "Wouldn't it be nice to have just one more before we leave." I said OK, so we did, then left the club and went home.

That started it all over again over a few months of wine with meals at the restaurants, then she bought some cans of beer and on and on until coming home and she was already in bed, reeking of alcohol. She would be in bed by 7 or 8 o'clock.

Only David was still home and he went to her and said, "Mom, I'm worried about your drinking." She said "Don't worry I'm fine, it just relaxes me, gives me energy, etc., etc., etc." Then in 1984 David died. She felt very guilty and depressed because his death was due to alcohol.

Elizabeth's depression became worse and with it came more and more drinking, and more confrontations. Finally, my anger, frustration, sadness, and confusion made me confront her in the middle of the night when I found a bottle of Vodka in the cupboard under her bathroom sink. She admitted to adding Vodka to her regimen. It was terrible daily for me to leave the house, go to the hospital, and to my office, worried about her and how she would be when I got home. During all her drinking she never left the house driving a car, all her drinking was done at home, and mostly at night.

After quite a scene, and after many months of my berating and demeaning words and sentences you don't want to see in print, she went to her bed, sat there and called Mary, our daughter, who was in college at the University of Colorado and asked her to find a place where she could go for treatment of alcoholism. Mary found a place in Denver that was a model for Betty Ford's treatment center in California. Elizabeth called the next day and made arrangements to get in as a patient. She flew to Denver and was admitted April I, 1986 into the Addictions Recovery Program, St Luke's Hospital in Denver, Colorado.

A few days later I received a phone call in my office from the director of the program, and he informed me of her admission and informed me that the entire family is required to attend the final week of the program, for my wife. I informed him very politely that would be impossible for me to do, because I was a doctor, and I was very busy with my very active practice and besides as a Physician I knew all about alcoholism and didn't need to attend that program. He politely informed me that he knew I probably did know all about alcoholism, and was very busy, but this is a 4 week program and each patient's entire family MUST come the last week for classes from 8AM until 5 PM daily, and if I elected not to attend she would not be discharged from this program until I do come.

I, therefore, agreed to the terms and made arrangements for Elizabeth's mother and all our kids who were in different colleges, to get to Denver and attend the classes. Mary who was in college at the University of Colorado elected strongly not to go with the family. She was asserting her independence. This was Mom's first challenge. Accepting things she could not control, because she really wanted Mary there.

We arranged for everybody, except Mary, to get to Denver, Colorado for the last week of Elizabeth's program, and our week of school. We stayed in a hotel in Denver and started the classes, and I must admit this was the best, most complete information about Alcoholism, and I learned more than I ever knew existed about the subject.

After the program and we were home, Elizabeth had to attend Alcoholic Anonymous (AA) programs locally. She went to AA meetings, and I told her I didn't want to go because I didn't want any body to know my wife was an alcoholic, I as a doctor was above that. Sometimes she would go to a meeting in Lakeland, or Haines City, or Winter Haven, but was a regular in Auburndale at the St Alban's Episcopal Church.

She continued this life and after a while I noticed her real dedication to this program. She started counseling newer ladies taking them to meetings and I began to worry about her safety, going to some of the out of the way places where some people lived.

I decided since nobody had mentioned my wife's attendance or involvement in the alcoholic program, they probably wouldn't find out if I attended some of the meetings. I could attend the "open" meetings. Only alcoholics could attend the "closed" meetings.

I attended my first meeting trying not to be known, I thought about wearing a disguise. To my utter surprise, I ran into a neurologist friend I'd known for years, a local attorney, the son of a doctor friend, wife of a neurosurgeon, a couple of nurses, and several of my patients. I even met some I didn't even know. Some of these people had been in AA for years and very dedicated to what they were doing and had been doing so for years, and none of them wore disguises. I learned nobody talks to anybody about who's there or not there. Nobody in AA gossips, I learned. My superiority and brilliance was dashed and crushed, so it seems I'm just like everybody else, no better and no worse. What a relief! Looks like if we're open to it, we can learn something about ourselves throughout our lives.

The AA program is just about perfect for people that are alcoholics, if they surrender to being an alcoholic, and follow the program as

it is presented. I have never seen anything as complete as this program. I believe this program will not fail. Only the people will fail if
they do not follow the program. I think the program would be good
for anybody and everybody, just for good down to earth living, day by
day, starting in the first grade of school.

I stopped drinking when Elizabeth entered the treatment center.
She told me I could keep on drinking if I wanted to. I had no reason to
continue drinking, even socially, I have never regretted one minute of
not drinking. I have supported her and praised her strength and loy-
alty to herself and her family for turning her life around. I am so
proud of my wonderful wife, and I love her more now than I think I
ever loved her.

As my practice grew I began to notice patients with upper abdominal pain of various severity and various locations in their abdomen.
Early I began to notice the ones with pain in the upper mid abdomen
with tenderness and seemed better with food intake, sometimes on
G.I. Series revealed gastric or duodenal ulceration. Then, I learned
over time, that they all didn't have acid in the stomach. I thought all
duodenal ulcers had way too much stomach acid, causing the ulcer. I
wondered why some had acid, some high amounts, and some had
very little, or none.

I began going the hospital early AM, and put a nasogastric tube
into the stomach, then taking the patient on a gurney to the X-ray
department. There I would get the help of a technician, fluoroscope to
see that the tube was properly placed in the stomach, and not curled
up in the stomach, and then go back to the floor. I would empty the
stomach, label the beaker and give the patient an injection of Pentogastrin, an acid stimulator. Each 15 minute aspirate emptying the
stomach, for 1 hour, then 1 hour later.

These beakers, labeled time-wise, were sent to the lab for acid
determination. Free acid was the amount in the fasting beaker.
Amounts of acid in the subsequent beakers were due to stimulation.
This was supposed to tell me if the patient would form acid when
they ate, to aid their digestion. Pentogastrin was supposed to simu-
late food intake. It is a powerful acid stimulator. I think sometimes a
much more potent stimulator than the patient produces with just
plain food. Others used alcohol as a stimulator. I felt like Pentogastrin was too powerful a stimulator and wondered if an intake more
like a meal would give a more accurate evaluation of the patient's
acid formation response. I felt the use of Pentogastrin was like
"wringing out that last drop of acid available," and wouldn't mimic a

meal, which may not cause acid stimulation at all in some patients. The ability to respond to food, I felt may be different in different patients. I changed my stimulator to beef bullion, knowing protein is a very good acid stimulator put into the stomach, instead of the most powerful laboratory stimulator Pentogastrin, which was nothing like a meal's stimulation.

I learned that some people that had no free acid, formed acid with Pentogastrin, and very little with beef bullion. Most people that had free acid did respond well to bullion. After many patients I tested, I learned some people with no acid, called Achlorhydria, formed gastric ulcers, and is supposed to sometimes be associated with stomach cancer.

Free gastric acid is also necessary to absorb vitamin B 12 from the intestinal track. The lack of free gastric acid can lead to developing Pernicious Anemia, over a slow long time. Apparently an injection of B 12 each month is necessary to protect from developing that type anemia.

I remember several cases I had of stomach cancer in my early years, but as time went by in my later years, I remember fewer cases. That may be due to less stomach cancers occurring, or because we began having gastroenterologists join our medical community and the patients saw those doctors rather than me, or better understanding of nutrition.

People that I tested all had symptoms. The ones with no acid seemed to get along with no pain or much less stomach pain if I put them on Acidulin, or 10 drops of hydrochloric acid (HCL) in water with each meal, using a glass straw. HCL could etch the teeth, so we used a glass straw and had them swallow quickly and rinse the mouth with water.

For years some people have a glass of wine, or cocktail before their meal. Alcohol stimulates production of gastric acid, thus aiding in digestion.

One of my patients with ulcer symptoms, a middle-fifties aged female, after a gastrointestinal series, revealed a rather large ulcer on the Greater Curvature of her stomach. The test for acid revealed no free gastric acid and no gastric acid after stimulation with bullion. Instead of using a barbiturate and belladonna, which was the usual treatment before Tagamet, and such, I talked with her and asked if she would let me try Acidulin to replace her acid and see if we could heal her ulcer, as well as help her stomach pain. I figured if God gave us acid for good digestion, and she had none, maybe replacing the acid would kind of bring her gastric physiology back to normal, and she would be better.

She consented, so after a month, symptoms were gone and re-X-ray showed total healing of the greater curvature ulcer. I was surprised, excited and happy that she seemed to get so much better. I began giving Acidulin to a lot of patients, and got a lot of them asymptomatic. None formed an ulcer while on Acidulin that I knew about. Maybe they did and found a new, better doctor to treat their ulcer, but nobody called me to let me know if that was the case.

Back in those days the medical staff had monthly medical department meetings and somebody would present an interesting patient, or subject to the doctors. I presented this lady's story and her x-rays to them. I was noted for trying things on my patients, and sometimes teased about what I tried. I don't think I harmed anyone, but who knows. I was fortunate never to have had a malpractice suit, or query that I was aware of. I have always been proud of that fact.

Today physicians usually don't try anything not suggested in the printed literature, and apparently use only accepted ways of treating patients. Maybe that's the way it needs to be. But trying new approaches to treatments usually is a way new treatments become accepted, someone thinking and trying possibly a new and maybe better way. I always got permission from each patient before I tried things. Some worked, some didn't but as far as I knew no one was harmed.

After Morrow Hospital opened, a local pastor's wife came to see me with left upper abdominal pain. Her husband had recently been called to a local church. She was complaining of rather severe pain, and examining her in the office, found her extremely tender in the left upper abdomen to my exam. There was no nausea, fever or any other symptom. I was concerned that she had some acute abdominal flare. Her past history was of several previous admissions in other areas of Florida for this same abdominal pain. One was in southeast Florida, another in a large hospital in Jacksonville, Duvall Medical Center, and another in a Tampa hospital. Sometimes the pain was milder, and just went away after a few days, so she saw no doctor. None of her previous admissions were successful in finding out what was wrong.

She agreed to being admitted to our hospital for an evaluation. I admitted her and ordered several blood test, an intravenous pyelogram, and barium enema. All tests were negative, so I added a chest x-ray and gastrointestinal series. These tests were also negative. She had no other symptoms, of nausea or diarrhea, only discomfort and major tenderness.

I racked my brain, and could come up with nothing else to do, so I went to her room to offer a referral to another doctor in Winter Haven or Lakeland. I sat down in a bed side chair, her head was to my right, and I laid my right hand on her left upper quadrant, and slowly moved my hand around while I was talking about her tests, and x-rays, and what she didn't have. I noticed a slight jump under my hand as it moved around, and noted I was not pressing hard on her abdomen, but a repeated little jump beneath my fingers at about the same place over and over. I said "does the hurt you?" She answered "Yes, sometime." I paid close attention to the spot, and each time I passed over the same place, she identified a small place on her abdominal wall that was consistently very tender. All around that area was not tender. I took a pencil from my pocket, identified the spot by pressure with the eraser end of the pencil. She would really jump when I did that at the same place. I then took a big handful of abdominal fat between my thumb and forefinger, pinching lightly, moving around until I found a spot where you might imagine a small BB in the tissue that I was squeezing between my thumb and forefinger. It was located and marked with a pen as the spot of a possible small neuroma.

I had heard of neuritis and neuromas, but I had never seen one to know it. So I thought I'd go the nurse's station and get some Novacaine and syringe with a long spinal needle and deaden the area and see if the pain would go away. I did get it and imagined the abdominal subcutaneous nerve running around the abdomen, and moved a couple of inches back toward the origin of the nerve and infiltrated up and down vertically subcutaneously, and deep, for about 4 inches so I would infiltrate the area of the nerve. I waited about 10 minutes and carefully palpated the area of pain and tenderness that I had marked with a pen. lo and behold, all her pain and tenderness had disappeared.

She was so happy, and so was I. Her problem had to be superficial, and not of deep intra-abdominal origin. I told her if she wanted me to do it, I could remove it in the AM, and maybe she'd never have this again. She agreed, and I called the operating room and set it up. The next AM, in the operating room, on the table I identified the spot before she was put to sleep, and put a long spinal needle into the spot passing it deep in her mildly obese abdomen down to the fascia of the rectus muscle, leaving it in place and the anesthetist put her to sleep. I made an elliptical incision horizontally above the needle and another below the needle with the lines meeting 2-3 inches on both sides of the needle, then went down to the fascia covering the muscle and remove all tissue down to the muscle. The nerve, skin, and fatty tissue were all removed from the area. We sutured the incision, made a nice scar, and with no more pain or tenderness, I sent her home next morning to follow up in the office. She never complained of this again while they lived in Auburndale, and in follow-up in my office she was very happy to have someone finally find out what was wrong with her.

This was the first of many patients who I found with the same story. Most I could attribute to what they did to flare it up bad enough to see a doctor. I was able to find the tender area by simply carefully palpating the area of their pain, and localizing the spot by pinching abdominal wall subcutaneous tissue then proving it to them by infiltrating the area with a local anesthetic and magically solving their pain problem, for the time being. These are mostly recurring if they do the same thing. I found that identifying their problem, they understood it and learned to live with it, or start on a few days of anti-inflammatory Advil or Aleve.

The actions and activities that people do to stretch an abdominal nerve, or bruise it, I identified as most were washing windows or cupboards requiring high reaching on tiptoes, or washing the top of their automobile, or a job requiring rather long time pressing the area against a hard object like a table or desk. Truckers with wide leather belts sitting for long distances while driving bruise a nerve some times. They also occasionally severely bruise the large sciatic nerve in their buttock sitting long hours on their large wallet, and causes weakness and numbness, and/or acute sciatica down a leg. This occurs in high school athletes like football, volleyball, tennis after serving, anything that might stretch or bruise the nerve, which is in the subcutaneous soft tissue.

One lady had pain in her right upper abdomen where most people hurt with gall bladder problems. I had evaluated her with gall bladder ultrasound, some blood tests, all negative, anesthetized the area with relief and explained this to her a number of times. She was a house cleaner for several people, a lovely person and we found out every time she did a lot of sweeping with a broom, the next day she would hurt, and come in. I hadn't seen her for several months. She wore a belt and when she bent over to sweep the layer of fat over the belt was squeezed while she swept and used muscular activity to clean. I felt she was contusing the subcutaneous abdominal nerve in that area of her abdominal wall. One day she came in again with her problem. I asked her how she was and she told me she went to another doctor in Winter Haven with a flare up. She was admitted to Winter Haven Hospital and was told nothing was wrong with her after her workup, and intimated it was in her head, and due to nervousness.

She returned to him once with a recurrence of pain and he referred her to the University of Florida Medical School Hospital, in Gainesville, Florida. She said she was put through a lot of tests, X-rays and was seen by several doctors. She was told the same thing, nothing turned up.

I tried again to go through all the reasons for these kinds of symptoms, and short of surgery to remove the nerve, nothing needs to be done except for her to understand this freaky diagnosis. I anesthetized her again, relieved her pain and she left. I continued seeing her for other problems but not for this. She finally understood and accepted her recurring difficulty, and got over her fear of these recurrences, and started taking Advil for several days, and found out the flare ups all go away within a few days. Removal of nerves sometime causes neuromas at the site of cutting the nerve, leaving continual problems.

I was reading an article in a surgical journal some years later, after finding many patients that I thought I had found this new problem. Many doctors wind up going to surgery to take care of various intra-abdominal surgical problems and finding nothing. The writer was writing on the subject "Differential Diagnosis of Acute Abdominal Pain," there was mention of abdominal neuritis as a cause not usually thought of. It has the name of Carnett's Syndrome, named in an article by Carnett in 1926 I believe. I looked it up on Google and find Carnett was right. A lot of patients go to surgery and wind up with no diagnosis.

If I had been aware of Carnett's Syndrome when I first recognized the problem in the pastor's wife, I would not have needed to do surgery on her. All the treatment would be is to explain the pain to the patient, and they need to believe it, learn how it comes about, and know they will probably have it flare from time to time. Most patients are scared because of not understanding the cause or why they hurt. If they do, most have been able to live fine with this weird syndrome. A few days of Advil or Aleve will settle the pain and soreness. Generally, patients with pain begin to worry about bad things like cancer, ulcers, kidney stones, or anything that they ever heard of that scares them. I sometimes had a hard time convincing them of the benign cause of such painful symptoms.

A new patient, named Heidi, and her husband came to see me. They recently moved to the area and needed a doctor. She was a pretty lady, about late 40s, thin, and spoke in a small, weak, and shy voice. The history was that she had chronic left abdominal pain for 15 years; she stated she had undergone 15 previous surgical procedures with no relief. She had been a dancer in Las Vegas for several years, and had to give up her career. So they moved from Vegas to Colorado Springs, was evaluated and operated several times there. She had undergone removal of both ovaries, and uterus, and had several abdominal exploratory surgical procedures, for adhesions and other obscure diagnoses. At any rate she admitted to being addicted to codeine, after all these years of pain requiring three to four tablets a day for the last 15 years, and wanted me to continue giving her that medication. After questioning her and examining her, I concluded she had Carnett's Syndrome. However, this was before I became aware of that as a named diagnosis.

I told her she had an abdominal superficial neuritis or neuroma. She agreed to a try of local anesthesia. I identified the spot of intense tenderness, injected the area, and all symptoms and tenderness disappeared. She had a hard time believing it, and still wanted Tylenol 3 to have at home. I agreed to give her only an prescription for 30 tablets with no refills. We followed her for several months, and she was unable to manage herself without her codeine. I got so I limited her to enough for 3 a day, for 30 days at a time. She invariably ran out with 3-4 days left. We limited her to the same pharmacy, and called him several times to see that she was not filling another doctor's prescription. I even called all of the area Pharmacies, and told them of her addiction and watch for other doctor's treating her also. I never caught her doing that.

I finally worried about my continuing to prescribe narcotics to an addict, so I referred her to a local neurosurgeon with the idea of him surgically removing the nerve. I thought this would give her a permanent numbness, therefore, permanent relief. He saw and examined her, came to the conclusion that she had a gynecological problem, and referred her to a Tampa gynecologist. The gynecologist told her she needed to undergo an exploratory operation to find the source of pain. They had already done that several times, so she refused surgery, and couldn't afford the cost.

The neurosurgeon explained to me if he removed the nerve, the addicted people are going to continue to complain. How do we know she really has relief, or not and continues with the same symptoms, and besides, sometimes the complication is formation of a neuroma at the site of the cutting of the end of the nerve, which is also a very painful thing.

I had a discussion with the family who were very supportive of her and also me, about the possibility of admitting her into a treatment center to treat the addiction, much the same as trying to solve an alcoholic problem. They were all very excited about that possibility, including Heidi. We found a good place in the Tampa Bay area. We referred Heidi and her husband to the facility, they went to the place, and consulted with them about her being admitted for treatment. They found out the treatment time is a required 6 weeks, minimum. They demanded a payment of $15,000, before admission, with the possibility of having to come up with more money later, if it turns up she would have to stay longer. They returned home with the inability to fund this treatment, so were back to the original state.

So I still had my nice lady with her pain. I did continue treating her until my retirement, calling pharmacists who by now were all my friends, helping me control strictly limiting her to no more than 90 tablets per month. She got so she would not even plead with me for more refills. After I retired, I guess she found someone to help her get her medication. Her daughter was working at Gessler Clinic in Winter Haven, Florida. Maybe she was taken care of there.

Looking back on her case, if one of her earlier doctors had known about Carnett's Syndrome, she could probably have had a much better life, and not become addicted to codeine, and not needed so many operations. I'm really glad she wasn't given Demerol, or one of the much stronger narcotics that are available now. Carnett's Syndrome was a fairly common problem in my practice and a simple one to evaluate, and manage, only if the doctor thinks about the possibility of this syndrome, to rule it out.

Over time I had some patients I was never able to diagnose. These people had sometime strange complaints, of vague right upper abdominal pain, or right flank pain, associated with nausea or sometimes without. Sometimes no pain, just nausea of some severity, sometimes very slight and fleeting nausea, sometimes with food, sometimes not. We would always think of gallbladder disease and get gall bladder series, subcutaneous abdominal neuritis like Carnet's Syndrome, and later when ultrasound became available, that replaced the gallbladder series. A plain X-ray of the gall bladder could usually find calcified gall stones. Cholesterol stones didn't show on X-ray so well, so the ultrasound could identify some of the stones. With all of our ability there were a few people that we just couldn't come up with the answer. They symptoms could generally be managed for the present situations; however, some continued to return to my office when flare-ups occurred. GI Series for ulcer disease were usually negative. The unknown was always a cause for concern, for the patient and for me.

Gail was a child patient of mine, had a couple of brothers, her wonderful mother Evelyn Jordan had worked for me and Gail also worked for me in my office, starting when she finished high school. Gail married Don Macklin and has a family and all are fine. Later Gail and her mother, Evelyn both worked for Winter Haven Hospital, and Gail continues to do so.

Some 8-10 years ago Gail came in with a history of suddenly feeling acutely nauseated and followed by fainting without obvious cause. Many of the episodes came as she was seated at a dinner table at home, or out at a restaurant, sometimes with the first bite of food. She would become acutely and severely nauseated, feel bad and go directly to the bathroom. She had on several occasions fainted in the restroom at home, and came close to fainting several times at a restaurant. She had been rushed by ambulance to the ER several times, was examined and nothing found and was sent home. She had no pain with her episodes.

She began to think that this had some thing to do with food, so she resorted to eating very carefully to avoid fainting. For over a year and a half, she basically ate plain bagels, plain turkey and bread sandwiches, plain baked potatoes, and pretzels. She said the good thing was that she lost 30 pounds, but felt pretty queasy most of the time, fearing fainting most of the time.

She had seen me over almost a 2 year period, many times. We had suspected gallbladder disease, emotional stress, heart murmur which we knew of (murmur that we had sent her to University of Florida cardiology department for, and was diagnosed as not a treatable or life threatening problem).We had ordered and receive 3 different gall bladder ultrasounds, lab tests, upper GI series, all reported as negative, no stones, or other disease. Pain had not been a part of any of her episodes. Nothing but her nausea followed by fainting. All these times I felt was gall bladder connected, but couldn't prove it. Sometimes with the first bite of food she'd get up and pass out.

The last time she was in, I instructed her to write down every bite of food she put in her mouth, the time, and if she had, nausea, fainting or dizziness and the time nausea started after she ate. She always denied any pain associated with her symptoms. She did list every bite for several months. During this time I was extremely frustrated and concerned, and happened to be talking to one of my surgeon friends, Dr. Cassidy of the Gessler Clinic about this case. He asked if I had done a PIPIDA study on her. I said I had never heard of it. He told me it is a radiological test of the gall bladder, and to be sure to have them do it and follow with stimulation by injection with Cholecystokinen, a hormone secreted by the cells in the intestine when food is put in the stomach. The PIPIDA is the chemical that is taken up by the gall bladder, and is seen on a visualization machine, the percent of excretion from the gallbladder is measured after injection of Cholecystokinen. He said he never heard of it either, but his sister had it done at Duke University when she had a nonfunctioning gallbladder, and this diagnosed it. I immediately went to the Radiologist and asked him to do one. He said they don't do them here, because no one ever asked them to do it. He would have to order the material and will do so, and let me know when they have available.

When Gail came in, she had recorded on a bunch of papers every bite of food she ever ate for months, and all of it added up to any little tiny amount of fat would trigger her symptoms. The best was when she was going somewhere on a trip; she ate couple of bites of a fat free bagel before she left. All was fine then a little later she ate ONE bite of a bagel with a very small smear of butter on it, within a few minutes her symptoms appeared, didn't faint but became weak and light headed and she stopped eating it.

I scheduled her for the Pipida study with stimulation. The result was positive; she had a very poor per-cent excretion of the bile from the gallbladder, and symptoms occurred on the table immediately on injecting the IV Cholecystokinen, and she almost passed out lying flat on the X-ray table. Happy, happy me, we found the diagnosis. Apparently, I guess, she had a very quick and violent stimulation of the vagus nerve, creating this sudden severe unusual symptom-complex.

Finally I had a diagnosis of an abnormally functioning gall bladder with very strange and peculiar symptoms, in this case. I referred her for cholecystectomy, with the surgeon doubting the diagnosis. It was done and showed many very small stones, and very mild gallbladder inflammation. None of this ever showed up on the several ultrasounds of the gallbladder or in any other way. She has been nearly symptom free for all these years since the gall bladder was removed. She reports a rare very mild episode of nausea.

She gave me a note once and stated, "Your persistence in resolving this gave me my life back. I remember waking up after surgery and feeling "calmness" in my stomach that I had not felt in a long time." This is what a physician lives for, a happy, successful ending in the mind of the patient, to what we try to do. I frequently go by her office at the Winter Haven Hospital where she works to see her, my good friend, and she calls me her hero. She states she has never had any further symptoms, which to me is remarkable.

This case of complete confusion told me there is always something that I didn't learn, so with all of the other cases I never found what was wrong, who had just as worrisome symptoms, I tried to remember. I went through their charts and called them up. I found 8 people who were still having undiagnosed pain and nausea, and I thought had gallbladder problems, agreed to undergo the Pipida scan with stimulation. Six of them did have positive tests and their gall bladders were removed, also had very small stones not picked up on ultrasound, and as far as I know are doing fine. I don't know about the other two or even some whose names I have forgotten. The Winter Haven Hospital has the PIPIDA scan available now.

# 8

# 50 Years of Investing

It has been said physicians are not very good businessmen. Ha!!! After my heart attack in 1959, it became apparent to me that physicians need a backup income when they have to be out of their office for any period of time.

So I felt the need, and urge to solve that problem for us. I began paying attention to possible ways for us to pay the bills, if I couldn't work. Nobody wants to pay a doctor if he can't be treated by the doctor, so no work, no income.

I noted various ideas in the newspaper advertisements, like collector plates, stamps, coins, antiques which we were already doing, citrus groves, stock market, and many others that came up from time to time.

Trying to furnish our first home was real expensive, so since Elizabeth was from Pennsylvania the cradle of Amish and Early American furniture, and we already decided to use antiques, because they were beautiful, usable, cheaper and good investments and would usually appreciate in value over time. We bought books, and educated ourselves about what was good and not good. We were taught by Luther Redcay, Elizabeth's father, the art of refinishing our early 1790 furniture and later, up to about 1840 when they began machine made furniture. All of our antique furniture was hand made from walnut, cherry, pine, curly and tiger maple woods that was shipped to us from Pennsylvania when we selected it during our visits there.

243

When she didn't have any thing to do except carry her pregnancies and take care of the house and kids, Elizabeth would spend hours stripping the old original paint and grime off of the woods. She was careful not to remove the patina from the wood, and then apply 3 to 4 layers of clear shellac to fill the grain, then 3 to 4 layers of Johnson's paste wax. She did a wonderful job and the beautiful furniture has graced our home for years. We furnished our 7 bedroom house with antique beds, chest of drawers, bedside tables and Windsor chairs. All were refinished beautifully. I was able to help her once in a while. As each child left they were given their furniture from their room. They also each had some favorite things in our home that they wanted, so they were given those things from throughout that we had accumulated in our 18 room home. Elizabeth had rented space in one of the nice antique shops in Lakeland, 10 miles west of Auburndale. She had a lot of nice antique glassware, some extra furniture and knickknacks, and some necklaces and earrings that she made. She stayed in business there for about ten years, until the owner left the area. Occasionally, when I went to her shop I would see something that I called "my best stuff." I would pick it up and take it back home. This created a mild storm associated with stronger words from the shop owner, but all of these things had "claim" in my mind because I remember where we were when we bought it, and I didn't want to give it up. I had a hard time letting go of my treasures.

When the kids were all gone from the home, and time for our retirement came, for some reason, there seemed to be still a house full of stuff. Over the years we would travel and stop at antique stores, also go to auction sales, and continue to pick up good stuff. We would take a van full of antiques to Flomaton Antique Auction House in Flomaton Alabama, right on the Alabama-Florida line above Pensacola, Florida, several times a year for about 10 years. We continued to find something we couldn't live without, as well as sell some things we could live without, which was rare. It was a fun time, but when retirement time came we sent 2 huge truckloads of stuff to a large auction house in Ashville, North Carolina. One chest of drawers, with inlays, on the drawers and back rail on the top was reluctantly sent to Ashville for sale because the auctioneer said it was beautiful, and he thought it would bring about $10-$12,000.00. I had bought it in an antique store after dickering about the price awhile, and had to pay $1800 for it. They wanted $2500.00 for it, and we had decided to keep it. We decided if it would bring that kind of money, we'd sell it. We put it in the auction. I couldn't believe it brought $34,500.00, with a 15% buyer's premium. It was evaluated by a professor from a North Carolina university who identified it as a Green County Tennessee chest, by some specific maker, identified by the style of inlay. We knew it was made about 1810-1820, but was unsigned.

During the years, the desire for antique furniture has increased, but the idea that you should carefully refinish the old stuff has changed. We didn't know by refinishing the antique, you lose a significant value of the piece. Now they warn you to LEAVE IT LIKE YOU FIND IT. NO REFINISHING IF YOU WANT TO RETAIN THE VALUE OF THE PIECE. They call it "The School of Grunge." Oh, well who knew? I think we wound up being pretty successful by using our antique furniture in our home, enjoying it, and we made some money in the overall investment for most of our married life. Brand new furniture winds up as second hand furniture, and a great loss at resale, until it becomes antique at 100 years of age, if it's made of real wood, and especially if it is hand made. We made enough money from the auctions to pay cash for our retirement home, which is good.

A collection of stamps, unused, bought at the post office in sheets, accumulated over time were sold at above face value, but I don't know how much we profited from them. They were sold as one lot to one collector. I never got enough, or have interest enough to learn what was good or bad. It was an easy thing to buy a sheet at a time, and accumulate. When the time came to liquidate, I didn't have the time to investigate the importance or the value of each sheet. Most of them commemorate something or somebody, so value accumulates and changes from time to time.

Coins attracted my attention in the late 1960s and I learned a lot from Claude Ray owner of a coin shop in Winter Haven, Florida for years. He educated me about gold especially $20 dollar Saint Gaudens gold pieces. He advised me to buy all I could when they were $30 dollars a coin. I bought one at a time, thinking I would give one to each of my kids. I slowly, one at a time accumulated 6, and then continued, until I had another 10 coins. We gave the kids theirs one Xmas, and they all still have them I think. Price of gold went way up in the '70s I think, and one of the kids needed and wanted his money, and sold it for $800. I still have mine, and right now gold is over $800 an ounce, making these numismatic coins worth more, but I don't know what. Other silver coins turned out to be a good collection, because the U.S. took the silver out of coins, so the prices are all way up, for the silver and numismatic value. I used to spend many a night going through bags of pennies, dimes, quarters and halves, looking for the numismatic more expensive coins. Some I found. I should have bought more silver and gold coins, like Claude used to tell me. He was a good friend, but sadly, he's been gone several years now.

We had been in the habit of attending auction sales of estates, looking to collect anything that one might find to start collecting, or add to a collection. We already began with antique furniture and glassware. Several auctioneers had sales that we had attended, like Marty Higgenbotham's, and Albritton's in Lakeland, Florida, Phil Riner's and Randy's Kincaid in Winter Haven, Florida and had picked up stuff. One thing we got interested in was Ivory. It was becoming scarce because laws were controlling it coming into the United States. People who attended auctions were aware of our interest in Ivory, because of what we had purchased from time to time at the auctions.

One day in my office a gentleman came in requesting to talk to me. He was escorted to my office to await me. When I walked in he was standing holding a long spiraled, ivory appearing pole almost 6 foot high. He asked me if I wanted to buy his ivory for $400.00. He had a Narwhal tooth. He told me he had been told that I would be interested because I had bought some ivory at sales. He gave me the story of collecting it by being on a boat in the Bay Of Disco (I believe, in far north—east of Canada). He shot the animal, drug it to shore and sawed off the Tusk to bring home.) He had recently come to our area, and had a newspaper picture of him standing with his specimen. I offered him $200.00, and after a while, he accepted, so I bought me a Narwhal tooth. I decided to save it in my office, wait until Christmas, and wrap it and present it to my wife for a Christmas present. I would tell her it was a Unicorn horn. At Christmas I wrapped it well, and that morning I presented my present to my lovely wife. After wondering, struggling to unwrap and open it, excitingly talking all the time, finally got it opened and was admiring my present, I said "A Unicorn horn for you, my dear" And up piped 6 or 7 year old David, and exclaimed, "Oh, a Narwhal tooth!" I was aghast at the kid's knowledge, and said, "Hush, how did you know?" He said, "I read about whales in the encyclopedia." I said "Oh, you just spoiled my joke." So everybody laughed.

When I first came to Auburndale, I wanted to buy an orange grove, but prices for a good grove was about $1500.00 an acre. I decided to wait until the prices came down, and when I had made some money, which was harder than I thought. After a few years, a friend, Roger Cheek, son of realtor Al Cheek, and I decided to become partners in buying and selling groves and other real estate. He was an antique dealer, quite knowledgeable, as well as a realtor, and quite knowledgeable. I was just knowledgeable.

One of our first deals was 2 lots that we bought in the brand new huge development south of Kissimmee, Florida, south of Disney World that had just recently begun, named Poinciana. We had them for several years, waiting for the population boom that was a lot slower than we anticipated. We decided to separate them, he took one and I took the other. He sold his in a New York newspaper want-add. I waited and waited, paying all the fees of ownership such as paving, electricity, sewage and taxes, and interest on the loan for purchase. Finally after 30 or so years public interest in the area developed, and we sold it for what we originally paid for it. I don't know how much money we lost on that investment. It was all the years of the above mentioned expenses. This was accompanied by a lot of discussions having to do with brains, common sense decisions, and stupid actions requiring money that wasn't readily available, requiring interest accumulation on debt. I kind of got sick of hearing about the same old thing.

With Roger out of my decision making about a future lot for our retirement house we began finding places we may want to live later. Lake Marianna, a beautiful lake between Auburndale and Lake Alfred, Florida, a small town east of us, had just opened up new lots on the lake and across the street. We arranged to buy one on the lake and 2 across the street. We wanted the one on the lake, and Granny, Elizabeth's mother, wanted one and we thought one of the kids wanted to move there later. None of our kids wanted to buy it so we sold it. Granny kept hers awhile then decided to sell it. Some years later we found a better one, and sold this Lake Marianna lot for a little profit.

A little later we bought a lot on Lake Hamilton. The Lake Region Yacht and Country Club is on that lake in Winter Haven, Florida, We were charter members of that club. We got rid of that one too, and bought one in Cypresswood Golf and Country Club in Winter Haven, Florida on the 6<sup>th</sup> fairway. A builder wanted to build a home on it so we sold it to him. We bought the last home lot on the lake in Gates of Lake Region. After our retirement, we bought our retirement home in The Enclave at Cypresswood, in Winter Haven, so we sold the lot at the Gates of Lake Region. We didn't make any money to speak of with all those transactions, we just moved money around.

The grove prices never came down, only up. Roger and I bought a grove together, and made out OK on a couple of crop years, and then Roger had a setback and couldn't pay his part of the mortgage. I offered to buy his half at a reduced price. He agreed. We had it taken care of by our friend Jere Stambaugh's grove caretaking business. We put this grove and it's fruit income and expenses, and the medical office with it's expenses and rent from me, in a ten year Clifford Trust for the kid's college education. That was a tremendous help. They no longer have Clifford Trusts.

Roger and I bought 150 acres of mostly swamp land, from an old gentleman for $15,000.00. He died soon after that, and before long Roger found some people in Miami looking for acreage in this area. They came up, looked at it, and bought it for $150,000.00 for investment. We divided the money, I put a good deal of it in oil well drilling, invested in several wells, usually at $1000 a unit. They were drilling in Michigan mostly, and we went to a couple of wells that they thought were going to be whoppers. When they knew about when they were going to drill into the level where the oil was going to flow from, we flew to the area and waited for the drill-in. They all turned out to be pathetic flows of oil, lasting for short time, months, and then they just capped them off as losers. I had one well that paid pretty good for a while, then it slowed a lot. It still, after about 30+years, pays us monthly, from 0 to $4monthly. I spent a lot of my money waiting for the big boom, which didn't happen. Elizabeth and I had a couple of discussions about that investment. There still is an occasional comment about them, even after all these years. But that's OK, I can take it.

One deal with Roger was a 5 acre piece developed in the area between Haines City and Poinciana, near Loughman, Florida. The area was a 30 acre piece cut in to 5 acres, and a few sold and mobile homes were in place and some people lived there. An older couple lived on the plot next to ours. We obtained ours in a swap deal with Realtor Joe Lombardi, a good friend and patient. On our piece, the last one in the row, contained 8 or 10, 55 gallon empty, old rusty drums scattered in one area. They had apparently been dumped, a good time ago. Roger, in all his dealings, found he couldn't keep up with this either, so I bought his half.

There began newspaper articles of a man who was developing neurological weakness and getting unable to walk. I got a visit from a state agency involved in pollution. He advised me of the drums, which had contained some waste chemical, rusted and leaked into the

ground and seeped down hill into my neighbors well; his water supply revealed the chemical that was in my ground. He said I was going
to have to move these barrels to Alabama where the nearest area
things like this can be safely deposited in a special regulated and
approved dump site, for the southeast U.S. Then I must clean up the
ground below these drums to get rid of the chemical in the ground.
I'm looking at a bunch of money I didn't have, and I wanted to just
run away. I told him how I wound up with the property, and he said he
would try and investigate where the drums came from. About 6-8
months later he called me and said he had identified that the drums
were from a large chemical plant in the Bartow area, and they had
contracted with a hauler to take them to Alabama, but the driver knew
of this remote land, isolated that he decided to just save driving to
Alabama, and dump them here, many months before I owned the
property. He told me the company had the responsibility, not me, so I
was off the hook. That was a close one, and I sold that 5 acres fast, for
a great deal—for the buyer. After this, there were a few in house
remarks, not very pleasing, but I can take it! I think the poor man who
lived next door continued with his neurological problem, and I was,
and am sorry.

Roger and I had a few more real estate deals that after a while, he
could not pay his share, so I found another friend, Dr. Charlie Curtiss,
Radiologist, to join me and buy his share. We finally sold our investments and maybe made a little money, but as a rule, doctors are not
such great business men.

I read advertisements of collector plates being a good investment.
They are easy to buy at $15-20 a plate, when they are issued monthly,
until the series of 12 months is over. It doesn't cost much, and the
wife never knows about them, and then you get the entire series. They
were easy to hide in my office. Then you can always find another
interesting series, like a flower plate a month, or a plate commemorat-
ing the revolutionary war, with war pictures, or individuals who
helped us fight the war, like Lafayette. Hummel plates are another
series. Known painters series is a good one. There are a number of
companies, like Bradford, making these investments available to certain business people like me who like to collect things that are going
to really appreciate.

If you are looking for a good way to get out of a marriage this is a
good one to try, up until you retire every thing goes smoothly, the
plates come monthly, you look at them and admire them, then store
them with the others that she doesn't know about, and forget'em.

They accumulate and you feel smug, like you know you're going to make a great profit when you retire and sell'em. Then the time come you decide to retire, quit your practice and sell your home. You suddenly wake up, and know you have to tell her, or sell'em, and there ain't no place that will, or wants to buy'em. You just mention to your wife you have a few things that she may want to help you take care of. Like liquidate stuff she didn't know was OURS. So she says "No problem I'll take care of them," through clinched teeth. Just tell your loving wife and let her find a place. Mine did real good, had the auction company come and pick them all up, take to their auction, and sell'em all for one small price. There was a lot of quiet around my house for a couple of weeks. I know she was thinking, and trying to find the right words to use discussing these items. I don't want to discuss this period in my life, even though it was real good!

There was a time the conversation could have just moved on beyond the discussion, very loudly, about stupid people doing stupid things with money. I solved that problem, by just shutting up. There is always somebody that will just buy anything, especially something they don't know anything about at auction, for a couple of bucks for 40 or 50 plates. Turns out I didn't make any thing on a whole bunch of all kinds of series plates, and some of them were really pretty, but we did have some tax deductions. It was very interesting to see and hear Elizabeth's discussions about that mode of investment.

Oh well, and then there were Beanie Babies, lots and lots of Beanie Babies, hidden in my office, and in a far away closet, and nooks in my big house. They came to light when we sold the big house. She was in the closet before I knew they were ready for closet check. I had to bring them out and she wanted to know "what are Beanie Babies? And why did you buy them?" I said "I don't know."

After Terry went back to St. Petersburg, he got interested in horse racing and went out to the Florida Downs racetrack in Oldsmar, Fla. north of Tampa. During our internship at Mound Park Hospital, and even after coming to Auburndale we would go to the Greyhound race tract and try to win betting. While Elizabeth was big and pregnant, we occasionally went with Terry to the horse race tract at Oldsmar, north of Tampa. Her being pregnant didn't keep us at home.

He and several other doctors met a horse trainer at the tract, who was a trainer for Ocala Stud Farms in Ocala, Florida, and got interested in putting together a group of owners and buy a racehorse for the trainer, Colonel Randolph Tayloe to train. Tayloe was well respected as a good, honest trainer, with a lot of experience, and was able to choose a good individual horse. They got into business, bought a couple of horses, trained them as young horses, took them to the tracks and raced them at Hialeah, Fla. racetrack in Miami and up into New England. They had a measure of success, and even bought a small farm in Ocala, to train horses. I couldn't invest with them because they put in too much money each, to begin their venture.

Colonel Tayloe told them about a filly at Ocala, that he thought a lot of, and suggested they buy her at the upcoming annual 2 year old sale. Terry's group already had horses and at the time couldn't afford to buy her. So—I talked to the Colonel and we made a deal, for him to train her for free, I would buy her, and we would go into partnership. We went to the auction at Hialeah and were really impressed with all of the known owners, public figures and breeders there. I loved the filly's name "FERTILE FIELD," I new this was a prophetic name for my new investment, this was a field I knew nothing about but I hoped it was going to be fertile. I immediately felt right at home, a big thoroughbred horse owner, racer, and breeder. At auction I bid up to my limit of $5000.00 and somebody else bought her. I was sad wanting to become a wealthy horse owner and breeder, and my world was shot.

A week or so later the Col. called me and said he had made a deal with Ocala Stud, who had been the buyer of their own horse because she didn't bring enough money. They would take the deal for $5000, and let us pay them 1/2 of the winning purse from her races, until we had paid the 5000. She was ours, in training as a 2 yr. old. Tayloe thought she had great speed, because she was extremely quick out of the gate, and outran all other 2 yr. olds at the farm. At this young age the length of the races for the first year is only 3 furlongs. The filly ran and won her first 4 or 5 races, easily. She was very fast and we were able to pay her off quickly and she was paying her feeding and veterinary fees. She was entered in some of the big named races for the next year for 6 furlongs and longer. We had some money in the bank and were really dreaming big.

Elizabeth and I took a trip to Miami to see her race a couple of times. On one occasion, we went out the night before to one of the night clubs having a Go-Go Dance contest. There was dancing until the contest, which was scheduled for later in the evening. We danced and drank, and drank, and after the contest we went back to our Americana Hotel room, pretty well looped. We got in bed about 1 AM. I wanted to go see my horse train early the next morning, about 6:30 to 7 AM.

It's a long drive from the Americana Hotel on Miami Beach down to Miami and on through town to Hialeah Race Track. The hotel operator woke me so I could go. I was really hung over. Elizabeth refused to get up and go, so I made myself get up and go. I got my car, began the trek, and noted I felt a little nauseated, but persisted—to see my horse train. Finally, in Miami I HAD to vomit, nothing open, I finally pulled over, in a residential area with some traffic, I sat upright as any sober gentleman would do, took the plastic waste bucket with flaps on opposite sides of the bottom to keep it upright on the transmission hump in the front floor, placed it against my upper chest and drooled my vomit into the container, trying to be as sophisticated as I knew I was, trying my best to keep my beard dry. I was hoping no human was watching me. When I quit vomiting the container was within an inch of overflowing the top. I saw no one staring at me, so I very carefully placed the full container back on the floor, started the car, eased on off and noted a canal in a residential area, with a road in front of a lot of beautiful homes facing the canal. I saw no one so I pulled up along the canal, eased out on the driver and canal side, eased to the waters edge, and slowly poured my vomit into the dirty canal, and sloshed out my container, looked nonchalantly out over the expansive body of water- a canal about 20 yards wide then stretched a little and moseyed on back to my car and drove my big headache on to the race track. I immediately found the rest room and washed up. I had an owners pass for the track, so I strutted up to the gate, presented my pass and was let in by somebody who was more sophisticated than I thought I was.

I found the proper stable and Colonel Tayloe and the grooms were just about to exercise the horse, which was a slow gallop around the track, then they walked her to cool her off. That was what I got to see. But I was happy and hung over. I went on back to the Americana Hotel, awoke my wife, and we decided to go back home, so we started driving. Elizabeth muttered something like, "This is ridiculous." I agreed with her in my aching head but she never heard it, so she never knew.

At the 6 furlong distance Fertile Field seem to tire and not able to win until she was dropped down in class. She had been in a higher class, $6000-10000 claiming. She won at 4-5000 class though. Then all of a sudden she was claimed at $5000. That means any trainer can claim any horse in any claiming race for that amount of money. They put the money up before the race, you don't know it, and after the race they walk up and take your horse and lead it to their barn, and it is their animal. So if you don't want to risk losing a horse, don't enter a claiming race. However you may not be able to race because that is what keeps it honest, and someone will claim the horse if they drop the horse down to a lower class race, and she is much better than others in the race.

Another time I went a sale in Ocala Stud, and bought a yearling filly for $100 dollars. This filly, Foreign Escapade, another excellent name that I could dream with, was bred well, in Georgia. The breeder had sent the farm hand down to bring the horse, for sale, and at auction they started trying to get 2500, no bids, kept dropping the price, it got to 500, I popped up and bid $100 dollars. No other bids, she was mine. I was excited and, whoever heard of someone buying a race horse for a hundred dollars.

On the way back to the barn area to see my horse, the farm hand from the breeding farm in Georgia stopped me. He told me he was supposed to buy her back if she didn't sell for a decent price, but that he had just gone out to buy a coca-cola and the horse came up for sale too quick. He wanted to buy her back, and pleaded with me until he finally gave up. I repeatedly told him my horse was not for sale. He figured he was going to lose his job, not my problem, it was my future.

I had no transportation for her, no way to leave with her. I asked the farm if we could leave her there until I could get back to get her. They agreed. I was excited, and decided to call her "C-NOTE." Then when I got home I asked Dr, Arnold Spanjers, Dr. Frank Zeller, and Dr. Bill Cottrell to be my partners, and share expenses. They all agreed and were excited to be racehorse owners. They also were physicians and not much on investments either, apparently.

One of Frank's friends had a horse trailer, we borrowed it, and I drove up to Ocala, picked up our horse, brought her back to Winter Haven to a small farm that Frank owned, and put her out. Frank's father was happy to feed and take care of her until we were able to put her in training as a 2 year old. We sent her to Hialeah Race Track and Colonel Tayloe to start training. Colonel Tayloe wanted to wait until the horse got larger and more mature before racing. When she was able to race as a 3 year old Tayloe said he wanted to send her back to Florida Downs in Oldsmar, Florida, just out of Tampa, Florida, and he referred her to another trainer at the Florida Downs, Mr. Camac a friend of Tayloe's.

In her first race, a 6 furlong race, all of my partners were at the track, excited. At the start our horse immediately took the lead, lead all the way around and was clipped by head, being barely beaten, wound up $2^{nd}$. I had my 16 MM movie camera trained on her to record her first race. I was watching through the lens ready to shoot the footage and followed the race the whole time and forgot to press the button to record it. So I got not one inch of her first race on film. I was very embarrassed, having watched it all through the eyepiece, and the other guys kidded me for a long time about that. We were all disappointed, but still happy. We had her for a year or so, she raced in all the tracks, in the east, generally in the lower class races, and we finally lost her in a $2500 claiming race. She had won enough to make her keep, but we didn't get rich, just a lot of fun.

I bought another horse, Helio Turn, bred north of Polk City; he won a few races and about fed himself, and was lost in a low claiming race. He was bred at one of the Fussell's farms north of Polk City, Florida. I had one more named Super Magic—we claimed that horse at a track in Orlando. He won a couple but we lost him to another claim. That just about got the horse racing bug out of my mind and I gave that up. I found out race horses are a little too large to hide from the wife, so there were a few conversations, some quite loudly expressed about investing, and investments; and I was informed that they are not the same. I also found out horses don't just stand around and wait to race. While waiting, they also just eat, and eat, and eat and somebody has to walk them and rub them every day, and clean out their stalls. Then, there is the veterinary care. My wife reminded me of all this insignificant stuff, having to do with live animals.

Terry had another group of 6-8 doctors, with me in it, bought a couple of sections of land near the gulf between Homosassa River and Crystal River, Florida, a vast flat section very low salt marsh. We got it for very little money, I don't even remember how much. We never got a bite on it for sale, and then there was grumbling among some about what to do with it. I finally gave my part in the land to the University of Florida and was able to deduct the value well above what I had paid for it.

I mentioned earlier that when Elizabeth was pregnant with John, she fell in the Rainbow River when the dock fell in with her on it at a cabin we bought. That was just out of town from Dunnellon, Florida. The old cabin was wood, one big room, with a wood floor, small bath room and kitchen, and the gas tank for cooking had to be delivered. It sat outside on a stand, and the pipes entered for the stove. I had Saturday office hours from 8 AM until 12noon. I rarely got through until 2 to 4 o'clock. If we planned to take the kids up for the weekend, I generally started off for the 2 hour trip early to mid afternoon. We would get there usually late afternoon, only to find the gas tank had been replaced with an empty one. Also Elizabeth refused to put the kids down on the wood floor, which happened to be almost covered with rat things and dead roaches, every time we arrived. So sweeping and mopping was first, starting the fire on the grill for the steak was next, then find someplace that was open to get some gas for the stove and hot water. Usually Saturday afternoon was closing time for people in Dunnellon, Fla. It was a royal chore to enjoy that little spot of heaven at that time in our lives. So after wanting to go and enjoying it, and worrying about who was stealing our gas, and besides a very rainy season that flooded the entire property for months with bass swimming all around our yard and under our cabin, we finally gave up, and quit wading into our property. More kids were coming interfering with our recreation places. So we chose to keep the kids, cut down on the investments that seemed not to be my forte, and sell the place. A lot of good and unusual memories of that place though, still run through my mind sometimes. Seems memories are made of the good times.

Another stint in real estate was at Paradise Point in Crystal River, Florida. We stayed at the motel there one beautiful weekend. We loved it and Jim Dicks the owner told us he was going to sell the rooms as units, like condo type ownerships in the motel. He would manage it as usual, rent the units for us, take a management fee, and send the balance monthly to us. That sounded real good, he did that, and we decided we needed 6 units, one for each kid. He financed them all for us and we were big unit owners. We had more than anybody, except Jim, so at the first meeting, the owners elected me President of the Association. Now I'm a brilliant motel unit tycoon. We selected what we thought were choice, first floor units. I remember thinking that these would be a good investment and I could pass one to each of our 6 kids when I died.

When we owned 6 units, we had a couple of unpredictable floods, water into most of our units, up about 2 feet on the wall. Furnishings were ruined, some walls had to be replaced, and mildew was a problem. Getting reimbursed by insurance, as usual, was very slow, and there were not complete paybacks—it was just a mess. It was and still is a beautiful location. As time went on not as many rentals were occurring so that rental income wasn't working so well for us. We had a problem paying our units off, so we talked to Jim and we agreed to return 4 of the units, and have 2 left that were completely paid off.

After several years a buyer came along and Jim sold the entire place that did help us recover most of our investment.

We have many fond family memories of Paradise Point, Crystal River, Florida, and Rainbow River out of Dunnellon, Florida. You can figure it's much better to rent a place for a weekend. If you own it, you think you have to always go to the same place on a weekend, or a vacation. You feel guilty not using the expensive place you own and going someplace new and different. I found out, by discussions with my wife, several times I might add, that investing in 6 units is a little too risky for most people, especially when you have 6 kids to educate. As I said, I thought at the time, we could leave 1 unit to each kid. The problem was that we lived too long, so far. We loved both of those beautiful clear Florida rivers.

Dr. Zeller, and three other gentlemen, had a partnership ownership of mining claims in a placer gold mine in Costa Rica. His son was down there trying to run the recovery in a running stream, and taking a very small amount of gold out. One of the others wanted to sell his fourth of the ownership. He offered it to me for less than he paid to get in, about $2500.00. I decided to do so, with high hopes. Now I own part of a gold mine, who wouldn't love that?

The group was trying to decide if it was worth spending the money to get heavy equipment down there to increase the operation production. I found a former gold explorer, a Geologist, with a lot of placer gold mine experience. We were able to pay his way to visit the site, and do whatever it takes to give us an answer of the real value of the claims that we had.

After his visit of a couple of weeks, his report was that it was, a mine but probably not worth a lot of money that it would take to get equipment in such a desolate area and the men it would take, to go there and operate it. And how much gold would they manage to steal? There were no roads to it, and would have to be made to even get into the area. That was about the end of that, but we did have some exciting discussions for several months of dreams and of what might have been. Elizabeth, my wonderful, smart, vocal and lovable wife, was part of even more exciting discussions regarding the gold mine.

As our kids grew and left home going out west, we would visit them. There are numerous Indian Tribes out there and I think each tribe learned long ago that the white man is a sucker for beautiful turquoise, silver squash blossom necklaces, rugs, and anything else that looks real pretty. After several trips we had our special traders in special places that we had to check out during each visit. As time went on we wound up with quite a few beautiful things. Anyway, these things are treasured, valuable investment items.

This lead my wife to try to start buying some semi-precious stones and make herself some necklaces and ear rings, and people talked her into making them some, so she has them in a few places for sale.

Attending some of the Indian pow-wows, I met a trader who also traded in antique African Trade Beads. These beads were made from 1490s, mostly in Venice, Bohemia, and Holland on into the 20$^{th}$ century. They are of glass with other colors of glass molded into them, making many different, beautiful beads that don't deteriorate. They were used at that time, as trade routes opened up, to take to Africa to trade for gold, ivory, slaves, and other products. Many beads were brought in, and traded, so Africa is where these things are found buried. They became desirable in the Hippy Generation years, and the girls all had them on, then they became quite popular, valuable and now somewhat scarce. They have many names such as Chevrons, rare 7 layers, 6 layers are scarce, Lewis and Clark beads, King beads, Bodom beads, Millefiori and many, many more different and beautiful. So, naturally, I became a connoisseur, and a collector and investor of a few nice beads. There have been a few scattered discussions regarding bead investing that seems to come up concerning a new availability of some desirable beads, from time to time. You win some and you lose some—discussions.

Sometime in the '70s or 80s Frank Zeller my Surgeon friend, asked me if I was going to the Gem Show in Tampa that weekend. I said "What show is that?" He explained that the House Of Onyx, out of Kentucky, was again coming for this years show of semi-precious stones, and he and Shirley, his wife, always go and maybe pick up some really great buys of precious stones, loose, not mounted, and you buy them at really no risk, because they will always buy back from you the same stone at least for what you pay for it, but maybe more, depending on the present prices. This sounded like a tremendous deal for experienced investors like me. Discount buying with a guarantee resale source, for at least what you pay for it, maybe more? We went, met Fred and his wife Shirley, owners of the company. Saw some fabulous stones, bought a few and were very happy with our new investment.

They would come to Orlando, or Tampa, and other Florida locales, with their wares for sale. We attended a few, always picking up a few beautiful stones. Each year the company invites some of their good customers to their store in Kentucky for special sales in their warehouse, at their expense to stay in a local hotel with meals. We were privileged to attend one of these sales. While driving to Kentucky, in very hot weather, our car air conditioning quit cooling. It was hot, hot and we didn't have time to have some mechanic put in a new one. We went to a store and bought an empty spray bottle and some water, and sprayed each other shirts and opened the windows to keep us cool all the way to Kentucky, and back home. We enjoyed our trip, bought a few things, and saw Mammoth Cave in its entirety deep into the earth, it was very impressive, and a long walk.

While there in the hotel, we ran into one of their hotels artists and some of his wonderful animal life paintings, and bought a few, like tigers in the snow, a flying eagle, and stuff like that. We met the artist and his name was Robertson. We still have our stone investments. A few years ago Fred, the owner, died suddenly of a heart attack. We were sad to hear about that. His wife Shirley still runs the business, and we still get fliers from her.

Some months later I called and spoke to one of the principals about selling some of our beauties that they had guaranteed to repurchase. I was told that since Fred had died that program was no longer in effect. Well that investment is still pending, but certainly did create fine fodder for discussion periods. Especially, from time to time when something triggers the mind of things I thought were forgotten.

There was a time that investing in stocks came up and interested me. One of my cousins, dead now, Bennett Waites, was a son of Mama's oldest sister Mattie. Bennett moved to our area, and Terry ran into him in St. Petersburg, Florida, after he moved back there. Bennett was an attorney and was instrumental in helping a group of business men start a company called "Reinsurance Investment Corporation." It would be a reinvestment insurance company. He told Terry this is the time to buy stock in this brand new company when the stock is cheap at $2.00 a share. Terry bought some, and so naturally I had to have some of my cousin's good investment. I couldn't bear to be left behind. I touted it to some of my doctor friends, and friends, and several agreed this was a good ground floor chance to invest and make some money. After a couple of years, the stock moved, gradually lower to about .50 cents a share. We all got scared and sold out as the stock just apparently went nowhere and was no longer listed. Bennett was very hard to get hold of and moved out of the area, later Terry found out he died.

But Terry had another friend, Mr. Cozart, president of "Automatic Merchandising," a company operating vending machines over the west coast of Florida, doing very well. I followed Terry into that investment, got quite a number of shares, and I was put on the Board of Directors, along with business people from Tampa. At the Directors meetings I became acquainted with Mr. Jack Eckerd, founder and president of Eckerd Drug Stores, others I have forgotten. After a few meetings, Mr. Eckerd resigned, citing that he was too busy to continue involvement. After another year or so, the company slowly declined and finally was sold after Mr. Cozart died.

Again, I sold my stock at a significant loss. It seemed that my wife was not the usual happy, loving, supportive wife that used to be easy to talk to, having changed to a raucous, loud, misunderstanding, shouting, unknown woman I had come to know associated with a few setbacks in my investing ventures, even though these meager losses were deductible.

And then there were metal houses. One of my other realtor friends and I were just talking about stuff. The conversation moved into a metal house that he was building for his mother on one of his lots. It was very interesting, and I wanted to know more. A company was looking for people to build them in different parts of the U.S. David was the one in this area. He had been offered stock in the company, and I got around to asking if I could invest in the innovative new concept. He had been offered a certain number shares, he could only buy some of what he was offered, so I was able to pick up the balance. David Watson paid for his, and I gave him a check for my part, $30,000.00.

These things looked really good to me. I watched his mother's home go up and it was really exciting. On a concrete slab, metal foundations were secured where the walls would be. Side walls are parallel, two 12 inch wide plates of steel, 9 feet long, about 3 inches apart, sandwiching about 3 inches thick foam insulation material. They were bolted together in a unit, making long planks that are bolted firmly to the steel base on the floor and to each other side by side, creating walls of the rooms, and the house. These also served as the roof. The homes would be termite free, insulated, water proof, and withstand hurricane winds. Heating and air conditioning costs are very low. After his mother's was built, and she moved in, I heard she was very happy with her new home. A couple of years ago, I was sorry to see in the paper that his mother died. I don't know who lives in the home now.

David built another home several blocks from the first one. He also got a contract to construct a school building, like the temporary building additions that they add to the school grounds, in the Orlando area.

I went up to see it, and was impressed with it also. But what do I know? Things were looking real good, and then the company suddenly apparently went into bankruptcy. It has been several years and I have heard nothing more about this fantastic, new, innovative way to build homes. It seems they are still building homes the old fashion way, as far as I can tell. After this latest real-estate-building investment, it was only a few days until the wife, being interested and involved in my life for a long time, suddenly brought up the venture for discussion. She had no knowledge of the new situation (bankruptcy) but she, doing a professional-FBI-like investigation, soon got the truth out of me, very, very, reluctantly. After new daily discussions, I finally told here "next time a good deal comes along, and when I get another $30,000, I'm just gonna turn it over to you and see how good you do. SO THERE!!!"

I stayed away from things a while, then we got an invitation to have a free dinner at one of the local restaurants, to hear a specialist investment broker talk about retirement investing. I thought it might be a good idea to hear a successful broker from the big city of Tampa, Florida explain how to do it—-make money in the stock market, or set up a retirement portfolio. My wife didn't want to go, but I convinced her I needed to learn how to get control of our retirement, so she went. We listened after a delightful meal—FREE, and took the broker to our home and talked some more. He convinced us that we could control everything, do it carefully, and he would help us to success. Bond Clinic bought my practice about this time so we put some money in an IRA and some money into our personal account.

He put us in some conservative income bonds, and things kept growing and we were doing very well. After a while, he would advise us to change some of these conservative things to better, and a little better percentage income. Things got better, so then one came along that really looked even better, so we put a lot of money in it. Within a few months, the bonds were in trouble, and stopped paying the dividend. He said they probably would have to pay every bond holder a smaller amount on the dollar after the bankruptcy hearings were over, in the next year or so, when they liquidated their assets, and they had a lot of assets. We are still waiting to hear from them. Well, the broker resigned from his company, and we are still waiting for SOMETHING, and his boss said nothing will probably come out of it. We had a number of discussions that repeatedly come up, when we talk about anything having to do with investing. But I still love her—wait-

ing for her to shut the hell up. (After she read this, she said—"it won't
happen!") On one of our trips, through Georgia, we decided to stay
off of the interstate highways and just meander over the smaller highways and go through some of the small towns. We came through a
small community, Cleveland, Georgia.

We stopped and looked through one of the flea markets and noted a
peculiar, ugly face made out of pottery. It was a gallon jug size, with a
small, frowning, pinched up, uuuugly, and I do mean ugly, facial
expression. I asked about it, and was told it was done by "One uv
them Meaders out tere outsid o' town at dere own famly kiln, name
uv Reggie Meaders. His brother is Lanier, is a real famous face-jug
maker." I just had to have it so I bought it. In several other shops in
town, there were face jugs by some of the brothers that we bought.
We learned Lanier, Edwin, John, and Reggie were the boys, and they
learned from their daddy, and mama Arie. The brothers are in their
80's, or are dead and the parents are dead.

We picked up several jugs, and went out to the family kiln and
met Reggie's son David Meaders who was there with his wife
Anita. David had been drinking and was real happy to see us. They
were "pottin' and fixin to put 'em all in the kiln and far 'em." I
showed him all the face jugs I had bought, so Elizabeth took a picture with me, and David, holding several of my new investment
face jugs. He was pleased and happy I had gotten a bunch of his
family's pottin.' We have occasionally picked up another Reggie's,
or Lanier's, or Edwin's jugs or pottery chicken. I was able to pick
up one of mama Arie's chickens, paid $2250.00 for it at auction,
and a couple of years later sold it at auction for $6500.00 to an
attorney from Gainesville, Georgia. We still look around for them.
Elizabeth kinda seems a little more lenient about some of these
things because she has picked up a few cute little animal pieces
that she likes, especially some of Billy Ray Hussey's pieces. He
pots in North Carolina, and he runs a frequent auction of Southern
Folk Pottery. Selling many good authentic, sometimes expensive
Face jugs and other really old Southern pieces, however, it does
seem to me her interest recently is waning, and my stuff is not as
cute as hers, but she notices my interest continues to burn brighter.
There has been, lately, some irritation notably arising from beneath
her calm, adult female predictable seething. I am at the present
time trying to be nice to her. For 50 years she has been harping on
having a savings account at the bank. I never would agree to stand

for that paltry interest, and most skilled investors, like me, would agree with me.

After all of this, and after reading all I have written, it is no wonder that my wife became an alcoholic. At the time of my investing I really believed I could make substantial money quickly. I had no idea of the anxiety and fear, the mother of my 6 children felt, scraping by to pay our bills.

# 9

# Office Visits and Patient's Comments and Quotes

## INTRODUCTION

These people are among my patients that walked through the hours and minutes of my life here in Auburndale. I can't remember a one of them that I wouldn't call a good friend, even the few that may have become angry with me, when I fussed at them, or took too long to see them in the office. Our town had several companies supporting a large Florida citrus industry. From the beginnings, in the late '30s '40s and '50s, many families migrated to this area to find jobs, from all areas in the south. Many were poor farmers where most did not have good foundation in education, and their children were taught their customs, ways of speech, and habits. All were good hard working honest people. I was privileged to treat many varieties of individuals and society levels. I felt comfortable speaking whatever level they came in speaking. I became friends with all of them, whether I was their friend or not. Most of what follows is sentences, or sayings, or comments that came out of the patient's mouth during my questioning them, or maybe a long winded comment I took down during my interview with them. They talk candidly if they have a good relationship with the doctor, and it's my responsibility to listen and respond to try to help them, or try to solve their worries or problems. Sometimes there is no

263

answer or solution. I tried to do the best I could. Some office visits and quotes that I have recorded seem to reflect the way many of my patients understand medicine and perceive their body parts, location, and functions, of how things anatomically, physiologically, and mentally, work.

I am really impressed with some of my patient's colorful, quaint and usual combinations of words, spoken in half-words, contractions, and "new spellings" of sounds of usual and common words that I try to copy to convey the way things were said to me. No one has any problem understanding what they mean to say, their meanings are clear.

The names in these two chapters are not those that spoke the quotes. They are just false names. I will try to choose some of the best of their comments. I included none of these patient's comments to degrade or diminish them. I consider all of them my good friends, and appreciate them allowing me to be part of their lives and my medical journey. I had saved these individual comments and phrases and always had the idea to put them in a short book, called "A Commode Book: For short reads while 'resting'." When I finally started that book, it dawned on me that the reader might want to know something about who wrote the thing, so I began trying to explain who I was, and it got out of hand and it wound up as an autobiography.

Note: For clarity, my patients' words will be and my words will not be in quotation marks, and paragraph breaks will separate different patients' quotes.

## COMMENTS AND QUOTES

One of my 60+ year old obese hypertensive ladies had married for the 3$^{rd}$ time. When she would return for follow up, I would always find that, after months and months, she had failed to lose any weight as I had ordered, asked, and even pleaded, for her to do. Her blood pressure was not controlled either, so we had a round every time she came in. On one of the last times I saw her she was brought in to the exam room, and was seated when I came into the room. Right as I sat down, she said, in her low key, usual slow talking voice, "Dr. Tanner, don't never tell me to lose weight no more, my husband won't let me." I asked her why. She said, "He says he wants to feel something between him and the mattress. That's why I ain't lost no weight." Somewhat surprised I assured her I certainly would follow their request, and I would continue to try and control her blood pressure.

She seemed pleased and I never spoke again to her about her weight. The weight and blood pressure never changed as far as I know.

§ § § § §

A young mother came in with her 7-8 year old daughter. I was their doctor and had seen them both before. When I asked the mother why she was there, she said "I want you to write a note to the school and tell them to keep my daughter out of Phys. Ed." I asked her why. The mother said, "She don't like it." I asked what was wrong with her. She said, "Nothin,' she just don't like the runnin' and stuff." I told her I can't just write a note for that, that I had to have a medical reason for me to request them to keep her out of Physical Education. I asked her why she doesn't write a note to them. She got very angry and loudly yelled, "DON'T YOU KNOW I'M DECLARED MENTALLY INCOMPETENT AND THEY WON'T BELIEVE ME?" I told her I didn't know that. She yelled, "YORE A DOCTOR AND CAN'T TELL THAT?" I told her no, but that I still couldn't just write a note, if she didn't have a medical reason to take her out of Physical Education. She yelled, "WELL, JUST MAKE UP SOMETHIN'!" I told her I couldn't just do that. She got up, jerked her daughter up and walked out telling me she was going to change doctors.

§ § § § §

One of my trucker patients came in to see me for heartburn, which he had had for 2 weeks. It started while he was on the road, and he got home from his run to the Chicago and mid- USA. He couldn't take the time for an evaluation with a GI Series, so I just started him on the medication Tagamet, which was one of the early new medications for gastric problems, peptic ulcer disease, hiatal hernia symptoms, heartburn, and the like. He was a long time sufferer with Psoriasis, and for years was being treated by dermatologists for the large plaques on both arms, elbows, knee areas, and some back areas. He was using prescription creams given by his doctors. After a month or so, he returned home and came in telling me his stomach got fine and his extensive psoriasis had nearly cleared up. He wanted me to keep him on Tagamet because he just knew that is what made his psoriasis so much better. I did that and saw him each time he came home over almost a year. One day I went in an exam room and met a new patient. She was from a town in Iowa. She stated she drove down to Auburndale to see me as a patient because of her friend, a trucker patient of mine with Psoriasis, told her that I had a treatment for Psoriasis that worked really well for his Psoriasis and she wanted some to see if it would help hers. I never had any idea that Tagamet would help Psoriasis. I explained the use of Tagamet, for stomach acidity, just happened to help my patient. She wanted it so I gave her a prescription for Tagamet 400 mgms to take 1 twice a day. I asked her to please let me know if it helped her. She was a very nice middle aged lady with rather severe psoriatic lesions on her arms and legs. She said she also sits out in the sun in the summertime and it seems to help. I knew Tagamet was in a class of H2 blockers, something like antihistamine drugs use for allergies, but never knew it was a possible use for Psoriasis. I have a letter from that patient named Joyce, address RR 1 Hinton, Iowa, postmarked May 7, 1981. Inside the envelope was a short letter I still have, and will quote: *"April 22, 1981. Dear Dr. Tanner. Will drop you a line to let you know how my psoriasis. They are almost completely gone. Very few spots left and they are looking real good. Only take 2 pills a day. Have had no side effects from them. Sure am happy about them. Thank you. Joyce."* I thought it was rather incredible that a patient, who knew one of my patients, would drive all the way to Auburndale from Iowa, for a possibility to be made better with her Psoriasis. I never heard from her again, and have no idea how she is. I often wondered how she got along.

§ § § § §

I was talking to one of my black preacher patients when he came in for his blood pressure check. He told me about his church. He said, "All them other preachers preach smoothin' to you. I preach truth, you got to get out of sin. You can't go back to you alcohol and you whores and all that other sin. Jesus won't save you in the sin, only out of the sin—so you got to quit before Jesus comes into you life. Come to our church. We have a shoutin' good time."

§ § § § §

I asked one of my smokers if he had quit smoking yet. He said, "I haven't finished quitin' yet."

§ § § § §

I had asked one patient to call me to get a lab report, he apologized and said, "I forgot to remember to call you about that."

§ § § § §

I was talking to a little 5 year old girl named Danielle, and she was proudly telling me—"I'm smarter than other kids. I learn quicker than other kids my age, and I never get into trouble."

§ § § § §

One of my long time patients, a 38 year old white female came in following a 4 day admission through the emergency room after suicide attempts. She said, "Got out 4 days ago and am extremely depressed. First I ran my car into a tree, and I didn't die. Then I smoked 3 packs of cigarettes a day and drank a lot of vodka, and I didn't die. Then my boyfriend moved out 2 weeks ago." I asked how long they were together and was it a long time. She said, "Yeah, but not a real long time. He keeps moving out with other women, and when he can't find none better'n me he comes back, and leaves again, over and over. I'm gonna' kick'm out for good."

§ § § § § §

A mother of one of my patients was asking to refill Amoxil and I asked her how many milligrams she was taking, 250 or 500 milligrams. She said, "I don't know because I never was good in math, and it was my worst subject in school."

§ § § § § §

A patient I won't name, who moved here from Alabama, had no kids, never learned to read or write except her name, adopted a friends child and raised him. Came in with a cold, and informed me, "I got no moist in my mouth and can't cough, and I lost my recipe for breathing." As I was talking to her, I asked about her child who now was 28-30 years old. She said, "I thought I'd make a mess of raisin' him; I ain't never had no kids of my own." I asked her why, and she replied, " 'Cause I was such a mess myself."

§ § § § § §

Lady: "I don't want to lose weight, 'cause I don't want to get long-jawed."

§ § § § § §

Arthritic man: "I got to keep walkin' to keep my knees from growin' together."

§ § § § § §

Dolph: "I'm sore all over. I fell out of a tree trying to flesh a squirrel out so them other boys could shoot 'im." Do you drink? "Yes sir, yeah, once in a while when I'm smokin'." Do you smoke? "Every night." Do you drink every night? "Mostly." How much do you drink every night? "6 pack." More? "Sometimes." 12 pack? "Yeah, a 12 pack or 2." Do you really drink two 12 packs every night? "Yeah." That's 24 beers! Every night! "Yeah." How you get up and go to work every day with a hang over? "No, I done learned how to get over that." How? "Just used to it." I gave him muscle relaxers and pain pills and warned him to not drink alcohol with these pills and to not drive a car with these pain pills. He said, "No, I gave up my license in 1982."

Emily: "I got a stuffed up nose. I didn't put no water on my head and I didn't sit up under no fan but my nose got all stuffed up. How come?"

§ § § § § §

A 51 year old, obese, edentulous, white female with chest pain for 3 days and she was very, very tired. She was scared to go to sleep these 3 days because she was scared she would die, and she wanted to be awake if she had a heart attack and died. She had a costochondritis (painful, tender, ribcage) and was quite tender over the left ribcage. I reassured her that she wasn't going to die, and gave her medication.

§ § § § § §

"I take cod liver oil for joint pains." I asked her did that really help, and she said, "I know one thing—it's sure got a fishy taste. What makes that?"

§ § § § § §

1967. A moderately obese patient and quite shy was sitting in a chair with her head down a little and her hands folded in her lap: Good morning, Helen, what's wrong with you today? "I aitches." You itch? "Yeh." Where do you itch? "Down'ere." Down where? "In ma'cat." In your vagina? "Yeh." I told the nurse to put her up for an exam. We had a time convincing her to get on the table, which she finally did for the nurse. When I came back in the room she was on the table, in stirrups with a towel over her face. I did the exam, with her face covered and found severe monilial vaginitis. She was given proper medication, and 2 weeks later she returned nearly completely well. She continued Rx another 2 weeks. I didn't see her again so I assume she was OK.

§ § § § § §

Eva came in complaining of poor vision: What's wrong with your vision? "I've got inheritance disease. Tampa doctors went back 7 generations and pronounced it that. One of my sons was gonna donate one of his eyes for a eye transplant but my eyes was too far gone." I sent her to an eye doctor.

§ § § § § §

Lottie: Wonderful elderly 80+ year old lady in with one of her daughters, I asked what she was in for. "I can't think fast like I used too. Can't think good no more." Daughter said, "She used to think of things most other people would forget. She thinks better at home than anywhere else, seems like. So she won't stay with other people."

§ § § § § §

A Down' Syndrome mother called and said, "She looks like she may be trying to start to run a fever." I asked her to bring her in.

Tia: "Give me something to keep me from dancing when I pee."

§ § § § §

A patient in for herself, speaking of a neighbor's child who is autistic: "His dad's a college professor and his mother is an investment advisor. He must have just got too many genes in his brain to make him act like that."

§ § § § §

24 year old female college student with severe nausea and vomiting: "Oh, I'm so sick!" I asked what happened. She said, "I drank 4 'Lay Me Down Sweet Jesus' in a bar last night." I asked her what that was. She responded, "Each has 7 different kinds of liquor!"

§ § § § §

Saturday 11-18-00. In with a sore throat, a patient asked for a note to stay off work 2 days. I asked him when he wanted to go back to work. He said, "I want next Thursday and Friday off." I asked him could he work Monday, Tuesday, and Wednesday. He said, "Oh yeah, just off next Thursday and Friday." I said sorry, no.

§ § § § §

I did a pre-employment physical, including a drug screen that was returned showing a positive test for marijuana. The patient said, "I don't use it but I was working outside and other people were smoking and my pores were open and I absorbed it into my body." I gave him his forms and reports, and told him to take them to his employer.

§ § § § §

In for a cough, elevated blood pressure and was cross-eyed: "I got a cough and I hope I ain't comin' down with that ole ammonia again.

§ § § § §

I got me a new job." What? "Cleanin' floors at the Ford place, you got to be good and get out of the way when they zoom all those cars around all the time." I asked him what happened to his custodian job at the nursing home. He said, "They fard me, said I wasn't doin' a good enough job after all these years. I even went to school to learn how to get a job- for 5 weeks, at Project Hope. They teach you all this stuff about how to get a interview, and I learned it good." I asked how many did he have. He said, "About 18 before I got my job and it's a good 'en too. I love it."

§ § § § §

Female, 75 years old: "I want a prescription for Restoril." I told her it may cause older people to have amnesia. She said, "They ain't never done me thataway. Give it to me anyway. I already don't know nothin.' I hurt. I got veins in my head as big as I got in my legs."

Do your ears hurt? "They don't hurt worth much."

§ § § § §

"I got gas from eatin' too fast." Well, slow down. "I can't, I need to hurry to get it done."

§ § § § §

84 year old lady: "I went shoppin' for one and a half hours and I want you to listen to my heart and tell me how I feel."

§ § § § §

82 year old female: "I'm floatified!" I asked what that was. She said, "I can't keep my balance."

§ § § § §

Lady: Had blood pressure elevated and an obese abdomen. I was telling her she just had to lose weight and get rid of this big abdomen. She said, "Wait just a minute, get off of that! That's all I got after 69 years!"

§ § § § §

Elderly man in the hospital with a stroke: Two weeks ago woke up at home and called 911 and told them he was lost and to come and find him and take him home. His wife had put him in the hospital for evaluation after that.

§ § § § §

James, 92 years old: How are you, sir? "Not so hot in places. He took out my left kidney 'cause he found a tumor bleeding on it. At least that's what he told me and I got a great big scar on my side. I don't know if he took it out or not."

§ § § § §

Jimmy, 62 years old: How are you? "Lousy! I know you can't make me look better but I sure hope you can make me feel better."

§ § § § §

Beverly, 43 years old: "I overtired myself and my nose bleeds."

§ § § § §

Young woman with unusually long fingernails: Where'd you get those long nails? "I just let 'em get away from me."

§ § § § §

Lettie: 1991, 87 years old, in to follow-up on fractured ribs, 10 day recheck. How have you been getting along? "If I hadn't been so sore I could a stood it better. I raised 10 children on a farm in Tennessee and women live longer 'cause they're always busy doin' something and house work. Men retire and sit down and die 'cause they ain't got nothin' to do."

§ § § § §

Merle: "I had a blazer put in my eye last year. Boy, when you come out of that place you can see just as goooood!"

Bill, college professor, fever, aches, flu symptoms: How do you feel? "As low as dog droppings on the bottom of your shoe!"

§ § § § §

Dave: "I have occasional diarrhea real bad and got to go right now!" Is it bad? "Well. I tell you sometimes it makes you want to be somewhere else."

§ § § § §

John, physical exam: OK, now I'll have to examine your prostate. "NO! I don't need that! It's perfect." How do you know? "My wife says I'm a perfect asshole." I did examine him, and his wife was right.

§ § § § §

A 74 year old man in my office, was drinking when he came in, and commented, "You can't drink this much marguerites and still be sober. Old age is messin' up my future!"

§ § § § §

Sarah, 80 years old: What are you eating? "Whatever my appetite calls for."

§ § § § §

65 year old white female: "I itch up inside—you know, where the gums are."

§ § § § §

Alvin, a delightful 88 year old white male: How are you? "I've been feelin' fine if I could just use myself... ole arthritis got me and won't let go. I've been tryin' to use up my heart medicine before I come back to get it all renewed at once but I got too many of 'em and now I can't wait to use 'em all up. My arthritis is killin' me. I'm learnin.' I'm learning more now than when I was young. All I knowd then was get up and go to work. I got a real big hernia and don't want it fixed—I just want to go out like I come in. I'll just wait 'til the Good Lord takes me out."

§ § § § §

Doing a physical: How are your bowels? "OK now, but sometimes they get better than they should be."

§ § § § §

82 year old lady with staples in her scalp from a fall, in for a recheck: "When can you take 'em out? I'm scared to walk under lightening. I might get zapped."

§ § § § §

"My head's been bangin' since yesterday. It's killin' me and getting' worse. It's jus' athobbin'."

Man and wife in together: Wife does the talking. What's your problem? "He's scared all the time. He got so he won't drive a car. He was a drunk and had all kinds o' phobias and wouldn't go to doctors or dentists. His teeth look like 40 acres of burnt out stumps."

§ § § § § §

Betty: "My nose is gettin' so it won't run no more. It all runs down the back of my throat."

§ § § § § §

Alma came to my receptionist's window and gave her this note for me: "Dr. Tanner, I have a bad cold and congestion. Have a lot of gas (unusual for me). Cough 'til I wet my pants. Finally get something up and it's clear. Tolerance a little low. Shortminded. Do you want to see me?" I had the nurse bring Alma into a room. After going over her complaints, I was examining her abdomen. She said, "Did you find anything?" I said that no, I thought it was all OK. "Well, I thought so but I just wanted you to bless it."

§ § § § § §

Ralph: Came in and obviously had been drinking, 69 years old with a very red face. When are you going to stop drinking? "If you had the trouble I have you'd be drinkin' too. I won't quit 'til my peter dies...about a year or so." Are you seeing other women? "Yeah." How many? "Three...my wife and two other women. The wife don't like it...but I gotta git all I can before it's gone. Workin' harder and harder ...really got to work to get it done."

§ § § § § §

Fred, 67 years old: "I guess arthritis has hit my left knee, I have to help it in and out of the car."

§ § § § § §

Sudie, 60 year old black lady talking about money: "I pays my bills, 'cause ain't no tellin' when I'm gonna need that person again. If you pays you bills you ain't gonna have nothin' to save."

§ § § § § §

Alma, 72 years old white lady with back pain: "you know...you pick beans and you stop raisin' up."

§ § § § § §

Louis, 77 year old black lady: "Thank you Dr. Tanner. I always think a whole lot of ya.' Yore the first one I think of when something happens."

§ § § § § §

"'Noise in my ear and the song stays in it all the time. The song is singing all the time."

Bertha, 58 year old black mother of teenaged daughter: She came in fussing and fuming about her pregnant daughter. She said, "That chile come home pregnant. That belly is the biggest thing on her. If you lay down with a man you better have a diaphragm up yore butt, or him got a condom! Uumph! I told her she done messed up her life now!"

§ § § § § §

Farmer came here from Alabama worked in citrus: "I'm real sick, vomiting. Et greens, and fat back and laid down on it and bumped 'em back up before. I was told before I came here don't eat no fat back and greens and stuff and lay down on it, and get sick. Never had nothin' this bad before. Yesterday AM went and got a half pint of Fleishmans vodka and forgot they told me don't drink no vodka and don't follow it with no greens and fat meat. I drank it and ate. In fifteen minutes I'm bad sick."

§ § § § § §

Older female: "I had 11 kids and I nursed 'em all. The last one was too greedy and I had to put 'im on a bottle."

§ § § § § §

Richard: "My mama's name is Henrietta, right now. She's just turned 60. Had a bypass aorta. My dad has what they call ulcers on both feet. He's got sugar. I've been known to drink a lot of sweet tea."

§ § § § § §

Susie, 84 year old black lady sitting on the side of the bed, 1999: New patient with high blood pressure and bad arthritis. After finishing my interview and exam, and was writing a prescription sitting in a chair, she chuckles and said to her daughter, "Um,-um,-um look at them little bitty feet ( looking down at my shoes). Mine's big! I wear size 12 shoe, what's them?" Seven. "Um-um, them's little bitty feet." Mine certainly looked little bitty compared to hers. I noticed the rather severe 'silver-fork' deformity of her right forearm, obviously an old Colle's fracture of long ago, maybe not set or treated. How long ago did you break your arm? "I disremember, I don't know. I didn't go to no doctor—we wrapped a kerosene rag around it, yeah. How'd you know that?" I just know. I wasn't born yesterday. "Oh."

§ § § § § §

Early in our practice, when Terry was with me, a lady came in to Terry and was complaining of a large lump in her stomach. Terry asked how big it was. She said, "Oh, about the size of a 32 grapefruit." She worked in the grapefruit sectionizing department of the

Adam's plant. Neither one of us knew what a size 32 grapefruit was. Turns out that it's a rather large size grapefruit.

§ § § § § §

In 1973, I received a letter from an elderly nice patient of mine that I will quote here, written in her shaky handwriting and her own personal language:

*"march 31, 1973*

*Mr. Tanner Please don't send me noe more bills for I dont owe you a dime. You owe me Plenty I an 82 years old but if get eney more of these Big bills from you ill see if I can't collect Paye for the Waye I was treated in that hospt I turned my lite on far help and I coued not get eney one soe I had to goe to bathroom and I sliped on sopy watter and it almost taken my life now my Dr says ill never be well again I am a nervis reck soe don't send noe more Bills to me if your heart was right you would send me several thousand dollars.*

*Josie"*

I have no idea how much she was billed for. I had my office personnel cancel the bill, whatever it was, and send her no more bills. And I did not send her several thousand dollars.

§ § § § § §

Here is a recipe given to me years ago by a patient whose grandfather used for his family who lived in the country. I was told it was good for arthritis, helps lose weight, and helps lower cholesterol. I didn't know the grandfather even knew there was a thing called cholesterol, anyway here it is: I don't know if it works or not, since I never gave it to anyone, in spite of my patient saying it really worked.

1/2 cup apple cider

1/2 gallon red grape juice

1/2 gallon apple juice

Take 1/2 cup daily.

§ § § § § §

"I had a cough a long time, but I wore it out—then it came back. You got anything for that?"

§ § § § § §

An obese lady with the left eye deviated to the left and upward, blind in that eye, and with an exceptionally fat lower lip: "I slept too hard and it caused my bad headache."

Carl: 48, heavy smoker, found he had Polycythemia (increase in red blood cells from heavy smoking decreasing the oxygen in the blood, stimulating overproduction of the red cell, therefore making the blood thicker, increasing chance of stroke, and/or cardiac disease). I told him he absolutely HAD to stop smoking, after explaining it to him. He said, "Stop? I can't, it ain't my fault. The government legalizes it and I'm addicted."

§ § § § § §

Ralph: "My wife has a cleanin' service an' works only 3 piece-a-day a week."

§ § § § § §

How are you? "Great—but I got over it."

§ § § § § §

How are you today? "I feel real dingy today."

§ § § § § §

How are you? "I'm havin' headaches in the head near where the brain is."

§ § § § § §

"I ain't feelin' good. I take 400 maggots of glucophage (for diabetes), and I got Playtex in service now."

§ § § § § §

"I got blowness in my stomach after I eat."

§ § § § § §

Tora, age 22, in to see me with his wife: I asked him how he was. He looked at his wife and said, "I got rectal bleeding and I cramp." I asked him how long he had been having cramps. He looked at wife again and said, "How long, I don't know." I asked him what color his blood was. He looked at his wife yet again and said, "What color?" She replied, "I don't know—you were in the bathroom!"

§ § § § § §

81 years old female: "My pain just keeps on goin.' Guess I'll have to die to over it."

§ § § § § §

Leatrice, 69 years old: I picked up her purse to place it on the table, and told her that boy, she had a heavy purse. She said, "That's because everything goes to the bottom of my purse."

§ § § § § §

Harry: "I'm spittin' up glompy stuff."

§ § § § § §

Marie, 80 years old: "I rubbed camphorated salve on the sole of my feet for my stuffed up nose. I hate to be sick worse'n anything else."

A female patient said after relating her problem with a boyfriend: "I'm cured of men."

§ § § § § §

An obese man with a large abdomen: I was telling him he must lose weight. He said," No, every night about 12:00 o'clock my belly turns to dick."

§ § § § § §

"I got ear wax. Put Murine ear drops in and burnt a candle outside my ear and didn't do no good."

§ § § § § §

"I hurt my leg and need some crunches."

§ § § § § §

Pierce 1992, complaining of abdominal pain: Is your pain bad? "Yeah! It's bad. You don't know but I do 'cause I'm wearin' it!"

§ § § § § §

Felicia, 22 year old white lady: Tell me your problem. "Well, I was cleaning my left ear and the cotton came off of the Q-tip in my ear and I can't get it out. It feels full in my ear. I put peroxide in the right ear and it didn't go through, so it must be plugged in there." Do you really think the peroxide would go all the way through? "Somebody told me it would, and would get it out." I was able to remove the cotton, and I think she learned a new way to remove it. She was reminded of the old suggestion, "Don't put anything smaller than your elbow in your ear."

§ § § § § §

Annie: I called her phone to give her a lab report. She answered, "I'uz asleep and had to come to the phone and tuk me a minute to thaw out so I could talk straight to you."

§ § § § § §

Dave, age 60: "I went to bed perfectly healthy and woke up in the middle of the night with severe pain in my foot." This was his first acute gout attack.

§ § § § § §

W.D., age 76: "I thought I'd been dealt a cancer. That stuff I had was real weakenin'."

§ § § § § §

"I got red spots all over me and I'm not sure if it's chidkin pots or not." It wasn't, only an allergic reaction.

§ § § § § §

"Other people have a hard time putting up with me—I don't know why they complain. I find it quite easy—I live with me all the time."

A parent wrote on the line for Chief Complaint before coming in to see me with her six year old. "He has coph and feavor and sore on thum."

§ § § § § §

Lonnie, 12-30-86: Came in with impetigo. "See here? Now I'm itchin,—Watch this!—(and he scratches) SEE? I told my wife, 'Itch around my rectum.'"

§ § § § § §

Vicky: "Everything I'm around I catch it fastly."

§ § § § § §

Jan,11-3-87: "I got VD again. Me and all my friends had it 4-5 months ago. I wasn't going back to that woman no more. She gave it to me and told me she messed up an old man with the same thing." Why did you go back? Doesn't she lay around with a lot of men? "Yeah, but that woman will make you fall in love with her every time, especially if you're weak. She wants somebody to keep her. I ain't weak—I just use her and let her try to make me fall in love with her. She's good, man."

§ § § § § §

Phone call for refill on fiorinal and valium: I replied that I can't and she must come into the office. She said "I can't, I'm too sick to see a doctor."

§ § § § § §

"Somebody must be pumping up that old man—he looks real juicy. Must weigh four hundred pounds."

§ § § § § §

Henry: Very, very deaf, eighty years old, in office with his wife, and she's talking, "Came home from the hospital today, weak but OK from gall bladder surgery. He got all mixed up in the hospital and I was afraid he'd never get straightened out again, him so deaf and all. I'd really have a mess, wouldn't I? Well, some old people get mixed up when they ain't even sick, don't they?"

§ § § § § §

An 18 year old black male with an eye infection: I asked him to put his name right there on that line. He said, "I got to put my name on the line?" Yes, and here's a prescription for your eye, go to the pharmacy. "I got to pay for it?" Yes, unless you have insurance. "I ain't got no money." I guess you have to borrow it. "Oh, OK."

§ § § § § §

Louis, 81years old, 9-17-87: "I don't use it for nothin' but to hold while I'm pissin.' Grandma used to say to her kids to control 'em she'll tear'em in two and shit in the middle of 'em. Husband'd take'um out behind the barn and talk to 'em kind as he could one time. Next time they'd get the snot kicked out of 'em. My kids, if I said something, they'd do it, sometimes I wish I hadn't said it, but it was said and had to stay said, so I had to stand by what I said. I'll have the wife call tomorrow, she ain't doin' nothin' but hangin' around the house and doin' her house work."

§ § § § § §

For: "My sister had heart surgery years ago, and now she's sick. She's having explosures with her heart several times a day and I'm stayin' with her."

§ § § § § §

For: In for abdominal pain: She's obese and getting heavier. I was complaining about her weight gain, high cholesterol, and not dieting. She was listening to me and looking at me out of the corner of her eye and when I was through, she waited a minute and said, "I like you for your docterin' but I don't like your ways . . . tellin' me to do stuff I don't want to do. I told the girls you were gonna' fume and fuss about me."

§ § § § § §

For: "I can't find nobody no better'n you nor no dumber'n you. I'd run up the wall backwards if you tell me I got cancer."

§ § § § § §

For, 3-17-87: "I chew tobacco. I'm the onliest one in our family to do it. My little friend, the one I babied with, taught me." She also was telling me about one of her friends who didn't like her doctor. "That bad ole Dr, he needs to be got!"

§ § § § § §

For: "I get mad at you sometimes, but not mad enough to quit."

§ § § § § §

I told a female patient she was obese. She said "I ain't never been obese before!"

§ § § § § §

For, 1992: "Friends tell me to change doctors when I complain of all this gas. I tell them your mind is nearly as sharp as it was in 1958 when I started coming here and I don't see no reason to change until it does. Do you? You'll tell me when your mind ain't as sharp, won't you?"

§ § § § § §

Teressa, 86, 12-3-87, Osteoporosis, bad back pain, hypertension and had a stroke: I told her I'd give her thirteen pills to take, one a day. She said, "No give me fourteen—thirteen is unlucky." She was checking the prescription I gave her, and she said, "You cheated me!" I asked her why. "You left one of the s's out in Teressa. Change it and give me what I'm entitled to!"

§§§§§§

Mrs. H., age 64, husband is 67, 1992: Tell me about your trouble, Mrs. H. "Well, he won't leave me alone. He can't ejaculate. He has a hard, puts it in and beats me tryin'to ejaculate, and it goes flat just like a balloon goes flat and he can't keep it in. He tries every night, it takes him about a month to finally ejaculate. Takes'im thirty to forty-five minutes of beatin' me before he does. He's killin' me. What can you do? He's been hurtin' in the left tetcycle." (This was before Viagra. I had no answer.) I suggested seeing a Urologist.

§§§§§§

Betty, 46: "My ear feels like my head's in a cloud...a real thick cloud!"

§§§§§§

Virginia: In to talk to me about dyspareunia (painful intercourse) "I have pain when he's enterin' me." Do you have pain during inter-course? "Not after he's in. He's not in long enough for much of a sen-sation. He's in and out." Do you reach a climax? "Only 1 in 10." Have you talked to him about that? Does he want to help you reach a cli-max? "Apparently not. He says he's making it alright. I talked to him about that but he ain't interested." She said she was 16 and he was 20 when they were married, and has been with him so long she's used to it.

§§§§§§

Wiley, 1-7-87: "I been down the horn...lived hard... cowboyed 7 years, range work. I drives a truck and 50 years old now, only shot for 40, and it really surprised me." How are you now? "About fair—got gout. Thing I ain't suppose to eat is the best to eat."

§§§§§§

Aug, 67 year old male, quite a talker: "My mama is 87 and chewed since age 6. Got throat cancer. Throat got as hard as a seasoned oak board. They couldn't saw through it and had to put a tube in'er throat. Tumor came from the strongest tobacco she could get...Kentucky Twist, or Hornet, none of this sweet mild tobacco. Dad did it too, and died from it, had high blood pressure and weighed 400 pounds. He loved pork and had a hog farm in Kentucky, and just wouldn't quit eatin' them hogs. Everybody tried to get'im to quit. He said he believed he'd just keep on eatin' them hogs and go when his time comes. I believe people do bad things to quicken them things, and dies sooner."

Mary, 12-30-86: "I had 21 for x-mas dinner. I had the flu in November but I overed it. I'uz too sick to come in and when I was better I didn't need to come in." Her husband is 80, and they've been married 8 years. She said, "He's vigorous. Takes care of 2 widder women's problems, fixes dryers, mows 2 people's yards, and he finally gave up smokin'." I asked her why. She said, "I kept after him since we got married and he finally quit. His inlaws came, ate daily with me and went every where we went. Nearly broke us up. Every Sunday dinner. One Sunday I left, they came and got mad...no dinner. They wanted to go with us every place we went. I stopped that— I didn't marry them! Went fishin' caught nothin' but them ole little bitty fry browns. I married for spite. Mad at my boy friend and married 25 year older. Mr. ...I got spited 40 years. I left him 17 months before he died at 87. He beat me. We were married 45 years. I left him, went home to my carpenter, 76 years old, and lived with him 6 years. Then he died of prostate cancer."

§ § § § §

What are you here for today? "Cold." How long? "A week." Sore throat? "Bad." Cough? "Yeah, bad." Cough up anything? "Yeah." What? "Thick blobs." What does it look like? "Snot." A lot? "Yeah." OK, take this medicine. "OK." Bring all your old medicine for blood pressure, next week. "OK."

§ § § § §

Male: "I got no appetite, mouth runs dry, and sticks to my teeth. Weak in my legs and all over...and my stems got an infection in it."

§ § § § §

David, 2000, at the Hospital Clinic, age 56: He said, "You don't know me do you?" No. "Don't you remember operating on me? You cut me from here to here (umbilicus to pubis with Dr. Zeller)." What was wrong with you? "I had pus coming out of my belly button." I remember, you had an infected Urachial Cyst. "Do you remember my daddy? Name Ralph." Oh yes, how is he? "Retired now. He don't know his ass from a hole in the ground, and he lives alone. I take care of him. We had to take his car away from him. He'd stop and sit at the green light, and take off on the red light. He can't remember nothin' either. I have to take him to the store and buy his food for him." What's wrong with him? "I just told you." Oh...!

§ § § § § §
William, February '81: "He used one of them big mayonnaise kind o' words for deafness."

Doris, 12-16-85, has a son to talk about: "He's 28 years old—they took a piece of his spine and half of his manhood out. They cut him across his stomach and up and down. Lost all his hair and half his manhood." (Testicular cancer?)

§ § § § § §
Louis, 81 years old, 9-15-87: "My dad in auto accident, got all banged up, had a stroke, and another finally got him at 85. Mom died 81 of kidney trouble. Have 4 sisters and 2 brothers, 83, 81, 79, and comes on down like that, 2-3 years difference. All healthy. All workin,' but that oldest one 83. She just gads around all the time."

§ § § § § §
Willie: "I am the real Willie…I'll be 65 over in the month of September…about the end sometime. Just write it up in September. My daddy's 70 or 80 in Birmingham. Cain't nobody stay with him 'cause he's so mean. But he is clean. Nobody can't stand him cleanin' all the time. Washes dishes before you're through eatin.' I don't know how many wifes he's had. Anybody ain't clean…gotta go! He runs 'em off. My folks from Chicago come down through there, can't wait to leave. He washes dishes too quick. He can't stand no nastiness."

§ § § § § §
Female patient sitting on exam table: I was trying to unbutton the top button of her shirt to listen to her heart. It was a very hard button to unbutton. She said, "Gosh, Doctor, you'd never be able to rape anybody, would you?" No, I've had no experience. "You wouldn't be able to have many affairs either, would you?" I meekly answered that I guessed not. I thought…What a failure I must be!

§ § § § § §
71 year old with a large hydrocele (large amount of fluid in scrotum): "I came to Jacksonville in 1926 and I was 17. When I was 19, started runnin' around with all them piece o' women and caught the clap. Floatin' down the Coast Line railroad with a different one every night."

§ § § § § §
69 year old female: "Our inlaws splunged on us all the time. I took over and run the sister-in-laws off. One had a love affair with my husband. He's 79."

§ § § § § §
Annie: "Worms ate my food value. They told me I didn't have no ulcers, but I just have ulcerative colitis. I stay on the constipated side

and don't got diarhea. Been x-rayed by a series of x-rays and won't never get well. Just treat it on a bad spell."

"Tooth broke. That's my teeth—they rot off at the roots. If you'd been in my mouth 76 years, you'd be rotten too."

§ § § § § §

"This rash is a mess on my shoulders and neck. When I spark it really drives me crazy with itching." (Had hot flashes).

§ § § § § §

"I get me a good hot cup of coffee, put little cream in it, and get me one of them Hydrops Chocolate cookies and pretty soon my bowels'll move."

§ § § § § §

"My back pain thowed a great big limp on me and had to bear on my wife to get in the house."

§ § § § § §

"My bowels never work normal. Once in a while nearly almost normal, then it'll skip a day then I have to push it out in little bitty balls and then gets almost normal but not never completely normal."

§ § § § § §

"My kidneys don't have the pressure they ourt to. They dribbles urine...stops and starts."

§ § § § § §

"I'm on a low salt diet. I cut salt WAY down...you know when you can eat cooked okra and just do get it off the fresh side...you know you done cut it down...or, a up egg! WOW!"

§ § § § § §

Wife with her husband, a diabetic: How long has he been a diabetic? She replied, "Ever since he found out in 1969. His mind ain't even as sound as mine."

§ § § § § §

"The only time I fart around people is when there's 3 people around me. When I let one, nobody knows who did it."

§ § § § § §

Doris: "I left him one time and had to come back to him. There's just something about him."

§ § § § § §

"I'm sedentary. As sedentary as I am I'm in pretty good condition."

§ § § § § §

"I feel like I been rode hard and put up wet. My throat's so sore I had to back up to swallow. They made me a set o' teeth a horse couldn't wear. I don't worry about getting old. I figger you got 2 choices...get old or die."

§ § § § § §

You got a job? "Yeah." Is it a good job? "Huh! It's just a got-job.
You work for free, just enough to eat with."
"I counted my pulse and it would skip 11 and go to 12."

§ § § § § §

"I don't feel like that lump on the couch I used to be."

§ § § § § §

"You ain't got to talk this behind me but she's a bitch and a doctor
sometimes needs to know something about my home life. She won't
let nobody tell her nothin'."

§ § § § § §

"I do farm work." Do you do any heavy work? "Naw, I just lift
things the tractor can't pull."

§ § § § § §

79 year old white female: "I can eat anything and it don't bother
me. I think I could eat a piece of iron and it wouldn't hurt me, if I
could chew it up. But I ain't got no teeth now."

§ § § § § §

"I been gappin' all day for 2 or 3 days." (yawning).

§ § § § § §

"In January I had the best bad cold I ever had. Didn't bother me
much."

§ § § § § §

"I coughed up blood and asked the Lord to stop it and he stopped
it. I have to take a little black pill to be excused every day."

§ § § § § §

Robert, 58 year old male, 12-12-86: Holding his testicles, he said,
"I got pain down here in both of my kidneys up to my stomach and
back down to my kidneys and I ain't got no taste. Food makes me
want to puke."

§ § § § § §

Jessie, 75, 4-2-86: New patient, elderly gentleman with severe
chronic obstructive pulmonary disease, and hypertensive cardiovas-
cular disease. He was stressed and very feeble. I gave him medication
and told him to take the medicine and if he doesn't get better to let me
know. He said, "OK. I'll just come back. If you don't know it today
you may know it tomorrow. I use 5 or 6 doctors around here trying to
find somebody who knows what'll help me. I'd just as soon pay you
as anybody else." 4-12-87, Jesse's wife, Lee Annie, 82, relates Jesse
was in hospital, and the doctor offered to put him in a nursing home.
He said no, and wife says they're getting along fairly good at home
with him. She said he just needs someone to fight for him when we
get into an argument. He's so short of breath he can't talk or yell loud

enough anymore like he use to, and win. On 6-9-87, Lee Annie is back to see me. Says, "Jesse is just barely here. He lays there lookin' like a frame with skin stretched over it." Good to see you losing weight and getting better. "Well, that's all I got. If you're poor the only thing you can have is good health." Jesse's wife in the office on 7-28-87 to tell me about her husband who died of COPD 6-26-87, two weeks after her last visit here. She said, "There was no betterin' for him. He just died."

§ § § § § §

New patient, very obese, I had given him medicine a week ago. He said, "Dr., you're so thin! Do you have all the organs in you that I have in me?" I said yes. He then said, "Dr., I'm suspicious of that medicine you gave me. I'm real shortminded."

§ § § § § §

James: "Dr., while being excused this mornin' I strained my back."

§ § § § § §

Mab: "When I was in my 30s never thought of all the things that foller. Thought I could do anything and eat anything forever. Now at near 70 got bad heart and blood pressure disease."

§ § § § § §

Debbie, 4-86: "I told my husband my ear was hurtin' and burnin' and was real, real sore. I kept on and on about it and he said 'you just act like a titty baby, now shut up.' So I did. Now it's worse and I'm here."

§ § § § § §

Male patient: "I used to be what's called a periodical drunkard. Now I work in a office as assistant in a dog pound. I trained the new dog pound director, and he gets the same pay. He's a disgusting neighbor and hurt me so deep. He's copying my hair and all. Valium 2 mgm helps, but 5 mgm too strong."

§ § § § § §

Vernon, being treated for prostate cancer, 70years old, 12-30-86: How are you Vernon? "Ooohhh, seems lak I ain't gettin' any younger. I think I got kidney trouble. Last time I had a intercourse, you know after my prostate operation several years ago, I cum back into my bladder. Well the last time it went back in there and ever since I been wantin' to pee a lot and seem hard to start and stop due to that stuff piled up in my bladder." When was the last time you had inter-course? "Oh, over a month ago was the last time she'd let me...and I got sinus trouble too. Probly from that backin' up...I must've really had a load."

§ § § § § §

Female patient: "I don't want to die as long as anybody else is livin.' My husband overused me and I'd get sore for a week."

Male: "I ain't got enough energy to say souie to hogs eatin' me up. My appetite's good. I eat anything from a gopher on up."

§ § § § § §

Female patient in hospital: Mornin.' You look better this mornin.' "I don't neither. I already got up and looked...you say that every mornin,' and I feel worse every mornin'."

§ § § § § §

1-7-87: My patient Barbara told me she and her husband were looking at a new house, walking around ooing and ahhing about how pretty the place was. Another lady also looking, came in from another room to be with them, and said "I just wanted to hear you see it."

§ § § § § §

New male patient in with stress: "15 years ago Dr. Moseley (Winter Haven Internist) told me I had worse case of nerves he ever seen in any man he ever took care of. You got to do something. He didn't help them they were so bad. What are you gonna do about them?"

§ § § § § §

Lottie, to follow up on her cough: Are you still coughing? "No, not no big sight now, just a little grunt once in a while."

§ § § § § §

Hubert, 8-14-7I: Do you drink? "I used to but I caught up on May 17, 1964. I was drunk as hell, sitting at a bar, and my 16 year old daughter came in and said 'Daddy, it's time to go home now.' When your 16 year old daughter comes in a bar to get you, that's bad. So I quit, and I vowed I'd save the money from the alcohol and smokin' I had quit. But I didn't save any money. I put in more food and bigger clothes every year. It wouldn't do for a man to see as far in front of him as he can see behind. He couldn't stand what he'd see was gonna happen to him. I'm retired now and do nothin' but I'm busier than I was before. Don't know how I had time to work."

§ § § § § §

Verla, 82 years, 1-16-87: "I do more than anybody I know of at my age. But I overdone it, cleanin' up the house for Christmas and company and just wore myself out and I'm deteratin' fast and hoped you could do me some good. Can't see good...Dr. called it deteratin' eyes... can't help 'em...nothin' to do."

§ § § § § §

Willie, very obese huge abdomen, 2-9-87, weighs 310, and short: I told him he's got to lose weight and get that abdomen smaller and do better for his high blood pressure. He said "Aww Doc, it's jes' unclaimed food."

Lonell, 5-4-87, nose: "I've blowed enough stuff out for it to be well."

§ § § § § §

Six year old, after surgery: "They gave me a shot and it made me disappear."

§ § § § § §

Ruth, quite obese, 6-24-87: "My breast have been sore ever since I've had 'em. I haven't had any kids so I haven't used 'em." While checking her thyroid in the neck, I said to swallow. She laughed and said, "I think that's where my problem is." Where? "In my throat, I swallow too much and too many times a day."

§ § § § § §

Mildred, 9-87: "It's a losin' battle...everything we do, and still die. It ain't the dyin' that's so bad...it's the getting' there."

§ § § § § §

Annie: "I got terrible arthritis and am very critical, so critical I can hardly walk on my hips. I tell you arthritis is critical stuff."

§ § § § § §

William, 81, 10-9-87: "I need somethin' to make my bowels more different than what they do."

§ § § § § §

Betty, 57 years old, 12-8-88: Abdominal pain. "My pain runs from up here in my chest to down there in my growns, on both growns."

§ § § § § §

Gracie, 81 years old, 11-21-88, 5 feet, 2 inches, weighs 225pounds: "I weigh 225, and that's too much. I got a cold 2 weeks." Been on medicine? "Yeah, I got that-uh-oh, you know, that stuff you buy at the drug store-oh-a-oh, yeah, Head and Shoulders for my cold and cough... no, that ain't it, it tastes different, -oh-uh- Alka Seltzer Plus that's it. Ain't no good, so I came here and saw a Chinese doctor. My daughter claims him for a doctor. I don't like him. I had 11 young'uns but never did lack for work!"

§ § § § § §

Bennie, 85 years old, 12-20-88: Did you get your hernia fixed? "Yeah, he pinched it back in and fenced it in so it cain't get out."

§ § § § § §

Mark, 72 years old, 12-1-88, back pain: "I got this terrible unnec-essary pain in my back. I'm the ugliest man in town, had 3 wives and a bunch o' women all my life. Bein' ugly didn't bother me none, and it didn't bother them women either. I just looked for the ones with a real strong stomach. I'm tired of this, I just want to die." No you don't! If you did you wouldn't be up here in my office every time you get a little ache or pain, scared to death you're gonna die! "Yes I do want to die, I just don't want to hurt. None of these things is fatal. The calendar's eatin' me up."

§ § § § § §

Nathan, 58, black, 11-28-88: "Had pain in my low back a long time. I works bended over all day long. I been working year in and year out and I think that's why my back hurts."

§ § § § § §

Cly, 69 years old, 9-2-88: "They x-rayed everything but my head, and they knew they won't find nothin' there. Sister said them dirty tracks are nothin' but bad memories."

§ § § § § §

Orville, 75 years old, 8-19-88: Have you had any tests? He said, "Aw, I've had it all. GI series, bavarian enema, and all those tests."

§ § § § § §

Mary, 89 years old, 8-15-88: "The Grime Reaper didn't want me, so I lived."

§ § § § § §

Barbara, 65 years old, 7-25-88: Nausea. "My stomach is so bloated and extended I'm on the verge of vomiting. Started last week when I got overcome by the sun working in the yard."

§ § § § § §

Carie, 41 years old, black female, fruit picker with a horribly deformed mouth and lower jaw from previous auto accident, 6-10-88: "Goin' to Louisiana to see my sister, I got a lots of nieces and things out dere, my husband doos. Dr. said I had a worriation ulcer, not no bleedin' ulcer, since my son was killed. My husband killed his only step-son, 9 year old, my son, 1981 in the livin' room. He got 1 year and a day. He's walkin' the streets now. Gonna kill somebody elses kid. I married in 1982 a older man. Peoples say all men ain't no good but some is. I say it's better to marry an older one. He's more settled and he got to get up and go to work in the mornin.' He can't run around all night lookin' for likker or drugs or runnin' up behind every woman out dere on the street catchin' all that shit and bringin' it home. He too old for that kinda livin' and we gets along good. I cooks good, he's getting' fat and I keeps 'im happy. Ain't got no reason to be lookin.' He tryin' to get me not to cook so good 'cause he's gettin' fat."

§ § § § § §

Leon, 84 years old, 7-19-88, in to follow up on his back pain: Are you any better in the back? "It's near bout close to it; it's about to get better."

Kelley, 74 years old, 7-1988: "They's 8 of us boys and ain't one of us ever had sugar (diabetes). My mother back in those days, had what was called 'mumblin' heart'."

§ § § § § §

Barbara, 50 years old, 7-21-88: "My other daughter had an auto accident, and was in the hospital 3 months. I don't think she's right in the head yet. They couldn't find anything wrong with her but some brain damage."

§ § § § § §

Mrs. M., 66 years old, 7-22-88, Vesicular rash on thumb: "I thought I was rotting away while I was still here."

§ § § § § §

Naomi, 71 years old, 5-6-88: "Stomach hurts, after I gets over it seems like I gets nervified and I just can't hold myself together."

§ § § § § §

R.R.: Do you cough? "Yeah, I've been coughin' up real good'uns." What? "Big blobs of yeller-green oyster lookin' things!"

§ § § § § §

Mildred, 52 years old, 5-13-88: "I took that Phleem cold, and cough it up. That's the reason I knew it was Phleem." (Phlegm.)

§ § § § § §

Barbara, 65 years, 2-1-88: 'I heard coco cola would eat up the bile when yur nausy (nauseated) and make you OK."

Jeanette, 55 years, 3-11-88: "I got so I have to wear a sedentary pad or I'll wet myself all over every time I cough or sneeze. My valves or somethin' are shot."

§ § § § § §

Sally: "The doctor said I locked the nerve in my swaller after I eat some chickin' due to my nerves."

§ § § § § §

I.M.: "Went swimmin' and got some more of that blabber in my ear."

§ § § § § §

Leonard, 60 years, 7-6-69: "I wore a stone 6 weeks in my tube. I loaned out to the bathroom and hit passed. (He passed a kidney stone spontaneously.) I hurt all over worse'n anyplace else."

§ § § § § §

A Mama about her son being bad: "I give him a good rakin' out about that. I come in ever nite jaded and can't even eat."

§ § § § § §

Cecil, 6-14-78: "I found out I gets severe migraine headache when I eats cabbage in cole slaw."

Forn, 71 years old: Patient told me her mother told her when she was born she had hair all over her face and wouldn't eat. She said, "Doctor told my mother the baby had cravins' disease and wouldn't eat 'til she got what she craved. Doctor said don't give the baby no bananas or no collard greens, or she'd die by one o'clock. They tried her on a banana, she ate it and got better, and all the hair disappeared." (Patients family were share croppers in Kentucky. And she never learned to read or write, except her name.)

§ § § § § §

Wallace, 58 yrs old, 8-30-90: Do you smoke? "No, I quit just in time, 15 years ago. It causes cancer now, after I quit. You really hear about people dyin' of cancer now."

§ § § § § §

Willie, 76 years old, 8-24-84: "Never was one to lay out an' get exposed to a lot of things. I always had a good place to eat and sleep- and just let the world go by."

§ § § § § §

Naomi, 57 yrs old, 1-24-86: "I begged my knee baby to let me lay down with my headache." How old is she? "Twenty-seven and my baby's twenty-five. I can't play like I'm 60 so I guess I gotta work." I asked her, what a knee baby is, since I'd never heard of that. "The one next to the baby." Oh!

§ § § § § §

Penny, 36 years old, 2-21-91: A new patient, beautiful, blond, and petite said, "I've been sick for 2 weeks and took everything and kept relapsin'." How do you feel? "I feel mostly like dawg doogie."

§ § § § § §

"She can't pray herself out of hell. I wake up a lot at night but I sleep good when I sleep. I ain't sleepin' with no woman in a funeral home."

§ § § § § §

"I don't feel good. I got 2 quarts of Old Turkey (liquor) and toddied on it all the time. Felt fine 'til it was gone."

§ § § § § §

"My wife sick." What's wrong? "Worriation, and my pants done got too big for me."

§ § § § § §

Verla, 84 years old, 7-13-91: 'I hurt in my wound (womb) (rubbing her lower abdomen), hurt bad yerstidy, and yerstidy I never had nothin' like it. I hurt right up here (rubbing her epigastrium), felt like a real bad pullin' on my navel cord. I taken Senokot for constipation and got diarrhea and had to eat a piece o' cheese to stop it!"

Irene, 70 years old, 12-27-90, on her return from Germany visit: "Swole up when my leg gave way walkin' down the Alps in Germany three weeks ago. I soaked a brown paper sack in vinegar and wrapped it around my leg and wrapped a towel around it 'til it dryed, and it took the swellin' down. I stopped my sleepin' pills. I used to see old people in crucial shape on them things."

§ § § § §

Bob, 63 years old, 3-1-91, severe bronchitis and bronchial spasm: How long you been smoking? "48 years." Don't you think, with your lung trouble, that's long enough and it's time to quit? "Naw sir! They ain't got so they quit tastin' good."

§ § § § §

Latania, 70 years old, 1-4-87: "Had gall bladder out, Thyroid out, Uterus out, Ovaries out, Appendix and tonsils out. My husband says I ain't nothin' but a runnin' chassis."

§ § § § §

Cly, 69 years old, 12-31-87, common cold: Do you cough? "Not much, just a regular cough, the one cigarettes left me." Have you stopped smoking? "Yeah, 5 years ago." You have to lose weight, you have diabetes and high blood pressure. "I did, I lost 15 pounds!!! But I gained it back over holidays I ate a bite of dressin' Thanksgivin' and Christmas and it came back. I made a pound cake and everybody raved how good it was and it was all I could do to keep my fingers off of it. I just took a little snitch a couple of times. I don't understand it!"

§ § § § §

Jack, 52years old, 12-29-87, Acute flu syndrome: "It just overtook me just in one night."

§ § § § §

Wanda, 52 years old 12-17-87, Flu: How are you? "Well, I've been better but I got over that thought, now I'm bad."

§ § § § §

Mrs. T. with her husband: She asked me, "Is that sore on his arm one of those unserious ones?"

§ § § § §

Josephine, 70 years old, 1985: Has chronic obstructive pulmonary disease, post-gastrectomy, macrocytic anemia, arthritis, osteoporosis, and digestive problems, came in to talk about her medications. I asked how she was doing. She said, "I'm in good shape for the bad shape I'm in."

§ § § § §

Lucile, 72 years old, 1-26-88: Worried about a lump on her upper back. "Seems lak I got a pone rightchere in my back." (She did, a soft tissue fatty tumor, a lipoma. She was reassured, and we would leave it alone.)

§ § § § § §

Roby, 55 years old, 3-21-88: Stepped on a nail yesterday, foot painful and swollen. I gave him a prescription, for antibiotic, pain pills, elevate and stay off of it, and hot Epsom salts soaks, and a Tetanus injection, and to return tomorrow. He said, "You know Doc. that foot's getting better already. That shot done it I know, that's the reason I come in. I was trained that way workin' for the company—go to the doctor time you hurt yourself!"

§ § § § § §

Joseph, 72 years old, 4-11-88: "I had a cold and whipped it and the flu got on me. Last year it relapsed on me 3 times. Sometimes I get a strong throat." What do you mean? "I mean it gets strong at night, cain't even swaller it's so strong. It hurts and holds my muscles in my throat and I ain't strong enough to swaller. I ain't got no resistence. When I get the flu I took co-tylenol and 3-6's, and other stuff. That way I've whipped the cold, sorta."

§ § § § § §

Bernice, 80 years old, 1978: "I lost 3 pounds, 159 to 156. I can tell it in my arms, they're wrinkly now. I think it's because I don't do any work. I just do crafts and knitting. I ought to do something to use my muscles."

§ § § § § §

J.L, 73 years old, 3-29-88: "I give out only when I'm up and about. Not when I'm sittin' around doing nothing. I think old age is my trouble now, every thing has gotten old. My trouble is my weight. It's hard for a man to lose weight or either gain it."

§ § § § § §

Mrs. J., 68 years old, 3-29-88: "Mik's in a bank now, he's rated high, doin' real good now. Pi, in Kissimmee doin' OK. First wife was a Yankee, couldn't get along, divorced. Now he's found another Yankee—couldn't let'er alone. She's got 3 grown kids, one's 23 yrs, old, she's 38 and Pi__'s only a boy, 30 yrs old. I'da stopped it if I coulda. But she loves him and he loves her. I'm old fashion and don't know what's happenin' in this world. Young men after older women and old men after younger women. Women take what they can get."

§ § § § § §

Ricky: "My marriage finally wore out, 13 years, 2 kids. Feels good to finish good."

How, 71 years old: "I'm up to 3 pieces a night. On Sunday, I'm in bed more than I'm out. I got a black friend and he cain't get it up, and him only 66 yrs old. His boss told 'im, when I died, he wanted me to will him his balls. He really needs them nuts."

§ § § § § §

"I want to sell a TV over the phone. I can be got at this number— 967-____."

§ § § § § §

W.C., 82 years old, 7-7-88: "How old are you DOC?" I'm 67! "Shiiit! I could piss over the barn when I was your age, flatfooted!!! You ain't old. You just look old!" (I thought) Thanks a lot.

§ § § § § §

For, 7-22-88, elderly, female, neck injury: "Headaches and necks ache all the time. I jes cry and cry tryin' to get better. I jes cain't wear that collar all the time—I jes want to vomit!"

§ § § § § §

Harney, 82 years old, 7-7-87: He had to sign a physical exam form I did, and I told him to write his name on this line. He did, then said, "You can look at it if you can read it or not."

David, 34 years old, 1989, in with epigastric pain: Hi, what's your trouble? "I got symptoms." Of what? "Innerjestion and rollin' stomac, and diaree."

§ § § § § §

Trecia, 33 years old, 2-4-89: "I'm not the type of person who can sit a long time and just get up and take off walking. I have to get all the crinkles out of my bones and muscles, or else I hurt to start walking."

§ § § § § §

My receptionist, Evelyn, came back to me after one of my patients left. It was one of my female patients I had just seen and she came to her saying she was highly insulted by me. Asking what happened, she told Evelyn that I had left the room for something, and she glanced at my chart and noticed I called her SOB on the chart. Actually I used SOB as short for describing the "Shortness Of Breath" she had described. Most physicians use this abbreviation. Evelyn was able to explain it to the happy patient. Now she was happy. I learned a lesson. I became more careful of where my charts were, and how I described things in my notes.

§ § § § § §

In 1986 the Bond clinic bought my practice and office, and took over the operation and billing for this part of their business. I stayed in Auburndale to continue in my same office. Apparently Agnes was one of my patients, I do not remember. She received a bill from the clinic for my services, and our office received a check from her with a small piece of paper in the envelope, with a hard to read handwritten note to me. The check was for $60, dated Aug.6, 1988. In the left lower hand of the check, on the "memo" line was written, "60 this is all you get." On the scrap of paper was written, "and your not my dr no more" and below that was written, "July 1988 I paid 60 Aug 60 July 75.40 total 195.45." Below that was written "don't send me no more bill Ill no send you a nother dime." I hoped Bond Clinic straightened that poor lady's bills out. I called the Bond Clinic billing office and told them to please help this lady, or cancel my bill. Well, you lose some and win some.

§ § § § § §

I continue to have these office encounters so far unrecorded, I think. However, I wonder if I have duplicated any. But I am not going to worry about duplications. Many of the patients have been in my office many times over the many years, and they may have mentioned the same things before, but not to my knowledge. If I do recognize it, I'll leave it out.

# 10

# More Patient's Comments and Quotes

More office visits, I am really unable to glean, and pick and choose. They all are getting' in here! If you're tired, close the book, go to bed, and read more tomorrow. I have found out there WILL be another tomorrow! Other people may enjoy the ones you don't. Just ignore any duplicates that I might have missed.

This is an exact copy and quote, of a typewritten 2 paged epistle from the elderly wife whose husband who was a little older, and seeming to be entering the . . . what we used to call "early senile" stage. I will copy this information exactly as she wrote it, and the spelling is hers. She always was sort of trying to boss, or correct, or help him through his years. I will change their names to Mary, and John:

CONFIDENTIAL HISTORY OF JOHN (their address), Auburndale, Florida.

Mother had bad nerves. She threatened to burn her house down while John was a youth. His mother had a hemorrhage at the base of her brain at age 77 and lost her mind. John had Asian Flu winter of '57-'58. He never got over it until after we moved to Florida in1963.

During this time his "friends" implanted in his mind that I was "putting on" those severe headaches to get him to do the housework. (I found this out after his nerves came so near snapping in '71, when he finally began to talk to me.) I had known there was something wrong, and had asked him numerous times to talk to me, but he refused. This had been about 10 years. He let outside influences cause him to leave home in October, '72. I invited him to supper the Monday night after Thanksgiving. After we ate, we sat in the living room talking. (He sat in the chair across from me. His tongue was hanging out the left side of his mouth, and he was drooling, just like a child I had taught who had brain damage. I didn't sleep much that night. A friend who was teaching at the same school he was told me he was dragging his left leg.

VERICOSE VEINS He told me about them in '82. I do not know how long he had them before he told me. A friend gave him advice wear support hose and take vitamins. They are better, but HE WEARS THE HOSE MOST OF THE TIME, DAY AND NIGHT.

HEART FLUTTERS There are times the vein in his forehead (left side) has stuck out, looking as it might burst. He said the Dr. in the army said his was a case of "nervous heart" and hasn't wanted to let the Dr. know he has this problem.

BAD NERVES Gets easily upset at small things.

HIS MEMORY IS BAD If I ask him to go to the store for one item, I have to write it down.

NO REASONING POWER ( Example: He opened the microwave to heat a hotdog. He found food I'd left in there and forgotten, so he ate his hotdog cold.)

UNCLEANESS He used to be VERY IMMACULATE, but now he goes for long periods of time wearing the same dirty clothes and not taking baths. When he does bathe, he washes the clothes he has on, and puts them back on as if he has no other clothes.

ATHLETE'S FOOT He contracted this in the army, and he doesn't bathe and change socks as he should.

DRIVING He cannot drive in strange places at all. He asks me to drive most of the time no matter where we are going. This is a complete 180 degree circle. I used to NEVER drive if he was in the car.

GETS MIXED UP He often tells me I'm going the wrong way, even when we are in familiar places.

EXTREME COLD NATURE Wears a coat when everyone else is "roastin'." Wants the windows and doors closed and no A/C.

SLEEPS A LOT Can sit in a chair and sleep 'til bedtime, then get up and go to bed and sleep all night. For the past three or four weeks he's been going to bed at 7 P.M. if we do not go someplace. Sleeps in day time, too.

TIRES EASILY

WALKS SLOWLY If I slow my pace to match his, he even gets slower.

CAT SCAN Is one indicated at this point?

X-RAYS AND BLOODWORK How much is needed to find out his problem?

NOW I'VE GOT HIM HERE, GIVE HIM THE WORKS: That finished her typed letter. She added this in her hand writing, "used to be a whiz in Math. Now when he has to borrow in subtraction, he asks me how to do it."

§§§§§§

For, 72 years old, 6-12-90: "I cough so long it gets serious. I think I'm gonna die but I kinda want to keep livin' 'cause I enjoy livin.' When I was a baby they had to unsoak my eyes, and their still lastin' me. The doctor told mama if I lived to have a period...I'd have a long life."

§§§§§§

Larry, 4-1991: A man came to the window asking to see me on personal business. The receptionist brought a note back to me to that effect. I told her to put him in my office. She did, and when I went in to see him, He said, "Dr., I just had to see you,—my wrist is killin' me!" He apologized for doing that' but I saw him any-way. He had a severe acute gouty arthritis right wrist, in severe pain. He got OK on medication, and became a patient, a tricky patient.

§§§§§§

Jesse, 46 years old, 7-19-90: "We love ice cream. Know it makes me fat but I take spells of cuttin' down. I don't mind getting' old, but I just don't want to go through it again."

§§§§§§

Thomas, 7-19-90: "I was trying to catch a cold and I couldn't catch it, tried and tried, sneezin' and runny nose then all of a sudden I caught it and it really clobbered me. I wish I hadn't caught it."

§§§§§§

Morene, 1990: "My right shoulder hurts. You know how you wake up and yawn and stretch in the mornin,' well, I can't yawn and stretch that arm. Movin' it a certain way sends pain all the way up to my ear!"

§§§§§§

Kincey, 73 years old, 5-23-86: Are you allergic to pills or any-thing? "Naw, it's only the side affects I'm allergic to."

Mayrine, 11-7-90: "My period stopped and started and stopped and started…a little and a lot. Then suddenly I had a period more normal than normal."

§ § § § § §

Middle aged female, 1975: "I had 7 head o' kids. I'd stand on Jesus's toes and say same thing. I ain't lyin'!"

§ § § § § §

Lottie, 87 years old, 1989, had 7 children, was sitting on the exam table: Scoot down to the end of the table. She said, "I can't scoot like I used to do. Had my knee injected and that helped a sight! Done real good and got almost like normal. Now it's all bad and hurtin' again." I injected it again for her.

§ § § § § §

Irene, 1989: "I hurt right next to my virginia."

§ § § § § §

Leonard, weighed 313 pounds, 6-7-90: "I had knee and leg pains. I got myself out o' bed and carried my ownself to the hospital emergency room and he told me my knees was sore and swollen. I knowd that! It just cost me a heap of money."

§ § § § § §

Leila, 61years old, 1990: "Some days I just feel disconnected, that's the only way I know how to describe how I feel. Today, now, I feel connected, and OK."

§ § § § § §

Debbie, 33 years old, 5-21-91: Do you ever examine your breasts? "No, I NEVER touch 'em. I just wear'em."

§ § § § § §

Gary, 6-22-99: Do you cough much? "Not such a terrible awful bunch."

§ § § § § §

Willie, 70 years old, 6-21-90: "He gave me drops. Ain't got no 'coma, no cataracks." What are the drops for? (He hesitated.) "Weeelllll, he calls hisself treatin' it. I donno what he's treatin.' It ain't hoped none, hits still the same."

§ § § § § §

How are you? "Well, old age got all the way down to my foot."

§ § § § § §

Chester, 7-90: "When it's cold and wet in the AM, I want to say DAMN!! Chicken and cows, they're all retired to do nothing, and they got time." I want to do a rectal. "I thought we settled that years ago, and weren't gonna ever do that again. It don't seem decent things to do to a man! If you're gonna do it to me, I at least ought to be able to do it to you!" I did do it to him.

§ § § § §

Vera, 90 years old, 7-6-90, in for exam, sitting on table, listening to heart and lungs: I told her to breathe deep. After a few breaths, I told her to lie down so I could examine her abdomen, feeling for liver and spleen. I told her to breathe deep. She kept breathing deep through my entire exam. Finally, I realized that and said, OK you can stop breathing now. She did stop, and in a short time she breathed deep again and said, "But I need to! Anybody 90 years old has got to breathe a lot."

§ § § § §

Irene, 71 years old, 6-6-9: She had a soft tissue mass, and had a CT abdominal scan for diagnosis. I told her that her lab work was all OK and the CT scan was all negative. She said, "Yeah, I knew that. Soon'az I saw it on the screen I knew I's normal. I couldn't believe how good and healthy all them things looked in there."

§ § § § §

Naomi, 70 years, 4-18-94: This was a unique, colorful, wonderful working black lady who at this visit got into a conversation about herself, and her life. I had treated her for many years before this. She moved here in 1969 to pick fruit. She was a tall, very thin lady, I thought way too thin to pick fruit. But she did, and a lot of it. These are my notes from that last visit. She said, "I worked from 15 to 70. Raised six, lost two. Seems not right. I raised 'em good to be so hardheaded now. But they off my hands now...but still hurts when they does things they wasn't taught. Cain't help bein' bothered. Now just walk aroun' and look at my flowers and gets off my mind. Chopin' cotton and pickin' it, 200-400 pounds (Louisiana). Came to Florida in the back of '69, with a baby 9 years old. I could get that cotton, get that stuff...400 pounds snappin' bowls, 200 to 300 pickin' it. Quit fruit last year, used to pick soommm fruit. Kids said I may slip an' fall offn' that ladder. Been kissed by the lord keepin' me here. Got two guns loaded, can't get to one, can get to othern."

§ § § § §

Mildred, 1-16-92: "I've got the weakest weakness I've ever been through."

§ § § § §

P.G.: "Can't pee. Won't come unless it calls. Not when I call on it."

Gertrude, 74 years old, 2-27-92: "They found I had a heart murmur on that machine (Echo). I guess I'm s'posed to have heart trouble. My mama and daddy both had it. So I guess I'm doomed and can't do nothin' about it. I hope not. I was sick the whole time I carried R___ (son) and kept on bein' sick for a whole year. L___ (husband) said, 'Now Honey, we got this kid and I need you to help raise 'im, so you got to get well. We ain't gonna have no more if you gonna get sick with'em. You got to raise this'n.' " Then she added, "R___ (son) divorced after 2 years. Wife wouldn't make M___ (their daughter) study."

§ § § § § §

Sam, 75years old, 1-17-92: "When you get 75, and the same stuff for 50 years…you kinda catch up."

§ § § § § §

Mildred, 1-15-93: "I got weight loss." Why? "I don't know, nerves I guess" What makes you nervous? She said, "Nothin,' I just made that up. I'm my own doctor, you know."

§ § § § § §

11-29-90, 69 year old white male: "Got pain ever since I had my right hernia fixed 25 years ago." Where is your pain? "Right here in my right Technical. There's a string attached to it and he pulled it up… too tight, because it was hangin' too low. He said it ort to be pulled up and he did. Cold weather pulls it up and it hurts…warm weather loosens it and it hangs, and is too heavy. Can anything be done to fix my technical on this side?"

§ § § § § §

Thomas, 1-15- 93: Age 78: "Smoking, because it gives me another chore to do and it keeps me alive to have something to do."

§ § § § § §

Mai, age 52, 6-6-91: (Taiwanese lady, hard time speaking, and understanding.). I was rattling on about all her lab work reports, and physical findings. I was doing a pelvic and she asked me about her mammogram. I told her the report was fine and was not changed from the last time and she could read the report if she world like. She said, "No, but I can read but I can't understand what I read, I can't even understand when you read it to me. I can't understand when you talk, even. So you 'splain it to me—slow."

§ § § § § §

Marshall, Age 77, 12-6-95: One of my old patients, in to see me about 3 weeks before I left my office practice to start working part time for the Hospital Express Care, overflow at the emergency room.

He, at this time, is in the early period of developing dementia. He is explaining things he has learned, and noticed. "You got to keep writing, if not you get to shaking. So don't stop writing. I also notice you develop saliva in your mouth watching TV. It'll fall out sometimes. I find that if you swallow once it takes it away a while. Does arthritis be more affective when it's damp? I notice morning worse, and when it dries out at noon it's better." Now I'll take blood for tests. "That blood is the life of the human being anyway, isn't it?" Yes. "So when you take that away, you don't have anything, do you?" No. "Well, you can take only a little!" OK. (I was amazed at the awareness and obvious recognition that Marshall has noted, not being apparently worried, but quick to inform me of ways he has learned to solve some of what he sees as new little problems of his daily living, that is occurring in his decline.)

§ § § § § §

Another of my very good longtime patients, and good friend Hannah, was in 10 days before I was leaving my practice, and commented how upset she was that I was stopping my office practice, and stated she had planned on dying before I retired from my office. I said, "Well, you've got 10 days." She just laughed heartily, and often reminds me of that, and is still living.

§ § § § § §

Gina, age 59, 10-91, sinusitis: " I have to get up in the morning and make unusual and loud noises for 15 to 20 minutes to clean all that stuff out up there."

§ § § § § §

Martin, age 30, 8-21-91, Down's Syndrome, obese, somewhat mentally deficient, long time patient, pleasant, likable young man, always smiling and cooperative. In for physical examination to be able to participate in Special Olympics: Hello, Martin. What are you going to do in the Olympics? "Bowl!" Do you bowl well? "Yeah, Good!" What do you bowl? "A ball! That's all I use!" Oh, well, good luck!

§ § § § § §

Mabel, age 71, 8-13-9 1: "I used to have bad ear aches. Mama put any thing in them ears anybody'd tell 'er to put in there. She even put urinate in my ears." Did it help? "No. You know what cured 'em?" No, what? "Prayer. A old lady came to the house one day sellin' Blair. Mama told'er about my ears. She said, 'Do you believe in prayer?' My mama said, 'Sure I do, we're God fearin' people.' She prayed over me and pain got better, and went away, and I ain't had no ear ache ever since then. I like to tell people about that 'cause the Bible says we ort to witness whenever we can. Anything I can do to help people is what I do, so they can pray and get healed. I ain't take'in nothin' away from doctors, 'cause I know God put 'em here on earth for somethin' and most of 'em do a lot of good. I know you have me."

§ § § § § §

Charles, age 49, 9-5-91: "I had a ear ache at 7 years old, over and over. My mama's old doctor in Indiana gave me a shot, and in just 2-3 days that ear pain was gone and I ain't had none since. Don't know what kind of shot it was but it shore worked on me. Wish I knew the name so I could give it to you to use and help ear-achin' people."

§ § § § § §

Charles, about 45 yrs, old, 8-13-91: "A week ago I started with a sore throat, aches, abdominal pain, and the flyin' shits started next day and been shittin' fast and hard ever since, and I'm wore out, and my belly hurts and I'm weak and shaky all the time now."

§ § § § § §

Linda, age 42, 11-5-90: Are you married? "Yeah, but separated 16 years. He went back to Mississippi. Come after me once to go back with him, but I didn't have no children so I didn't HAVE to go back with him. You don't need to if you ain't got no children." Why did he leave? "I run 'im off. He's just like a stop sign. You know what that is, don't you?" No. "Well, he just keep on stoppin' at all these places before he got home and wasn't nothin' left for me when he got home. He was all wore out and all I got was a back when he turned over in the bed." You got a boy friend? "Yeah, but we separated 3 weeks ago, and I got to get me a nudd'in. I got nature too, you know, and it's got to be satisfied. You know, the old cow goes into heat sometimes, a lot o' times!" Why'd he leave? "When they lay up and don't work and want me to cook and work and take care of him I kick'em out. I can get me a nudd'in . You can find good'uns sometime. You just have to keep tryin'."

§ § § § § §

Gracie, age 80: How are you? "I'm doin' fine 'cept for my head parts. Got a cold, and all them grandchildren. I had eleven children and got a bunch of grandchildren from 'em." How many? "I don't know. I had all midwifes."

§ § § § § §

Gladys, age 71: "The doctor fussed at my blue jeans. He told me I was old enough to come out of 'em."

Jonie, "I was too close built. Had two C-Sections. Couldn't do pap smears."

§ § § § §

Age 65, male, from Louisiana: "Had eighteen kids. Lived next to RR tracks. Every mornin' the 5:15 train came by—it was too early to get up and too late to go back to sleep. And my nose runs like a sugar tree."

§ § § § §

Alice, 62 years old, 2-4-93: "Every time I eat chocolate, or sweets, I have pappillations in my heart."

§ § § § §

Norman, 7-26-93: "Sore throat and a cough. Everybody I know has it. The trouble with down here is it's always warm here and the germs don't ever get a chance to hibernate."

§ § § § §

Barbara, age 69, 3-4-93: "Long years ago every time I'd wash my feet, and bend over to dry them I'd hurt in my stomach, and later I had gall bladder and stones removed. Bending over like that caused gall stones."

§ § § § §

Doug, age 71, 4-4-94: "Obstruction go, urine flow, in the name of Jesus. Speaking the prostate down, too, works! I get rectal bleeding from sittin' on roofs roofin'—twisting my butt-hole out and I bleed. OK after I heal up."

§ § § § §

Blanch, age 72, 1989: "Forty years ago I had leg clot. Was told I'd drag my leg rest of my life if the new medicine didn't work. Next mornin' it worked. Two others died. I told my husband—he was alive then—I'd take a chance, if he'd feed my three week old baby."

§ § § § §

Blanch, age 81, 3-8-93: She had bilateral leg tingling and aching, I thought it might be low salt syndrome since she had diarrhea off and on 10 days and may be dehydrated. Put her on Lodine and saltine crackers, and forced fluids. She called and said she forgot the saltines, and that her stomach hurt, and that she read in the TV Guide a Captain on a ship made his sailors eat saltines to keep from getting sea sick and nauseated. She said that now she knew why I wanted her to eat them and that I knew what I was doing, and said that she was starting to feel fine. Just wanted to call to apologize and let me know it was her fault, not my fault, that she got sick.

Joe, age 75, 3-25-94, had a flu and cold, for follow up: How are you, Joe? "Well, I'm OK I guess. I didn't get around my cold until this mornin.' Been a long time but I'm better now."

§ § § § § §

A mother: "Without you bein' at my house you wouldn't know my misery with my kid. He's got as much brains as half again as much as is in that glass, and it empty."

§ § § § § §

Female, 12-26-86: "I got a cold and bad teeth and they drain all that bad stuff in my stomick and give me stomick trouble. I saw a doctor a year ago and he said I had gall stones. Then he said I had a deodental ulcer." Did he do an x-ray of the stomach? "No, he only did a Pap test. Gave me Tygomet and got me better. I don't eat no spicy food, or anything with acid in it. I drink only acid free coffee. Do everything right 'cept one thing—still smoke. My stomick still hurts."

§ § § § § §

Willie, had a brain tumor, and nearly blind, came in with urinary tract infection: "Last Thursday started my symptoms." When was the last time before that you had intercourse, or been with a woman, that you may have caught something from? (Patient thought a while). "HE-HE, I can't member last time I ever fooled with a woman, years ago and didn't do it good then."

§ § § § § §

James, age 55, 12-24-86: "My ears are hurting; left was badder and now is better, still can't hear around me." Patient had external otitis, and I irrigated and removed the debris. He said, "Now I can hear the world! WOW!"

§ § § § § §

Female patient asked me, at one of her office visits, "Doctor, do you know why God created man?" I said no. She said, " 'Cause dil-does can't mow the grass!"

§ § § § § §

Riley, age 45, 3-2-94, Hypertension: "Found me a new piece, and called her up. She said come over in the mornin.' I went over and just had to stuff it in, 'cause of that Hytrin. Tried my wife and still had to stuff it in." Do you have, or find other new pieces? "Yeah, lots of 'em." How often do you have sex with your wife? " 'Bout 2 a week, them others in between." Does your wife know? "Naw." You'll get caught one of these days, and she's probably gonna shoot you. "She sho will if she finds out. But there's too much good stuff out there goin' to waste."

William, 6-25-90: "Had a colonoscopy, nothin' ever hurt me like that! Just before I died, I told 'im, 'One more gasp, and I'm gone if you don't stop.'"

§ § § § § §

Mildred, age 65: "Just before my pan-hysterectomy, my husband told the doctor to leave the box that they came in."

§ § § § § §

Aug, age 65, 6-11-90: "I was much of a man 'til I had that prostate, messed me up. Used to go to Rainbow Club with a bottle. I'd drink cokes, and give the booze to the girls. I could drive home, and they'd go with me. I'd pick one; send them others home. I'd get through, send her to the bathroom to clean up, then could get her again 3 more times as soon as she'd clean up and come back."

§ § § § § §

Aug, age 69, 6-13-94: "My brother, A____, no where near crazy, but he just ain't quite rite in his mind. Quit drinkin' just in time, four brothers alcoholic. Dad alcoholic. He was stoned out of his mind all the time, and when he was, he knowed more than any doctor or lawyer about everything. He died last year."

§ § § § § §

Annie, 9-4-87, in to follow up on a dog bite: "That was my brother George's daughter Annie's baby John's dog that bit me. And do you know ain't one of 'em ever asked me how my leg was."

§ § § § § §

Unknown male patient: "My wife had this female trouble and jist had 'er nutrus took out, and caint do no work around the house. My daughter, 19 year old died with that jumpin' kind of cancer." (Melanoma.)

§ § § § § §

"Caint sleep? Float yer tongue!"

§ § § § § §

Man and wife sitting in the exam room, I'm telling him that he has to stop smoking. His wife told me to be quiet. Patient said to his wife, "Aw, it's OK, it don't bother me, if it makes him feel better to get it off his chest."

§ § § § § §

Male patient: "I felt as good as common until 2 o'clock when I woke up with my belly about to kill me."

§ § § § § §

Eula, 74 years old from Indiana, 11-16-87: "I got a bad sore throat. Been nearbout tryin' to take a sore throat for years. Ov a nite it's terrible!"

"Aspirin takes the scream out of my headache."

§ § § § § §

"I felt froggy again and wanted to lose weight. Had a bunch of blood testes."

§ § § § § §

A wife wanted me to "Give'im a physical going over."

§ § § § § §

Annie, 73 years, 1-6-87: "Nerves ain't any good. Fell apart yers ago. Now jist jerk and spasms. They ain't no good. Fever I had one time ate 'em up. Colitis later finished 'em up. A nerve pill is all I had to do'em any good."

§ § § § § §

"I use to have pretty teeth. Now all abcessed up in the roots. Been treated with ulcerated stumik, and had a heart attack but no heart damage. I'd pick 600 pounds cotton then 200, then 200, then another 200 pounds, but bruise my teeth draggin' the bag. Was livin' in Culman, Alabama. I was stout. My brother 'n me used to fight and hit each other with hickory limbs with no shirt on, and we used to crack hickory nuts with our teeth. Our friends, the Estrige boys would hit their calf in the head with their fist, then butcher 'em, five of 'em."

§ § § § § §

Susie, 79 years old, 6-26-87, weight 101: Had been losing weight and was worried. "Never know what yer children will turn out to be, so I went up to Kersey's (funeral home) and made my own funeral arrangements, jes like I wanted. I taken all the pills you described fer me. I eat hearty and gonna live 'til 100, Lord willin.' Mr. Kersey said it wouldn't cost no more if I did." She didn't.

§ § § § § §

"My mind ain't very long. I don't remember nothin'."

§ § § § § §

Female, middle aged, obese: "I got a discharge with a very loud odor."

§ § § § § §

Husband and wife in together: Wife said, "His stomach was out of shape and we went to the Mayo Clinic. They told 'im he has a 'one-type-stomach,' and can't eat but one type food, eggs and grits for years. He got well and had no trouble after 20 years of this." Husband said, "I felt better than I thought I was."

§ § § § § §

White male: "I hurt right down here in my secrets."

Wife said "I feel like I'm clamped together. Don't have too many intercourses 'cause he a diabetic and can't much. He don't care and I ain't that way anyway. It's either my back or my front hurtin'."

§ § § § § §

Wife: "We didn't have no sex life for 2-3 weeks. Something wrong with his equipment."

§ § § § § §

V.C., 4-13-87, 84 year old patient, bald headed with dandruff: "I used to have beautiful hair as a boy. It was straight and scraggly growin up, but when I got to lookin' at girls I wanted it curly. My other sister told me to drain the sap out of grape vines and shampoo my hair with that, and that'll do it. I did, and my hair got curly and stayed that way, 'til I lost it." Wife, Lois, age 74, was with him and she cut into the conversation and said, "It sure worked because he was curly headed when I met him, until he went bald. I wish we knowd what kind of grapevine it was 'cause we could'a made a fortune." Lois continued to talk: "My father had a head of hair he couldn't do nothin' with. A barber told him if he cut it all off and shaved his head, when it came back in he could control it, then he'd have a head start on it. He went to a campground meeting in West Virginia and met his first to-be wife for the first time after his head was shaved. She hated men with bald heads. He had a terrible time getting' her to like him, but they were married a year later."

§ § § § § §

Sam D., 74 year old trucker, in with his wife 12-86: Wife said I had told him a year ago his neck arthritis was due to not rolling his driver's window up while driving. Patient said, "I took your advice and kept my window rolled up and my neck arthritis never got no worse. Wish I'd a knowed the wind would cause neck arthritis. I'd a rolled it up before."

§ § § § § §

Patient with gonorrhea: "I took 2 pills I had left from before, and it done every thing but clear up!"

§ § § § § §

Louise, 60 year old, 4-17-87, had a severe acute gall bladder attack and subsequent surgery. She had a known gall stone for years not bothering her: "I knew it was coming, but I was hoping I'd die with something else before it happened."

§ § § § § §

Tommy's wife called to tell me her husband was going to call me "to see how much time he's got left."

Marie, age 70, 9-1689, advanced diabetic, with the recent loss of 3 gangrenous toes: "It's taken 70 years to grow my regular toes and much slower to regrow 'em."

§ § § § § §

An elderly black patient: "I got a nillybout brand new hose for sale, and my son's got 4 gooses for sale at 25 dollars for all, or I'll trade 'em."

§ § § § § §

On the way out, a patient volunteered, "We're lookin' for a little small dog, one that'll stay little when it gets big. We want one that somebody will give away. We don't believe in buyin' and sellin' dogs."

§ § § § § §

Gertrude, 5-14-91: "I'm jigglin' inside."

§ § § § § §

Nathan, 1-14-90, obese, jolly, happy, good patient, black: "I cain't pay for all 'dis today, but I kin along. Dat's somthin' I cain't keep none of. Looks like I jes got to spend it jes time I gets it. But I'll pay you." And he always did.

§ § § § § §

Male patient: "I went to the emergency room 'cause I had pain and swellin' in my left testament."

§ § § § § §

62 year old female patient I hadn't seen in quite a while, 2-14-71: How did you get that old? "Well, it just got to be my turn."

§ § § § § §

Irene, age 71, 6-6-91, hypertension in for checkup: "I used to have a restaurant in a little ole bitty town in south east Missouri, down in the boot heel, a good'n, too. Home made pies was my callin.' Truckers used to stop all the time for a cup of coffee and a piece of pie, all and any kind. Had a hard time closin' at night; them guys'd know I'd stay and give 'em a piece o' pie if they caught me there."

§ § § § § §

"I'm getting'fat—my clothes look like they was melted and poured on me."

§ § § § § §

"I've been feelin' do-less last few weeks."

§ § § § § §

Nellie, 66 years, 2-13-87: "I had a hysterectomy 30 yrs. ago, and on autopsy it showed cancer." (I examined her feet.) You have fungus on your feet! "Fungus? I have not!!" Yes, you have fungus ! "Ain't that from nastyness? I ain't nasty. I bathe every day, and sometimes twice." I reassured her that it was like an infection on the skin, not nastyness. We treated it and cleared her fungus.

§ § § § §

James, 29, 1-20-87: What do you do? "Laborer for the city." Do you like it? "Yeah!" You gonna do that the rest of your life? "Hell, yeah, I love it. I got a good job."

§ § § § §

Estelle, 83, 3-20-87: "I got to see the doctor quick! I was sittin' on the commode going to the bath room and something fell out of me. It didn't hit the water, so I pushed it back in me. I need to know what it is before you take it out—I may need it!" She had strained at stool, causing a complete uterine prolapse. I assured her that she didn't need it any more, and referred her to a gynecologist for either surgery, or to be fitted with a pessary.

§ § § § §

"My head be dizzy, my stomach upset, I feel weak, arms, legs hurtin,' and I feel sick."

§ § § § §

Did you ever stop smokin'? "Yes." How? "I got saved and the Lord just took away the taste for it, and healed me."

§ § § § §

Buford, 58 years old, a long time patient, and a known heavy drinker. In for a cold and cough 4-10-87: Now this medicine is gonna taste bad. "I don't care, I can take it. As much bad whisky and crap I used to drink, I can take anything. People used to give me BAD whisky. I knowed it was bad 'cause they wouldn't drink it. If it was any good they'd a drunk it. I don't drink no more, 'cause I got saved the last Sunday night in September, 1986. Quit smokin' too. Cain't stand it! Won't let nobody around me smoke! Praise the Lord!"

§ § § § §

Juanita, 36, 4-7-87: "I was in the hospital 2 weeks before they could take'm out. Tonsils were so bad they exploded when they hit the air when he took'm out the doctor said."

§ § § § §

Donald, 7-87: "We moved so fast and ain't had time to change addresses yet."

§ § § § §

Rita, 34 years old, 12-14-87: "I got sick way over in the day like 4 o'clock or somethin.' Loss of appetite, whole head feels dumb, dizzyness, nauseated, weakness in arms and legs, chest feels full, and head feels confused."

Ralph, 50 years, 9-27-88, pain in right shoulder: "I uz up on top of a ladder, hit twisted and thoad me and I fell down amongst it. Hurt me rightchere and rightchere and rightchere (rubbing shoulders and hips). I rubbed DMSO on it, and took care of it, but it still ain't better."

§ § § § § §

For, 72 years, 11-18-88: "We're getin' too fat—me, husband and son decided we weigh too much. So the other night we decided not to eat nothin' for supper, and the next day did you know we didn't lose nuthin'on them scales? So my son sat down and poured him a plate of syrup and put about a cow pie blob of peanut butter in it and ate it and next day didn't gain a pound! So he said 'see, I can eat it and it ain't fatenin'.'"

§ § § § § §

Joan: I was taking a throat culture, and I commented that's good, no gagging. She said, "Yeah I know, my husband makes me practice all the time. I got pain in my low back and down my leg, and comes and goes. I guess that's the way it's supposed to be."

§ § § § § §

Ladon, 56 years, 1-30-89, ill, severe bronchitis, URI, advanced Chronic Obstructive Pulmonary Disease, in with his wife, who said, "Tell him about your legs, too." Patient says "Yeah, Doctor they cramp all the time—what makes that? And that pain goes up to my left ear and out." Wife said, "And tell him about that rash in your privates."

§ § § § § §

Jason, one of my patient-family's sons, 15 yrs old, 5-30-89: He was in my exam room, and had written a fake prescription on one of my pads that weren't supposed to be in the room, but were in my room. He had written for: 1. Morphine and Demerol, 2. Cocaine, Acid, Advil, 3. Any others you can think of. When I entered the room, he presented this to me, as a joke. His problem was a severe ingrown toenail that he had been plagued with, with recurrences for a long time. He said, "I usually wear thick white athletic socks, but the things hurt so bad in my last baseball game because my spikes are too short for me; I had to wear my tux socks, and it still nearly killed me in the game." We're supposed to keep our prescription pads out of the patient rooms. There was in house conversation about that!

§ § § § § §

New patient, Marie 84 years old, 1986: Good morning, how are you? "I ain't hittin' on all of 'em, I got pain in my right knee, and I'm hoppin' like a frog!"

An older patient: Are you smokin'? "Now don't be too hard on me. I done quit down some. I'm down to a pack a day from 7 packs a day. I had a bad ear ache but I overed it on my own. My chest hurts."

§ § § § §

Harry, 75 years, 1-20-90: Any diabetics in your family? "Yes, strong diabetics on my grandmothers side, and none on my grandfathers side."

§ § § § §

Jeffery, male, 75 years old: What's your problem? "I got chiggers on my gentiles."

§ § § § §

Betty, 63year old female, 11-3-88: "I'm dizzy; seemed like my head wanted to go ahead of me."

§ § § § §

Robert, 51year old male, 1983, grove worker, allergic to arthritis medication: "I'm aitchin on my arms. It's a full time job all night jes scratchin' it. My wife told me to stop scratchin' else people'll think I got the itch. I told her, 'Hell, woman, I do have the itch or I wouldn't be scratchin.' "

§ § § § §

Verla, 84years old, 12-20-89: "I been here a long time, and seen my 84th birthday and hurt all over at times. Sometimes when I stop my body, my head keeps agoin' and I wants to fall on the ground. My chest tight and nose stopped up. I taken some castor oil and loosened my chest up some, but got tight again but I can't keep takin' castor oil—it'll loosen me all up and probably run me all out the other end. So I stopped and came to you. My throat's OK; I rubbed it with turpentine just to keep it from gettin' sore."

§ § § § §

James, 31year old trucker, 9-19-88, wife has left him for other men 2-3 times: "We're back together again now. I think she's either grown up or finally got a sense of humor now to take me like I am. I got this creeping eruption (larve migrans, subcutaneous larve of dog and cat hookworm, causes intense itching). I'm 31 years old and ain't never had nothin' like that. It itched so bad I been doin' everything they all told me to do. No help. One guy told me to get that propane stuff that you charge a butane lighter with and freeze it. I did that and it all turned white and I knew I messed up right then. When it thawed, it blistered, and I think the little thing got pissed off, 'cause it really itched then and ain't stopped yet."

Marie, 12-90: "I made a new revolution this year—stop smokin.' I got a son dyin' of cancer, 40 years old and done been cut to pieces. Now they want to cut in his head but he won't let'em. I told him to live as long as he can."

§ § § § § §

Mary, 4-22-88, patient talking about her neighbor: "She was diabetic and clogged up. They told 'em to give'er salts, and castor oil, and it busted her colon and she died. She was 89 yrs. old."

§ § § § § §

Lessie, 5 -21-88, in for a urinary problem, feeling her abdomen: She said, "Had a herni and the stitches didn't take and left that pucker. My yurn acts purty plenty when I go, not jes a little bit. I hope I get over this and it ain't serus."

§ § § § § §

For, 4-25-88: "I got one in town now. He's nice-seeming." How long are you going to live? "Oh, I don't know. I never figgered it out."

§ § § § § §

Ray, 4-26-88: What are you here for? "There's a place on my feet that gets tangled up with my nerves in my foot and hurts like hell sometimes walking." (Claudication.)

§ § § § § §

Ollie, 78years old, 4-88, talking: "I got fifteen kids, married in 1931. Had one wife. First two kids died, all others living. I was a farmer in the Gainesville area. I had to have some hands on my farm. Nine were girls and four were boys."

§ § § § § §

Sarah, 1988: "I got arthritis, bursitis, neck, shoulders, upper back and chest. I think it's pressing on my lungs and I can hardly breathe."

§ § § § § §

Karen, 4-27-88: "My husband left for another woman. I asked him, and he told me, 'If you hadn't asked me the truth, we'd still been together! It's all your fault!' He says I'm too fat. She's fatter and shorter. He says I wear too much blush. She wears a bottle of make up, and you can't even see her eyes. She looks like a street lady."

§ § § § § §

Joseph, 67years, 4-26-88, phone call with me: "My wife can't take that last medicine you fixed for her." What is it? "I don't know the name of it but hits a big red capsule and she thinks it's the one she couldn't take last year and it done her the same way, dizzy like that anner air." What is it? "Hits that great long red..." Get the bottle and read the label. "OK, let's see now...well hit ain't right here with these...wait'll I go and find it...hyar hit is...D A R V...no, that ain't it…jes a minute…hyar it is…C E P H…no that ain't it, wait a minute …T E T R A…" Tetracycline? "Yeah…hit made her the same way before, she thinks." Why didn't she tell me when I asked her what she couldn't take…penicillin…and stuff? "She didn't think of it, I guess." OK, I'll give her something for dizziness.

§ § § § § §

M.G., 58, 5-5-88: How are you today? "I've always been in good health until the last week or so, and it looks like I outgrew it and got sick."

§ § § § § §

Joe, 67 years, 4-19-88, had bad chills and fever walking in the flea market: "I have the flu and you got to get out and see how you are once in a while, when you got the flu,…else how you gonna know if you're getting' better? Saturday I got to feelin' better but undoubtedly my condition wasn't no better and I got bad walkin' around at the flea market. Yore medicine wanted to bind me up a little bit and I tuk prune juice and Black Draught and got OK. I don't go fishin' any-more. I guess I'll quit. Always somethin' gets in the way." Do you ever get diarrhea? "No, except only when that stuff runs around here and gets everybody sick, I get my share of it but nothin' bad—-I jes wait and it goes away." Two weeks later Joe is back for a check on his flu. "I don't worry about my money, I ain't got none to worry about. I like boiled chicken backed behind my rice. Every time I get out to check myself out I have a relapse and get sick again. I jes quit checkin' myself out. The flu'll jes have to go away itself."

§ § § § § §

For, 1988: "I got so nervous. I was so proud when my company left I couldn't stand it."

§ § § § § §

A.B: "I got a piece o' carpet for sale. It's used but just like new. It ain't all blemished up. Have 'em call 425…"

§ § § § § §

Cordean , 1988: "I'm doin' jes what you told me to do…eat fish and skinnin' back the chicken I eat."

§ § § § § §

C.D.: "Their baby is 2 weeks out."

§ § § § § §

Jean, 37 years old, 6-27-89: "When I was young I hemorrhaged…I sat on the commode when I was on my period, about 15 years old and I suddenly started to bleed like you'd cut off a chicken head and he bleeds from the neck, you know? That's why I later had to have a par-tial hysterectomy cut off."

Aug: This gentleman was a pompous, nice, outgoing braggart spinning what I think were "tales" of his successes and excesses. 64 years old, called himself "A Tennessee Boy." Never came in without relating one of his many stories, or suggestions. 11-15-88: "You got to treat women nice, buy 'em dinner and drink and expect nothin' in return. Give 'em time and they'll fall for you. I invite 5 or 6 at my home, after eatin' and talkin,' one would stay, alternate every night. I had more sex than 3 banty roosters. Women love me. My neighbors use to say I lived better'n Elvis Presley."

§ § § § § §

Bobby, 28 years old, 9-26-88, came in complaining: "My nuts is sore." After exam I found a very tender right undescended testicle. I asked him when it started. He said, "I slipped and nearly fell down, felt like somebody grabbed my balls and it's still sore." I discussed this with him and wanted him to see an urologist, and probably they would recommend removal of that undescended testical. "I don't want nobody messin'with my manhood!" I told him with one left, there would probably be no change, and asked how many kids he had. "Two, but we don't want no more, but I just want my dick to get hard some more." I explained it won't be any different. He said, "It'll be OK, if it's just as good as it is."

§ § § § § §

James, 72, 5-31-88: "I'm thowin up. I thowed up so much and hard, I'd a thowed up my shoe soles if I wasn't standin' on 'em."

§ § § § § §

For, 72 years, 11-11-88: "I didn't have no kids of my own. Thought the Lord didn't want me to have none and I was afraid to get one, but I prayed and adopted him, but I was scared I'd mess him up since the Lord didn't intend for me to have none of my own, but he's done good and I'm proud and I know the Lord is proud of him and me, too."

§ § § § § §

Willie, weighs 302 pounds, 7-13-89: "I'm all a time busy. I love to be busy. I'm gonna go 'til I die! Jes like a bullet...go like hell then "chunk!" stop...drop...hit the ground...dead!." I asked how long ago he stopped smoking. "15 years." I asked if he ever wanted another cigarette. "Yeah, every night after supper I could smoke a 90 foot long cigarette! The left knee and leg swells if I walks a lot on it. I jes rub and pour white alcohol on it...gets it drunk and it gets smaller and comes on down common with the other'n." I checked for phlebothrombosis.

Jimmie, 7-89: "Take right now, like that muscle in the calf of my leg is justa thobbin.' I got a water bed with no heater under it, that ain't no good for me, is it?"

§ § § § § §

I returned a phone call: What are you doing? She said, "Who, me? You caught me right in the middle of doing nothing. I need some thing for head lights." (Head lice.)

§ § § § § §

Chester, 81years, 10-29-87: "I'm layin'off of cholesterol to get it out of me; then I can go another 81 years 'til it comes back. My wife's worse'n a dog about meat—she can't stop it. I ain't never been sick 'cept them fits (convulsions). I'd smoke a pipe big, then go to bed and have a fit. Ain't had none since I quit smokin'."

§ § § § § §

Wife of a boss on the job: "I got to get him out a that job—he just sits around and all the others like to sit there and help him."

§ § § § § §

David, 7-89: "My folks all died, but they didn't have nothin' serus."

§ § § § § §

Allen, 35 years old, 9-2-89: "I got three things wrong. One, got a knot on my nut sac. Two, got hard of hearin' in my right ear and started turnin' my bad ear to whoever was talkin' so I could exercise it and get to hear better. Three, constipated...don't never get notified any more that I got to shit. I used to get notified every day."

§ § § § § §

Mary, 1989: "Too much goin' on in my neighborhood. Dog barkin' on one side, a black woman prayin' 2-3 o'clock in the mornin.' Another crazy woman down the street hollerin' all the time outside. They took her to the asylum and she's back out. Crowin' rooster in the back yard. They killed a man in a store two doors down, and robbed it again Saturday night."

§ § § § § §

"I took wax out'a this ear and put it in the other'n, to grow some."

§ § § § § §

Lennie, 52 years, 10-11-89: "I saw another doctor, and he said I might have arthritis and gave me medicine. But I don't go on MIGHTHAVE and I didn't take it. I want to know what it exactly is. Another thing...I'm getting' older an' I'z trying not to claim arthritis. I jes work it off; I don't never get down under no sickness."

George, 78, 11-17-89, bowels: "When I got to go I got to go or I won't have to go. I had one big ole hemorrhoid cut on and they cut one of my pucker muscles."

§ § § § § §

Helen, 6-20-89: You gained weight. You have to lose it. "My goodness, I got a fast fork I guess."

§ § § § § §

Inell, quaint straight laced 70 yr. old, in for hemorrhoids and didn't want to be examined: I need to diagnose you, get up on the table. "OK." Spread out. "No." I can't see you down here. Spread out, Inell! "I don't want you to see me!" How about if I close my eyes? "Well, how can you examine me then?" I can't, that's why you need to spread out! You're no different from any other lady I been looking at for 34 years! "Yeah, but that'n is MINE!" Yes, and you can keep it, I don't want it 'cause I got mine at home! (My mission was finally accomplished.)

§ § § § § §

James, 48 years old, 2-28 89, says he was in waiting room 1 1/2 hours: "Damn, I thought you'd gone home, or forgot, or somethin.' Mama said she was goin' on to get her oil changed and gas up and come back and get me, but she'd a had enough time to get a overhaul and engine rebuilt by now." (A very busy morning, I apologized.)

§ § § § § §

An employer sent a patient to me for exam. He called my receptionist after the patient got back to work, with a note from me. He said, "I thought my employee saw Dr. Tanner but this note is signed by somebody else!" She said, "That's Dr. Tanner's signature." He said, "No it ain't!" She said, "Yes it is, does it look like it says Paul A Jones, or something like that?" He said, "Well, maybe." She said, "It says, Paul A. Tanner, Jr. M.D." He said, "Where?"

§ § § § § §

A belligerent black lady walked into my full waiting room, holding her 16 year old very thin, timid, rather small son tightly by his upper arm to the desk loudly announcing, "This boy's done been with some old girl and he's done got a dose of the clap and needs to see the Doctor!"

§ § § § § §

Janet, 35 years old, 5-15-89: "My 15 year old boy run away from home with an 18 year old he got pregnant! She done him dirt, got'im in bed and inticed'im to do it. Wouldn't you know it, the first piece'o ass he ever got, she got pregnant!" I asked if he was big enough to have a kid and take care of it. She said, "I don't know. I shamed him into not lettin' anybody look at him down there since he was 18 months old. I kept sayin,' 'Shame, shame, that ain't for nobody but you to see,' so I ain't seen it since he was 18 months old. I don't know how big it is. It wasn't very big when I saw it last!" (After that conversation, I tried to state my questions in a little better worded sentence.)

§ § § § § §

Judy, 38 years old, married 18 years, works in a factory, 2-12-89, complaining of dyspareunia (painful intercourse). Pelvic exam revealed some tenderness in the joint between the coccyx and the sacrum: She said, "The pain interferes with our sex life." I asked her how often she had sex. She chuckled, "Ha ha. Oh I don't know, uh, well, only about 4 to 5 times a week, but you know it hurts me when we do, so we've had to cut it way down." Oh!

§ § § § § §

Carol, 35years old, 3-7-89: "I've got a sweet feelin' in my stomach." What's that? "You know, like you feel when you eat a bunch of Snickers all at once!" (I still don't know.)

§ § § § § §

Merie, 55 years old, 8-89, husband, 68 years old: "I need to talk but I don't know how." I reassured her and advised...just start talking and we can get it going to whatever it is. She reluctantly started, "You're my Doctor, so here goes...When they operated and did a hysterectomy, they told me I'd either go sex crazy...or just plain crazy, and now I'm in trouble. Last year or so I can't get enough sex, and my husband can't do it but once in a while. He starts, can't keep it hard, gets mad and quits and I nearly go crazy 'cause he gets off and leaves me alone and won't do nothin.' I get mad and get up and leave the house and walk around and cool down and then I'll talk to him again." I suggested a referral to a Gynecologist. This was a little out of my world, and before Viagra.

§ § § § § §

Mary, 68 years old, 3-7-89, acute bronchitis, and bronchial spasm: She said, "I blame this on that old cloud cover we had last week. It was pink and everybody's been sick since then. I think there was something in it and got me sick."

§ § § § § §

Lillie Mae, 62 years old, 2-3-89: "I keep a hungry streak in my stomach. I eat but I still keep that hungry streak there."

1987. Save the old cloth adhesive tapes for Bill. He makes turkey calls out of them. (This was a note I left for my office staff. They had just about quit making cloth adhesive tape, and we had some left over. Bill needed it for his turkey calls.)

§ § § § § §

Christina, 15 year old, 2-28-89, has acute otitis media and acute pharyngitis: "My ear was hurting really good last night. I tried to get my Mom to say something last night. It hurt so good I wanted her to say a bad word. She won't let me. I ain't old enough."

§ § § § § §

Rick, 24 years old, 2-16-89: "We like you! You know my Mom. She used to see you a lot with her nerves. You remember her? We lost Dad two and a half years ago and Mom's been better. You notice she ain't been in here in a long time. We sure do miss Dad though."

§ § § § § §

Sara, 2-7-89: "I collapsed into my ankles. I didn't fall over like I usually do. I'm dizzy and confused in the front of my head."

§ § § § § §

Ralph, 58 years old, has chronic obstructive pulmonary disease, diabetic and hypertension: How are you? "All right...almost all right, I guess...I got too much cold and can't shake it. I usually use Comtrex but I started a day too late and no good now. I got bad lungs and was supposed to die 3 years ago." Are you a smoker? "Yes, and a damned good one too." How much do you smoke? "Three to four packs a day." Don't you think that's kind'a dumb to keep smokin' with lungs like you have? "No, because when I quit smokin' I always gain weight...every time, that's what happens. If I gain 10 pounds, I'm so short of breath so bad I nearly die. I can't breathe at all if I gain weight. Smokin' keeps my weight down so I can breathe." Do you drink? "Of course, and a lot of it, too." How much? "Well, I sit with a friend late afternoon every day and each kill a 6-pack then go home and get serious—Canadian Mist, vodka, scotch, or what ever,... about a 1/2 to 1 gallon a week. Probably ain't got no liver. It's pickled and I'm scared to stop. If it starts workin' it'll probably shock my consti- tution to death."

§ § § § § §

Lillian, 74 years old, 1-27-89: "Kid across the street in the hospital with pneumonia and I'm sick. They call it a respiratory infection pneumonia, or somethin' like that, and it's contagious they say. I ain't never heard of no respiratory disease that's contagious. They called it something that starts with somethin' like syndrome, or somethin'."

Naomi, 65 years old: "Bad back pain. I got a bad pain in my back and I was goin' to leave for my sister's funeral tomorrow afternoon, but I told 'm I had to postpone it until I get well. I don't feel good right now."

§ § § § § §

Hollis, 48 years old, 9-16-88: "All my energy just drains down to my bottom and I have to sit down to make it better."

§ § § § § §

Serdinea, 72 years old, 1-2-89: Have you had an exam of your uterus? "No, I haven't had a public exam in over 10 years."

§ § § § § §

Susan, 37 years old, 1-6-89: "I got low thyroid for 2 years." How did you find out about it? "Well, I got sick, stiff neck, weak, sore throat and got coherent. They told me at the emergency room to get tests and that's what came back." How long you been off medicine? "Three months." How long have you lived here? "Oh, going on several years. I'd a been down here a long time ago if I'd a known you were here." How far do you live from here? "Four to five blocks. I don't get out of the house much."

§ § § § § §

Ralph, 6-8-89: How much do you smoke? "Two packs a day between 4 and 8 AM, then only one pack all the rest of the day." How much do you drink? "Not much; one liter of vodka a week." Why? "I drink a lot of grapefruit juice to lose weight, and I hate to waste it all and not put vodka in it."

§ § § § § §

George, 74 years old, 12-23-88, stomach pain: Do you have stomach trouble much? "Yeah. Do you remember Dr. Simmons?" Yes. "Well, he was a good doctor. He examined my stomach and I was told I had a incomfection. I don't know what that is, but he gave me a shot of penicillin daily for a week. I got better but he told me I'd just have to live with it. But the medicine you gave me helped me so much—I had no pain...no nothin,' and I can even eat apple pie and it don't hurt me. It used to hurt bad."

§ § § § § §

Frank, 45 years old, 3-30-89, in my office with a low back strain, he began talking about a coworker: "He claims to be a Christian but he tries to take everybody he can. I don't trust 'im, even if he is a Christian, all the way. I'll back a Christian all the way. I believe in God myself, but he seems to be a funny Christian. I don't smoke, drink, or tell lies; and work hard raisin' four kids and give a man 110% work for his money."

Edna, 82 years old, 4-20-87, talking about her medications: I asked
her did she know the name of what she was taking. She said, "Yes but
I can't think of it, and I noticed I couldn't hear the phone ringing."

§ § § § § §

James, 38 years old, 2-27-89: While listening to his heart, he spoke
very seriously and very apologetically to me, and said, "I just got up
out o' bed so you may notice my heart is slow and ain't got itself
warmed up to runnin' normal yet."

§ § § § § §

Leonard, 72 years old, 4-13-89: He said "I got to go up to Haines
City to fiddle for Mr. Webb to beat the spoons. They play dulcimers
and fiddles. He's won 3-4 plaques, and $20 a time or two, but he ain't
never give me a dime to play for him. He orta share. I told 'im once
he could jes' whistle or hum for himself for his own music."

§ § § § § §

Lillian, 71 years old, 4-10-89: "Lord, I'z up all nite a-wettin' and
hurtin.' I had to go to the druggist for eeze. He give me this ...(bottle
of pyridium)...and it helped but my pee is all red! jes like blood! I
tho't he'd ruint me. But hit slowed down how much I wet and didn't
burn so bad. I jes need you to get me all the way well." (Pyridium,
urinary antiseptic over the counter, but does dye the urine red and
every thing it gets on.) I reassured her.

§ § § § § §

Louis, 67 years old, 4-11-89, smoker, diagnosed cancer of the
lung, had surgery, worried: "This cancer scare has got me all nervous
and I smoke more. I eats bought biscuits." (He died later of his disease.)

§ § § § § §

Gracie, 71 years old, '88, hypertensive: "I got old age pides (blem-
ishes) on my face." How long have you had them? "When I clam up
the tree to pick that fruit and the ladder broke."

§ § § § § §

Eva, 68 years old: "My daddy's 92. Fell at home a week ago, fractured neck and back, and is paralyzed from the waist down. They said
if anybody would over'n it, he would. They said he had determination."

§ § § § § §

E.G., 74 years, 1987: "I got ten kids and only one of 'em is bad.
One son went to jail with another guy, fightin' another, got a broken
jaw. My son only hit 'im a couple of times, to help 'im."

§ § § § § §

D.M.: "I had a kidney operation and just overin' it."

Eddie, 66 years old, 5-12-89: "Hi Doc. I got one of them bad summer colds. I can fight off them winter colds but I cain't do nothin' with them summer colds. It started with a chest cold and tight cough and wheeze wasn't too bad—but then it went up to my head and got a head cold and them summer head colds make me feel BAAAD! I got cataracts now, and heart trouble, and circulation leg trouble. Seems like everything's attackin' me all at once. Somethin' will kill me, I guess!"

§ § § § § §

Rita, 31 years old, 5-10-89: "Yersterday my hands and feet were take'in and goin' numb and then my head was take'in and getting' dizzy and my fingers were take'in and getting' blue so I went to the emergency room and they didn't even do a blood count!"

§ § § § § §

Shirley, 58 years old, 5-12-89: "I got cholesterol and been on a diet and lost 30 pounds." How? "If it tasted good I'd spit it out."

§ § § § § §

Gertrude, 67 years old, 5-11-89, was speaking of their auto wrecks: "Leonard had three, and I had two. We got to git rid of that car, it keeps getting' into wrecks. I try not to pay no attention."

§ § § § § §

Ross, 68 years old, 3-16-89: Trucker lived in Wilmington, Del. Earlier, he had been given shots of Halotestin, male hormone for his low libido, was in my office for a D.O.T driver's physical: "I was living with my divorced wife. I found a 45 year old waitress I wanted, but she was married. Last year her husband died. I found out a couple months later. She was a good looker. I took her out and she's sex crazy, so I married 'er. I don't need Halotestin no more. She gave me lovin' last night and again this mornin' so I wouldn't get horny before I got back on my truck. She loves it like I do. We do it almost ever' day. My old wife is mad 'cause I left. She couldn't turn me on and didn't want to try much neither but now she's always callin' me and wants me back for some lovin' when I get back to Wilmington. I jes' go by and give her a little once in a while when I'm in town. But I sure got me a good and hot one now at home. She's always ready."

§ § § § § §

For, 5-10-89: "Yeah, (son), been married for 5 months but couldn't go on because she wouldn't do, you know, that thing married people do. She said her mama and daddy didn't do that so she wasn't going to do it. So, M. jes' had to leave."

322 PAUL ALEXANDER TANNER, JR., M.D.

Ru, 63 year old, '89: "I've always been a minute person. Do it now and get done."

§ § § § § §

Dewey, 78 years old, 5-15-89: "I get sick at my stomach and want to vomit but I never was no hand to vomit when I had to. I hurt all over worse'n anywhere else."

§ § § § § §

T.R., 72 age, 1987: "I'm bald headed and the sun on it makes my nose and sinuses plug up!"

§ § § § § §

Howard, 22 years old, 6-6-89: "Dr. said I had a genital defect in the left big toe."

§ § § § § §

T.Y., 72 years, female: How are you today? "I've felt better before. I was hurting so bad last night I was scared to go to sleep."

§ § § § § §

Mark, 70 years old, 2-17-86: (I was doing a history.) Do you have any headaches? "Doc., I never had no headache in my life until October 17, 1956." You've had headaches since then? "Yeah, ever since I got married to this woman on that date. I didn't have none with them other women. This'n'll drive anybody crazy. There's always somethin'! Grits too watery or too stiff, eggs too soft or too hard, biskits too hard, too soft, too tall or too flat, too salty, or not salty enough. Nothin' jes ain't never right!" Why don't you get another wife? "Waaait a minute, Doc. I never said everything was bad. She's the best in bed I EVER had, so I can put up with a lot to keep what I got. I don't know what the next one'd be like nohow."

### Chief Complaints

These are a list of Chief Complaint entries on the patient chart filled out by the patient, prior to his entry into the HOSPITAL OUT PATIENT CLINIC, FIRST CARE, where I worked This is what the patient says is wrong with him and collected over three to four days.

SOAR THROAT

MAJOR HEAD ACK, STUFF NECK

PUSSY EYES

RECK (WRECK)

RESPIRATORY IMPECTION

UPI

SICK, SORE THARRT

HEAD ACKE, ACKE ALL OVER

KEIDRY TROBLE

COLIFLOUR EAR

NICK AND BACK PAIN

LOOK AT TOES

EXTREMELY SORE THROAT, STIFNESS OF NECK. PUSS IN THROAT

STREPTH THROAT

TAKE OUT BOXS (skin staples used to suture a laceration several day ago.)

NOT SURE

SPRAINED FOOD

PENN WORMS

THOART

PUSS COMING FROM EYES

INTENSE SORE THROAGHT

"PROBLRMS WITH PENIS"

EFFECTIVE FINGER

JOINT MICE RADIOLOGY REPORT OF KNEE XRAY

WATER STOP

CHESD

SORE THREAT

PRINCIPAL PULL MUSSLE

LEFTED EAR

RISEN

STRIPE THOAT

KEEP SHITTING MYSELF

SOARS IN MOUTH

CUMMING BLOOD

NEED A PERK FOR MEDICINE

PLATEX IN SERVICE

EX RAY ANKLE

HIGH BLOOD PREASHER AND SHOULDER PAIN

LITTLE PEE PEE IS SWOLLEN

TAKING 200 MAGGOTS OF GLUCOPHAGE TWICE A DAY

BED-A-WEEK NOT GETTING BETT

STAFFY HEAD

SCORE THROAT

### More Patient Comments and Quotes

Tom, 4-26-91: "I caught cold from my daughter." How old is she? "Eight years old…eleven years old. She used to be eight years old."

§ § § § § §

Roger, 74 years old, 4-20-91: (Doing a physical exam I announced to him that I was going to do rectal exam.) Bend over the table and put your elbows on it and stick your butt out. "You mean like you break a shotgun?" Yeah.

§ § § § § §

For: "I got a crooked swaller and it's getting' wore out, swallerin' too much. I cain't lose no weight. How come?"

§ § § § § §

Fannie, 67 years old, 4-6-90: What's your trouble? "I got that ole arthritis and cain't hardly raise that arm…You hear what I mean? I don't want to take nothin' for pain. I know you can get attached to that stuff, BAD! If I keep my bowels open I know I do a lot better most of the time, you hear what I say?"

§ § § § § §

David, weighs 222 pounds, hurt his back lifting 100 pound steel object with another man: "Me and him outweighed that damm steel four times but it still hurt my back."

§ § § § § §

Female, 40 years old, 3-1990: Are you having trouble today? "Yes, I burn and sting when I pee." Where do you hurt, where you urinated from, or on the skin around your vagina? "It's right in my T hole, that's where it hurts mostest."

George, 77 years old, 4-2-90: What's going on George? "I have spells of weakness and dizziness and got to sit down." Do you have any nausea or vomiting or diarrhea? "No, but I do have trouble with my bowels. I had an operation for hemorrhoids and they had to cut one of my pucker muscles. When I got to go, I better."

§ § § § § §

Robert, 4-10-90, cough: He said, "When I cough with my dentures in, I swaller mucus right down. If I can get one up it's mucus, and do good with dentures in and spit'em right out. My wife gets after me to cough it out and spit it out. She says I shouldn't swaller it, it'll make you sick."

§ § § § § §

Enrique, 5-11-90, has severe moniliasis, rash, bilateral groin areas: "I had that rash three years. Went to a doctor and didn't help, so I said 'Lord God if you want me to have this, I'll just have it and take care of it.' " (I treated him, and cured it all up, with a little time.)

§ § § § § §

Gertrude, 73 years old, 6-1-90: "I been trying to have a headache, which I don't need, and I been thinkin' about fallin' because of my eyes, I think. Let's see...what else I can figure up to tell you about what's makes allergies with medicines. Let me see now...what else is wrong with me. I have the worse time pickin' out somethin' to eat... 3-4 mouthfulls and don't taste good. If I did anything I'd be losin' weight but it ain't so, I don't lose no weight. I think I'm goin' crazy. For 2-3 weeks a little worse and worse 'til now. I'm jes plum sick. I jes don't know. When my back hurts, if it would keep on I'd be in a real fix and couldn't stand it. Then it quits and jes a few minutes I'm OK. My body jes ain't workin' out."

§ § § § § §

Louise, 6-5-90, has a severe left ankle sprain, with fracture of the left lateral malleolus, for follow up: "It's funny how it don't hurt until it hurts, then it really hurts. Then it really makes you sick at your stomach." Sorry. "That's OK. It could be worse, and it has!"

§ § § § § §

"My feet and legs hurt all the time but I grown to that and put up with it."

§ § § § § §

"My daughter has that fast eatin' rare cancer." (Melanoma.)

§ § § § § §

William, 69 years old, 8-9-90: What's your trouble? "I had a sudden onset of frequency, and burning and getting' up at night the last few days." Where is the pain? "Right down here in the base of my unit there."

§ § § § § §

Gladys: "I came in because I've enjoyed poor health as long as I want to."

§ § § § § §

Wallace, 8-18-90, long time smoker: "I was a 3 packs a day smoker, way back when they didn't cause cancer."

Merle, 77 years old, 8-23-90: "I don't sleep! I don't sleep good enough to go to bed."

§ § § § § §

William, 73 years old, 12-8-87, patient returns for follow up on his urinary tract infection: "My wife made me come back. She's dyin' to get on livin.' I can't until you release me to go back to my usual duties."

§ § § § § §

Jean, 46 years old, 7-15-86: "I been so weak I can't even spit over my own chin."

§ § § § § §

Mildred, 12-5-87: I phoned her to return her call. She said, "Lawww, it's like the White House around her, the way that phone rings." You've got to quit smoking! "I AM!!! I quit every now and then. It won't be long before it's permanent."

§ § § § § §

Elicia, 12-7-87, severe tonsillitis: "It's worse'n havin' a baby!"

§ § § § § §

Cathy, 29 years old, 10-25-90, severe vaginal itching: Called me, and said, "I was so busy trying to ignore it I got to scratchin' so bad and so often and made it bleed. Now I can't stand it. The itchin is drivin' me crazy."

§ § § § § §

Male, age 55, 4-25-71: "I got this baaad chest pain all over my body!"

§ § § § § §

Frances, 12-18-90: "These insensible people keep bringing in these goodies, and sweets, for me and my fat daughter. If I can catch'em before she does, I get'em outa the refrigerator and give'em to some of my other kids for their kids." (She and her daughter are very obese.)

§ § § § § §

Harry, 67 yrs old: "I have trouble moving my bowels occasionally, so I stand up and let it drain down there to the bottom...You know, the last place it goes to before it exits your body...and it helps."

§ § § § § §

Patricia, 12-27-96: "That sleepin' pill wired me wide awake all night. If I felt good enough I could'a got up and cleaned house...but I ain't never felt THAT good."

§ § § § § §

11-29-96: I was working in hospital clinic, Express Care, and treated a male with a little cut. Among the things I told him to do was to use Neosporin ointment to dress his laceration. He commented, "Neosporin, that's the best stuff in the world...It'll heal up a cat's ass and hair it over in 24 hours!"

§ § § § § §

Larry, age 50, 9-20-96: Patient previously had a stroke, and has diabetes. After my exam, blood pressure check, and heart check, I told him his heart and lungs sounded normal and his blood pressure was normal. He said, "My heart and blood pressure is a lot better shape than I am."

§ § § § § §

New female patient from Wisconsin: "My doctor is Dr. Lewis Hanover up in Racine. Do you know him?" No, does he know me? "I don't know."

§ § § § § §

"I lives way up yonder on the other side of nowhere. If it don't eat me first, I'll eat anything!"

§ § § § § §

Robert, 3-23-96: Older boy brought in his little brother, and said, "Mama say he got a loud smell from the nose."

§ § § § § §

Mother in with a child that stepped on a nail: "My kid needs a Technical shot."

§ § § § § §

Patient's comment, "If I got any worse, I'd be dead."

§ § § § § §

Patient's comment, "I ain't no doctor, but when I got up this mornin' feeling so bad I knew I was sick!"

§ § § § § §

One of my patients "prescription" for arthritis of the fingers: "Take a flat bowl, put white raisins in the bottom and cover them with gin, place under a fan until the gin evaporates. Then put them in the refrigerator, and eat 8 to 10 each day." I never tried this remedy. I just copied it down some years ago.

§ § § § § §

Mabel, 69 years old, 11-5-90, very obese diabetic: You've just got to lose weight! She said, "I try but I just cain't! I've had it so long I just cain't get rid of it."

§ § § § § §

Patient in after a fall, 2-4-96: "I fell worse'n I thought. I fell yerstidy on my right knee, now my left wrist swole up."

§ § § § § §

Thomas, 79 years old, 1-24-94: "Sunday afternoon I was watchin' football at the kitchen table. I suddenly woke up and found myself sleepin.' I never sleep in day time. But with a cold I only get about two hours sleep a night. Probably the reason. I treat myself with an old German remedy: onion cut up in a jar. Add 1 cup of sugar. Let it sit a day. Use 1 teaspoon for cough and mucus."

§ § § § §

This is the same Thomas, 11-8-94, age 80 now, his wife died 3 years ago: "She gave me many good long years of marriage. I nursed her after all the doctors up north gave up on her. I got a wheel chair and took her for lunch every day, and sometimes just drove around-going nowhere...just driving. I use psychology on her, like the old fairy tale I read about when I was a child...about the dyin' girl in the bed...The father painted a leaf on her window. The girl said she wasn't going to die before that leaf fell to the ground. She lived on that strength of next year. When my wife Marie would get so discouraged I'd tell her 'Just hang on 'til next year, and then you're gonna take care of me and cook my meals for me.' It kept her going a long time, getting' to next year. She always had hopes for next year." This man had more love and more concern, and gave all the complete care for his wife, with no other help. Much more than husbands I saw in similar situations. She was obese, sweet quiet lady, with advanced diabetes that gradually caused dry gangrene of several toes, that is, the toe's vascular supply literally disappeared and the toes turned totally black, hard, and died and dropped off. He kept her clean and immaculate. It was an honor to have known them, and him. In my later years of practice we found a cancer on his tongue, with nodes in the neck. He was referred to the appropriate cancer specialists. I don't think any surgery was done, and he died a few years after I retired. I continued to receive yearly personal Xmas cards from him 'til his death. He was a wonderful man.

§ § § § §

Jewell, 88 years old, 6-90, seated in a chair, I wanted her on my table to examine her: She said, "Well, let me prize myself up outa' the chair. My back is killin' me."

§ § § § §

Aug, 65 years old, hypertension: "You need to change my medicine 'cause I'm doin' too good for my age. Girls just love me! My daddy eat hisself to death. Died at 63 and weighed over 400 pounds, an inch shorter than Fred (brother). Had to get a special suit o'clothes and casket to bury 'im in. He had a hog farm and loved his pork. Clay died at 41—Little Red we called 'im). Vomit up pieces of his liver and bled to death. Herbert died of brain stroke, age 40 in 1980. We would'a sued 'em but for him vomitin' up pieces of liver big as quarters. Fred was gonna marry a little old woman from Tennessee, but she wouldn't marry him 'cause he's a drinkin' and wouldn't quit."

§ § § § § §

Aug, 1993: "Took my girl friend out for a free dinner yesterday. I been goin' square dancin'—take a girl home every night. Can't go as much anymore. I sleep in the bed or on the couch. I don't bother 'em only when they want to be. I even had a policeman's wife."

§ § § § § §

This ends the voluminous peculiar writing of what I called "My Book" for the lack of a better title, until I wound up with what turned out to be my autobiography, with all my collected patient comments and quotes. Then I just called it 'My Whole Life and 48 Years of Small Town Family Medical Practice." I have no idea how to write a book…as you can see, if you read even one paragraph. I started to call it "Doctorin'," or "Patient's Moments in Time," or "Often Late To See The Doctor, Because He Took So Much Time With Other Patients."

I remember one new patient, who sat in my office 30 minutes, got up and left. A few days later I received a bill for his time, for waiting, $50.00. I failed to pay him, and was a little worried that he may turn me over to a Collection Agency.

Paul Alexander Tanner, Jr. M.D. August 14, 2008

Grandchildren! 2001: In the main picture, James with his wife Andrea and their children. Left to right: Their daughter, Fiona Elizabeth, 4; James' stepdaughter (and Andrea's daughter) Jessica, 17; his stepson Nick, 15; Andrea, James, and his stepdaughter Stacey, 13. In the inset, James with his son Garrick Alexander, age 11, driving our boat in Lake Ariana. Four times a year, James flies to Georgia, where Garrick lives with his mother Karen, and drives him down to see us.

2003: Mark and Kathy with their four boys. Left to right: David Vincent, 13; Luke William, 8; Charlie Martin, 4; Anthony Andrew, 12.

2003: Paul III (left) visiting John and John's wife Billie in their home on Lake Juliana in Auburndale. Visiting from California, Mary (right) and her daughter Isabella Jane Grimaldi.

2006: In the main picture, Mary with her husband Maurizio and their then 5-year-old daughter Isabella. In the inset, with my brother Dr. Terry Tanner and Terry's wife Lynn on Terry's 80th birthday.

Printed in the United States
140531LV00004B/5/P